ARON NIMZOW
MASTER OF PLANNING

ARON NIMZOWITSCH –
MASTER OF PLANNING

ARON NIMZOWITSCH:
A Reappraisal

RAYMOND KEENE

B. T. Batsford Ltd. *London*

First published 1974 by G. Bell and Sons, Ltd

First Batsford edition 1991

© R. D. Keene 1974

ISBN 0 7134 6898 X

A CIP catalogue record for this book is available from the British
Library.

Typeset by Lasertext, Stretford, Manchester
and printed in Great Britain by Dotesios Ltd, Trowbridge, Wilts

for the publishers,
B. T. Batsford Ltd,
4 Fitzhardinge Street,
London W1H 0AH

A BATSFORD CHESS BOOK
Adviser: R. D. Keene, GM OBE
Technical Editor: Andrew Kinsman

ARON NIMZOWITSCH –
MASTER OF PLANNING

INTRODUCTION BY RAYMOND KEENE

I was delighted when B. T. Batsford invited me to prepare a fresh
edition of my book on Aron Nimzowitsch, the great chess thinker
and aspirant for the world championship in the late 1920s and early
1930s. Nimzowitsch's influence on subsequent generations of players
has been enormous, his espousal of his own defence the Nimzo–
Indian, 1 d4 ♘f6 2 c4 e6 3 ♘c3 ♗b4, helping it to become perhaps
the most popular and effective weapon against 1 d4. I have very
little to add to what I wrote in this book in the mid-1970s except
to stress the value of Nimzowitsch's long range planning. Study of
his games will be of immense benefit to the chess student who wishes
to follow a thematic strategic line. By studying Nimzowitsch's games
it is possible to prepare such plans for one's own chessboard battles
and then carry them out, secure in the knowledge that the intellectual
spadework has been done well in advance by a master of the art.

Games which are particularly valuable in this sense are the
thematic dark square domination against Maroczy from Bled 1931,
the superlative demonstration of good knight against bad bishop
against Henneberger at Winterthur 1931, the strangulation against
Tartakower in Nimzowitsch's greatest tournament triumph at
Carlsbad 1929 and the ruthless exploitation of doubled pawns
against the two times world championship challenger Bogolyubov
from that same tournament. An absolute masterpiece of planning
was his game against Johner from Dresden 1926 which I give in this
book on page 64. It has inspired many subsequent generations of
masters and grandmasters and I cite it here once more with slightly
different annotations.

JOHNER – NIMZOWITSCH, *Dresden*, 1926. *Nimzo–Indian Defence*
1 d4 ♘f6 2 c4 e6 3 ♘c3 ♗b4 4 e3 0–0 5 ♗d3 c5 6 ♘f3 ♘c6 7
0–0 ♗xc3 8 bxc3 d6 9 ♘d2 b6 10 ♘b3 e5 11 f4 e4 12 ♗e2 ♛d7
13 h3 ♘e7 14 ♛e1 h5 15 ♗d2 ♛f5 16 ♔h2 ♛h7

The completion of a remarkable concentration of Black forces on
the king's flank which more or less paralyses White's chances for
freedom of action. In particular it should be noted what a miserable
role is now played by the White bishop pair.

17 a4 ♘f5 18 g3 a5 19 ♖g1 ♘h6
20 ♗f1 ♗d7 21 ♗c1 ♖ac8 22 d5
♔h8 23 ♘d2 ♖g8 24 ♗g2 g5

With White tied up in knots the
time has come for Black to start his
own assault in earnest.

25 ♘f1 ♖g7 26 ♖a2 ♘f5 27 ♗h1
♖cg8 28 ♛d1 gxf4 29 exf4 ♗c8 30
♛b3 ♗a6 31 ♖e2 ♘h4 (diagram)

As so often happens when one side
has been strategically outplayed
wonderful combinations begin to
arise naturally from the position. Thus, had White chosen to defend
himself with 32 ♘d2 then Black could sacrifice his queen most
aesthetically with 32 ... ♗c8 33 ♘xe4 ♛f5 34 ♘f2 ♛xh3+ 35 ♘xh3
♘g4 mate.

32 ♖e3 ♗c8 33 ♛c2 ♗xh3 34 ♗xe4

If instead 34 ♔xh3 ♛f5+ 35 ♔h2 ♘g4+ with mate to follow.

34 ... ♗f5 35 ♗xf5 ♘xf5 36 ♖e2 h4 37 ♖gg2 hxg3+ 38 ♔g1
♛h3 39 ♘e3 ♘h4 40 ♔f1 ♖e8 White resigns

IN

MEMORY OF MY MOTHER

WHO TAUGHT ME CHESS

CONTENTS

TOURNAMENT AND MATCH RECORD, 1904–1934

Date	TOURNAMENT	Placing	+	=	–	
1904	Coburg (Hauptturnier A)	6	9	3	4	
1905	Vienna	6	3	10	5	Double Round
1905	Barmen (B)	15–16	3	6	8	
1906	Munich	1	7	3	0	Double Round
1907	Ostende (Master Tourn.)	3–4	14	10	4	
1907	Carlsbad	4–5	8	9	3	
1910	Hamburg	3	8	5	3	
1911	San Sebastian	5–7	3	9	2	
1911	Carlsbad	5–6	11	9	5	
1912	San Sebastian	2–3	8	8	3	Double Round
1912	Vilna	4	6	9	3	Double Round
1913	St. Petersburg (Russian Ch.)	1–2	12	3	2	
1914	St. Petersburg (Grandmaster T.)	8	1	6	3	
1919–20	Göteborg	12	1	7	5	
1920	Stockholm	2	11	2	1	Double Round
1923	Copenhagen	1	6	4	0	Double Round
1923	Carlsbad	6–7	8	4	5	
1924	Copenhagen	1	9	1	0	
1925	Baden-Baden	9	7	8	5	
1925	Breslau	2	6	3	2	
1925	Marienbad	1–2	8	6	1	
1926	Semmering	4–5	9	5	3	
1926	Dresden	1	8	1	0	
1926	Hanover	1	6	1	0	
1927	New York Candidates' Tourn.	3	6	9	5	Quadruple Round
1927	Berlin	2–4	5	2	2	
1927	Copenhagen	2–3	$3\frac{1}{2}/5$			

Date	TOURNAMENT	Placing	Score			
1927	Keckskemet	2–3	8	7	1	
1927	Niendorf	1–2	4	3	0	
1927	London (Int. Tourn.)	1–2	7	2	2	
1927	London (Imperial Ch. Club)	1	7	3	0	Double Round
1928	Berlin (Schachge-sellschaft)	1	8	4	1	
1928	Kissingen	5	3	6	2	
1928	Berlin (Tageblatt)	2	4	6	2	Double Round
1928	Copenhagen	1	4/5			
1929	Carlsbad	1	10	10	1	
1930	San Remo	2	8	5	2	
1930	Lüttich (Liège)	3–5	3	6	2	
1930	Frankfurt a.m.	1	9	1	1	
1931	Winterthur	1	7	1	0	
1931	Bled (Veldes)	3	8	12	6	Double Round
1933	Copenhagen	1	5	1	1	
1934	Stockholm	2	6	2	2	Double Round
1934	Zürich	6–7	6	6	3	
1934	Copenhagen	1	$6\frac{1}{2}$/8			Swiss

MATCHES

Date	Opponent	Place	Score		
			+	=	–
1905	Spielmann	Munich	4	5	4
1908	Spielmann	Munich	1	1	4
1911	Leonhardt	Hamburg	0	1	4
1913	Alekhine	St. Petersburg Play-off	1	0	1
1920	Bogoljubow	Stockholm	1	0	3
1922/23	Brinckmann	Kiel	4	0	0
1931	Double round matches v. leading Swiss players	Bern	8	3	2*
1934	Stahlberg	Göteborg	2	2	4
1934	Stoltz	Stockholm	2	3	1

Nimzowitsch was never as comfortable in match play as he was in tournaments and in fact he lost more matches than he won. Probably his greatest match success was his tie with Alekhine, but this match was of minimal duration.

* Bern 1931: Double-round Matches against seven leading Master players of Switzerland:

Nimzowitsch	0	½	Naegeli	1	½
	0	1	H. Johner	1	0
	½	1	Voellmy	½	0
	½	1	Zimmermann	½	0
	1	1	Grob	0	0
	1	1	Gygli	0	0
	1	1	Michel	0	0
	10½			3½	

ACKNOWLEDGEMENTS

Only rarely can an author claim that his book is exclusively his own work. In the present case I must acknowledge aid from a variety of quarters.

First I must thank Harry Golombek, who provided the initial impulse for the book and who gave me access to his extensive library, without which valuable contemporary references would have been unobtainable.

In this respect too I am indebted to Bob Wade and Lothar Schmid, the latter via Henrich Fraenkel ('Assiac' of the *New Statesman*), and also to Annette Goodman for her help with historical research.

The translations from German in this volume are largely my own, but Nimzowitsch's alternative languages (Russian and Danish) are, unfortunately, beyond my grasp. For the translation from Russian of Nimzowitsch's own account of his career I must thank John Sugden of St. John's College, Cambridge, while George and Gitte Botterill were responsible for those of Nimzowitsch's notes carried over from Danish.

For general technical advice and aid I must record my debt to Kevin O'Connell, Les Blackstock and Shirley Blackman, and for permission to reprint the late Hans Kmoch's parody I am grateful to Colonel Ed Edmondson of the U.S. Chess Federation.

Finally I must thank Michael Varvill of G. Bell & Sons Ltd., without whose patient enthusiasm this book would never have seen the light of day.

London   RAYMOND KEENE
September, 1973

EXPLANATION OF SYMBOLS

+ =	Slight advantage to White.
= +	Slight advantage to Black.
±	Clear advantage to White.
∓	Clear advantage to Black.
+ −	White has a winning advantage.
− +	Black has a winning advantage.
‡	After a move in the text indicates the position of a diagram.

CHAPTER I

WHY WRITE ABOUT NIMZOWITSCH?

Aron Isaewitsch Nimzowitsch (November 7, 1886–March 16, 1935) was one of the world's leading Grandmasters for a period extending over a quarter of a century, and for some of that time he was the obvious challenger for the world championship. Nimzowitsch, however, belongs to that select group of players (which includes Rubinstein, Keres and Reshevsky) who were not granted the opportunity, for various reasons, to play a match for the world title at the time when they had reached the peak of their form.

Aside from his practical achievements Nimzowitsch was a great and profound chess thinker, second only to Steinitz, and his works— *Die Blockade*, *My System* and *Chess Praxis*—established his reputation as one of the father figures of modern chess.

Yet Nimzowitsch has not received the recognition in the English speaking world that he deserves. Some masters have run their own publicity campaigns with great skill, but Nimzowitsch's works were uncompromising and suffered from the disadvantage that they did not cover the most successful phases of his career. We all know a few famous Nimzowitsch games, such as the blockade against Johner, or the zugzwang game versus Sämisch, and these particular games are reprinted again and again to the detriment of other equally spectacular masterpieces. It seems to me a waste that these identical games should be printed *ad infinitum* whenever someone has to write something about Nimzowitsch, when so much superb unknown material does exist.

As an indication of the extent, or otherwise, of our knowledge of Nimzowitsch I would like to enquire whether we even understand how to spell his name. I have seen Nimzowitsch, Niemzowitsch, Nimzovitch, and Nimzovich. The English translation of *Praxis* has settled for a compromise and uses versions (ii) and (iv)! I have adopted version (i) because that is the way Nimzowitsch wrote his own name after the Great War. Before then he used version (ii) so I imagine that is also valid. All other versions are quite simply incorrect.

At the age of thirteen I came across *My System* and, without really understanding it very much, I played through all the complete games and was overwhelmed in a way which I hope will affect some of the readers when they see Nimzowitsch's masterpieces from this volume.

Here are two of the games from *My System* which impressed me when I first studied the book.

Consultation game played simultaneously with three others, Uppsala, 1921. White: Brodd, Paulsson and Mandel—Black: Nimzowitsch.*

Nimzowitsch Defence to the KP

1. P—K4, N—QB3; 2. P—Q4, P—Q4; 3. P—K5, P—B3; 4. B—N5/b5, B—B4; 5. N—KB3, Q—Q2; 6. P—B4, B × N!! A brilliant conception which enables him to fight successfully for control of the vital d5 square. **7. R × B, 0—0—0; 8. P × P.** On P—B5 Nimzowitsch planned ... P—KN4 followed by ... B—N2. **8. ... Q × P; 9. B × N, Q × B; 10. 0—0, P—K3; 11. B—K3, N—K2; 12. Q—K2, N—Q4; 13. KR—B1, Q—Q2; 14. R—B4, K—N1; 15. Q—Q2, R—B1; 16. N—K1, B—K2; 17. N—Q3, KR—Q1; 18. Q—B2, P—KB4; 19. R—QB1, P—KN4.** With the centre secure Nimzowitsch undertakes a powerful wing diversion: **20. N—B5, B × N; 21. R × B, R—N1; 22. Q—K2, P—KR4; 23. B—Q2.** Not Q × P ... P—N5. **23. ... P—R5; 24. P—R4, P—N5; 25. P—R5, P—R3; 26. P—**

N4, P—B3; 27. R—N1, Q—KB2; 28. R—N3, P—B5‡; 29. Q—K4, P—B6; 30. R—B1, P × P; 31. K × P, QR—B1; 32. R—B1, P—N6!; 33. RP × P, P × P; 34. P—B4. Of course, **34. R × P, R × R +; 35. K × R** would be horrible for White. **34. ... N—K2; 35. B—K1, N—B4; 36. R—KR1, R—N5; 37. B × P, Q—N3; 38. Q—K1, N × B; 39. R × N, R/1 × P; 40. R—R3, R × P; 41. Q—B2, R × R +; 42. R × R, Q—K5 +; 43. K—R2, Q × P; 44. K—N2, Q—Q4 +.** White resigns. Compare the finish of the game with that of Diez del Corral–Petrosian on page 125.

NIMZOWITSCH–RUBINSTEIN, Dresden, 1926. *English opening*
Awarded the prize for the best-played game

1. P—QB4, P—QB4; 2. N—KB3, N—KB3; 3. N—B3; P—Q4;

* To avoid confusion I should point out that this game appears in some German language books (and in the one-volume translation from German into English of Pachman's work on the middlegame!) as 'Beratende–Nimzowitsch'. There is no contradiction involved, for 'Beratende' is the German word meaning 'consultation partners'.

4. P × P, N × P; 5. P—K4, N—N5; 6. B—B4, P—K3; 7. 0—0, QN—B3; 8. P—Q3, N—Q5; 9. N × N, P × N; 10. N—K2, P—QR3; 11. N—N3, B—Q3; 12. P—B4, 0—0; 13. Q—B3, K—R1; 14. B—Q2, P—B4; 15. QR—K1, N—B3; 16. R—K2, Q—B2; 17. P × P, P × P; 18. N—R1!!‡ A wonderful idea. White has in mind the manœuvre N/R1—B2—R3—N5, in conjunction with Q—R5, as a method of assaulting the position of Black's king.

When I first read *My System* I was so impressed by this game that I deliberately created situations in my next few games where the move N/N3—KR1 was possible, in the belief that this mystical retreat would somehow result in a miraculous increase of energy in my position, irrespective of whatever else may have been happening on the board at the time.

18. ... B—Q2; 19. N—B2, QR—K1; 20. KR—K1, R × R; 21. R × R, N—Q1; 22. N—R3, B—B3; 23. Q—R5, P—KN3; 24. Q—R4, K—N2; 25. Q—B2. Another brilliant idea. The threat to the QP forces Black to withdraw either his Q or his KB from the defence of his K side. **25. ... B—B4; 26. P—QN4, B—N3; 27. Q—R4.** Back again and with redoubled strength. **27. ... R—K1** (or 27. ... R—B3; 28. N—N5, P—R3; 29. N—R7 × + −) **28. R—K5!, N—B2.** If 28. ... R × R; 29. P × R, Q × P; 30. Q—R6 + or 28. ... P—R3; 29. P—N4, P × P; 30. P—B5, Q × R; 31. P—B6 +, Q × P; 32. Q × P. Mate.

These beautiful variations are just an indication of what Nimzowitsch saw. **29. B × N, Q × B; 30. N—N5, Q—N1; 31. R × R, B × R; 32. Q—K1!** A decisive change of front. **32. ... B—B3; 33. Q—K7 +, K—R1; 34. P—N5!!‡** Who would expect the death-blow to come from this quarter? If Black plays 34. ... P × P he is mated as follows: 35. N—K6, P—R4; 36. Q—B6 +, K—R2; 37. N—N5 +, K—R3; 38.

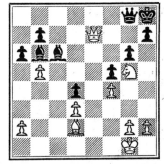

B—N4! In view of this, Rubinstein elects to surrender a piece but that too is obviously without hope. **34 ... Q—N2; 35. Q × Q +, K × Q; 36. P × B.** For the record the final moves were: 36. ...

P×P; 37. N—B3, P—B4; 38. N—K5, B—B2; 39. N—B4, K—B2; 40. P—N3, B—Q1; 41. B—R5, B—K2; 42. B—B7, K—K3; 43. N—N6, P—R3; 44. P—KR4, P—N4; 45. P—R5, P—N5; 46. B—K5. Black resigns.

I would like to stress here that my book is in no way intended as a replacement for Nimzowitsch's *Chess Praxis* and *My System*, in fact it should be read in conjunction with these two volumes from the great man's own hand. Of course it has not been possible to avoid touching on the same ground as Nimzowitsch covers himself, but where this has occurred (as is the case with his famous victories against Johner, Dresden, 1926, or against Sämisch, Copenhagen, 1923) I have adopted a completely different standpoint from that taken by Nimzowitsch himself.

Nimzowitsch's own books stop at 1928. This is unfortunate, since the period of his greatest successes, when he had claim to be the crown prince of the chess world (owing fealty only to the then champion, Alekhine) set in at the close of his creative literary career. Although he did continue to write for magazines he ceased to update his major works. In this sense, then, I hope that my book will come to be regarded as a continuation of his *Chess Praxis* covering the years 1928–1934. For this period I have made liberal use of Nimzowitsch's own notes which would otherwise have languished forgotten in the pages of now defunct magazines or chess columns, which are only accessible to bibliophiles. Indeed, most of these later games have never appeared in English.

To repeat—I strongly recommend that this book should be read in conjunction with *My System* and *Chess Praxis* for, in many cases, I have felt it superfluous to requote at length his ideas which appear in these excellent volumes. The English translation of *My System* is, by and large, very good and makes a brave effort to capture the spirit of Nimzowitsch's original German, but, unfortunately, the same cannot be said of the translation of *Chess Praxis* which I find a poor, maimed torso of Nimzowitsch's original. If you have no alternative read the translation by all means, but if you possess the merest smattering of German I urge you to read the original. It is well worth the effort. In this book the translations from *My System* and *Chess Praxis* are largely my own.*

Apart from the translations of Nimzowitsch's own works the only other English language publication to have appeared concerning Nimzowitsch was a book by Reinfeld which came out in the late

* 'Chess Praxis' is the title used in the English edition of *Die Praxis Meines Systems* which should actually be rendered as 'My System in Practice' or possibly 'My System in Operation'.

1940s. That was almost thirty years ago and I think the time for a reappraisal is ripe. To be honest I feel that Reinfeld also skated round some of the deeper issues involved in Nimzowitsch's play by concentrating in his collection on the master's more obviously attractive exploits. There does exist a work published at roughly the same time as Reinfeld's effort which does considerably more justice to Nimzowitsch. This is by B. Nielsen, but it is written in Danish.

CHAPTER II

'HOW I BECAME A GRANDMASTER'

(Extracts from a brief autobiography published by Nimzowitsch in 1929 as a Russian booklet, now translated for the first time.)

An argument on a topic of practical importance: which age in life is the most suited to a first acquaintance with the principles of chess?

I was eight years old when I first became acquainted with chess. Yet in spite of the fact that I made immediate progress and apparently(!?) continued in the same stride later on, I now boldly maintain that my chess development would have proceeded more harmoniously, and moreover more painlessly, if I had learned the game *not in childhood but in adolescence*. The reader will soon ascertain that my development up until 1906 (I was born in 1886 in Riga) was extremely one-sided: a strong combinative ability at the expense of positional play. This could have been avoided without any drawbacks, merely by waiting a little and teaching me to play chess at a more mature age.

At this point I should like to discuss with the reader a question which lacks neither general interest nor a special interest for the teacher of chess. How about elucidating the attitude which underlies the supposedly rational demand that a child should, if possible, never waste a minute of his time but cram himself with endless studies? If this demand stems solely from a feeling of solicitude towards the child, then why is Latin (for example) still taught in Western schools, and why does a course of study in bourgeois Europe (e.g. in the venerable Faculty of Law!) consist almost entirely of *ballast*, useless to no one, which is ruthlessly brushed aside the minute examinations are over? And why—to turn again from the law student to the child at elementary school—why are all boring and tedious things, such as the learning of any sort of 'principles' and 'elements', considered *highly propitious* for a child, when an adult would show revulsion if expected to concern himself with such uninteresting matters?

May we describe a feature of domestic life which will help us, perhaps, to find our bearings in the matter at issue? In central Europe, in petty-bourgeois circles, there is a widespread view that women should never on any account sit with their arms folded, and therefore they sew or embroider, etc., even when out visiting. The case is a clear one: such a view is an obvious manifestation of the master-and-slave attitude to woman, which has still not fully died out. After all, in the Middle Ages woman was essentially a slave. Isn't our attitude to children based on a similar feeling? At all events, it is time to renounce the notion that a child ought to work unceasingly, and that it is to him that any boring and tedious occupations are especially suited!

If the process of studying 'principles' is a boring one, then in no case (particularly where chess and music are concerned) should one impose these principles on a *child*; wait until he is older. But if you do nevertheless require a child to master them, *then do your utmost to make them interesting, lively and attractive*! The feeling of grey monotony ought, for a child, to be an unfamiliar feeling!

The process of studying the first principles is based on imagination, but at the same time calls for logic; hence *the ideal age for a beginner must be considered adolescence, and by no means childhood*!

> *I begin to play combinatively, but increasingly I lose all vital contact with chess realities, i.e. with the demands of positional play.—On how one ought to study first principles*

My first acquaintance with the principles of chess took place under the sign of *solemnity*. In our family chess was regarded with great respect, for our father, himself an ardent devotee of the game, more than once held forth to us on its astonishing beauties. I would often ask him to show me what it was all about, but Father always refused, saying that 'it's too soon for a lad like you to be thinking about chess'. In the end he consented, however, and this hallowed occasion was arranged for my name-day in my ninth year. Yet I remember being a little disappointed, since the moves of rook, bishop, knight, etc., seemed to me devoid of all combinative interest. I ought to mention that even before becoming acquainted with chess I had a strong penchant for combination as such, since all the efforts of my teachers, and of my father first and foremost, had been specifically aimed at fostering in me a gift for association and a love for that world of scholastic argument and intricate sophistries which is so well known to anyone who has ever been concerned to study the Talmud.

Nevertheless, my disappointment soon gave way to a feeling of keen curiosity. About three weeks after my first lesson, Father showed me some combinations, including a smothered mate (White: Kh1, Qc4, Ne5; Black: Kh8, Qb2, Ra8, P's h7 & g7. 1. Ne5—f7 +, Kh8—g8; 2. Nf7—h6 + +, Kg8—h8; 3. Qc4—g8 +, Ra8 × g8;

4. Nh6—f7 mate), and three months after that, as a reward for progress at school, he demonstrated to me Anderssen's 'Immortal Game'; I not only understood it, but at once fell passionately in love with it.

Playing frequent games with Father, I quickly took a combinative path, but for a long time my stock of strategic concepts remained extremely meagre. By way of characterising Father's pedagogic method, I ventured to remark on the following not uninteresting detail. Now and then Father would explain to me that a central pawn-couple (e.g. on e4 and d4) must only be advanced to the fifth rank with caution. And I am, of course, quite convinced that Father, being a player of master strength, perfectly understood the danger— of a purely *positional* character—of an over-hasty advance: often, of course, it permits an enduring restraint (blockade) of the reckless pawns (e.g. white pawns on e4 and d5; a black knight blockades on e5). It would seem that such an argument, of a purely *positional* character, could not fail to prove useful; yet despite this, Father supported the rule he had stated chiefly by *abstract* considerations: the position of the pawns on e4 and d4 is more rich in possibilities, i.e. one may play either e4—e5 or d4—d5, according to circumstances.

Thus it was that I became more and more estranged from the inexorable realities of chess and began to lose myself in the clouds; and I grew more and more receptive to the idea that it's really no use racking your brains thinking how to create a good position, since the possibility of combinations which the opponent doesn't expect arises equally in bad positions and good ones! Such was the spurious point of vantage I had finally arrived at. . . .

Before proceeding to criticise the method of instruction I have characterised above, I shall insert a few facts from the early part of my chess career.

1. The first of my games to appear in print was played when I was eight and a half. It was published in the *Rigaer Tageblatt* and testifies clearly enough to the presence of a remarkable gift for combination.

2. Nevertheless, throughout the period 1894–1902, I generally had occasion to play only rarely, and exclusively with first category players—of course, I received odds.

3. Notwithstanding the fearfully anti-positional nature of my style, I gradually reached the point where my father had to limit the odds he gave me to a knight. This occurred in 1902. In the same year I went abroad. This commences a *new* period of my chess career.

Before proceeding with the narrative, let us do some summing up. The reader has no doubt managed to grasp that errors were committed, on the part of the teacher, in the early period of my development—otherwise my style of play (in 1902) would not have been so uneven. What did these errors consist in?

Let's begin at the beginning, i.e. by criticising my very first lesson. I was 'shown the moves'. Was that the proper thing? 'Well of course it was,' my esteemed reader will say. 'You can't dispense with that.' But the whole point is that in this case the reader is mistaken: *the method referred to is fundamentally false.* You cannot take a boy who is completely new to the game and immediately confound him by demonstrating that the rook moves so and the bishop thus, and the pawn crawls forward at such a ridiculous snail's pace; that the knight hops crazily all over the place, and the queen can go anywhere it pleases; that the rook moves and captures in straight lines, but the pawn moves straight forward and takes diagonally, etc. The only thing to result from all these demonstrations will be an impression of dreariness: information of this kind which the novice takes in is purely *formal*, without a trace of vitality or substantiality, and hence its multifariousness can only accentuate the feeling of dreariness. . . . No, it is not thus, but quite otherwise, that one must teach the first principles. *A bit less formal ballast and a bit more substance—that is the basic principle!* But let us show concretely how we consider that the first two or three lessons should be conducted.

First lesson. Familiarisation with the board. Understanding of the dividing line between White and Black—and of the central point of the board.

Rook. Understanding about ranks and files. Exercises and problems. . . .

The reader will, I hope, have grasped our basic idea: from the very start we are *playing*, fighting, battling, and have no intention of giving precedence to any formal data. And we are inclined to ascribe a decisive significance to the initial impression formed by the pupil after his first lesson. One has to gain his interest, he must feel straightaway that this is a game in which *victory* is both possible and gratifying!

With the study of the *queen* (second lesson) it is not a bad thing to introduce the concept of the fork, i.e. the simultaneous attack on two enemy pieces, which has, incidentally, been partially touched on in the first lesson. And here again, use practical examples and combinations. . . .

The third lesson is devoted to a study of the *pawn*. The pawn attacks an enemy piece. The pawn protects its own piece (a series of examples). The pawn protects (creates) a strongpoint. . . .

If the strongpoint method of thinking can be acquired with comparatively little trouble, the problem of the knight presents a considerable obstacle to the novice. And to us this seems natural; to some extent, a healthy instinct protests against the form of motion peculiar to a knight. Of course, much can be achieved by sensibly chosen examples, and the knight, that wily offspring of the human fancy, will finally come to seem familiar and intelligible. But the teacher must beware of excessively complex examples, for all '*Rösselsprünge*' merely emphasise the 'distressing' circumstance that the knight is, by nature, an 'imaginary' piece, i.e. it has, so to speak, no bonds with living reality. Exercises like the following are desirable: White: Ng2; Black: Bd6 (White moves exclusively)—how can the knight capture the bishop? . . .

On the delights and torments of combination

The principal error that was committed in my case was not, of course, the fact that *the first lessons* fell short of what we now consider ourselves entitled to expect of an ideal chess pedagogue. For, as I was endowed with a considerable store of active imagination, the 'formalistic' spirit of the first lessons was quite incapable of extinguishing in me an intense love of chess. Considerably worse was another circumstance: Father had, apparently, no wish to face up to the fact that I clearly evinced a hypertrophy of combinative thinking. A hypertrophy of this sort cannot be left out of account; measures must be taken to combat it. Quite naturally, these measures should bear the character of *influence through positional ideas*. But in what should such influence consist? If one feeds a beginner with various considerations of a positional character, the result achieved will be this: the novice's frail organism will prove unequal to *assimilating* this wisdom. He will, perhaps, remember isolated rules, but his positional sensitivity will not be improved by this at all—and yet it is the possession of such sensitivity that constitutes the main criterion, and decisive symptom, in the process of curing an 'over-combinative' player.

There is a way out of this situation, as follows. Let us recall that certain mineral salts, which are hard for the human organism to assimilate, can be assimilated quickly and effectively if only they are introduced into the organism in the form of a chemical compound, combining them with other (organic) substances. Now that's just how we too should proceed; let us try to produce, as it were, a chemical compound of dry positional sagacity with a vigorous and perspicuous exposition of the 'elements'. On these elements I have written nearly a whole book; it is to them that I devote the first (and, partly, the second) section* of my work *My System* (the third section is devoted to positional play in its chemically pure form). Without in any way intending to advertise my work, I submit that in

* *My System* was originally published in five instalments (sections).

this context I am nevertheless entitled to recommend it; the chess tragedies I experienced in my youth give me the right to do so. I should like to show the combinative player the way to cure himself positionally, and no one, surely, will blame me for that. Ah, those tragedies! Those interminable combinative onslaughts, inevitably foundering on the dry positional sense of a sober, and sometimes poorly gifted, opponent!

But let us return to the 'elements'. By this term we mean the file, the seventh rank, the passed pawn, the discovered check, the pin, the pawn chain, etc. In the first section of *My System* I set them out in detail and formulate a whole series of laws for their purposive use. The essence of this method of instruction consists, as I see it, in the very fact that in a way that is entirely unnoticed by the student the laws amount to a notable store of positional wisdom. Let us illustrate this by an example.

The positional rule that the entire struggle, in its essence, amounts to a struggle between two forces, namely the pawns' tendency to advance (lust to expand) on the one hand and the tendency to block-ade the pawns on the other—this rule, or this way of formulating it at least, is difficult for a beginner to grasp. It's a different matter if the same rule is served with a sauce which shows the two tendencies, not as existing in their own right, but as though they were merely an interesting feature of one of the elements (the passed pawn). Viewed in this light, our rule will appear quite comprehensible, and its appropriation cannot fail to develop the beginner's 'flair for blockade' and with it his positional sense. (Subsequently, of course, the rule can and must be elaborated.) This simple law of ours about blockad-ing passed pawns may be stated thus: one must endeavour to blockade the opponent's passed pawn. It is in this sense that a study of the elements, in the first section of *My System*, can be useful to a 'combinationalist'.

If the beginner does not belong to the combinative type, then, before anything else, he must learn to combine. To all novices of *this* kind we recommend a study of P. Romanovsky's book *The Middle-game*.

The period 1902–1906—Anxiety about the 'elements'—I discover . . .
not America, no, but my 'born enemy'—The first serious encounter
with him, and the 'pronouncement' he made on that occasion

In the first year of my stay abroad I played chess assiduously, to the extreme displeasure of my father, who had demanded uncon-pitionally that I should pass an additional examination and enter a university. At the beginning of 1903 I moved from Königsberg to

Berlin, where, among other things, I made the acquaintance—and later became the friend—of O. S. Bernstein and B. M. Blumenfeld. With Blumenfeld I played scores of games, and also with the master von Scheve and the American D. G. Baird. Considerably surpassing me in strength, they would often nevertheless stumble into bad positions, for at times I found combinations which no one else would even have thought of. All the same, I lost the vast majority of games, because *without possibilities for combination* I was completely at sea. I had no positional directives at all; never, for example, did it enter my head to weaken the opponent's black (or white) squares prior to occupying them, or to arrest the enemy breakthrough at its origins, etc. I went all out to attack, rushed forward with my pawns and set combinative traps. I used to perceive such traps with uncommon rapidity and execute them with confidence, easily and boldly calculating five or six moves ahead, or more. I recall, for example, that in a game played between Bardeleben and the student Nisniewitsch it scarcely took me *half a minute* to work out a striking combination something like the following: White: Kg1, Qb1, Rc7, Be4, P's a3, b2, g2, h3; Black: Kh8, Qc5, Rf2, Nh5, P's g7, h6; Black to move. The win is achieved thus: 1. ... Rf1 + ; 2. K × f1, Ng3 + ; 3. Ke1, Qe3 + ; 4. Kd1, Qe2 + ; 5. Kc1, Qe1 + ; 6. Kc2, Qxe4 + ; 7. Kc1, Ne2 + and 8. ... Q × b1.

In 1904 I took part in a tournament for the first time (Hauptturnier in Coburg) and gained sixth prize. Inspired by this success, I travelled to Nuremberg to 'play a few games with Tarrasch'.

Permit me at this point to recount a little episode of chess psychology which was destined to play an immense rôle in the history of my development. In one game I had been playing, a position had arisen characterised by a pawn chain. Let us suppose that these moves were played: 1. e4, e6; 2. d4, d5; 3. Nc3, Nf6; 4. Bg5, Be7; 5. e5, Nfd7; 6. B × e7, Q × e7. In this position (approximately) I was *pained by the thought* that 'I could play 7. Nf3 or I could play 7. f4', and that this dilemma, in its essence an agonising one, could only be fully resolved by *someone's discovery of the laws or principles for the exploitation of the pawn chain as such*. In other words, in a purely intuitive sense, the thought dawned on me that there exist strategic *elements* and that they were, so to speak, seeking their ideologue and 'lawgiver'.

That I myself could emerge as such an ideologue—this thought did not even enter my head; and at the time, generally speaking, this episode did not seem to me at all meaningful or deserving of attention. But in 1904, when my recollection of this slight and quite innocuous story had had time to evaporate completely, the following thing happened to me. While analysing a game of mine played during Coburg, 1904, together with a certain master (whose name will be disclosed later), I happened to convince myself that my rook manœuvres from the 'd' file to the 'h' file and back were not at all necessitated by the strategic données. On the extreme right flank the position was this: White Rh1, Pg5; Black Rh8, Pg6. 'You should have played Rh1—h6,' the master proclaimed in portentous tones. 'Why?' I asked, still not giving in, 'I mean, the move I played in the game, Rh1—d1, wasn't bad.' This modest assertion of mine drew forth the following reply, in a tone which permitted no argument: 'No, you *had* to play Rh6, *because that's the thing to do in cases like this*!' I distinctly recall how, upon these words, which produced a tremendous effect on me, there arose in me the memory of the above-mentioned episode with another element, the pawn chain; and how, at that moment, I made a definitive resolve: 'There *are* laws and rules for the utilisation of both the pawn chain and the file, and somehow or other I must find them!'

A curious quirk is that the master who—quite by chance and involuntarily, to be sure—gave the decisive jolt (impulse) to my eventual revolutionising of chess strategy and the overthrow of the pseudo-classical style, was none other than Tarrasch himself, i.e. the very leader of that trend which was fated to disappear from the scene on account of my discoveries; in other words, with his own weighty utterance Tarrasch actually dug his own grave!

If at that time I was already aware that Tarrasch was my antagonist, I still had no inkling that he was my 'born enemy'. But our relations were soon destined to become strained. This is how it happened. Two months or so after the 'Rh6' incident, Tarrasch granted me the honour of playing a serious game with him (see page 90). My opening play, as usual, was most bizarre, partly because, at that time, as explained above, I was generally ill-versed in 'positional play', but partly because I was already consciously avoiding well-worn paths, and, in particular, regarded the dogmas of the then dominant school not without a certain scepticism. A lot of spectators gathered (although the game had an informal character), for, knowing the richness of my combinative imagination and mistakenly equating this with playing strength, they expected, if not an equal contest—for Tarrasch was then at the height of his fame—then, at any rate, a game full of absorbing interest.

After the tenth move, Tarrasch, folding his arms across his chest, suddenly made the following pronouncement: '*Never* in my life have I had such a *won game* after ten moves as I have now!' The game, incidentally, ended in a draw. But for a long time I could not forgive Tarrasch for the 'insult' he inflicted on me in front of all those onlookers.

Soon afterwards this game was published, to the great annoyance of Tarrasch, who considered that in publishing it I was virtually committing a crime. As it happens, the game was not published by me at all, but by someone else, a certain von Parisch, and this against my wish. But the fact remains that we became enemies and remained so until 1907. Later I shall relate the curious, and for Tarrasch entirely characteristic, episode of our reconciliation. For the present I declare that, had it not been for a feeling of animosity towards Tarrasch, I should never have learned to play chess properly. To play better than Tarrasch—that was the formula of all my yearnings in the period 1904–1906. To all my readers I can give the pleasant advice, 'If you wish to achieve results, *select a born enemy* and attempt to "chastise" him by toppling him from his pedestal.'

I believe it is necessary, however, to add the following: if my feeling of enmity towards Tarrasch was *aroused* by personal motives, it was not *sustained* by them (for, from 1904 onwards, we never had any further quarrels), but by that profound antagonism of an ideological nature of which I was so acutely aware right from the very beginning of our acquaintanceship. Tarrasch, to me, always meant mediocrity; it is true that he was a very strong player, but all his views, his sympathies and antipathies, and above all his inability to conceive any new idea—all this clearly attested to the full mediocrity of his cast of mind. I myself, who paid homage to genius, could in no way be reconciled to the fact that *mediocrity* should stand as the *leader* of the dominant school! This fact, for me, was a veritable outrage!*

The Barmen† fiasco in August 1905 as the final and decisive stimulus: at last I settle down to work! (1906)

At the beginning of 1905 I took part in the Vienna tournament (I— Schlechter, II—H. Wolf; I finished sixth out of ten competitors, ahead of Albin, Neumann and others). My play created an impression (see pages 93–94). The same is true of the match with Spielmann which followed (+4 −4 = 5), and I began to imagine, in all seriousness, that I was on the point of obtaining the master title. In this, however, I failed to reckon with the fact that during my stay abroad my nerves had become wrecked. The endless wandering between chess coffee-houses, the irregular mode of life and the complete absence of definite work—all this, taken together, had a highly detrimental effect on my nervous system—and I began to play impetuously (in a reckless attacking style, as in the very early days of my youth) and badly.

---

* I would stress that the views expressed here are entirely Nimzowitsch's own.
† Or Wuppertal.

In August 1905 I played in the Barmen combined tournament and
. . . came to grief (+ 3 − 8 = 6). At the time I thought this collapse
was a terrible disaster for me, yet today I am convinced that it
provided 'salvation from an almost hopeless situation'. Without
this 'saving grace' bestowed by providence, my state of affairs would
have proved catastrophic.

Embittered by the mocking attitude to myself which I encountered
from the critics in the Barmen tournament book, I decided to give up
the chess coffee-house life, cure my nerves, and afterwards sit down
to some fundamental work on chess.

I sat down to work in the first half of 1906, in Zürich, where I had
enrolled myself as a student (the fact is that I was able to present, not
only my technical high school certificate—which by itself would have
been insufficient—but also a favourable reference from one of the
teachers at the school, affirming my supposedly remarkable aptitude
for mathematics). After two or three months of diligent work I had
made enormous progress.* Let us examine: (1) the psychological
factors in this achievement, (2) the plan of study.

I consider that the factors which alleviated my task were—apart
from the supply of combinative talent I possessed—my bitterness due
to the Barmen reversal, my strong dislike for Tarrasch, and that
deep-seated 'anxiety about the elements' described in the foregoing
chapter.

A superficial analysis of the games played at Barmen was sufficient
to show me that a principal weakness was my bad handling of the
openings (I knew of no defence to 1. d2—d4). A deeper scrutiny of
the games convinced me, in addition, that I had completely failed to
master the art of consolidating my position. This is revealed, e.g. by
my game with Forgacs, in which I pressed forward on the flank in a
wholly antipositional fashion.

By that time the tournament book of Nuremberg, 1906, had
appeared, with commentaries by Tarrasch. I gave the book to a book-
binder, asking him to insert a clean white sheet in between every two
pages of the text. I then began investigating a number of games,
predominantly those of Salwe, Duras and Forgacs; and also M. I.
Tchigorin's games with Black. The results I arrived at I immediately
wrote down on the inserted pages. Each time I would 'play' on one
side or the other, either with White or with Black; first I would try to
find the best move, then I would look up the move played in the
game. In this manner the game would last six hours or so, at the
least. I studied consolidation on the following lines. In one of Salwe's
games there arose a characteristic position with an isolated queen's
pawn: White Nf3, Pd4; Black Nd7, Pe6 (and lots of other pieces on

* With chess, not mathematics!

each side). It turned out that White has no cause for *hurrying* to occupy the point e5 with the knight; within a few moves the Black knight embarked on a journey, seeking to settle on d5, and thus the point e5, *without any effort on White's part*, was still left in his hands. This state of affairs was at once registered on the blank page; the main thing was not the purely technical content of the manœuvre, but, so to speak, its psychological peculiarities: 'Often squares are weakened automatically!' 'Don't hurry', etc. At the same time, with a sort of anxious interest, I gave ear to the slightest 'stirrings' of the open file, the seventh rank, and passed pawns. It was then, in fact, that I discovered the concept of the 'outpost on an open file' (see *My System*, section I). But I derived the greatest pleasure of all from proving the fallaciousness, and quite often the general superficiality, of Tarrasch's views and comments. I learned a great deal from this.

It is curious that I refrained altogether from working through any master games played in the attacking style, e.g. by Spielmann, Marshall or Leonhardt. Nor did the games of Tarrasch seem to me at all useful for the improvement of my style.

The final result of my zealous efforts was the following: (1) I had worked out a detailed plan of defence against 1. d2—d4, namely: 1. ... Nf6 and 2. ... d7—d6 (following in Tchigorin's footsteps). (2) I had acquired the knack of playing a slow, waiting game. And I was already at a loss to understand how I had been capable of making sacrifices without precise calculation (as I had done, alas, at Barmen!). (3) A further important achievement was the fact that, owing to an intensive scrutiny of certain games, I had begun to understand the strategy of blocked positions; in particular, I had mastered the principles of the pawn chain, and to some extent those of centralisation.

Let us now forget that my own case is being discussed, and imagine, in my place, any combinative player whose talent has not yet come to maturity. Can we recommend to him the same plan of self-improvement that I adopted in 1906?

In order to understand this question, we must take account of the following. In 1906 the position of a chess student was far more difficult than it is in the heyday of chess education in which we are now living. At that time, in 1906, one had to discover the positional principles for oneself, whereas today I venture to assert that—owing, in a significant measure, to my discoveries (in my works, *My System* and *Chess Praxis*)—the principles have already been discovered. Not only are the 'elements' set forth for the student's inspection, but the concepts of centralisation, blockade, prophylactic, etc., are clearly formulated and substantiated.

And yet the method I adopted in 1906 can even now be recommended without hesitation. Let us visualise a young combinative player slowly playing through a game by Capablanca, move by move. A position arises, let us say, in which our combinationalist is 'burning with curiosity' to know which of the available *attacking* continuations was given preference; he looks, and discovers that Capa played what seems like a completely passive move. The combinationalist is astounded, perhaps even distressed; but on closer analysis he convinces himself of the concealed *strength* of this move. Such is the *sensation* created by a purely manœuvring move (instead of the expected attacking move).

This is a 'sensation' ('shock') to which I am inclined to ascribe an enormous significance from a pedagogical point of view. Try as you will to preach him centralisation, the combinative player will keep making thrusts on the flank; whilst in all probability the 'sensation method' (this is what we shall call it henceforth), which we have just demonstrated, can influence his style of play in a decisive manner. And therefore, in addition to a study of *My System*, we propose this sensation method to the combinationalist, as a very reliable antidote to the superficiality of his own combinative style.

Moreover, the art of consolidation is directly dependent on the state of one's nerves and the steadiness of one's character. Capablanca must be acknowledged as the best consolidator of all time (he has carried the art of prophylactic manœuvring to unprecedented heights). But Capa is a *sportsman*, a man without nerves, a man with an utterly placid psyche. Hence our advice: combinative player, take part in sport, take frequent walks in the fresh air, do deep breathing exercises, endeavour to be tranquil, do gymnastics by Müller's system, etc. [*sic!*].

For we are convinced that the late Schlechter was right in maintaining that *every combinative player can become a master of the first category if things are arranged properly.* This is all the more true in our own day (Schlechter voiced this opinion as early as 1905, in spite of the fact that chess teaching was then sleeping sweetly in its cradle), for obviously we are now living in the golden age of chess teaching. Combinative talent plus a text-book plus a proper management of affairs (evenness of temper!) must surely add up to a master's playing strength.

On the other hand, people who play few combinations *may develop* their combinative ability. It is also possible, incidentally, to do without combinations. John, e.g. who possessed no imagination at all, still became a very strong master.

My results have their effect: I become a master. On my truce with Tarrasch (1907), and what followed after that 'truce' (1907–1914)

My very next performance—in Munich, November, 1906—bore the mark of a major success. In the double-round tournament containing the masters Spielmann, E. Cohn and Przepiorka (the other participants were Elyashov and Kürschner), I won first prize with 8½ points out of 10, two whole points ahead of the second prize winner. My play was not only distinguished by solidity, as in my game against Cohn, it also shone with a wealth of ideas. I remember, e.g. the start of my game with Elyashov (I had Black): 1. e4, e5; 2. Nf3, Nc6; 3. Bb5, Nd4; 4. N × d4, exd; 5. f4? I now devised the following manœuvre over the board: 5. ... Qh4 + ; 6. g3, Qe7; 7. 0—0, Qc5! There followed: 8. Bd3, h5; 9. Kg2, d5; 10. exd, Nf6! with a very promising game (I won quite quickly).

At the beginning of 1907 I took part in the master tournament at Ostend. Tarrasch was playing in the premier tournament. We came together each day in a café, yet in spite of all my efforts he absolutely refused to notice me, i.e. he simply ignored the fact of my existence. Meanwhile, I was continuing on my victorious way: in the first two weeks I scored 7½ points out of 9. Then, suddenly, a miracle occurred: Tarrasch saw the light! On that day I had beaten W. Cohn. I went into the café; Tarrasch was there already. I had hardly set foot inside, when Tarrasch came rushing up to me, beaming with delight and holding his arms out. 'At long last I've come across you! How pleased I am with your success! Aren't you going to show me some of your games? How pleased I am with your success!!' The apotheosis of opportunism! Trampling the weak in the dirt and pandering to the strong! At that moment I perceived, with particular clarity, the total *mediocrity* of Tarrasch's nature.

My *search for new paths*, adumbrated at Barmen and Coburg, was, as it were, grounded on a more solid base with the improvement of my playing technique. If the opening experiments which I tried out at Barmen (e.g. 1. c4, c5; 2. Nc3, g6; 3. e3, Bg7; 4. Nf3, Nf6; 5. d4, cxd; 6. exd, 0—0; 7. Be2, *Nc6*; 8. *d5, Nb8*, followed by the occupation of the c5 square—Caro *v.* Nimzowitsch) suffered disaster at that time, owing to my lack of corresponding technique, there was no question of this in the following years.

In 1907 I started to play, with the White pieces, 1. Nf3, d5; 2. d3, and if Nc6, then 3. d4, leaving Black's knight awkwardly placed, obstructing the advance c7—c5. In 1910, in bold defiance of Tarrasch, I began to give an obvious preference to cramped positions, e.g. the Hanham variation, etc.

The challenge was taken up, and from that moment on Tarrasch began disparaging me in the press, in the most ruthless fashion. The favourite epithets he levelled at me were *hässlich, bizarr*, etc. All that now appears ridiculous to me, but how it made my blood boil at the time!

In 1912 I narrowly missed winning the grandmaster tournament at San Sebastian (the fact is that owing to nerves I lost a crucial game against Rubinstein and had to be content with sharing second and third prizes with Spielmann). Tarrasch did not fail to chuckle gloatingly: 'It would have been a *scandal* if such anti-aesthetic play had gained the victor's crown!'

I continued to undermine Tarrasch's 'strong'(?) position: the variation 1. e4, c5; 2. Nf3, *Nf6!* and then the attempt at resuscitating the old variation 1. e4, e6; 2. d4, d5; 3. *e5*—all this slowly but surely weakened the position of the Nuremberg champion. In bringing back the variation with 3. e5 I set myself the task of a 'reductio ad absurdum' of the old conception of the centre. In 1912 I published my games with Salwe (1911) and Tarrasch (1912), by which I attempted to show that the old conception of the centre, upheld by Tarrasch, was outdated.

In 1913 I discovered a method of play which since then has attained so much popularity: 1. d4, Nf6; 2. c4, e6; 3. Nc3, Bb4— *without d7—d5*; or 1. d4, Nf6; 2. c4, e6; 3. Nf3, *b6*, also without a subsequent d7—d5, and with this the position of Tarrasch as a generally acknowledged teacher of chess understanding was conclusively destroyed.

On the triumph of my ideas, and my successes as a grandmaster, 1923–1929. Some concluding advice

After the end of the war the correctness of my revolutionary views on chess became generally recognised. Variations which had seemed so strange and whimsical when these ideas were invented gradually acquired rights of citizenship.

Conversely, Tarrasch's theory (on the arithmetical centre, fast development, etc.) began to provoke nothing but a smile.

Parallel with this I achieved even greater successes in practice, which secured me the title of grandmaster. I consider my greatest success to have been, not the first prizes at Marienbad, 1925, London, 1927, and Berlin, 1928 (in the last two cases I finished above Bogoljubow), but the first prize at Dresden, 1926, where I scored 8½ out of 9 *and came no less than 1½ points ahead of Alekhine!* And, in my opinion, it was at Dresden that I played my best games.

There is little else to say, and we could proceed to the games section with a clear conscience; yet I should like to say a few more words about the 'elements' (i.e. about the time when I was finally working them out).

Having felt 'anxiety' about them as early as 1902 (see chapter 5), I was still for a long time unable to surmount the enormous difficulties which confronted me. Isolated portions, e.g. the idea of the outpost, and also the new understanding of the pawn chain, were conceived by me in the period 1911–1913.

But in as much as any new system demands detailed elaboration as well as intuition, the definitive creation of my system must be dated in the period 1917–1923. The fact is that the author of the proverb *discendo discimus* is right ('By teaching, we ourselves learn'). That is what happened to me. From 1917 onwards I started giving chess lessons, which I conducted in strict accordance with a policy I had previously chosen, namely the teaching of the elements. In this fashion I assembled a mass of necessary details on the file, the seventh rank, the passed pawn, etc. After this, I was able in 1925 to proceed with a clear conscience to the presentation of the collected material in the book *My System*. . . .

In parting I should like to give a few more pieces of advice.

Take a thoughtful attitude towards chess. Understand that a *thorough* acquaintance with one element is more effective in improving your positional sense than a superficial acquaintance with all the elements. The treatment of an element is full of 'positional value'. . . .

Try to memorise as *few* variations as possible! Positional sense ought to liberate you from enslavement to 'variations'. And therefore: endeavour to develop in yourself this positional sense! . . .

Even more important is analysis! Analyse an opening you are interested in with friends (whose strength slightly exceeds yours). But your analytical work should on no account be confined to the openings; you should also analyse a variety of typical positions.

Thus we recommend: (1) playing through a limited number of games thoroughly; (2) a thorough study of the elements (using the book *My System*); (3) a thorough acquaintance with a modest number of typical situations by means of comprehensive analysis.

To sum up: a serious approach to the matter is indispensable!

A. Nimzowitsch

Here, at the beginning of 1929, ends Nimzowitsch's own account of his career.

I would like to add a few points to this narrative and also bring it to the close of Nimzowitsch's life.

The upheavals of the Great War, the Russian Revolution and the subsequent civil war in Russia interrupted Nimzowitsch's successful chess career in no uncertain fashion. For six years after 1914 Nimzowitsch played no serious chess and at some time in 1920 (earlier perhaps) he fled from his home town of Riga to Scandinavia. Precisely why he took flight we do not know, but we do know that Bolshevik and irregular German armies were at large, and at war with Latvia in its struggle for independence, at this time and this fact may not have been unconnected with Nimzowitsch's sudden departure. Shattered by his experiences (whatever they may have been) in his war-torn country Nimzowitsch's return to international chess at Gothenburg in 1920 was a disaster, but he gradually recovered and began to play himself back into form.

In 1922 Nimzowitsch settled in Denmark and stayed there for the remainder of his life, living in one small rented room in Copenhagen. One has the impression that Nimzowitsch's life-style in Riga had not been un-affluent, but it seems that all this changed after his exile.

During the years 1925–1929 he worked his way towards his ultimate goal—the world championship. His own narrative closes just prior to his greatest triumph: the first prize at Carlsbad, 1929, ahead of Capablanca, Spielmann, Rubinstein, Vidmar, Euwe and Bogoljubow. His result at San Remo the following year confirmed his position as 'Crown Prince of the chess world', and Alekhine himself expressed the opinion that Nimzowitsch was his worthiest opponent, but the match never came about. It is unlikely that Nimzowitsch would have been able to unseat Alekhine, but his claims were certainly superior to those of the official challenger, Bogoljubow, who twice met the world champion in abortive matches in 1929 and 1934.

From 1929 onwards Nimzowitsch made the fine scores of 4/5 versus Bogoljubow, 1½/2 versus Euwe, who did unseat Alekhine shortly after Nimzowitsch died, 2½/3 versus Flohr, who was generally regarded as Alekhine's most likely challenger apart from Euwe, and also plus scores against Lasker, Vidmar and Spielmann.

Nimzowitsch's results at the great tournaments of San Remo and Bled were excellent and (apart from a comparative failure at Liège where he tied third) these successes were backed up by a number of first prizes in smaller tournaments (Frankfurt, Winterthur, Copenhagen) in which the general standard of his play was outstanding. He was less successful in matches versus Stoltz and Stahlberg, the rising

Scandinavian stars, but Nimzowitsch was never a particularly accomplished match player, an observation which reinforces the feeling that he would not have succeeded in a challenge match versus Alekhine. Indeed, Nimzowitsch suffered repeated defeats at the hands of Alekhine in the years 1930–1934, although previously their results against each other had been reasonably balanced (+ 5 − 3 = 9 to Alekhine).

After 1931 Nimzowitsch took no part in major tournaments for three years—possibly as a result of increasing ill health. His emergence in 1934 at Zürich was not worthy of his former achievements, although he did win an 'immortal' N ending versus Lasker, and it was clear from this tournament that Nimzowitsch could no longer be regarded as an automatic candidate for the world title. He did win a Nordic tournament in Copenhagen later in 1934, but a few months after that he was dead. 'Nimzowitsch's death at the beginning of 1935 was a severe and unexpected blow to the chess world' (Stahlberg).

Bjørn Nielsen, Nimzowitsch's Danish biographer, wrote: 'Shortly before Christmas, 1934, Nimzowitsch had to be admitted to the Bispebjerg Hospital where he lay hopelessly ill for three months. At the beginning of March, 1935, he was moved to Hareskov Sanatorium and here he succumbed to a lung infection (pneumonia). On March 16, 1935, the Grandmaster, only forty-eight years old, breathed his last.'

CHAPTER III

A DISCUSSION WITH BENT LARSEN

At various stages throughout this book I allude to connections between Nimzowitsch and Larsen. As we all know Larsen is Denmark's most successful player and his chess-formative years occurred some time after Nimzowitsch's death in 1935, the year in which Larsen was born, when the great Master's influence amongst Danish players was considerable.

Larsen is not only Denmark's leading player, but one of the most successful tournament players of our era—as Nimzowitsch was of his—and many of Nimzowitsch's aggressive ideas are to be observed in Larsen's approach to tournament chess. Larsen, like Nimzowitsch, is an uncompromising fighter over the board and often controversial and outspoken in his published comments.

In this interview, conducted exclusively for this volume, Larsen gives his views on Nimzowitsch's influence over the succeeding generations of Grandmasters.

Question: What do you regard as Nimzowitsch's main contributions to the advance of chess theory?
Larsen: Well, in my opinion his original contributions were not as great as most people think because so much in Nimzowitsch can be found already in Steinitz, but he did emphasise certain things that Steinitz neglected, things that were very much against Tarrasch and so on. The funny thing is that Nimzowitsch's most famous book is called *My System*, and it's not a system. It's part of a system. It is not a whole system. Nimzowitsch's writings meant very much for the development of certain important ideas, but it's hard for us to see now if these ideas would have developed independently of Nimzowitsch in other writers; but it does look as if he passed on some ideas to, for instance, a player like Petrosian. For example: the blockading knight. This is one of the parts of his 'system' which comes across very strongly. Donner once told me that Euwe lost a game—I think it was Amsterdam, 1950, against Pilnik—and afterwards Euwe didn't understand the mistakes he had made; and to Donner, to me, to Pilnik, to a lot of people it was obvious that Euwe had allowed his opponent a strong position where he had this blockading knight, and it seemed as if Euwe didn't understand this, which was really strange.

Other Dutch players have also told me that Euwe never understood Nimzowitsch. But to me Nimzowitsch is something I absorbed very early in my chess development, which is why I have some difficulty in isolating his specific achievements, because when you take some of Nimzowitsch's ideas I simply say: 'Yes, of course!'

I didn't learn so much from *My System* because I only started to read it when I was seventeen. By that time I had already got most of Nimzowitsch in a more easy, more popular, way, you could say, because we have in Danish a very good book—in memory of Nimzowitsch—written by Björn Nielsen and there most of the games are given with Nimzowitsch's own comments. A lot of these things I learnt when I was about fourteen years old: but this story of Donner's about Euwe's game with Pilnik has made me think— maybe these things we find in Nimzowitsch were not so obvious earlier on.

Question: Would you associate any ideas with Nimzowitsch rather than with any other writer or player?

Larsen: Yes. Play on squares of a certain colour. This is very often something like a blockading knight, or a knight against a bad bishop, but it can mean different things: it can be opposite-coloured bishops, for instance. The way he sees these weaknesses developing on squares of one colour. That, to me, is one of the most typical things in Nimzowitsch; and it is the one thing I would mention as very significant.

What I don't understand at all in *My System* is why he talks so much about this 'seventh rank absolute' because it normally arises in the endgame. It's very nice, of course, but others have seen that too and I don't know why he stressed it so much and made it a part of his system—which, as I say, is not a system. But this play on weaknesses of one colour—that is to me very typical Nimzowitsch.

In this respect one game that made a very strong impression on me when I was about fourteen is the ending von Gottschall–Nimzowitsch with rooks and opposite-coloured bishops. There are other such endings and I could have learnt the same things just as well from a game of Spielmann's with Alekhine, but I did learn it from the Gottschall–Nimzowitsch game.

Question: Do you think that Nimzowitsch affected many of the modern Grandmasters?

Larsen: I think he affected Portisch when Portisch was very young. It is hard to see now, but when Portisch was young he had many of Nimzowitsch's ideas. Korchnoy too, but above all Petrosian, and maybe also Bronstein; but it is difficult to see these things when we come to the Soviet masters, since very few of them have really studied Nimzowitsch. Petrosian has, because his teacher was

Ebralidze,* the great admirer of Nimzowitsch; and Bronstein has, but most of the others have probably not studied Nimzowitsch very much. I don't know what Nimzowitsch literature exists in Russia. Not too much, and his influence comes only in an indirect way. I don't think the other Russians have studied him. They know Alekhine well, much better than they know Nimzowitsch. And other Grandmasters . . . I don't think Fischer has studied Nimzowitsch in detail; Capablanca perhaps in his case.

Question: To what extent has your own style been influenced by Nimzowitsch?

Larsen: The main influence stems from my study of his games when I was fourteen. Part of these things also come from other Danish players who knew Nimzowitsch personally in Denmark. So it is rather difficult for me to pin-point his precise influence because part of it came through some of the other Danish players.

When I was fourteen or fifteen we had very little chess literature in Denmark. We did have, for instance, Euwe's opening theory and later Euwe's middlegame books and so on. But at a certain time in my development I found out that they were very bad for an advanced player, and Nimzowitsch became then for me more or less the author of the only book that could help me to get away from these Euwe books, which, I admit, are very good for the ordinary club player. But once you've reached a certain strength you get the impression that everything that Euwe writes is a lie.

There is something that I often say and Nimzowitsch says it himself: 'Everything is Nimzowitsch-My System, every move is Nimzowitsch-My System because it is either centralisation or decentralisation.' He sometimes made jokes with this and thereupon others said that he first played his games and didn't think of his system, but then afterwards because he had written this book or these books he had to fit the games into his system.

There is this in Nimzowitsch that he is very flexible, although people sometimes tell stories about his opposition to Tarrasch as if he were very narrow-minded. But he is very flexible, and his system, which is not a system, is full of these contradictions and paradoxes. And this is one of the nicest examples: he sometimes has these things about decentralisation in such a way that you don't really understand

* 'The greatest influence on Petrosian's style was his trainer, at the Tbilisi Palace of Young Pioneers during the ages of thirteen to fifteen, the master Archil Silovanovich Ebralidze (1909–1960). He introduced Petrosian to Nimzowitsch's book *Chess Praxis*' (R. G. Wade in *Soviet Chess*). Nimzowitsch's influence on Petrosian can most clearly be traced in the latter's prophylactic or preventive style. The main influence on Korchnoy is the idea of 'Heroic Defence'—deliberate choice of inferior or difficult variations in order to set the opponent problems.

(R.D.K.)

what's going on. A man who always preaches centralisation—and here he suddenly writes about the 'instructive decentralisation'. Nimzowitsch, when you study him, doesn't try to tell you that it's all very easy, and that was very good for me at that period of my chess development.

Nimzowitsch was also very much of a fighter; he was a player who was not afraid of difficult positions. In Denmark he certainly had a very strong influence in his time and although he was very much a foreigner he became accepted in a way. He was a very strange man, but people more or less liked him, also because he had a certain humour. In Denmark there are all these stories about Nimzowitsch and a lot of people tell about his persecution complex—how he was sure that the waiter in the Industrieverein wanted to poison him, and so on.

But how he influenced my style it is difficult to say precisely.

*   *   *

Four points in this conversation with Bent Larsen particularly caught my attention. They were (i) the formative influences affecting Nimzowitsch's theories, (ii) his trouble with Tarrasch, (iii) the question 'Is it a system?' and (iv) the positional themes of Nimzowitsch's writing and play. I decided to have a closer look at them.

(1) INFLUENCES AFFECTING NIMZOWITSCH

('As a chess thinker Nimzowitsch is comparable with Steinitz. If Steinitz was the father of modern chess Nimzowitsch was the formulator of many of the so-called hypermodern conceptions.' DR. EUWE)

The influence of Steinitz on Nimzowitsch's ideas is apparent even in such surface details as opening variations. For example, look at the first few moves of Steinitz–Showalter, Vienna, 1898:
1. P—K4, P—K3; 2. P—Q4, P—Q4; 3. P—K5(!), P—QB4; 4. P × P, N—QB3; 5. N—KB3, B × P; 6. B—Q3, KN—K2; 7. 0—0, N—N3; 8. R—K1, and White later won by means of an alternating attack in the centre and against Black's K side.

However, in this volume I am more concerned with the influence exerted by Nimzowitsch than with the influences which shaped his own style and ideas in his formative years, so here I shall only touch briefly on the subject. How does Nimzowitsch himself approach the question? In *My System* he wrote: 'First came Steinitz; but what he had to say was so unfamiliar, and he himself was so towering a figure, that his "modern principles" could not immediately become popular. There followed Tarrasch who took hold of Steinitz's ideas and served them up diluted to the public taste. Steinitz was deep and great but deepest and greatest in his conception of the centre.'

Admiration indeed, and what Nimzowitsch must have had in mind were games such as Lasker–Steinitz, game 7 World Championship Match, 1894: **1. P—K4, P—K4; 2. N—KB3, N—QB3; 3. B—N5, P—Q3; 4. P—Q4, B—Q2; 5. N—B3, KN—K2; 6. B—K3, N—N3; 7. Q—Q2, B—K2; 8. 0—0—0, P—QR3; 9. B—K2, P × P;** Steinitz cedes White an arithmetical advantage in the centre, but not a genuine one. Moves like this were the spiritual ancestors of Nimzowitsch's treatment of the Hanham defence and of later (modern) developments in similar vein (see page 41) **10. N × P, N × N; 11. Q × N, B—KB3; 12. Q—Q2, B—B3; 13. N—Q5, 0—0; 14. P—KN4, R—K1,** with a fine position for Black.

Another example is the following, in which Steinitz operates precisely according to Nimzowitsch's theory of over-protection—four years before Nimzowitsch was born!

STEINITZ–WEISS, Vienna, 1882

1. P—K4, P—K3; 2. P—K5, P—QB4; 3. P—KB4, P—Q4; 4. P × P ep, B × P; 5. P—KN3, B—Q2; 6. N—KB3, B—B3; 7. B—N2, N—B3; 8. 0—0, QN—Q2; 9. P—Q3, 0—0; 10. QN—Q2, N—N3; 11. Q—K2, Q—B2; 12. P—N3, B—K2; 13. B—N2, P—QR4; 14. P—QR4, N/B3—Q4; 15. N—B4, N—N5; 16. QR—K1, N/3—Q4;‡ 17. N/3—K5, B—B3; 18. Q—B2, B—K1; 19. P—KN4, R—Q1; 20. P—N5, B—K2; 21. N—N4, N—QB3; 22. Q—R4, N—Q5; 23. B—K4, P—B4; 24. P × P ep, N × P/3; 25. N × N +, B × N; 26. Q × P +, K—B2; 27. B—N2, R—KN1; 28. N—K5 +, K—B1; 29. R—B2, P—QN4; 30. P × P, B × P; 31. B—KR3, R—K1; 32. R—

K4, B—B3; 33. R × N, P × R; 34. B—R3 +, B—K2; 35. B × P. 1—0.

I am indebted to R. N. Coles' *Dynamic Chess* for drawing my attention to this game and it is difficult to better his explanatory comments: 'Nimzowitsch realised that Tarrasch had simplified and diluted the original Steinitzian practice, and that some of the old master's deeper conceptions had been omitted altogether. He found that Steinitz had conceived the idea of a strong central square which he had controlled but not necessarily occupied continuously. Steinitz's view, as Nimzowitsch understood it, was that when a strong square had been established, like White's K5 in the Weiss game, it became a nerve-centre for the radiation of attacks and threats, and therefore all pieces were developed so as to be brought into relation with the strong square. When a large number of pieces were developed so that they all defended the strong square, that square was, as Nimzowitsch put it, "over-protected". He affirmed that from the over-protected square all these pieces could quickly exert their maximum influence.'

Related to the Weiss game was Steinitz' handling of the defence in his encounter with Lasker (White) from Hastings, 1895. This time Steinitz strongpointed the e5 square without first emptying it of his KP:

1. P—K4, P—K4; 2. N—KB3, N—QB3; 3. B—N5, P—QR3; 4. B—R4, P—Q3; 5. 0—0, N—K2; 6. P—B3, B—Q2; 7. P—Q4, N—N3; 8. R—K1, B—K2; 9. QN—Q2, 0—0; 10. N—B1, Q—K1; 11. B—B2, K—R1; 12. N—N3, B—N5; 13. P—Q5, N—N1; 14. P—KR3, B—B1; 15. N—B5, B—Q1; 16. P—KN4, N—K2; 17. N—N3, N—N1; 18. K—N2, N—Q2. Intellectually this game makes a profound impression but practically Steinitz' play was too provocative. Lasker won the game by means of direct attack.

Certainly Nimzowitsch examined the games of Steinitz and quarried out from the raw material of the great man's practical exploits a coherent theory which had applications in many different directions, but it would be a foolish over-simplification to regard Nimzowitsch's teachings as an updated, pseudo-carbon copy of Steinitz. At the start of the 20th century the situation facing the aspiring chess enthusiast, anxious to increase his chess wisdom, was roughly as follows: there were three great chess pedagogues from whom one might seek enlightenment. (Lasker the then world champion was regarded as the practical player *par excellence* and only much later on was it realised that his games also contained the basis for a psychological theory of chess. To his credit Nimzowitsch was one of those who recognised this fact.) The three teachers I have in mind were Steinitz, Tarrasch and Tchigorin. There is no doubt that Nimzowitsch utterly rejected the doctrines of Tarrasch and that he went back to the original Steinitzian source in his quest for knowledge but, to an extent which has hitherto been overlooked, Nimzowitsch also scanned the games of Tchigorin* in his search for chess truth. What Nimzowitsch produced from his investigations into the past was undeniably and indelibly his own, but it was to Steinitz and Tchigorin that Nimzowitsch turned for his initial guidance.

I close this section with one of Tchigorin's classic games. Whether Nimzowitsch had studied precisely this one, or just games of the same style by the great Russian master, is not strictly relevant. What is of relevance is the way in which Tchigorin dominates and blockades

---

* Nimzowitsch mentioned this in his brief 'autobiography' (page 16 above).

the entire White position (with its bishop pair) by exploiting to the full the resources of his knights. In this game we can see the rudimentary stirrings of a theory of blockade and restraint, which was later formulated by Nimzowitsch himself.

LASKER–TCHIGORIN, Hastings, 1895. *Q.P, Tchigorin's Defence*
1. P—Q4, P—Q4; 2. N—KB3, B—N5; 3. P—B4, B × N; 4. NP × B, N—QB3; 5. N—B3, P—K3; 6. P—K3, B—N5; 7. P × P, Q × P; 8. B—Q2, B × N; 9. P × B, KN—K2; 10. R—KN1, Q—KR4; 11. Q—N3, N—Q1; 12. Q—N5 +, Q × Q; 13. B × Q +, P—B3; 14. B—Q3, N—N3; 15. P—KB4, R—QB1; 16. K—K2, 0—0; 17. R—N3. Much stronger would have been P—B5 breaking open the position for the bishops. After the text Tchigorin succeeds in implementing the blockade. One of Nimzowitsch's achievements was to elaborate an openings repertoire that successfully brought about blockade situations as a logical consequence of the initial moves:

17. ... P—QB4;   18. QR—KN1, P—B5; 19. B—B2, P—B4; 20. B— B1, R—KB2; 21. B—R3, R—QB3; 22. B—B5, R—R3; 23. P—QR4, N—QB3; 24. R—N1, R—Q2; 25. 25. R/3—N1, N/N3—K2; 26. R— QN2, N—Q4; 27. K—Q2, R—R4; 28. R/1—N1, P—QN3; 29. B—R3, P—N3; 30. R—N5, R—R3; 31. B— B1, N—Q1; 32. R—QR1, N—KB2; 33. R/5—N1, N—Q3.‡ It would have been more accurate to play ... P— KN4 at once.

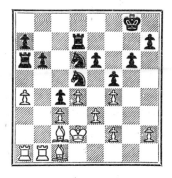

34. P—B3, N—KB2; 35. R—R3, P—KN4; 36. K—K2, NP × P; 37. P—K4!, N—B3; 38. B × P, N—R4; 39. B—K3, P—B5; 40. B— B2, R—R4; 41. R—N1 +, K—B1; 42. R/3—R1. It looks as if White can lift the blockade with 42. P—K5 but in that case Tchigorin had planned: 42. ... P—N4; 43. B × P, N × P; 44. R—N8 +, K—B2; 45. P × N, P—N5!; 46. P × P, R × P + ; 47. K—B1, N—B3 – + ; 42. ... P—K4; 43. R/QR1—N1, N—N2; 44. R—QN4, R—B2; 45. B—N1, N—K3; 46. R—Q1, N/3—Q1; 47. R—Q2. He had to try P × P; after the text Black can win.

47. ... N—B3; 48. R—N5, R × P; 49. P × P, N/2 × P; 50. B—R4, R—KN2; 51. K—B2, R—N3; 52. R/2—Q5, R—R8; 53. B—Q8, N—Q6 + ; 54. B × N, P × B; 55. R × QP, R/8—KN8!; 56. R—B5 +, K—K1; 57. B—N5, R/3 × B. White resigns. Had he played 57.

R × P Black would have delivered mate by means of 57. ... R/3—
N7 + ; 58. K—K3, R—K8 mate.

(2) *THE TROUBLE WITH TARRASCH*

('... very much against Tarrasch and so on...')

Nimzowitsch's feud with Tarrasch is notorious and has been
mentioned elsewhere in the volume in Nimzowitch's own words
(page 11). From Nimzowitsch's comments we can see that, prior to
1914, opposition to the great Dr. Siegbert Tarrasch, the leading
German master (apart from Lasker), the 'world tournament champion' (a title Tarrasch gained at Ostend, 1907) and challenger to
Lasker's individual title, provided the spur to Nimzowitsch's own
remarkable progress. The animosity between these two outstanding
writers and practical players meant that their clashes over the board
were needle sharp. Many of their encounters are well known (perhaps
too well known). The very first game they ever played together 'under
serious conditions' is to be found in the games section. I have chosen
this game alone to appear with detailed notes precisely because it is
virtually unknown. Nimzowitsch's celebrated victory with 3. P—K5
in the French Defence can be located in the theoretical survey, while
the remainder of their decisive encounters I have assembled here
with brief notes. It will be seen that Nimzowitsch won the majority of
games but to Tarrasch belongs the honour of the greatest brilliancy.
I mean, of course, the game from St. Petersburg, 1914.

Complete record of score between Nimzowitsch and Tarrasch:

Location and date	Nimzowitsch's result
Nuremberg, 1904	½
Hamburg, 1910	1
San Sebastian, 1911	0
San Sebastian, 1912	1½/2
St. Petersburg, 1914	0
Gothenburg, 1920	½
Carlsbad, 1923	1
Baden-Baden, 1925	½
Breslau, 1925	1
Semmering, 1926	½
Kissingen, 1928	1

[+5 = 5–2: 7½–4½]

(i) TARRASCH–NIMZOWITSCH, Hamburg, 1910. *Q Gambit, Tarrasch
Defence*

1. P—Q4, P—Q4; 2. N—KB3, P—K3; 3. P—B4, P—QB4;
4. P—K3, N—KB3; 5. N—B3, N—B3; 6. B—Q3, B—Q3; 7. 0—0,
0—0; 8. P—QN3, P—QN3; 9. B—N2, B—N2; 10. Q—K2, QP × P;

11. NP × P, P × P; 12. P × P, R—B1; 13. QR—Q1? (13. P—QR3!),
13. ... N—QN5; 14. B—N1, B × N; 15. P × B, B—N1; 16. P—
QR3, Q—B2; 17. P—B4, Q × KBP; 18. P—B3, N—B3; 19. N—K4,
KR—Q1; 20. K—R1, N—K2; 21. B—B1, Q—B2; 22. N × N +,
P × N; 23. Q—N2 +, N—N3; 24. B—R2, K—R1; 25. P—B4, N—
R5; 26. Q—R3, N—B4; 27. P—Q5 (27. B—N2! intending Q—KB3.
'Observe now how Black answers "dynamics" with "statics"; he
hems in and blockades the pawns at c4 and d5 to the utmost'—
Nimzowitsch in *Chess Praxis*), 27. ... R—N1; 28. B—N2, R—N3;
29. R—KN1, QR—N1; 30. R × R, R × R; 31. R—KB1, Q—B4;
32. Q—KB3, B—Q3; 33. Q—B2, Q × Q; 34. R × Q, B—B4; 35.
R—N2, K—N2; 36. R × R +, RP × R; 37. K—N2, B—Q5; 38. B—
B1, B—K6; 39. B × B, N × B +; 40. K—B3, N—B4; 41. B—N1,
N—Q3; 42. B—Q3, P—K4; 43. K—N4, P—B4 +; 44. K—N3, P—
B3; 45. P—KR4, K—B2; 46. B—K2, N—K1; 47. K—B3, K—K2;
48. K—K3, N—N2; 49. B—B3, K—Q3; 50. B—Q1, N—R4; 51.
P × P +, P × P; 52. K—Q3, K—B4; 53. P—R4, N—B3; 54. B—K2,
N—K1; 55. K—B3, N—Q3; 56. B—B1, P—K5; 57. K—Q2, P—
B5; 58. K—B3, P—B6. 0–1.

(ii) NIMZOWITSCH–TARRASCH, San Sebastian, 1911. *Scotch Game*
1. P—K4, P—K4; 2. N—KB3, N—QB3; 3. P—Q4, P × P; 4.
N × P, N—B3; 5. N × N?!, NP × N; 6. B—Q3, P—Q4; 7. P × P,
P × P; 8. 0—0, B—K2; 9. P—QB4?!, 0—0; 10. P × P, N × P;
11. B—K4, B—K3; 12. N—B3, N × N; 13. P × N, Q × Q; 14.
R × Q, QR—Q1 ∓; 15. B—K3, P—QB4; 16. B—B3, R × R +;
17. R × R, R—N1; 18. P—KR3, R—N7; 19. B—Q5, B × B; 20.
R × B, R × RP; 21. P—QB4 (21. B × P?, R—R4 – +); 21. ... R—
R8 +; 22. K—R2, R—R4; 23. P—B4, P—B3; 24. K—N3, K—B2;
25. K—B3, P—QR3; 26. P—R4, R—R5; 27. B × P, R × P; 28.
B × B, K × B; 29. R—KR5, P—R3; 30. R—R5, R—B3; 31. K—N4,
R—N3; 32. P—B5, K—B2; 33. K—R5, P—N3 + (!); 34. K × P
(34. P × P +, K—N2; 35. R—R2, R—N4 +; 36. K—N4, P—
R4 +; 37. K—B3, P—R4 followed by ... K × P and Black has
made some progress), 34. ... P × P; 35. R × BP. (He could also
hold the game with 35. R—B5, P—B5; 36. R—B7 +, K—K3;
37. K—N6 =.) 35. ... R—N1; 36. K—R5?? (36. K—R7!, R—N4,
37. R × R, P × R; 38. P—N4! =); 36. ... R—N4; 37. K—N4,
R × R; 38. K × R, P—R4; 39. K—K4, P—B4 +. 0—1. (40. K—Q3,
P—B5; 41. K—B4, K—N3 – +).

(iii) NIMZOWITSCH–TARRASCH, St. Petersburg, 1914. *Q Gambit,
Tarrasch Defence*
1. P—Q4, P—Q4; 2. N—KB3, P—QB4; 3. P—B4, P—K3; 4. P—

K3, N—KB3; 5. B—Q3, N—B3; 6. 0—0, B—Q3; 7. P—QN3, 0—0; 8. B—N2, P—QN3; 9. QN—Q2, B—N2; 10. R—B1. Q—K2; 11. BP×P (11. Q—K2!?), ... KP×P; 12. N—R4, P—N3; 13. N/4—B3, QR—Q1; 14. P×P, P×P; 15. B—N5, N—K5; 16. B×N, B×B; 17. Q—B2, N×N; 18. N×N. ('The guardian of the King's field leaves his post for a moment, assuming wrongly that 19. Q—B3 is a major threat'—Tartakower. If 18. Q×N, P—Q5; 19. P×P, B×N; 20. P×B, Q—R5), 18. ... P—Q5!; 19. P×P (19. KR—K1!), ... B×P+; 20. K×B, Q—R5+; 21. K—N1, B×P!; 22. P—B3 (22. K×B, Q—N5+; 23. K—R2, R—Q4—+); 22. ... KR—K1; 23. N—K4, Q—R8+; 24. K—B2, B×R; 25. P—Q5 (25. R×B, Q—R7+ or 25. N—B6+, K—B1; 26. N×R, Q—N7+), 25. ... P—B4; 26. Q—B3, Q—N7+; 27. K—K3, R×N+; 28. P×R, P—B5+ (... Q—N6+!); 29. K×P, R—B1+;

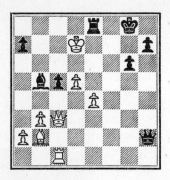

30. K—K5, Q—R7+; 31. K—K6, R—K1+; 32. K—Q7, B—N4. ‡ Mate.

(iv) NIMZOWITSCH–TARRASCH, Carlsbad, 1923. *English Opening*
1. N—KB3, N—KB3; 2. P—B4, P—B4; 3. N—B3, N—B3; 4. P—Q4, P×P; 5. N×P, P—K3; 6. N/4—N5, B—N5; 7. B—B4, 0—0 (7. ... P—Q4!?; 8. N—B7+, K—K2; 9. N×R, P—K4; 10. B—Q2, P—Q5; 11. N—Q5+, N×N; 12. P×N, Q×P; with compensation for the lost material, is an idea of the inventive Yugoslav analyst Velimirović. However, 10. B—N5! is a probable refutation.) 8. B—Q6, B×B; 9. N×B, N—K1 (9. ... Q—R4; 10. P—K3, P—QR3; 11. B—K2± Polugaievsky–Gligorić, Belgrade, 1969); 10. P—K3, Q—N3; 11. R—QN1, N—K4; 12. N×N, R×N; 13. B—K2, Q—B3. (The beginning of a bad plan. Black should have developed his Q side, although his position would remain inferior even in this case.) 14. 0—0!, N×P; 15. R—B1, P—Q4; 16. P—QN3, N—Q3; 17. N—N5, N×N: 18. R×Q, P×R; 19. Q—B2, B—Q2 (nominally Black has sufficient material for the Q but his pieces are passively placed and his dark squares very weak); 20. B×N, P×B; 21. Q—B7, KR—Q1; 22. Q—N7, P—QR4; 23. R—B1, QR—N1; 24. Q—R7, R—R1; 25. Q—N6, P—R5; 26. P—KR3, P×P; 27. P×P, B—K1; 28. P—B4, B—Q2; 29. R—B7, B—K1; 30. K—R2, R/Q1—N1; 31. Q—B5, R—Q1; 32. Q—B3, R/R1—N1; 33. P—KN4, R—R1; 34. K—N3, R—Q2; 35. R×R, B×R; 36. Q—B7, B—K1;

37. P—R4, P—R3; 38. P—R5, K—R1; 39. P—N5, K—R2; 40. Q—K7, K—N1; 41. K—B2, R—R7 + ; 42. K—K1, R—R1; 43. K—Q2, R—N1; 44. K—Q3 and here Black exceeded the time limit. 1–0.

(v) NIMZOWITSCH–TARRASCH, Breslau, 1925. *English Opening*
1. N—KB3, N—KB3; 2. P—B4, P—B4; 3. N—QB3, P—Q4; 4. P×P, N×P; 5. P—Q4, P×P; 6. Q×P, P—K3; 7. P—K3, N—QB3; 8. B—N5, B—Q2; 9. B×N, B×B; 10. N—K5, N×N; 11. N×B, Q×Q; 12. N×Q, N—Q4; 13. B—Q2 + = (White threatens to take over the QB file); **13. ... B—B4?!** (13. ... B—K2!); **14. N—N3, B—N5?!** (14. ... B—N3! to protect c7 from invasion); **15. R—QB1, R—Q1; 16. B×B, N×B; 17. K—K2, K—K2; 18. R—B4.** (There follows a classic illustration by Nimzowitsch of how one should exploit greater control of terrain in a R + N ending.) **18. ... N—R3** (18. ... N—B3; 19. R/1—QB1!± ;) **19. KR—QB1, R—Q2; 20. P—B4, KR—Q1; 21. N—Q4, P—B3; 22. P—QR4, P—K4; 23. P×P, P×P; 24. N—B3, K—K3; 25. P—QN4, P—QN3; 26. R/1—B2!.** (Nimzowitsch makes the following penetrating comment to this move: 'One of those unpretentious moves which are more disagreeable to a cramped opponent who is threatened on all sides than the worst direct attack.' and: 'the finest moves are after all waiting moves!'), **26. ... P—KR3; 27. P—R4** (gaining space on both wings), **27. ... R—Q3; 28. P—KR5, R—Q4; 29. R—KN4, R/4—Q2; 30. R—B6 + ; R—Q3** (or 30. ... K—B4?; 31. R/6—N6 and mate follows).
31. R—N6 + ‡, K—K2 (31. ... K—Q4; 32. R/QB×R +, R×R; 33. P—K4 +, K—B3; 34. P—N5 +); **32. R×P +, K—B1; 33. R×R, R×R; 34. R×P, N×P; 35. N×P, R—K3; 36. N—N6 +, K—N1; 37. N—K7 +, K—B1; 38. N—B5 + −.** There followed: **38. ... N—Q4; 39. P—N4, N—B5 + ; 40. K—B3, N—Q6; 41. R—R8 +, K—B2; 42. R—KR8, N—B4; 43. R—R7 +, K—N1; 44. R×P, R×R; 45. N×R +, K—B1; 46.**

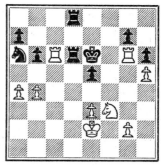

N—B5, N×P; 47. P—R6, K—N1; 48. P—N5, K—R2; 49. K—N4, N—B4; 50. K—R5, N—K3; 51. P—N6 +, K—N1; 52. P—R7 +, K—R1; 53. K—R6. 1–0.

Their Last Game

(vi) NIMZOWITSCH–TARRASCH, Kissingen, 1928. KP, *Nimzowitsch
Defence with colours reversed* (and actually, by transposition!)

**1. P—K3, P—K4; 2. N—QB3, P—Q4; 3. P—Q4, P × P; 4. Q × P,
N—KB3; 5. P—K4** (reaching exactly the position that would occur
after: 1 P—K4, N—QB3; 2. P—Q4, P—Q4; 3. P × P, Q × P;
4. N—KB3, P—K4), **5. ... N—B3; 6. B—QN5, B—Q2; 7. B × N,
B × B; 8. P—K5, N—K5** (or 8. ... N—Q2; 9. N—B3!, B—B4;
10. Q—KN4); **9. N × N, P × N; 10. N—K2, B—K2** (10. ...
Q × Q!; 11. N × Q, B—Q2 intending ... 0—0—0); **11. B—K3,
Q × Q; 12. N × Q, B—Q2; 13. 0—0, 0—0; 14. KR—K1, P—QB4;
15. N—K2, P—B4; 16. P × P ep, P × P?** (16. ... B × P!; 17. QR—
Q1, B—N5! = e.g. 18. B × P, KR—B1 or 18. P—QB3, P—QN3);
**17. N—B4, R—B2; 18. QR—Q1, B—KB1; 19. R—Q2, R—K1;
20. P—KR3, B—B3; 21. R/1—Q1, R—B2; 22. N—Q5, R—B2;
23. B—B4.** (Changing the guard. In Nimzowitsch's eyes it was
necessary to blockade even such pawns as Black's KP here which is
only 'passed' in the sense that no opposing pawn exists on the same
file.) **23. ... R—B1; 24. N—K3, P—B4; 25. N—B4, R—B3; 26.
N—R5, B—K1; 27. R—Q8, R × R; 28. R × R, K—B2; 29. R—N8,
P—N3; 30. N—B4, R—K3; 31. R—N7 +, R—K2; 32. N—Q6 +,
K—K3; 33. R—N8** (if 33. R × R +, K × R; 34. N × BP + Black
would have been able to put up stiff resistance with his two bishops),
33. ... B—R3! (if 33. ... K—Q2; 34. N × BP, R—K3; 35. R—
N7 +, K—B3; 36. R × KRP, R—B3; 37. R—QB7 +, K—N4;
38. P—KN4, B—N3; 39. B—K5, R—B2; 40. R × R, B × R; 41.
B—Q6! neatly winning a bishop); **34. B × B, K × N; 35. B—B8,
K—B2** (subtle defensive play by Tarrasch, but he still cannot avoid
the loss of a pawn); **36. R—R8, K—N2; 37. R × P +, K × R; 38.
B × R, K—N2; 39. K—R2, P—QB5; 40. K—N3, K—B1; 41. K—B4,
K—Q2; 42. B—N4, K—K3; 43. B—B3, B—Q2; 44. P—KN3,
P—N4; 45. K—N5, K—B2; 46. P—KR4, B—B1; 47. K—R6, K—
N1; 48. P—N3, P × P; 49. BP × P, P—B5** (49. ... B—Q2; 50.
B—N4, B—K3; 51. P—QR4 or 50. ... B—K1; 51. K—N5,
B—Q2; 52. K—B6); **50. P × P, B—Q2; 51. K—N5, K—B2; 52.
P—B5, B—B3; 53. K—B4, K—K2; 54. K—K5, B—K1; 55. K × P,
B—B3 +; 56. K—K5, B—K1; 57. K—Q5, B—B2 +; 58. K—B5,
B—K1; 59. B—K5, B—Q2; 60. K—N6, K—B2; 61. P—B6, B—K1;
62. P—B4, K—K3; 63. K—R5, K—B2; 64. P—N4, K—K3; 65. P—
R4, P × P; 66. P—N5. 1–0.**

(3) 'IS IT A SYSTEM ...?'

(... or a set of highly relevant *aperçus* of a positional and tactical
nature formulated by a gifted chess master?)

This is a question, I must admit, about which I cannot reach a firm conclusion. At first I accepted Nimzowitsch's teachings at their face value as a system. Then I was stricken with doubt: now I incline, once again, to the view that a 'system' of sorts does exist, bodied forth in a fashion undertaken by no other chess master or writer. It is, however, shot through with paradoxes. For example: one of Nimzowitsch's main strengths over the board was his ability as a fighter and an acute tactician, yet the appeal to a 'System' (= higher order of principles) does a lot to underplay the element of struggle. *My System* could equally aptly be titled 'My Struggle',* but does not a system deny struggle? All too often one is tempted to write of an impressive Nimzowitsch victory: 'all according to system', but this sentence sweeps the element of uncertainty, of struggle, right under the carpet, and, by an annotational sleight of hand, consigns to oblivion all those games in which Nimzowitsch followed his own theories as best he could, and finished up by suffering annihilation. Precisely to avoid this deception and to avoid giving the impression that Nimzowitsch's opponents were cyphers or punch bags against whom he demonstrated the superiority of his theories I have included a number of games in this collection which Nimzowitsch did not win. A rounded picture of a chessmaster can only be provided by his wins, draws and losses.

So, perhaps Larsen is right; perhaps the writings of Nimzowitsch are brilliant insights into the essence of chess, but still only part of a system. But a system can also be something more humble, yet still of immense value: an 'explanatory hypothesis', and who can deny that Nimzowitsch's writings have brought enlightenment to countless devotees of chess?

Ultimately, I suspect, this is a question about which the reader should form his own judgement by study of the original text.

(4) *POSITIONAL THEMES*
(a) The blockading knight
(b) Play on squares of a certain colour.

It is a rather artificial exercise to isolate such themes from Nimzowitsch's play as a whole: in fact it is even artificial to isolate them from each other. The blockading knight can be equally germane to a prophylactic manœuvre as it can be to play on squares of one colour. The point of adumbrating these themes in isolation, far from suggesting that they can operate in a vacuum in Nimzowitsch's games, is to draw the reader's attention to them in order to enhance his appreciation when they reappear in unison, and possibly obscured by

* Both over the board and in conflict with Dr. Tarrasch.

variations. Indeed, all of them will recur frequently in this collection of Nimzowitsch's games, and it is good to establish common ground and an acceptable terminology in advance of the later, more detailed discussion.

(a) *The Blockading Knight*

Ideally the rounded chess master should not harbour an idiosyncratic affection for one or other of the two minor pieces. However, Nimzowitsch did, and it is quite obvious from his games that he had a penchant for closed positions where he could exploit to the utmost the blockading potential of the knight. In his pamphlet *Die Blockade* Nimzowitsch gives away his preference for the knight by postulating the following fantasy position in which two knights dominate rook, bishop and two pawns. (White: Kg3, Nd4 and e5; Pa5, b5; Black: Kg8, Ra8, Bc8; Pa7, b7, d5, e6.) It is certainly hard to envisage winning plans for Black in his super-blockaded state. However, in *My System*, which was published after *Die Blockade*, Nimzowitsch allowed his fantasies an even freer rein. The identical position occurs there too but with the addition of a White pawn on h5, and now: 'White has winning chances!' You will see from the examples which follow that Nimzowitsch was also capable of constructing fantastic blockading possibilities for his knights over the board.

MATTISON–NIMZOWITSCH, Carlsbad, 1929, *QP, Nimzowitsch Defence*
1. P—Q4, N—KB3; 2. P—QB4, P—K3; 3. N—QB3, B—N5; 4. N—B3, B × N + ; 5. P × B, P—Q3; 6. Q—B2, Q—K2; 7. B—R3,

P—B4; 8. P—N3, P—QN3; 9. B—KN2, B—N2; 10. 0—0, 0—0; 11. N—R4, B × B; 12. K × B?, Q—N2 + !; 13. K—N1, Q—R3; 14. Q—N3, N—B3; 15. KR—Q1, N—QR4; 16. Q—N5, Q × Q; 17. P × Q, N—B5; 18. B—B1, P—QR3; 19. NP × P, R × P; 20. P × P, NP × P; 21. N—N2, N—Q4; 22. R—Q3, KR—R1.‡ Black's blockading knights, firmly established on light squares, create an impression both of power and of pictorial beauty. The same could also be said of the next example. **23. P—K4, N—K4.** White resigned.

MANNHEIMER–NIMZOWITSCH, Frankfurt, 1930. *French Defence*
1. P—K4, P—K3; 2. P—Q4, P—Q4; 3. N—QB3, B—N5; 4. P × P, P × P; 5. N—B3. White handles the opening in stereotyped

fashion and soon contracts an incurable light square weakness, with Black's knights masquerading as physicians. **5. ... N—K2; 6. B—Q3, QN—B3; 7. P—KR3, B—KB4; 8. B × B, N × B; 9. 0—0, B × N; 10. P × B, 0—0; 11. Q—Q3, N—Q3; 12. N—N5, P—KN3; 13. B—B4, Q—B3; 14. B—Q2?** It was essential to remove one of Black's knights. **14. ... P—KR3; 15. N—B3, K—R2; 16. N—R2, Q—R1.** Not just a case of Nimzowitsch's sense of humour gaining the upper hand. White threatened N—N4 and if **16. ... Q—N2; 17. N—N4, P—KR4; 18. B—R6 + −. 17. Q—K3, Q—N2.** Now this move is safe. **18. Q—B3, N—K5; 19. B—B1, P—B4; 20. Q—Q3, N—R4; 21. P—KB4, Q—Q2; 22. N—B3, Q—B3; 23. N—K5, Q—K3; 24. R—N1, P—N3; 25. K—R2, N—B5; 26. B—K3, P—KN4; 27. P—N3, R—B3; 28. QR—K1, R—KN1; 29. B—B1, P—N4; 30. N—B3, P—KN5; 31. P × P, R × P; 32. N—N1, R/3—N3; 33. R—B3, Q—N1; 34. N—K2, P—KR4‡; 35. K—N2, P—R5; 36. R—R1, R—R3; 37. R—R3, Q—N3; 38. B—K3, Q—R3.** White is helpless against Black's plan of annexing the QRP. **39. B—B2, Q × P; 40. B—K1, P—R4.** The finish is not lacking in humorous touches. **41. K—B1, Q—N8; 42. N—N1, P—R5; 43. K—K2, P—R6; 44. R—B1, P—R7.** White resigns.

Observe that Black's 38th move threatened ... N—N7 'checkmating' White's Q.

For a discussion of Nimzowitsch's slightly strained relations with the bishop pair I suggest you consult the notes to Nimzowitsch–Kmoch (page 193).

b) *Play on Squares of a Certain Colour* ('The way he sees these weaknesses developing on squares of one colour—that is one of the most typical things in Nimzowitsch.')

There follow three examples from Nimzowitsch's tournament career of a winning campaign carried out exclusively on squares of one colour (two dark and one light).

In each case the units involved are major pieces and opposite bishops, since the question of the exploitation of a colour complex involving a knight has been covered in the previous section.

NIMZOWITSCH–O. BERNSTEIN, Vilna,
1912
Position after 31. ... R—Q2.

White's winning chances reside in (i) the unfortunate position of the Black K—note that the White K does not intervene at all until a late stage of the ending—and (ii) White's dark square grip, especially the possibility of B—B8 attacking Black's KNP. Once Black loses his g7 pawn White will have little difficulty in creating a passed KRP. From the diagram the game continued: **32. P—KR4, P—R4; 33. P—KN4, P—N4.** (In the interests of exchanging the Q side pawns.) **34. P—R5, P×P; 35. P×P, P—R5; 36. P×P, B×P; 37. P—R5, R—R2; 38. B—B8, B—N8; 39. R—B1, B—Q6; 40. R—Q1, B—B4; 41. B—N4, R—R1; 42. R—Q6+, K—B2; 43. P—QR6, R—R1.** White was threatening 44. B—R5+, K—N1; 45. R—Q8+, K—R2; 46. B—N6+; a variation which highlights how important it is to have threats against the enemy king if one is seeking to win an opposite bishop plus rook position. **44. B—B5, B—N5; 45. P—R6, P×P; 46. P×P, K—N1; 47. K—B2.** Hitherto White has dominated the entire Black army with his R+B but now his K also enters the battle with decisive effect. **47. ... B—B4.** So powerful are the dark squares that Black's bishop hardly seems to count at all. **48. K—B3, P—N5; 49. B—K3, K—R1; 50. R—N6, R—KB1; 51. R×NP, P—B3; 52. B—B5!, R—B1.** Or ... R—B2; 53. R—N7!+ – ; **53. P×P, R×B; 54. P—B7, R—B1; 55. R—N7, B—Q6; 56. R—K7, B—N4; 57. K—B4, R—R1; 58. P—KR7, B—R5; 59. K—K5.** The king penetrates via the dark squares. **59. ... B—N4; 60. K—B6, P—K4; 61. K—N7.** Black resigns.

VON GOTTSCHALL–NIMZOWITSCH,
Hanover, 1926
Position after 20. ... B—Q2.

'A dead draw!? By no means. There is still a great deal in the position and the game is only just beginning' (Nimzowitsch).

21. R—B5, R×R; 22. P×R, B—B3; 23. P—B3, P—B3; 24. K—B2, K—B2; 25. R—Q4, P—QR4; 26. P—KN3? He should have done some-

thing for his light squares, e.g. 26. P—QN3, B—Q4; 27. R—Q3
followed by P—R3 and he can resist successfully. **26. ... P—
R5; 27. P—B4, P—R4; 28. P—R3, R—R1; 29. R—Q1, K—N3;
30. R—Q4, K—B4; 31. B—Q2, R—KB1; 32. B—K1, P—K4;
33. P × P, P × P; 34. R—R4, P—KN4; 35. R—QN4, K—K3 dis. + ;
36. K—K2, P—K5; 37. B—B2, R—B6; 38. R—N6, K—K4; 39.
R—N4, K—Q4; 40. P—R4.** A zugzwang position had been achieved
in which White had to give ground somewhere. The text cedes Black
more light squared territory on the K side (which is soon invaded by
Black's K) but 40. R—N6 shed a pawn after ... P—R5; 41. P × P,
P × P; 42. B × P, K × P and R × KRP. There was even a way for
White to lose a piece on move 40 by R—Q4 + ... K × P; 41. R × P
dis. + ?, R × B +. **40. ... P × P; 41. P × P, R—R6; 42. R—Q4 +,
K—K4; 43. R—Q8, B—Q4.** 'The win is not too difficult now;
in spite of annoying checks the Black army, now welded into a
homogeneous whole, creeps ever nearer' (Nimzowitsch). **44. R—
K8 +, B—K3; 45. R—Q8, K—B5; 46. R—B8 +, B—B4; 47. R—B7,
R—R7; 48. R—K7, B—N5 + ; 49. K—K1, K—B6; 50. R—B7 +,
K—N7; 51. K—Q2, K—B8; 52. K—K3, B—B6; 53. B—N3, R × NP;
54. B—Q6, R—N6 + ; 55. K—Q4, K—B7; 56. R—N7, P—K6;
57. B—N3 +, K—B8; 58. R—KB7, P—K7; 59. R—K7, B—B3.**
White resigns.

Nimzowitsch-Vera Menchick, Carlsbad, 1929. *French Defence*
**1. P—K4, P—K3; 2. P—Q4, P—Q4; 3. P—K5, P—QB4; 4. Q—
N4, P × P; 5. N—KB3, N—QB3; 6. B—Q3, Q—R4 + ; 7. N/1—
Q2, KN—K2.** Nimzowitsch recommended ... Q—B2. **8. 0—0,
N—N3; 9. R—K1, B—K2; 10. P—KR4, B—B1.** An unhappy sort
of move. Black has treated this difficult variation with a certain lack
of finesse. For superior methods I suggest the reader consult the
relevant section of the theoretical survey. **11. P—R5, KN—K2;
12. N—N3, Q—B2; 13. N/N3 × P, N × N; 14. N × N, B—Q2; 15.
B—KN5.** The dark squares loom up. **15. ... P—KN3; 16. QR—B1,
N—B4; 17. B—B6, R—KN1; 18. B × N, KP × B; 19. Q—K2, Q—
N3; 20. P—QB3, B—B4; 21. P—QN4, B × N; 22. P × B, B—K3;
23. R—B5.** Black is now held in a dark square vice. **23. ... K—
Q2; 24. Q—B3, Q × P; 25. R × P +, K—K1; 26. R—QB1, B × R;
27. Q × B, Q—N3; 28. Q—B3, P × P; 29. Q—QR3, Q—K3; 30.
R—B7.** The last link in the dark square attack. 1–0.

CHAPTER IV

THE INFLUENCE OF NIMZOWITSCH ON MODERN OPENING PLAY

'Nimzowitsch's contributions to openings theory were of such importance that it is difficult to think of anyone who had a comparable influence in our time' (Harry Golombek).

INTRODUCTION

There are many ways of categorising great chess masters, and one legitimate method is to divide them up according to whether or not they were restricted in their achievements to practical play (really Lasker and Capablanca belong to this class since they left behind them no coherent corpus of advanced theoretical writings). Tarrasch and Nimzowitsch belong to the other type which is composed of masters whose impact and success can also be judged by the durability of their theoretical utterances. When evaluating Nimzowitsch, then, we cannot ignore the question of the extent to which he has, in his games and writings, influenced that highly important aspect of modern chess: the theory of openings.

GENERAL POINTS

There are three general ways in which Nimzowitsch has influenced modern opening theory:

(1) Nimzowitsch was the first master to lay immense stress on the creation of doubled pawn complexes, and this theme runs through many of the opening variations which we associate with his name. Indeed, doubled pawn play is an essential part of the general theory of prophylaxis (or restraint), which forms the very basis of positional play, according to Nimzowitsch (*My System*, p. 118) '... in what do I see the idea of true position play? The answer is short and to the point—in prophylaxis.' We illustrate general point (1) with a modern game by Petrosian which, in my opinion, betrays clear indications of the Nimzowitschian influence apropos doubled pawns.

PETROSIAN–NILSEN, Nimzowitsch Memorial Tournament, Copenhagen, 1960. *Dutch Defence*
1. P—Q4, P—KB4; 2. B—N5, P—KN3; 3. N—Q2, B—N2; 4. P—QB3, N—KB3; 5. P—K3, P—Q3; 6. KN—B3, N—B3; 7. Q—

N3, P—KR3; 8. B × N, B × B; 9. P—K4, P—K4; 10. B—N5, K—
B1; 11. B × N, P × B; 12. P × KP, QP × P; 13. Q—R4, Q—Q3;
14. N—N3—heading for the blockading square QB5. 14. ... B—
Q2; 15. R—Q1, Q—K2; 16. N—B5!, B—K1. The way in which
Black's bishops are never given a chance is highly reminiscent of
Nimzowitsch. 17. P—QN4, K—N2; 18. 0—0, R—KB1; 19. Q—
R6, P × P; 20. N—Q2, P—K6; 21. N/2—K4!, P × P +; 22. R × P,
B—N4; 23. R × R, K × R; 24. N × B, P × N; 25. Q—N7 winning the
rook. Black resigned.

(2) Nimzowitsch frequently employed Black defences when playing
the White pieces, and therefore with an extra tempo. Playing an
opening with 'colours reversed' is now the stock-in-trade of many
modern masters. Nimzowitsch frequently opened with 1. P—K3,
sometimes transposing into the Nimzowitsch defence to the king
pawn (1. P—K4, N—QB3) with colours reversed. His real speciality,
however, was to play the Queen's Indian reversed (commencing with
1. N—KB3 and 2. P—QN3, or 1. P—QN3 immediately).

(3) It should be noted that the aim of the Black defences we
associate with Nimzowitsch was not so much to equalise as to
counter-attack and unbalance, either by provoking the foe (his
special variation of the Sicilian with 2. ... N—KB3), inflicting
weaknesses on the enemy (3. ... B—N5 in the French and the
Nimzowitsch–Indian Defence) or by inviting weaknesses, or even
cramp, in his own structure in order to obtain compensating advantages (1. P—K4, N—QB3 and 4. ... N—B3 in the Caro Kann). The
notion of the early Black counter-attack, rather than concentration
on equalisation, is now firmly embedded in modern chess thinking.

SPECIFIC OPENING VARIATIONS

(1) *Philidor Defence, Hanham Variation*
1. P—K4, P—K4; 2. N—KB3, P—Q3; 3. P—Q4, N—KB3; 4. N—
B3, QN—Q2.
This was very popular with Nimzowitsch but is hardly played at
all nowadays. However, perhaps we can observe Nimzowitsch's
influence in the related lines of the King's Indian Defence, popular-
ised by Bronstein, where Black plays ... KP × QP and then operates
in the half-open K file against White's KP. A very good example too
occurs in some related lines of the Pirc/Modern complex; for example
Gipslis–Hort, Havana, 1971, opened with 1. P—K4, P—Q3; 2. P—
Q4, P—KN3; 3. N—KB3, N—KB3; 4. QN—Q2, B—N2; 5. B—K2,
0—0; 6. 0—0, N—B3; 7. R—K1, R—K1; 8. P—B3, P—K4;
9. P × P, QN × P; 10. N × N, R × N!; 11. B—B3, Q—K1; 12. P—
B4, R—K3; 13. Q—B2, B—Q2; 14. N—B1, B—R5; 15. Q—Q3,

B—B3; **16. N—N3, Q—K2‡** and White's entire war effort had to be devoted to the defence of his KP which Black 'merely' restrained.

Teichmann–Nimzowitsch, Carlsbad, 1911, is a case of the strategy of restraint in this line advocated by Nimzowitsch: **1. P—K4, P—K4; 2. N—KB3, P—Q3; 3. P—Q4, N—KB3; 4. N—QB3, QN—Q2; 5. B—QB4, B—K2; 6. O—O, O—O; 7. Q—K2, P—QB3; 8. P—QR4, Q—B2; 9. B—N3, P—QR3; 10. P—KR3; P×P; 11. N×P, R—K1** (commencing restraint operations against the white KP); **12. B—KB4, B—KB1; 13. P—KB3, N—B4; 14. B—QR2, N—K3!; 15. B×N, B×B; 16. Q—Q2, QR—Q1; 17. KR—K1, B—B1; 18. QR—Q1, N—Q2!; 19. N—B5, N—K4; 20. N—Q4, P—KB3; 21. K—R1, Q—KB2; 22. Q—KB2, Q—N3; 23. P—QN3, N—B2; 24. K—R2, R—K2; 25. N/Q4—K2, P—KB4!; 26. N—N3, P×P?** (Precipitate. Nimzowitsch gives instead 26. ... QR—K1; 27. P×P, B×P; 28. N×B, Q×N; 29. B—N3, R×R; 30. R×R, R×R; 31. Q×R, Q×QBP); **27. N/B3×P, P—Q4; 28. N—QB5, QR—K1; 29. N—Q3, R×R; 30. R×R, R×R; 31. Q×R, Q—K3; 32. Q×Q, B×Q; 33. B—K3.** Black should now have contented himself with a draw; he wished to get more and lost the game ...' (Nimzowitsch). The continuation of this game can be found in *My System* (game 2).

(2) *King's Pawn—Nimzowitsch Defence*

Nimzowitsch's own defence to **1. P—K4: 1. ... N—QB3.** This line really has gone right out of fashion (not that it ever reached the heights). On the rare occasions when it is brought out of the closet players tend to continue, after **2. P—Q4**, with 2. ... P—K4 rather than 2. ... P—Q4 which is the 'echt Nimzowitsch' method, as in te Kolsté–Nimzowitsch, Baden-Baden, 1925: **2. ... P—Q4; 3. P—K5, P—B3!?; 4. P—KB4, B—B4; 5. N—K2, P—K3; 6. N—N3, P×P; 7. BP×P, Q—Q2!?; 8. N×B, P×N; 9. B—QN5, P—QR3; 10. B—K2, P—KN3; 11. O—O, B—R3!; 12. B×B, N×B; 13. Q—Q2, Q—N2?** (... N—B2!); **14. N—B3, N—K2; 15. B—B3, R—Q1; 16. N—K2** (16. N—R4!), **16. ... P—KN4; 17. P—B4, O—O; 18. Q—N4, P—B3; 19. P—KN3, P—B5!; 20. P×BP, P—N5; 21. B—N2, N/3—B4; 22. Q—N3, P×P; 23. Q×P+, K—R1; 24. Q—B3, P—KR4; 25. QR—Q1, P—R5; 26. R—Q3, N—Q4; 27. Q—Q2, R—KN1; 28. B×N, P×B; 29. K—R1, P—N6; 30. P×P, P×P; 31. K—N2, N—R5+; 32. K—N1, QR—KB1;**

33. N×P, Q×N+; 34. R×Q, R×R+; 35. K—R2, R/6—N2; 36. Q—Q3 (36 P—B5!, R—R2; 37. K—N3, N×P+; 38. R×N, R×R; 40. Q—R5!, R—N2+; 41. K—R4 = Nimzowitsch), **36. ... R/1—KN1; 37. R—KB3, N×R+; 38. Q×N, R—R2+. 0–1.** Interesting, if not completely correct.

Larsen has played the system on a few occasions. Jimenez–Larsen, Havana Olympiad, 1966, continued **2. ... P—Q4; 3. N—QB3!, P×P; 4. P—Q5, N—N1; 5. B—QB4, N—KB3; 6. B—KN5, P—KR3; 7. B—B4, P—R3; 8. P—QR4?, P—K3; 9. P×P, B×P; 10. B×B, P×B; 11. Q×Q+, K×Q, 12. 0—0—0+, K—B1; 13. P—B3, P×P; 14. N×P, B—B4** and Larsen went on to win the ending. Larsen played the same line against Keres at Stockholm later the same year, which varied with **5. B—KB4, N—KB3; 6. B—B4, P—QR3?!** (Keres suggested 6. ... P—KN3); **7. Q—K2!, P—QN4; 8. B—QN3, P—B4; 9. P×P e.p. N×P; 10. R—Q1, Q—R4; 11. B—Q2, N—Q5; 12. N×KP, Q—Q1; 13. Q—K3** with advantage to White—better development and no weaknesses.

Nimzowitsch, when playing this line, frequently obtained positions typical of the French. An example is Kmoch–Nimzowitsch, Niendorf, 1927: **2. N—QB3, P—K3; 3. P—Q4, B—N5!?; 4. KN—K2, P—Q4; 5. P—K5, P—KR4; 6. N—B4, P—KN3; 7. R—K3, B×N+?!; 8. P×B, N—R4; 9. B—Q3, N—K2; 10. N—R3, P—QB4; 11. B—N5, P—B5; 12. B—K2, QN—B3; 13. B—B6, R—KN1; 14. 0—0, Q—R4; 15. Q—Q2, N—B4; 16. KR—Q1, K—Q2; 17. N—N5, R—B1; 18. P—KR3, K—B2; 19. P—KN4‡** and, despite White's winning position, Nimzowitsch later succeeded in turning the tables and broke through with his Q side pawn advance to win (cf. *Chess Praxis*, game 50). The real significance of this is that in *Chess Praxis* Nimzowitsch mentions, in the notes to his 7th move, the possibility of ... B—B1, which is even now regarded as a rather advanced idea.

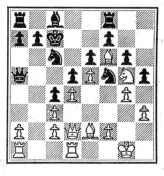

Another example of this 'French' treatment is Dr. Vajda–Nimzowitsch, Kecskemet, 1927: **1. P—K4, N—QB3; 2. P—Q4, P—Q4; 3. N—QB3, P—K3; 4. P—K5, KN—K2; 5. N—B3, P—QN3; 6. N—K2, B—R3; 7. P—B3** (Boleslavsky recommends 7. P—KN3! followed by B—R3, 0—0 and R—K1), **7. ... Q—Q2; 8. N—N3, B×B; 9. N×B, P—KR4; 10. B—N5, N—R4; 11. Q—K2, P—R3; 12. N—K3, Q—N4; 13. P—QN4, Q×Q+; 14. K×Q, QN—B3; 15. N—K1, N—N3; 16. N—Q3, B—K2; 17. B×B, QN×B;**

18. P—KB4, N—R5; 19. P—N3, N/5—B4; 20. N×N, N×N; 21. K—B3, P—R4; 22. P—QR3, K—Q2; 23. P—R3 (23. KR— QN1!), 23. ... P×P and Black is better.
Or Brinckmann–Nimzowitsch, Niendorf, 1927, which varied from the above with 7. N—N3, B×B; 8. K×B, P—KR4; 9. B—N5, Q—B1; 10. Q—Q3, N—N3; 11. P—B3, P—R5; 12. N—K2, B—K2; 13. P—KR3, B×B; 14. N×B, QN—K2; 15. K—N1, P—KB3; 16. N—B3; Q—Q2; 17. K—R2, P—QB4 and once again Black was better.

Nimzowitsch's influence with this defence can be seen in the Andersson/Petrosian method of playing the French (this should also be compared with the game against Thomas in the section on the Winawer variation of the French). A modern example, seemingly played by Nimzowitsch himself, is Olafsson–Petrosian, Bled, 1961, which went 1. P—K4, P—K3; 2. P—Q4, P—Q4; 3. N—QB3, B—N5; 4. P—K5, Q—Q2; 5. Q—N4, P—KB4; 6. Q—N3, P—QN3; 7. P—KR4, B—N2; 8. B—Q3, N—QB3; 9. KN—K2, 0—0—0; 10. B—Q2, N—R3; 11. P—R3, B—K2; 12. B—QN5?, QR—N1; 13. Q—Q3, N—B2; 14. 0—0—0, K—N1; 15. N—B4, Q—B1; 16. N/3—K2, N/3—Q1; 17. Q—QN3? (better 17. P—QB3, P—B4; 18. K—N1), 17. ... P—B3; 18. B—Q3, P—B4!; 19. P×P, B×P; 20. N—R3, N×P; 21. B—KB4, N/1—B2; 22. B—QN5, K—R1; 23. N—Q4, N—N3! (with the awkward threat 24. ... P—K4); 24. Q—R4, B×N; 25. B—Q7, Q—B1; 26. R×B, P—K4; 27. R—N4, P×B; 28. R×NP, N/2—K4; 29. R×B, K×R; 30. P—R5, Q—Q3; 31. P×N, Q×B; 32. Q×BP, N×P. 0–1. Nimzowitsch would have approved, in particular, of Petrosian's delayed ... P—QB4, and also of the effect that this move then had on White's position. The reader might also like to compare this more recent case:

CAMPOS–PETROSIAN, San Antonio, 1972

1. P—K4, P—K3; 2. P—Q4, P—Q4; 3. N—QB3, B—N5; 4. P—K5, P—QN3; 5. N—B3; B—B1!?; 6. B—K2, N—K2; 7. 0—0, N—N3; 8. R—K1, B—K2; 9. P—KN3, P—QB4; 10. P—KR4, P—KR3. Prophylaxis or provocation? A paradox exists with Petrosian too in that despite his great preventive proclivities he frequently allows his opponent a completely free hand in the opening, leaving him to his own devices to an even greater extent than did Nimzowitsch. 11. B—Q3, N—B1; 12. P—R4, P—R3; 13. P—QR5. Give a man enough rope ... P—B5.‡ The typical Nimzowitschian treatment of such situations. 14. B—B1, P—QN4; 15. B—Q2, N—QB3; 16. B—R3, P—N5; 17. N—K2, N×RP; 18. P—R5, N—B3; 19. N—R2, Q—N3; 20. B—K3, P—R4;

21. P—N3, B—R3; 22. N—QB1,
B—QN4; 23. P—B4, P—R5; 24.
P×RP, R×P; 25. R×R, B×R;
26. N—B3, N—QR2; 27. P—B5,
N—N4; 28. R—B1, N—B6; 29.
Q—K1, B×P; 30. P—B6, P×P;
31. P×P, B—Q3; 32. Q—Q2, B—
K5; 33. N—K5 and 0–1.

Ulf Andersson has also played
several games with the above line.
You will see that I am attempting
to establish some sort of identity
between Nimzowitsch and certain modern players, notably Petrosian
and Hübner and, most of all, Larsen, who seems to use a lot of
Nimzowitsch's openings—perhaps because they *are* unusual—and
also has a lot of Nimzowitsch's faults; a comparison which will
recur. Petrosian and Nimzowitsch do show similarities in attitudes
and concepts, but of course chess personalities are very complex,
and one could not say that Larsen and Petrosian are at all close!

(3) *French Defence—Winawer Variation*

1. P—K4, P—K3; 2. P—Q4, P—Q4; 3. N—QB3, B—N5. This is
known on the continent as Nimzowitsch's variation. His main contribution was to demonstrate in many games that the once feared
4. P×P is by no means a refutation of 3. ... B—N5. A signal
example of this was Yates–Nimzowitsch, Semmering, 1926:
1. P—K4, P—K3; 2. P—Q4, P—Q4; 3. N—QB3, B—N5; 4. P×P,
P×P; 5. B—Q3, N—K2; 6. N—K2, 0—0; 7. 0—0, B—N5;
8. P—B3 (White later suffers from the weakness at K3), 8. ...
B—KR4; 9. N—B4, B—N3; 10. QN—K2, B—Q3; 11. Q—K1,
P—QB4; 12. P×P, B×P+; 13. K—R1, QN—B3; 14. B—Q2,
R—K1; 15. N×B, RP×N; 16. P—KB4, N—B4; 17. P—B3,
P—Q5; 18. P—B4, Q—N3; 19. R—
B3, B—N5 (conquering K6); 20. P—
QR3, B×B; 21. Q×B, P—R4; 22.
N—N1, R—K6; 23. R—Q1, QR—
K1; 24. Q—KB2, Q—N6; 25. R—
Q2, N—Q3; 26. P—QB5, N—B5;
27. B×N, Q×B; 28. R—B2, Q—
Q4; 29. R—B1, Q—K5.‡ Black's
position is clearly superior.

Another example of the way in
which Nimzowitsch reduced the fearsome reputation of the exchange

Winawer is Marshall–Nimzowitsch, New York, 1927: **5. N—B3, N—K2; 6. B—Q3, QN—B3; 7. P—KR3, B—K3; 8. O—O, Q—Q2; 9. B—KB4, B × N; 10. P × B, P—B3; 11. R—N1, P—KN4; 12. B—N3, O—O—O; 13. Q—K2, QR—K1; 14. KR—K1, N—B4; 15. B × N, B × B; 16. Q—N5, N—Q1; 17. Q—B5, P—N3; 18. Q—R3, K—N2; 19. Q—N3, N—B3; 20. N—Q2, N—R4; 21. Q—N2, R × R +; 22. R × R, R—K1; 23. R × R, Q × R; 24. Q—N1, K—B1** (24. ... Q—K7 is also good); **25. Q—Q1, Q—K3; 26. N—N3, N—B5; 27. N—Q2, N—R6; 28. N—B1, N × P; 29. Q—R5, B—Q6; 30. Q—Q1, Q—K5** and Black eventually won.

Finally Spielmann–Nimzowitsch, Copenhagen, 1923: **5. B—Q3, N—QB3; 6. N—K2, KN—K2; 7. O—O, QB—B4; 8. N—N3, B—N3; 9. N/B3—K2, Q—Q2; 10. P—KB4, P—B4!; 11. P—QR3, B—Q3; 12. P—N3, N—KN1; 13. B—N2, N/3—K2; 14. P—B4, P—B3; 15. Q—B2, N—B3 = ‡.**

Once Nimzowitsch had succeeded in demonstrating that the Winawer was viable against the exchange line, this whole variation became considerably more popular and quite respectable. It is interesting to note that, once again, this is a variation where the stress centres on a doubled pawn complex. The variation has been bequeathed in modern chess to R. Byrne, Botvinnik,* Uhlmann, Petrosian and Korchnoi, to name but a few.

The theory of the 'Andersson/Petrosian' line, which seems to have been born in Nimzowitsch's treatment of his own defence (above), was further elaborated in his game against Thomas from Carlsbad, 1929. **1. P—K4, P—K3; 2. P—Q4, P—Q4; 3. N—QB3, B—N5; 4. P—K5, P—QN3!; 5. Q—N4, P—KN3; 6. B—KN5, B—K2; 7. B—Q2, B—R3; 8. B × B, N × B; 9. Q—K2, N—N5** (Nimzowitsch, in the tournament book, suggested that the retreat . . . N—N1 would be more dynamic); **10. Q—N5+, Q—Q2; 11. Q × Q +, K × Q; 12. O—O—O, P—KR4; 13. N—B3, N—QB3** (heading for QB5); **14. N—K2, P—R4; 15. P—QR4, N—R2; 16. K—N1, N—R3; 17. P—R3, P—QN4; 18. P × P, N × P; 19. P—B4!, P × P; 20. R—QB1, N—B4; 21. R × P, P—QR5; 22. K—R2, R—QR3; 23. N—N5, B × N; 24. B × B, N—K2; 25. R—N4, P—QB3; 26. B × N, K × B; 27. N—B3, R—Q1!; 28. N—K2, N—B2; 29. R—N7, R—Q2; 30. R—QB1, N—Q4; 31. R × R +, K × R; 32. N—B3!,**

---

* Especially his games in the U.S.S.R. during the 1930s and 1940s—for which see Botvinnik's own book of selected games.

K—K2! (not 32. ... N—B5; 33. P—KN3, N×P?; 34. N—K4 and
Black's knight is trapped); **33. N×N+, BP×N; 34. K—R3,
K—Q2; 35. R—B3, R—R1.** ½–½.

Compare with this modern game by Ulf Andersson: Spassky–
Andersson, Dortmund, 1973—as above up to **5. ... B—B1;
6. N—B3; Q—Q2; 7. P—KR4, P—KR4; 8. Q—B4, B—R3;
9. B×B, N×B; 10. Q—K3, P—QB4; 11. Q—K2, N—B2;
12. B—N5, N—K2; 13. B×N, B×B; 14. Q—Q2,** and now ...
P—B5 is =.

Nimzowitsch had a fondness for playing ... P—QB5, blocking
the Q side, for example Steiner–Nimzowitsch, Berlin, 1928, opened
**1. P—K4, P—K3; 2. P—Q4, P—Q4; 3. N—QB3, B—N5;
4. P—K5, P—QB4** ('This challenge, as will soon be seen, is not
meant seriously and the pawn presently passes by in peace'—Nimzowitsch); **5. B—Q2, N—K2; 6. P—QR3, B×N; 7. P×B, P—B5?;
8. P—KR4, P—KR4; 9. B—K2, N—B4; 10. P—N3, P—KN3;
11. B—N5, Q—R4; 12. Q—Q2** ('the White QB's diagonal has a
crippling effect and Black's counter-blockade by the N at KB4 soon
proves untenable'—Nimzowitsch), **12. ... N—B3; 13. B—B6,
R—KN1; 14. N—R3, K—Q2; 15. N—N5, N—R3; 16. P—B3,
K—B2; 17. P—N4, R—K1; 18. B—N7, N—N1** and Black is
repulsed all along the line. After **19. P×P, P×P; 20. P—B4**
Black's position can no longer be held.

A happier example was Becker–Nimzowitsch, Breslau, 1925:
**1. P—K4, P—K3; 2. P—Q4, P—Q4; 3. N—QB3, N—QB3;
4. N—B3, B—N5; 5. P—K5, B×N+; 6. P×B, N—R4;
7. P—QR4, N—K2; 8. B—Q3, P—QN3; 9. N—Q2!, P—QB4;
10. Q—N4, P—B5; 11. B—K2** (11. Q×NP, R—N1 and ...
P×B), **11. ... N—B4; 12. N—B3, P—KR3; 13. Q—R3, K—Q2;
14. P—KN4, N—K2; 15. N—Q2,
Q—K1; 16. P—KB4, K—B2; 17.
B—QR3, B—Q2; 18. Q—KB3, P—
KR4!;‡ 19. N×P!, N×N; 20. B×N,
P×P; 21. Q—N2, N—B4; 22. B—
Q3, B×P!!** ('A lunch under danger-
ous conditions!'—Nimzowitsch); **23.
B×N, P×B; 24. Q×QP, B—B3;
25. Q—Q6+, K—B1; 26. P—Q5,
R—KR3; 27. P—K6, B×P!** (27. ...
R×KP+ was also possible); **28.
Q×B, Q×P+; 29. Q×Q+, R×Q+.**

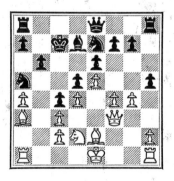

'White now has a piece for two
pawns, but his own pawns are weak'—Nimzowitsch. Black won
after a variety of adventures.

A number of modern masters also share a fondness for ...
P—QB5, among them being Petrosian, Korchnoi, Bronstein and
Botvinnik. A recent example is Ostojic–Botvinnik, Wijk aan Zee,
1969: **1. P—K4, P—K3; 2. P—Q4, P—Q4; 3. N—Q2, N—KB3;
4. P—K5, KN—Q2; 5. P—KB4, P—QB4; 6. P—B3, N—QB3;
7. QN—B3, P—B5!; 8. P—KN4, P—QN4; 9. N—K2, N—N3;
10. B—R3, P—KR4!** Black has already equalised, and he went on to
win.

Nimzowitsch's swan song with the **3. ... B—N5** variation was his
win against Lasker from Zürich, 1934 (page 303).

Before concluding this discussion of Nimzowitsch's handling of the
French Defence from the Black side we must mention his original
treatment of the Orthodox variation—which has points in common
with his own defence and his interpretation of the Winawer.

Sämisch–Nimzowitsch, Berlin, 1928 (Schachgesellschaft), **1. P—
K4, P—K3; 2. P—Q4, P—Q4; 3. N—QB3, N—KB3; 4. B—N5,
B—K2; 5. P—K5, N—N1!?** This unusual move, or rather the
strategic conception underlying Nimzowitsch's interpretation of
this move, contains in itself the quintessential Nimzowitschian
paradox: provocation and prevention, under one roof, as it were.
White will naturally wish to administer sharp punishment for the
'insult' involved in returning the N to its initial square, e.g. Levy–
Heidenfeld, Dublin, 1968: **5. ... N—N1; 6. B—K3, P—QN3;
7. P—KN4?!** But such violence may later react to White's disadvantage, especially if he continues in like vein. As to prophylaxis:
with White's pawn chain established on dark squares and with
White in possession of a 'territorial plus' on the K side Black must
overprotect the K side light squares (f5/g4/g6) to forestall a K side
pawn avalanche by White along the lines of (eventually) P—KB4/
P—KN4 and P—KB5. Bizarre though it may appear **5. ... N—N1**
achieves far more in the direction of the said overprotection (since
the N can redeploy via e7 or h6 to f5) than does **5. ... KN—Q2.**
The disadvantage, of course, is the 'anti-development' of a piece, but
so long as Black avoids a premature ... P—QB4 the position will
remain closed and virtually impervious to break through; and, after
all, is d7 such a marvellous square for the Black KN? **6. B—K3,
P—QN3; 7. Q—N4?!** In a detailed discussion of the whole ...
N—N1 variation (*Chessman Quarterly*, 1970) the Irish International
John Moles recommended **7. P—KR4!** giving as a reasonable continuation: **7. ... P—KR4; 8. B—K2, P—N3; 9. N—B3, B—R3;
10. Q—Q2, B × B; 11. N × B, N—QB3** followed by ... Q—Q2 and
... O—O—O. Perhaps White is slightly better, although Black's set-up
is extremely tough. **7. ... P—N3; 8. P—KR4, P—KR4; 9. Q—N3?!
(9. Q—R3!?), 9. ... B—R3; 10. N—B3, B × B; 11. K × B, Q—Q2;**

12. P—R3, N—QB3; 13. R—Q1,
N—R4; 14. N—KN5, N—R3; 15.
B—B1, 0—0—0; 16. Q—Q3, K—N1;
17. R—R3, QR—KB1; 18. K—N1,
N—B4; 19. N—K2, Q—Q1‡; 20. P—
KN3, P—B4; 21. P×P, P×P; 22.
K—N2, Q—N3. Black's plan is to
attack White's KP until P—KB4
becomes necessary and then to
eliminate White's advanced N (...
B×N/g5) at a moment when White
cannot recapture with his B. (Nimzo-

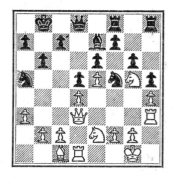

witsch). 23. P—B4?! Playing it at once saves Black a lot of trouble.
23. ... B×N; 24. RP×B, R—B1; 25. R—R2, KR—Q1; 26. K—
R3, P—Q5; 27. Q—KB3, R—Q4; 28. P—N3, P—B5; 29. P—
QN4, N—B3; 30. P—B3, P—Q6; 31. N—N1, P—Q7!! Intro-
ducing a deep and beautiful combination, one of the most im-
pressive I have ever seen. 32. R/2×P. After 32. B×P, R/1—Q1
the pin is overpowering. 32. R/1×P is also unplayable since the
N hangs. 32. ... R×R; 33. B×R, R—Q1. Threatening ... R—
Q6×NP. 34. Q—K2. On 34. B—B1 Nimzowitsch planned ...
R×R; 35. Q×R, Q—B7; 36. N—K2, K—B1!; 37. Q—R4, Q—
B6 − +. If 37. P—R4, N/3—K2 followed by ... N—Q4 and ...
N—K6 − + and White is paralysed. A wonderful variation. 34. ...
R—Q6; 35. N—B3, Q—Q1; 36. R—KB1, Q—Q4; 37. R—B2,
P—R5! The climax of the combination. White loses his Q. Observe
the remarkable paralysis that has seized White's pieces after the
inspired pawn sacrifice on move 32. 38. P×P, N/3—Q5; 39. P×N,
N×QP; 40. Q×R, P×Q; 41. N×N, Q×N; 42. K—N3, Q—K5??
With 42. ... Q—R8! Nimzowitsch could have crowned his outstanding combination. White cannot prevent the loss of the QRP
and a Black victory is assured. After the text Sämisch succeeds in
protecting his QRP and, unbelievably, Black's advantage is insufficient to win. After further serious errors by White Nimzowitsch
did eventually win from this drawn position on move 88.

(4) *French Defence—3. P—K5*
1. P—K4, P—K3; 2. P—Q4, P—Q4; 3. P—K5. Yet another of
Nimzowitsch's brain children, but it is not very popular now—
though there are occasional surges of interest in the Milner–Barry
gambit line.
   After 3. ... P—QB4 Nimzowitsch frequently played 4. Q—N4
which, however, is now right out of fashion and rarely employed. An
example of Nimzowitsch's handling of the line is Nimzowitsch–

Szekely, Kecskemet, 1927: **4.** ... **P×P; 5. N—KB3, N—QB3** (the modern discovery is 5. ... P—B4; 6. Q—N3, N—K2; 7. B—Q3, N/K2—B3; 8. 0—0, N—Q2; 9. P—QR3, N—B4; 10. P—N4, N—K5; 11. Q—B4, P—R3, Gumprich–Platz, Berlin, 1950, but why not simply 7. N × P?); **6. B—Q3, KN—K2; 7. 0—0, N—N3; 8. R—K1, Q—B2; 9. Q—N3, B—B4; 10. P—KR4, K—B1; 11. P—R5, KN—K2; 12. P—R6, P—KN3; 13. P—R3, P—R4; 14. B—KN5, N—KN1; 15. QN—Q2, P—B3?! 16. N—N3!, P—N3; 17. P × P, Q × Q; 18. P × Q, B—Q3; 19. B—N5, N—R2; 20. KN × P, K—B2; 21. P—B4, P—K4; 22. P × P, P × N; 23. B—K8 +, K—B1; 24. P—B7, B—KB4; 25. N × QP, B—B4; 26. QR—Q1, N—N4; 27. P × N = Q +, R × Q; 28. B × N, K—B2; 29. P—Q6. 1–0.**

Nimzowitsch–Haakanson, Kristianstad, 1922, was a signal success for this system. It varied from the Szekely game with **6.** ... **P—KB4; 7. Q—N3, KN—K2; 8. 0—0, N—N3; 9. P—KR4, Q—B2; 10. R—K1, B—Q2** (10. ... B—B4 was essential); **11. P—QR3, 0—0—0; 12. P—QN4, P—QR3**

(12. ... K—N1 would have been rather better); **13. P—R5, KN—K2; 14. B—Q2, P—KR3; 15. P—R4, P—KN4; 16. P—N5, P—B5; 17. Q—N4, N—QN1; 18. P—QB3, R—K1; 19. P × P, K—Q1; 20. R—QB1, Q—N3; 21. P—R5, Q—R2; 22. P—N6, Q—R1; 23. R—B7, N—KB4; 24. N—QB3!, B—K2; 25. N × QP, N × QP; 26. N × N, P × N; 27. Q × B + ‡. 1–0.** A remarkable case of asphyxiation!

Nimzowitsch also played 4. N—KB3 quite frequently. 4. ... P × P is the most logical reply; Nimzowitsch–von Freymann, All Russian Championship, 1914, continued **5. Q × P, N—QB3; 6. Q—KB4, Q—B2; 7. B—QN5, N—K2; 8. 0—0, N—N3; 9. Q—N3, B—Q2; 10. R—K1, 0—0—0; 11. B × N, P × B; 12. B—N5, R—K1; 13. P—B4, P—B3?!; 14. B—B4!, B—N5; 15. N—B3, KR—B1; 16. BP × P, KBP × P** (16. ... KP × P; 17. N × P!); **17. P × BP, B × P; 18. B × P, N × B; 19. N × N, B—B4; 20. R—K2, B—N2; 21. N—N5, Q—N3; 22. R—QB1, Q × N; 23. KR—B2, K—N1; 24. R × B, R—B1; 25. N—Q3 +. 1–0.**

It would seem that von Freymann had not learnt a great deal from their meeting in the All Russian Championship, 1912: **5. N × P** (instead of 5, Q × P), **5.** ... **N—QB3; 6. N × N, P × N; 7. B—Q3,**

Q—B2; 8. B—KB4, P—N4?; 9. B—N3, B—KN2; 10. Q—K2, N—K2; 11. 0—0, P—KR4; 12. P—KR3, N—B4; 13. B—R2, P—N5?! (Nimzowitsch will be only too pleased to take control of his KB4); 14. R—K1, K—B1; 15. N—B3, Q—K2; 16. B × N, P × B; 17. Q—K3, R—R3; 18. N—K2, P—B4; 19. N—B4, P—Q5; 20. Q—Q3, Q—Q2; 21. Q—B4, Q—B3; 22. P × P, B—R3; 23. Q—Q5, Q × Q; 24. N × Q, B—B5 (Black has not been able to capture the pawn because of P—K6!); 25. N—B6, RP × P; 26. B—B4, R—N3; 27. N—Q7 +, K—K2; 28. N × P, R—QB1; 29. P—N4, B—KR3; 30. QR—Q1, B × B; 31. R × P, R—KR3; 32. R × QB, QR—KR1; 33. K—B1, R—R8 + ; 34. K—K2; R × R + ; 35. K × R, B × P; 36. N—Q3, B—Q3; 37. P—R4, P—R4; 38. P—N5, R—R8 + ; 39. K—K2, R—R7; 40. N—B4, B × N; 41. R × B, R × P; 42. P—B4, R—N8; 43. R × BP, K—K3; 44. R—Q5, R—N8; 45. R—Q8, K—K2; 46. R—QR8, R—N5; 47. P—B5, R × RP; 48. P—N6, R—N5; 49. P—B6, R × P; 50. P—B7. 1–0.

Two other interesting games in this line, in which Nimzowitsch's opponents answered 4. N—KB3 with moves other than 4. ... P × P, are:

NIMZOWITSCH–SPIELMANN, San Sebastian, 1912

4. ... N—QB3; 5. P × P, B × P; 6. B—Q3, KN—K2; 7. B—KB4, Q—N3; 8. 0—0, Q × NP; 9. QN—Q2, Q—N3; 10. N—N3, N—N3; 11. B—N3, B—K2; 12. P—KR4, Q—N5; 13. P—QR4, P—QR3; 14. P—KR5, N—R5; 15. N × N, B × N; 16. P—QB3, Q—K2; 17. B—R2, P—KB4; 18. P × Pe.p., P × P; 19. N—Q4, P—K4; 20. B—KB5 with a strong attack, duly converted into a win.

NIMZOWITSCH–LEONHARDT, San Sebastian, 1912

4. ... Q—N3; 5. B—Q3, P × P; 6. 0—0, N—QB3; 7. P—QR3, KN—K2; 8. P—QN4, N—N3; 9. R—K1, B—K2; 10. B—N2, P—QR4 (better 10. ... P—QR3); 11. P—N5, P—R5; 12. QN—Q2 (threat: 13. P × N, Q × B; 14. R—N1 followed by P × P), 12. ... N—R2; 13. B × P, B—B4; 14. B × B!, Q × B; 15. P—B4, P × P; 16. N—K4, Q—Q4; 17. N—Q6 +, K—K2; 18. N × QBP, Q—B4; 19. B × N, RP × B; 20. Q—Q6 +, Q × Q; 21. P × Q +. 1–0.

Nimzowitsch played what is now known as the Milner-Barry gambit rather infrequently, but he had one particular success which must have given him very great pleasure:

NIMZOWITSCH–TARRASCH, San Sebastian, 1912

4. P—QB3, N—QB3; 5. N—KB3, Q—N3; 6. B—Q3, P × P;

7. P×P, B—Q2; 8. B—K2 (not the pure Milner–Barry, which should not be bad for Black after 8. O—O, N×QP; 9. N×N, Q×N; 10. N—B3, P—QR3! and it is not clear that White has enough compensation for the pawn. It may also be possible for Black to play 10. ... Q×P; in a recent game Westerinen scored a fine success with this over Bisguier: 11. R—K1, Q—N1; 12. N×P, B—Q3; 13. Q—R5—13. *Q—N4! is stronger*—13. ... K—B1; 14. N—B3, N—B3; 15. Q—R4, B—B3; 16. B—KN5, B—K4 − +; **8. ...**

KN—K2; 9. P—QN3, N—B4; 10. B—N2, B—N5 +; 11. K—B1‡, B—K2 (keeping up the pressure on the QP, but Nimzowitsch shows that Black should have played 11. ... O—O!; 12. P—KN4—*12. B—Q3, P—KB3; 13. B×N, P×N+ =*—12. ... N—R3; 13. R—KN1, P—KB3; 14. P×P, R×P!; 15. P—N5, R×N!; 16. B×R—*or 16. P×N, R—B2*—16. ... N—B4; 17. R—N4, B—K1; 18. Q—K2, QN×P; 19. R×N!, N×R; 20. Q—K5, B—N4 +; 21. K—N2, N—B4; 22. B×QP—*if 22. N—QB3, B×N; 23. B×B, P—Q5*—22. ... P×B; 23. Q×N, R—KB1; 24. Q×QP+, R—B2!; 25. Q—Q4, B—B4 and White must resign); **12. P—KN3, P—QR4?; 13. P—QR4, R—QB1; 14. B—QN5, N—N5; 15. N—QB3!** (Louis Paulsen–Tarrasch, Nürnberg, 1888, had gone 15. B×B+?, K×B; 16. N—QB3, N—QB3; 17. N—QN5, N—R2; 18. N×N?, Q×N; 19. Q—Q3, Q—R3!, and Tarrasch won a fine ending after the exchange of queens), **15. ... N—QR3** (in *Dreihundert Schachpartien*, the second edition published in 1909, Tarrasch gives 15. ... B×B; 16. N×B, N—B7 with the threat of ... N—K6 +; this Nimzowitsch shows to be harmless: 17. R—QB1, N—K6 +; 18. P×N, N×P +; 19. K—K2, N×Q; 20. R×R +, K—Q2; 21. R×R, N×B; 22. R—QB1 and wins). **16. K—N2, N—B2; 17. B—K2, B—N5; 18. N—R2, N—QR3; 19. B—Q3, N—K2; 20. R—QB1, N—B3; 21. N×B, N/R3×N; 22. B—N1, P—KR3; 23. P—KN4, N—K2; 24. R×R +, B×R; 25. N—K1, R—B1; 26. N—Q3, P—KB3; 27. N×N, Q×N; 28. P×P, R×P; 29. B—B1, N—B3; 30. P—N5, P×P; 31. B×P, R—B1; 32. B—K3, Q—K2; 33. Q—N4, Q—B3; 34. R—KN1, R—KR1; 35. K—R1, R—R5; 36. Q—N3, R×QP** ('Despair! B—N5 was threatened as also Q×P'—Nimzowitsch); **37. B×R, N×B; 38. Q×P, Q—B6 +; 39. Q—N2, Q×Q +; 40. R×Q, N×P; 41. P—KR4.** 1–0.

After his game with Tarrasch Nimzowitsch decided that 6. B—Q3 was too risky, and in subsequent games (before he discovered 4. Q—N4) he developed the KB on a more modest square, K2, although this cut out the possibility of reaching the position from his Salwe game (cf. page 104). Here is one example: Nimzowitsch–Spielmann, Stockholm, 1920: **6. B—K2, P×P; 7. P×P, N—R3; 8. N—B3, N—B4; 9. N—QR4, B—N5+; 10. B—Q2!** (10. K—B1? was played by Nimzowitsch just prior to this tournament in the third game of his match with Bogoljubow. There followed: 10. ... Q—Q1; 11. P—QR3, B—K2; 12. P—QN4, 0—0; 13. KR—N1, P—B3; 14. P—N4, N/B4×P; 15. N×N, N×N; 16. Q×N, P×P; 17. Q—Q2, P—QN3; 18. P—KN5, P—Q5!; 19. B—QB4, P—QN4!; 20. B×NP, Q—Q4; 21. Q—K2, P—K5; 22. B—QB4, P—Q6; 23. Q—R2, Q—Q5; 24. R—N4, P—Q7; 25. Q×P, Q×B+; 26. Q—K2, Q—N6; 27. N—B5, B×N; 28. P×B, B—R3. 0–1), **10. ... Q—R4; 11. B—B3, B—Q2** (a subtle idea of Hübner's is 11. ... P—QR3! as in Kupreichik–Hübner, Sombor, 1970: 12. P—N4, N/4—K2; 13. Q—N3, P—R4; 14. P×P, R×P; 15. P—QR3, B×B+; 16. P×B, R—N1; 17. N—N6, B—Q2; 18. P—KR4, N—Q1; 19. R—KN1, B—N4; 20. P—R4, B×B; 21. K×B, N—B1; 22. N×N, R×N; 23. K—Q3, R—KB4 and Black went on to win), **12. P—QR3, B×B+; 13. N×B, P—R4; 14. 0—0, QR—B1; 15. Q—Q2, Q—Q1; 16. P—R3, N—R4; 17. QR—Q1, Q—N3; 18. KR—K1, N—B5; 19. B×N, R×B; 20. N—K2, B—R5; 21. QR—B1, B—N6; 22. R×R, B×R; 23. N—N3, N—K2; 24. P—KR4, N—N3; 25. N—B1, B×N; 26. R×B, N—K2; 27. R—B1, 0—0; 28. P—QN4, N—B4; 29. R—B5, Q—R3; 30. Q—B3** with a grip on the QB file which sufficed for victory.

(5) *Caro Kann*

1. P—K4, P—QB3; 2. P—Q4, P—Q4; 3. N—QB3, P×P; 4. N×P. This was another favourite of Nimzowitsch's, but he did not like the generally quiet situations generated by the classical 4. ... B—B4, preferring the tense struggles that resulted from 4. ... N—KB3 and after 5. N×N+ the recapture with the KP. Asztalos–Nimzowitsch, Bled, 1931, went **5. ... KP×N; 6. P—QB3, B—Q3; 7. B—Q3, 0—0; 8. Q—B2, P—KR3; 9. N—K2, Q—B2; 10. B—K3, N—Q2; 11. Q—Q2?!** (better 11. 0—0—0, R—K1; 12. P—KN4!), **11. ... R—K1; 12. N—N3?, B—B5!** and Nimzowitsch was beginning to get on top.

Nimzowitsch, on occasion, played the alternative fifth move recapture 5. ... NP×N. His game against Leonhardt at Carlsbad, 1911, must have been one of the first games with this idea. Lasker–

c

Nimzowitsch, St. Petersburg, 1914, continued **6. B—K2** (nowadays 6. P—QB3, B—B4; 7. B—QB4 or 7. N—K2 would more likely be played), **6. ... B—B4; 7. B—B3, Q—R4 + ; 8. P—B3, P—R4!?** (intending to prevent White castling K side); **9. B × RP, N—Q2; 10. B—N4, B × B; 11. Q × B, 0—0—0; 12. N—K2, P—K3; 13. B—B4, Q—QN4; 14. 0—0—0, N—N3; 15. N—N3?** (15. P—QN3 would leave White with a safe though difficult game—Lasker), **15. ... Q—Q4; 16. K—N1, Q × NP; 17. QR—N1, Q × BP; 18. N—K4, Q—R5; 19. Q—B3, N—B5; 20. K—R1, P—KB4; 21. N—N5, B—Q3; 22. B—B1, R—Q2; 23. R—N2, B—B2; 24.**

KR—N1, N—Q3; 25. Q—K2, N—K5; 26. N—B3, Q—R6;‡ (26. ... Q—R4 is probably better); **27. P—R3, P—R3; 28. B—K3, KR—Q1; 29. K—R2, R—R1; 30. K—R1, KR—Q1; 31. K—R2, R—K1; 32. R—N8, R × R; 33. R × R +, R—Q1; 34. R—N7, R—Q2; 35. R—N8 +, R—Q1; 36. R—N7, R—B1** (again 36. ... Q—R4, threat 37. ... B × P); **37. P—B4, N—B3** (better 37. ... K—Q1); **38. B—N5, N—R4; 39. R × P!, R × R; 40. Q × P +, R—Q2; 41. N—K5.** ½-½. Nimzowitsch should certainly have won this game. Nimzowitsch also pioneered the method with 4. ... N—Q2 as in his game with Kostic (White), Bled, 1931: **5. KN—B3** (we now consider as the main line 5. B—QB4, KN—B3; 6. N—N5, P—K3; 7. Q—K2, N—N3; 8. B—Q3!), **5. ... N/1—B3; 6. N—N3, P—K3; 7. B—Q3, P—B4; 8. P × P, N × P; 9. B—N5 +, B—Q2; 10. B × B +, Q × B; 11. Q × Q +, N/4 × Q; 12. P—B4, B—N5 + =.** Smyslov and Petrosian have upheld the honour of this variation in contemporary practice.

As White, against the Caro Kann, Nimzowitsch had a sneaking admiration for his French move: 3. P—K5. He played it in a game against Giese (cf. *My System*, p. 120), and in the following game where he suffered a calamitous reversal.

NIMZOWITSCH–CAPABLANCA, New York, 1927

1. P—K4, P—QB3; 2. P—Q4, P—Q4; 3. P—K5, B—B4; 4. B—Q3, B × B; 5. Q × B, P—K3; 6. N—QB3 (6. N—K2 is more usual), **6. ... Q—N3; 7. KN—K2, P—QB4.** (A possibility favoured by Nimzowitsch as Black in such positions—e.g. his game versus Duras from San Sebastian, 1912, was ... Q—R3. Capablanca had borrowed that idea to beat Atkins at London, 1922.) **8. P × P, B × P;**

**9. 0—0, KN—K2; 10. N—R4, Q—B3; 11. N × B, Q × N; 12. B—
K3, Q—B2; 13. P—KB4, N—B4** (it is rather amusing to compare
this with the Vajda–Nimzowitsch game in section 2); **14. P—B3,
N—B3; 15. QR—Q1, P—KN3; 16. P—KN4?** (creating a perma-
nent weakness. Better 16. B—B2), **16. .... N × B; 17. Q × N, P—
KR4; 18. P—N5, 0—0; 19. N—Q4, Q—N3; 20. R—B2,
KR—B1; 21. P—QR3, R—B2; 22. R—Q3, N—R4; 23. R—K2,
R—K1; 24. K—N2, N—B3; 25. R/K2—Q2, R/K1—QB1; 26. R—
K2, N—K2; 27. R/K2—Q2, R—B5!; 28. Q—R3, K—N2;
29. R—KB2, P—R4; 30. R—K2, N—B4!; 31. N × N +, NP × N;
32. Q—B3, K—N3; 33. R/K2—Q2, R—K5; 34. R—Q4, R/B1—
B5; 35. Q—B2, Q—N4; 36. K—N3, R/B5 × R; 37. P × R, Q—B5;
38. K—N2, P—N4; 39. K—N1, P—N5; 40. P × P, P × P; 41. K—
N2, Q—B8; 42. K—N3, Q—KR8; 43. R—Q3, R—K8; 44. R—
KB3, R—Q8; 45. P—N3, R—QB8!** (Zugzwang); **46. R—K3,
R—KB8.** 0–1. One might suppose from this game that Capablanca
had carefully read *My System* and then used all the theories contained therein against their inventor!

Did Nimzowitsch's patronage of 3. P—K5 influence Tal's
adoption of it? He certainly interprets it in a completely different
way from Nimzowitsch, e.g. Tal–Pachman, Bled, 1961, which
went on 3. .... B—B4; 4. P—KR4, P—KR3; 5. P—KN4, B—Q2;
6. P—R5 with a quite different set-up to that employed by Nimzowitsch.

Later in life Nimzowitsch took to playing what we now call the
Panov–Botvinnik Attack: 3. P × P, P × P; 4. P—QB4. Botvinnik is
another player whose openings are influenced by Nimzowitsch, who
played this line before anyone had heard of Panov or Botvinnik!
Nimzowitsch–Alekhine, Bled, 1931, went (after 4. P—QB4),
**4. .... N—KB3; 5. N—QB3, N—B3; 6. N—B3, B—N5; 7. P × P,
KN × P; 8. B—QN5, Q—R4; 9. Q—N3!, B × N; 10. P × B, N × N;
11. B × N +?** (It was Alekhine, against Winter at London, 1932, who
improved on this with 11. P × N, P—K3; 12. P—Q5!), **11. ....
P × B; 12. Q—N7?, N—Q4 + ; 13. B—Q2, Q—N3!; 14. Q × R +,
K—Q2; 15. 0—0.** (If 15. P—QR4, N—B2; 16. P—R5, Q × NP:
17. Q × RP, Q × R +), **15. .... N—B2; 16. B—R5, N × Q;
17. B × Q, N × B; 18. KR—B1, P—K3; 19. R—B2, B—K2;
20. R/1—QB1, B—N4; 21. R—Q1, R—QN1; 22. R—B5, N—Q4;
23. R—R5, R—N2; 24. R—Q3, B—Q1; 25. R—N3, R × R;
26. R × P +, N—B2; 27. P × R, B—B3; 28. R—N7.** (If 28. R—R4,
N—N4!), **28. .... B × P; 29. R—N8, B × NP; 30. P—R3, P—KB4;
31. K—B1, N—Q4; 32. K—N2, B—K4; 33. R—QR8, N—B5 + ;
34. K—R2, N—Q6 + ; 35. K—N1, N—K8; 36. R—R7 +, B—B2.**
0–1.

(6) *Sicilian*

Nimzowitsch's contribution to the theory of the Sicilian falls into three distinct compartments:

(A) **1. P—K4, P—QB4; 2. N—KB3, N—QB3; 3. B—N5.** This line was strongly recommended in *Chess Praxis* where Nimzowitsch writes of 'the triumph of the bizarre and ugly move' (*Siegeszug* being translated as 'triumph', but it actually means triumph in the sense of a Roman triumph—perhaps 'victory march' is a better translation). An amusing example of the victory march in progress is Nimzowitsch–Gilg, Kecskemet, 1927, which went **1. P—K4, P—QB4; 2. N—KB3, N—QB3; 3. B—N5** (note that this move seems to plan the exchange of bishop for knight at great speed); **3. ... Q—B2** (modern theory centres around 3. ... P—KN3, which gives Black about equal chances); **4. P—B3, P—QR3; 5. B—R4** (a change of heart?), **N—B3; 6. Q—K2, P—K4; 7. 0—0, B—K2; 8. P—Q4, BP × P** (better 8. ... P—Q3. Now Black is in a bad way); **9. P × P, N × QP; 10. N × N, P × N; 11. P—K5, P—Q6.** (Or 11. ... N—Q4; 12. P—K6, P × P; 13. Q × KP, N—N3; 14. B—KN5, Q—Q1; 15. B × B, N × B; 16. Q—N3, Q × B; 17. Q × N); **12. Q—K3, N—Q4; 13. Q—N3, P—KN3; 14. B—N3, N—N5; 15. B × P +, K—Q1; 16. B—R6, N—B7; 17. N—B3, N—Q5** (if 17. ... N × R then 18. N—Q5, Q—B3; 19. B—K3, P—Q3; 20. B—N6 +, K—Q2; 21. P—K6 mate); **18. Q × QP, Q × P; 19. KR—K1, Q—B3; 20. R × B.** 1–0 (20. ... K × R; 21. N—Q5 +, or 20. ... Q × R; 21. Q × N).

(B) **1. P—K4, P—QB4; 2. N—KB3, N—QB3; 3. P—Q4, P × P; 4. N × P, P—Q4!?** This was played for the first time by Nimzowitsch against Rubinstein at Carlsbad, 1923. That game continued with 5. P × P—modern theory has also elaborated:

(a) **5. B—QN5, P × P; 6. N × N, Q × Q +; 7. K × Q, P—QR3; 8. B—R4!** (8. N—Q4 +?, P × B; 9. N × P, B—N5 +; 10. K—K1, R—Q1—10. ... 0—0—0!—11. QN—B3, P—B4!∓, von Holzhausen–Nimzowitsch, Dresden, 1926), **8. ... B—Q2; 9. N—B3, B × N; 10. B × B +, P × B; 11. N × P, P—K4; 12. K—K2!, P—KB4; 13. N—Q2 + =.**

(b) **5. N—QB3, P × P; 6. N × N, Q × Q +; 7. K × Q, P × N; 8. N × P + =.**

(c) **5. N × N, P × N; 6. P × P, Q × P; 7. N—Q2!, N—B3; 8. B—K2, P—K3; 9. 0—0, B—K2; 10. B—B3, Q—Q3; 11. Q—K2, 0—0; 12. N—N3** and this represents White's best line.

(C) **1. P—K4, P—QB4; 2. N—KB3, N—KB3!?** The Nimzowitsch variation. This was the spiritual forerunner of Alekhine's defence, and therefore of crucial importance to one entire stream of development in modern chess.

Nimzowitsch first played this line against Spielmann at San Sebastian, 1911, and it is worth quoting Nimzowitsch's comments on the opening:

'This set Spielmann thinking. After some minutes I raised my eyes from the board and saw that my dear old companion in arms was quite disconcerted. He looked at the knight, now confidently, now suspiciously, and after much hesitation gave up the possible chase started by P—K5 and played the more circumspect 3. N— QB3. Next year I tried 2. ... N—KB3 on Schlechter, and in the Book of the Congress we find the following note to this move by Tarrasch: "Not good, since the knight is at once driven away, but Herr Nimzowitsch goes his own way in the openings, one, however, which cannot be recommended to the public."

'Ridicule can do much, for instance embitter the existence of young talents; but one thing is not given to it, to put a stop permanently to the incursion of new and powerful ideas.' (It is worth noting that 1911 was the year that Diaghilev produced *Petrushka* and two years before Thomas Mann's *Tod in Venedig*, set in 1911, was published; and two years before Stravinsky's revolutionary 'Rite of Spring' (written in 1911–1912) was put on in Paris—and the initial opposition to that was immense! *R.D.K.*)

This remarkable game went on **3. N—QB3, P—Q4; 4. P × P, N × P; 5. B—B4, P—K3; 6. 0—0, B—K2; 7. P—Q4, N × N; 8. P × N, 0—0; 9. N—K5, Q—B2; 10. B—Q3, N—QB3; 11. B— KB4, B—Q3; 12. R—K1, P × P!; 13. P × P, N—N5; 14. B—KN3, N × B; 15. Q × N, P—QN3; 16. P—QB4, B—R3; 17. QR—QB1, QR—QB1; 18. Q—N3!, P—KB3; 19. Q—R4?** (19. P—B5, B × N; 20. P × B =), **19. ... P × N; 20. P × P, B—R6!; 21. Q × KB, B × P; 22. R—K4, Q—Q2; 23. P—KR3, B—Q4; 24. R—K2, Q—N2; 25. P—B4, Q—KB2; 26. R/K2—QB2, R × R; 27. R × R, Q—N3; 28. Q—QB3** (28. R—B3, P—KR4; 29. P—KR4, R × P), **28. ... B × RP!; 29. B—R4, B—Q4; 30. B—K7, R—K1; 31. B—Q6, Q—K5; 32. Q—B7, P—KR3; 33. R—KB2, Q—K8 +; 34. R—B1, Q—K6 +; 35. R—B2, P—QR4; 36. B—K7, Q—K8 +; 37. R—B1, Q—K6 +; 38. R—B2, K—R1; 39. B—Q8, Q—K8 +; 40. R—B1, Q—K6 +; 41. R—B2, Q—K8 +; 42. R—B1, Q—KN6; 43. R—B2, R—B1; 44. Q × QNP, R × P; 45. B—K7, P—R5** ('a passed pawn, plus a mating attack, a wicked affair'—Nimzowitsch); **46. K— B1?, Q × P +. 0–1.**

Nimzowitsch used to answer 3. P—K5, N—Q4; 4. N—QB3,

with 4. ... N × N, for example Michell–Nimzowitsch, Marienbad, 1925: **5. QP × N, P—QN3** ('a conception of hyper-modern boldness' —Nimzowitsch. **5.** ... P—K3 does not have a very high reputation, though: **6. B—KB4, N—B3; 7. B—B4, Q—B2; 8. 0—0, P—QN3; 9. R—K1!, P—KR3**—*even worse is* . *9*... *P—B4; 10. N—R4, P—N3?; 11. N × BP!, N—R4; 12. B—Q5, B—QN2; 13. N—Q6 +, B × N; 14. P × B, Q—B1; 15. B—R6, R—KN1; 16. Q—B3, B × B; 17. Q × B, N—B3; 18. QR—Q1, N—Q1; 19. Q—N5, N—B3; 20. Q—B6, P—KN4; 21. R—K5, 1—0* which was an unmitigated disaster for Black in Gurgenidze–Lein, U.S.S.R. Championship, 1967 —**10. N—Q2, P—Q4; 11. P × P.** e.p., **B × P; 12. B × B, Q × B; 13. B—N5, 0—0; 14. N—B4, Q × Q; 15. QR × Q, N—K2; 16. N— K5 ±**, this is modern theory on the line); **6. B—Q3** (very dangerous for Black here is the sacrifice 6. P—K6 intending to follow-up with N—K5), **B—N2; 7. B—KB4, Q—B2; 8. B—N3, P—K3; 9. 0—0, B—K2; 10. N—Q2, P—KR4; 11. P—KR3, P—KN4; 12. B—K4** (12. N—B4!), **12.** ... **N—B3; 13. R—K1, 0—0—0; 14. N—B4, P—N4; 15. N—Q6 +** (arriving too late), **15.** ... **B × N; 16. P × B, Q—N3; 17. B—B3, P—KN5; 18. P × P, P × P; 19. B × P, P—B4; 20. B—B3, R—R2; 21. K—B1, P—K4; 22. B × N, Q × B; 23. P— B3, P—K5; 24. P × P, R—N1; 25. B—B2, P × P; 26. Q—Q2, P—K6; 27. Q × P, Q × P + ; 28. K—K2, R—B2; 29. K—Q1, K—N1; 30. R—KN1, R × B!; 31. R × Q, R/B7 × R; 32. P—N3, R—N8 +** and won easily.

A further parallel between Larsen and Nimzowitsch is evident in the game Larsen–Spassky from the U.S.S.R.–World match, 1970, which went: **1. P—QN3, P—K4; 2. B—N2, N—QB3; 3. P—QB4, N—B3; 4. N—B3, P—K5; 5. N—Q4, B—B4; 6. N × N, QP × N** (obtaining the same position as above, but with colours reversed— another Nimzowitsch theme—this type of position would not appeal to many players!); **7. P—K3, B—B4; 8. Q—B2, Q—K2; 9. B—K2, 0—0—0; 10. P—B4, N—N5; 11. P—N3, P—KR4!; 12. P—KR3, P—R5; 13. P × N, P × P; 14. R—N1, R—R8; 15. R × R, P—N7; 16. R—B1, Q—R5 + ; 17. K—Q1, P × R = Q + .** 0-1.

Nimzowitsch never played the pawn sacrifice line, the modern, but unsound, method of handling the variation: 3. P—K5, N—Q4; 4. N—QB3, P—K3; 5. N × N, P × N; 6. P—Q4, N—B3; 7. P × P, P × P; 8. Q × P, Q—N3; 9. B—QB4, B × P + ; 10. K—K2, 0—0; 11. R—B1, B—B4; 12. N—N5, N—Q5 + ; 13. K—Q1, N—K3; 14. N—K4! (the bone-crusher), 14. ... P—Q3; 15. P × P, R—Q1 (15. ... B × P??; 16. N × B, R—Q1; 17. B—B4!, N × B; 18. Q × P +, K—R1; 19. Q—N8 +. 1-0. Unzicker–Sarapu, Siegen Olympiad, 1970); 16. Q—R5!, B × P; 17. B—Q3!, P—B4; 18. R × P, N—B1; 19. R—B1, Q—Q5; 20. B—Q2, B—QN5;

21. B × B, Q × B/N5; 22. P—QR3, Q—K2; 23. K—Q2 wins, Planinc-Dobrev, Varna, 1970.

The nearest Nimzowitsch ever came to this was Yates–Nimzowitsch, Carlsbad, 1929: 5. N—K4, P—B4; 6. N—B3, N × N; 7. QP × N, B—K2; 8. B—KB4, Q—N3; 9. P—QN3, Q—B2; 10. B—Q3, P—QN3; 11. Q—K2, P—B5!; 12. P × P (12. B × QBP?, P—QN4), 12. ... N—B3; 13. O—O, B—N2; 14. KR—K1, O—O—O; 15. QR—Q1, B—B4!; 16. N—Q2, P—KN4!‡

Any discussion of this line would be incomplete without the following game.

YATES–NIMZOWITSCH, London, 1927

3. P—K5, N—Q4; 4. B—B4, N—N3; 5. B—K2, N—B3; 6. P—B3, P—Q4; 7. P—Q4, P × P; 8. P × P, B—B4; 9. O—O, P—K3; 10. N—B3, B—K2; 11. N—K1 (better 11. B—K3, O—O; 12. R—B1 following by establishing a knight outpost on QB5), 11. ... N—Q2; 12. B—N4!, B—N3; 13. P—B4, N × QP; 14. N × P!, N—QB3! (14. ... B—QB4; 15. P—N4); 15. N × B, Q—N3 +; 16. K—R1, N × N; 17. Q—R4?! (17. Q—K2 with the idea of B—K3 is better), 17. ... P—KR4; 18. B—R3, B—B4; 19. Q—R3, Q—N4; 20. K—N1, N—QN3; 21. Q—KB3, N/N3—Q4; 22. P—QN3, Q—N3 +; 23. R—B2, R—QB1; 24. B—Q2, R—R3; 25. R—Q1, B × B; 26. Q × B, N—B4; 27. Q—Q3, R—N3; 28. N—B3, R—N5; 29. P—KR3, R—N6; 30. P—QR4, N—R5; 31. K—B1, R—B3; 32. P—R5, Q—Q1; 33. K—N1, N—B4; 34. K—R2, P—R3; 35. Q—N1, Q—K2; 36. N—Q4 (loses. Better 36. R—QB1), 36. ... Q—R5; 37. B—K1, N × P; 38. R × N, R × RP +; 39. P × R, Q × R +; 40. K—N2, N—K6 +. 0–1.*

(7) *Queen's Gambit Declined—Tarrasch—Swedish Variation*
1. P—Q4, P—Q4; 2. P—QB4, P—K3; 3. N—QB3, P—QB4; 4. BP × P, KP × P; 5. N—B3, N—QB3; 6. P—KN3, P—B5. The main line of this variation was worked out, for White, by Nimzowitsch in his game against Stoltz, at Stockholm, 1934: 7. B—N2, B—QN5; 8. O—O, KN—K2; 9. P—K4, P × P (9. ... O—O is

---

* Note the independent existence of two Black army corps in the above game and compare with Stalberg–Nimzowitsch (page 293). To 37. ... Q—R5 Nimzowitsch wrote: 'As the detachments which have been cut off cannot get back to the army, the army comes to them.'

regarded by modern theory as the main line continuation, but it also is good for White: 10. P×P, KN×P; 11. B—N5!, B—K2; 12. N×N, B×B—*12. ... Q×N?; 13. N—K5!*—13. N×B, Q×N/ N4; 14. N—K3! with a strong initiative for White); **10. N×P, B—KB4?!** (Or 10. ... 0—0; 11. Q—B2!, Q—Q4—*11. ... N×P?; 12. N×N, Q×N; 13. B—K3 and 14. Q×P*—12. B—K3, N—N3; 13. N—R4, Q—QN4; 14. N×N, RP×N; 15. P—QR3, B—K2; 16. P—Q5, N—R4; 17. P—Q6, B—Q1; 18. N—B3±; Reshevsky–Stahlberg, Zürich, 1953); **11. N—K5!, Q×P; 12. Q×Q, N×Q; 13. P—QR3, B×N; 14.**

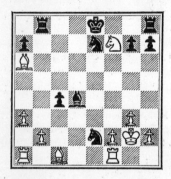

B×B, B—B4; 15. B×NP, QR— N1; 16. B—QR6 (±), 16. ... N—K7+; 17. K—N2, B—Q5; 18. N×KBP!,‡ N×B (18. ... K×N; 19. B×P+); **19. N×R, N—N6; 20. QR—Q1, P—N3; 21. N—B7, K×N; 22. B×P+, K—B1; 23. B×N, B×NP; 24. R—Q3, B×P; 25. R—B3+, K—N2; 26. R—QR1, B—B4; 27. R—B7+, K—R3; 28. R—R5, B—N3** (cutting off the rook, but 28. ... B—Q3; 29. B—K6); **29. R—R4, N—B4; 30. B—K6, N—Q5; 31. B—Q7. 1–0.**

Nimzowitsch himself played the Swedish/Tarrasch, as *Black*, in his match with Stoltz, which shows that he was not so dogmatic as people sometimes like to paint him.

(8) *Queen's Gambit Declined—Exchange Variation*
1. P—Q4, P—Q4; 2. P—QB4, P—K3; 3. N—QB3, N—KB3; 4. B—N5, QN—Q2; 5. P×P, P×P; 6. P—K3, P—B3; 7. B—Q3 is the modern move-order. This line was enthusiastically taken up by Nimzowitsch (as White) in the late 1920s, at approximately the same time as Alekhine was adopting a similar variation in his 1927 title match versus Capablanca (e.g. game 32). It is hard to tell which came first. Here is an early Nimzowitsch example:

NIMZOWITSCH–ROMIH, Match game, London, 1927
7. ... B—Q3; 8. Q—B2, P—KR3; 9. B—R4, Q—R4; 10. 0—0—0, B—N5; 11. KN—K2, B—K2; 12. K—N1, N—B1; 13. P—KR3, B—K3; 14. P—B3, P—R3; 15. P—R3, B—Q2; 16. B×N!, B×B; 17. P—K4, N—K3; 18. P—K5, B—K2; 19. P—B4, N—B2; 20. P—B5, N—N4; 21. KR—B1, Q—N3; 22. B×N, RP×B; 23. N—B4, P—N5; 24. QN×P!, P×N; 25. N×P, Q—R4; 26. N—B7+, K—Q1; 27. N×R, Q×N; 28. P—Q5, Q—B1;

29. Q—K4, R—K1; 30. R—B1, Q—N1; 31. P—K6, B—QN4; 32. Q—Q4, P—QN3; 33. P—Q6, B—KB3; 34. P—K7 +, K—Q2; 35. Q—Q5, B × R; 36. Q—B6 mate.

Another case was: Nimzowitsch–Spielmann, Bad Kissingen, 1928, which went **7. ... B—K2; 8. KN—K2, 0—0; 9. Q—B2, R—K1; 10. 0—0—0!** (for 10. 0—0 see the Botvinnik game which follows), **10. ... N—K5** (10. ... N—B1 is better, and Taimanov now gives 11. P—KR3, Q—R4; 12. K—N1, B—K3; 13. P—B4, QR—B1 with about equal chances); **11. B × N!, P × B; 12. P—KR4!, B × B; 13. P × B, Q × P; 14. N × P, Q—N3; 15. P—B3, N—B1; 16. N—B4, Q—B4; 17. R—R5!, Q— Q2; 18. P—Q5‡.** (If 18. R/1—R1, Q—Q1 not 18. ... P—KR3?; 19. R × P!), **18. ... P × P?** (18. ... P—KB4 would have limited White to a good ending: 19. P × P, Q × P; 20. Q × Q, P × Q; 21. N—Q6, R × P; 22. N × P, B × N; 23. R × B, but ...); **19. N × P, Q—B3; 20. Q × Q, P × Q; 21. N/5—B6 +, P × N; 22. N × P +, K—R1; 23. N ∧ R, B—N5; 24. N—B7!, R—B1; 25. R—KN5, B—K3; 26. N × B,**

N × N; 27. R—QR5. 1–0. So impressed was Spielmann that he adopted the idea himself—Spielmann–Thomas, Carlsbad, 1929— **12. ... P—KB4; 13. Q—N3 +, K—R1; 14. N—B4, N—B3; 15. P—R5, N—Q4; 16. B × B, N × B; 17. N—N6 +, N × N; 18. P × N, B—K3; 19. R × P +, K—N1; 20. P—Q5, P × P; 21. N × QP, R—B1 +; 22. K—N1, Q—N4; 23. R/1—R1, Q × P (g6); 24. R—R8 +.** 1–0.

Botvinnik also later took up this method, but against Keres in the 1952 U.S.S.R. Championship he played **10. 0—0, N—B1; 11. QR— N1** which is not such a satisfactory method, even so he scored a memorable success: **11. ... B—Q3; 12. K—R1, N—N3; 13. P—B3!, B—K2; 14. QR—K1** (the attack in the centre and on the K side, as demonstrated by Nimzowitsch, is stronger than the Q side advance that Botvinnik had planned when making his 11th move), **14. ... N—Q2; 15. B × B, R × B; 16. N—N3, N—B3; 17. Q—B2, B—K3; 18. N—B5, B × N; 19. B × B, Q—N3; 20. P—K4, P × P; 21. P × P, R—Q1; 22. P—K5, N—Q4; 23. N—K4, N—B1; 24. N—Q6, Q—B2; 25. B—K4, N—K3; 26. Q—R4, P—KN3; 27. B × N, P × B; 28. R—B1, Q—Q2; 29. R—QB3, R—KB1; 30. N—B5!** (winning at least the exchange), **30. ... R/1—K1; 31. N—R6 +, K—B1; 32. Q—B6, N—N2;**

33. R/3—B3, R—B1; 34. N×P, R—K3; 35. Q—N5, N—B4; 36. N—R6, Q—N2; 37. P—KN4. 1–0.

(9)   *Modern Benoni—Nimzowitsch's Method*

NIMZOWITSCH–MARSHALL, New York, 1927

1. P—Q4, N—KB3; 2. P—QB4, P—B4; 3. P—Q5, P—K3; 4. N—QB3, P×P; 5. P×P, P—Q3; 6. N—B3, P—KN3; 7. N—Q2 (Nimzowitsch rejected the more forthright 7. P—K4 on account of: '7. ... B—N2; 8. B—Q3, 0—0; 9. 0—0, P—QR3; 10. P—QR4, R—K1; 11. P—R3, P—N3 followed by ... R—R2—K2. Even 10. ... B—N5 and ×N would have been playable.' The two procedures mentioned by Nimzowitsch here have become absolutely main line methods for Black in the handling of the Modern Benoni in contemporary tournament chess). **7. ... QN—Q2; 8. N—B4, N—N3; 9. P—K4, B—N2; 10. N—K3!** (It is interesting to compare the third Spassky–Fischer match game, which went 8. P—K4, B—N2; 9. B—K2—*9. N—B4 would have transposed to Nimzowitsch's method*—9. ... 0—0; 10. 0—0, R—K1; 11. Q—B2, N—R4; 12. B×N, P×B; 13. N—B4, N—K4; 14. N—K3, Q—R5 = + and Spassky's variation on Nimzowitsch's idea had failed. This line has since been strengthened in Gligorić–Kavalek, Skopje, 1972, which went 11. P—QR4, N—K4; 12. Q—B2, N—R4; 13. B×N, P×B; 14. N—Q1, Q—R5; 15. N—K3, N—N5; 16. N×N, P×N; 17. N—B4±), **10. ... 0—0; 11. B—Q3, N—R4!?** (11. ... R—K1?!; 12. 0—0, P—B5; 13. B—B2, B—Q2; 14. B—Q2!, R—QB1; 15. K—R1, R—B4; 16. P—B3, N—B1; 17. P—QR4, P—QR3; 18. N—K2!, N—K2;

19. B—N4, R—QB1; 20. B—B3!, K—R1; 21. Q—Q2, N/K2—N1; 22. B—Q4, P—QN4; 23. P×P, B×P; 24. Q—B3‡, N—R4; 25. B×B+, N×B; 26. N—Q4, Q—N3; 27. R—R2, Q—B4; 28. KR—R1, P—KR4; 29. B—Q1?!, K—R2; 30. R—R5!, N—R3; 31. B—R4, R—QN1; 32. N/K3—B2!, R—N2; 33. N—N4, Q—B2; 34. N×P, B×N; 35. B×R, N×B; 36. R×N. 1–0. Keene–Pritchett, British Championship, 1972, a recent game which was directly inspired by the Nimzowitschian approach.) **12. 0—0, B—K4; 13. P—QR4, N—KB5; 14. P—R5±.** For the full score of Nimzowitsch–Marshall see page 182.

(10) *Queen's Indian*
1. P—Q4, N—KB3; 2. P—QB4, P—K3; 3. N—KB3, P—QN3.
This was Nimzowitsch's own idea. He also claimed responsibility for
1. P—Q4, N—KB3; 2. P—QB4, P—K3; 3. N—KB3, B—N5 +,
though this was effectively stolen by Bogoljubow, which didn't do
him much good in the end as it is now known as the Bogo-indian! Of
the individual variations of the Queen's Indian Nimzowitsch is
specifically responsible for three:
(A) **4. P—KN3, B—R3.** Nmzowitsch explains this idea as follows:
'3. ... P—QN3 aimed at centralisation by ... B—N2; in order to
weaken the effect of this move White played 4. P—KN3, intending
B—N2, but at the same time left his QBP uncovered. This was the
signal for the second player to start an attack against the White
QBP. Grünfeld—Nimzowitsch, Breslau, 1925, continued: 5. Q—R4,
P—B3; 6. B—N2, P—QN4; 7. P × P, P × P; 8. Q—Q1, B—N2 and
Black, having eliminated White's QBP, has at least an equal game.'
[9. 0—0, B—K2; 10. QN—Q2, 0—0; 11. N—N3 and now ...
B—B3! to hinder P—QR4.]
Another example was Pirc–Nimzowitsch, Bled, 1931: **5. QN—Q2,
B—N5; 6. Q—B2, B—N2; 7. B—N2, B—K5; 8. Q—Q1, B × QN;
9. B × B, P—Q3; 10. 0—0, QN—Q2; 11. B—B3, Q—K2; 12. R—
K1, 0—0; 13. B—R3, B—B4! =.** The reader should also consult
Nimzowitsch's game against Sultan Khan, page 251.
Valcarcel–Larsen, Las Palmas, 1972, is a modern example of this
line: **5. Q—R4, P—B4; 6. B—N2, B—N2; 7. 0—0, B—K2;
8. N—B3, 0—0; 9. R—Q1, P—QR3!; 10. P—QR3, P × P;
11. N × P, B × B; 12. K × B, Q—B2 =.**
(B) **4. P—KN3, B—N2; 5. B—N2, B—K2; 6. 0—0, 0—0;
7. N—B3, P—Q4** (strange that Nimzowitsch should introduce this
rather classical set-up). For a Nimzowitsch game with this line see his
famous win versus Sämisch, page 81.
Nowadays this line is sometimes employed by Larsen (that name
again!).
(C) **1. P—Q4, N—KB3; 2. N—KB3, P—QN3.** This, the Marienbad variation, was introduced by Nimzowitsch against Rubinstein at
Marienbad, 1925—see page 162.

(11) *Queen's Pawn—Nimzowitsch Defence* (*Nimzo-indian*)
1. P—Q4, N—KB3; 2. P—QB4, P—K3; 3. N—QB3, B—N5.

Nimzowitsch's most famous strategic invention, although it had been
played previously (by accident!?) in 1883! Englisch–Blackburne,
London, 1883: 1. P—Q4, P—K3; 2. P—QB4, N—KB3; 3. N—
QB3, B—N5; 4. B—Q2, 0—0; 5. N—KB3, P—QN3; 6. P—K3,

B—N2; 7. B—K2 (7. B—Q3 would be played today), 7. ... P—Q4; 8. 0—0, QN—Q2; 9. N × P, N × N; 10. P × N, B—Q3; 11. P × P, P × P and, thanks to some most ingenious play, Blackburne went on to draw the game.

The specific variation 1. P—Q4, N—KB3; 2. P—QB4, P—K3; 3. N—QB3, B—N5 was introduced into tournament practice by Nimzowitsch, as Black, against Janowsky at St. Petersburg, 1914: 4. P—K3, P—QN3; 5. B—Q3 (nowadays 5. KN—K2 is very popular, to avoid the doubled pawns), 5. ... B—N2; 6. N—B3, B × N + ; 7. P × B, P—Q3; 8. Q—B2, QN—Q2; 9. P—K4, P—K4; 10. 0—0, 0—0; 11. B—N5, P—KR3; 12. B—Q2, R—K1; 13. KR—K1, N—R2; 14. P—KR3, KN—B1; 15. N—R2, N—K3; 16. B—K3, P—QB4; 17. P—Q5, N—B5 with a draw on move 60. But in his invention of the 'ideal Queen's Gambit', where Black forgoes altogether the occupation of the centre by his pawns (*My System*), is it possible that Nimzowitsch was influenced by some of Tartakower's games from Carlsbad, 1911, such as the following? Salwe–Tarta-

kower: 1. P—Q4, P—K3; 2. P—QB4, P—KB4; 3. N—QB3, N—KB3; 4. P—K3, B—N5; 5. B—Q3, B × N + ; 6. P × B, P—B4; 7. N—K2, P—Q3; 8. 0—0, P—K4; 9. B—R3, P—QN3; 10. Q—N1, P—N3; 11. P—B3, 0—0; 12. B—B1, N—B3; 13. B—Q2, B—R3; 14. P—K4, P—B5; 15. P—QR4, N—QR4; 16. Q—R2, R—B1; 17. QR—B1, K—R1; 18. K—R1, P—KN4; 19. P—N4, P—KR4; 20. P—R3, K—N2; 21. R—KB2, R—KR1‡ ∓ (0–1 36).

A Dutch, admittedly, but the manner of play against the doubled QB pawns and the whole concept of blockade evinced by this game is ominous. Clearly there was some cross-fertilisation between the livelier minds of the pre-1914 chess world. The new ideas were not the sole intellectual property of Nimzowitsch!

The imposing strategic ideas with which Nimzowitsch stamped his own invention were the absolute importance of the doubled pawn complex, which frequently arises, and the necessity for general restraint of the white position. These themes are both in evidence in P. Johner–Nimzowitsch, Dresden, 1926: 4. P—K3, 0—0; 5. B—Q3, P—B4; 6. N—B3, N—B3; 7. 0—0, B × N (the ancestor of the Hübner variation which is discussed next); 8. P × B, P—Q3; 9. N—Q2! (if 9. ... P—K4; 10. P—Q5, N—QR4 then 11. N—N3 'will bring the aggressive black knight back to reason'), 9. ...

P—QN3; 10. N—N3? (10. P—B4 was better, the text move could have been delayed), 10. ... P—K4; 11. P—B4, P—K5 (now White is faced with the problem of what to do about the restriction of his K side); 12. B—K2, Q—Q2 (another restrictive manœuvre gets under way . . .); 13. P—KR3, N—K2; 14. Q—K1, P—KR4!; 15. B—Q2, Q—B4; 16. K—R2, Q—R2 (... and the strange destination is reached—White's K side pawns aren't going anywhere); 17. P—QR4, N—B4; 18. P—N3, P—R4; 19. R—KN1, N—R3; 20. B—KB1, B—Q2; 21. B—B1, QR—B1; 22. P—Q5, K—R1; 23. N—Q2, R—KN1; 24. B—KN2, P—KN4; 25. N—B1, R—N2; 26. R—R2, N—B4; 27. B—R1, QR—KN1; 28. Q—Q1, P × P; 29. KP × P, B—B1; 30. Q—N3, B—

R3‡; 31. R—K2 (31. B—Q2, R—N3; 32. B—K1, N—N5 +; 33. P × N, P × P +; 34. K—N2, B × P; 35. Q × B, P—K6 would have been pretty—the mate at KR3 can only be parried by 36. N × P and then the queen is lost), 31. ... N—R5; 32. R—K3 (or 32. N—Q2, B—B1; 33. N × P, Q—B4; 34. N—B2, Q × P +; 35. N × Q, N—N5 mate), 32. ... B—B1; 33. Q—B2, B × P; 34. B × P, B—B4; 35. B × B, N × B; 36. R—K2, P—R5; 37. KR—N2, P × P + +; 38. K—N1, Q—R6; 39. N—K3, N—R5; 40. K—B1, R—K1. 0–1. 'One of the best blockading games that I have ever played.' In an interview granted to C. H. O'D. Alexander after Hastings, 1972–1973, Larsen remarked that Johner–Nimzowitsch was probably the game by another Master which had exerted the deepest influence on his own style.

The above game represents one of Nimzowitsch's ideas that has really made the big time in modern chess. There follow three recent examples of the way in which this line has made the grade:

NAJDORF–HÜBNER, Wijk aan Zee, 1971

4. P—K3, P—B4; 5. B—Q3, N—B3; 6. N—B3, B × N + (the same procedure—exchanging without provocation—as in the Johner game); 7. P × B, P—Q3; 8. P—K4 (8. 0—0, P—K4; 9. Q—B2, Q—K2; 10. N—Q2, 0—0; 11. P × BP!?, P × P; 12. N—K4, P—KN3; 13. N × N +, Q × N, Taimanov–Hübner, and 8. N—Q2, P—K4; 9. P—Q5, N—K2; 10. 0—0, 0—0; 11. Q—B2, P—KN3; 12. P—B4, P × P; 13. P × P?, B—B4, Addison–Hübner, both games from Palma, 1970, are also very Nimzowitschian in their concept), 8. ... P—K4; 9. P—Q5, N—K2 (the central blockade is achieved);

10. P—N3, P—KR3?! (10. ... N—N3!?), **11. N—R4, P—KN4; 12. N—N2, Q—R4; 13. Q—N3?** (13. B—Q2 would be much better), **13. ... B—R6; 14. 0—0, 0—0—0; 15. R—N1, Q—B2; 16. P—B3, K—N1; 17. R—B2, KR—N1; 18. N—K3, B—B1; 19. K—B1?!** (19. N—B5!? could be tried), **19. ...**

QR—B1; 20. K—K1, N—K1 (Black can manœuvre at will—White has no relevant pawn breaks at his disposal); **21. N—B5, N×N; 22. P×N, P—B3; 23. P—N4, R—R1; 24. B—K3, P—KR4; 25. B—KB1, R—B2; 26. P—KR3, Q—Q2; 27. K—Q2, N—B2; 28. P—QR4?, R—K2; 29. R—K1, N—R1; 30. P—R5, Q—Q1; 31. Q—R3, R/1—R2; 32. R—N1, P—N3; 33. B—Q3, R—QN2‡.** Black won on move 52.

OLAFSSON–ANDERSSON, Reykjavik, 1972

4. P—K3, P—B4; 5. B—Q3, N—B3; 6. N—B3, B×N+; 7. P×B, P—Q3; 8. N—Q2, P—K4; 9. 0—0, 0—0; 10. N—N3, P—K5 (another way of setting up a blockade); **11. B—B2, Q—K2; 12. P—B3, R—K1; 13. K—R1, P—KR3; 14. N—Q2, KP×P; 15. NP×P, P×P!** (the blockade has been lifted, but White's position will be riddled with weaknesses as a penance); **16. BP×P?, Q×P; 17. N—K4, Q×QP; 18. Q×Q, N×Q; 19. N×N+, P×N; 20. R—KN1+, K—B1; 21. B×P+, K—K2; 22. B—K4, B—K3; 23. QR—N1, QR—N1; 24. B×P, B×P; 25. B—K3, N—N4; 26. B—QR6, N—R6!; 27. R×R, R×R; 28. B×P, R—QR1; 29. B×B, N×B; 30. B—Q4, K—K3; 31. R—N2, K—B4; 32. R—K2, N—K4; 33. K—N2, P—Q4; 34. B—B2, R—KN1+; 35. B—N3, P—Q5** and Black won a long ending thanks to his passed QP and more centralised position.

The Hübner/Nimzowitsch finally reached the summit on July 20, 1972: SPASSKY–FISCHER, game 5: **4. N—B3, P—B4; 5. P—K3, N—B3; 6. B—Q3, B×N+; 7. P×B, P—Q3; 8. P—K4, P—K4; 9. P—Q5, N—K2; 10. N—R4, P—KR3; 11. P—B4!?, N—N3!; 12. N×N, P×N; 13. P×P** (better to maintain the tension with 13. 0—0, 0—0; 14. P—B5!. Black's trump card in this line is the rigid pawn formation, which doesn't suit White's bishop pair), **13. ... P×P; 14. B—K3, P—N3; 15. 0—0, 0—0; 16. P—QR4, P—QR4; 17. R—N1, B—Q2; 18. R—N2, R—N1; 19. R/N2—KB2, Q—K2; 20. B—B2, P—KN4; 21. B—Q2, Q—K1; 22. B—K1, Q—N3; 23. Q—Q3, N—R4; 24. R×R+, R×R; 25. R×R+,**

K × R; 26. B—Q1, N—B5‡ (Nimzowitsch would have loved this—
restraint, blockade, doubled pawn
complexes *and* an outpost on an open
file); 27. Q—B2??, B × P!. 0–1.

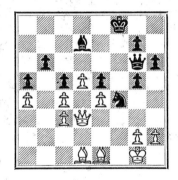

In the above line a favourite move
of the Dutch Grandmaster Donner is
11. P—B3, but this should not terrify
Black, e.g. Donner–Portisch, Skopje,
1972: 11. ... Q—R4!; 12. Q—B2,
P—KN4; 13. N—B5, N × N; 14.
P × N, B—Q2; 15. P—KR4, P—N5;
16. P × P, N × NP; 17. B—K2, R—KN1; 18. B × N, R × B;
19. B × P, B × P!; 20. Q × B, Q × P + ; 21. K—B2, Q—N7 + ;
22. K—K3, R × NP. 0–1.

One of the most popular continuations in Nimzowitsch's day was
4. Q—B2, an example of which is Rubinstein–Nimzowitsch, Bad
Kissingen, 1928: 4. ... B × N ! (sometimes Nimzowitsch took his
ideas to extreme lengths. It is all very well to exchange, without
provocation, when the knight can only be recaptured by the NP, but
when it's protected by a *piece* ... !); 5. Q × B!, N—K5; 6. Q—B2,
P—Q4; 7. P—K3, P—QB4; 8. QP × P, N—QB3? (8. ... Q—R4 +
followed by ... Q × BP would be better); 9. N—B3, 0—0;
10. B—Q2!, Q—K2; 11. R—B1!, Q × P; 12. P × P, Q × Q (12. ...
Q × QP?; 13. B—B4, Q—KB4; 14. B—Q3); 13. R × Q, P × P;
14. B—N5!, B—Q2; 15. B × N!, P × B (15. ... B × B; 16. N—
Q4±); 16. N—K5, B—B4; 17. N × QBP, KR—K1; 18. R—QB1,
P—QR4; 19. P—B3, N—Q3; 20. B × P (20. N × P was correct),
20. ... P—Q5? (Nimzowitsch misses the chance of 20. ... N—B5;
21. B—N4, N × NP!; 22. N—K7 + , K—R1; 23. N × B, N—Q6 + ;
24. K—K2, N × B); 21. B—N4!, R × KP + ; 22. K—B2, R × RP;
23. B × N, R × NP + ; 24. K—N3, B—Q2; 25. N × P, P—R4;
26. KR—K1!, P—N4; 27. P—R3 (27. R × R??, P—R5 mate would
have been a mistake), 27. ... R—Q6; 28. QR—Q1, R—B6;
29. R—K7, B—R5; 30. R—QR1, P—R5 + ; 31. K—N4, R—B5;
32. B—K5. 1–0.

The fondness for playing ... B × N even when this move does not
double the white QBP's is a rather idiosyncratic characteristic
shared with Nimzowitsch by Larsen. It has cost them both a lot of
points. There follow some more of these disasters:

BOGOLJUBOW–NIMZOWITSCH, Breslau, 1925

1. P—Q4, N—KB3; 2. P—QB4, P—K3; 3. N—QB3, B—N5;
4. N—B3, P—QN3; 5. Q—B2, B—N2; 6. P—QR3, B × N + ;

7. Q×B, P—Q3; 8. B—N5, QN—Q2; 9. P—K3, N—K5; 10. B×Q, N×Q; 11. B—R4, N—K5; 12. N—Q2, N×N; 13. K×N, P—QB4; 14. P—B3, P—QR4; 15. P—QN3, P—B3; 16. B—Q3, K—K2; 17. B—N3, P—R3; 18. P—KR4, KR—QB1; 19. P—R4, KR—KR1; 20. P—R5, QR—KN1; 21. K—B3, N—B1; 22. QR—Q1, P—K4; 23. P×KP, QP×P; 24. R—Q2, P—KN4; 25. P×Pe.p., N×P; 26. B×N, R×B; 27. KR—Q1, B—B1 (27. ... B×P! would retain some hope of salvation); 28. B—R4, R—B1; 29. P—N3, P—K5; 30. P×P, B—N5; 31. R—KB1, K—K3; 32. R—Q5, R—K1; 33. R—B2, B—R6; 34. P—K5, P—B4; 35. P—K4, R—KB1; 36. R—Q6+, K—B2; 37. R/2—Q2, P×P; 38. R—B2+. 1–0.

RUBINSTEIN–NIMZOWITSCH, Berlin, 1928

1. P—Q4, N—KB3; 2. P—QB4, P—K3; 3. N—QB3, B—N5; 4. Q—B2, P—Q3; 5. P—K3, P—B4; 6. B—Q3, N—B3; 7. N—K2, P—K4; 8. P—Q5, B×N+; 9. Q×B, N—K2; 10. Q—B2, 0—0; 11. 0—0, N—N3; 12. N—N3, R—K1; 13. P—B3, B—Q2; 14. B—Q2, P—QR3; 15. P—KR3, P—QN4; 16. P—N3, Q—N3; 17. K—R2, P—QR4; 18. QR—N1, P—N5? (... KR—QN1! intending ... Q—Q1 and ... P—R5); 19. P—B4, P×P; 20. P×P, N—B1; 21. B—B1, Q—Q1; 22. Q—KB2, P—R5; 23. B—N2, N—N3; 24. QR—Q1, P×P; 25. P×P, R—R2; 26. QR—K1, R×R; 27. R×R, N—B1; 28. B×N!, Q×B; 29. N—K4, Q—R3; 30. P—B5, R—R6; 31. R—QN1, R—R3; 32. P—N4, P—B3; 33. K—N3, B—B1; 34. R—K1, B—N2; 35. Q—K2, N—Q2; 36. N×QP!, R×N; 37. Q—K8+, N—B1; 38. R—K7, P—N3; 39. Q—B7+, K—R1; 40. R—K8, R—Q1; 41. Q×BP+, K—N1; 42. Q—K6+, K—N2; 43. P—B6+. 1–0 .

Both Nimzowitsch and Larsen seem to underestimate the bishop pair in the hands of the opponent, although Larsen denies this charge in his book of selected games.

UHLMANN–LARSEN, Hastings, 1972–1973

1. P—QB4, N—KB3; 2. N—QB3, P—K3; 3. N—B3, B—N5; 4. Q—B2, 0—0; 5. P—QR3, B×N; 6. Q×B, P—Q3; 7. P—Q4, P—QN3; 8. P—KN3, B—N2; 9. B—N2, QN—Q2; 10. 0—0, Q—K2; 11. P—N3, P—K4; 12. P—Q5!, P—QR4; 13. N—R4, N—B4; 14. B—N2, KR—K1; 15. Q—B2!, P—QN4!? (active counter-play is needed); 16. N—B5!, Q—B1; 17. P—B4!, NP×P; 18. P×KP!, P×KP; 19. P×P, N/B4—Q2; 20. B—B1!, N—N3; 21. B—K3, N—N5; 22. B×N, P×B; 23. Q—K4, Q—B4+; 24. K—R1, P—R4; 25. P—R3!, N—B7+; 26. R×N, Q×R; 27. R—KB1, Q—B4; 28. Q—R4!, Q—B1 (28. ... P—N3 fails

against 29. N—R6 +, K—R2; 30. Q—N5!); **29. Q—N5!, P—B3; 30. Q—N6, R—K2; 31. B—K4!, Q—K1; 32. N—R6 +, K—B1; 33. R × P +. 1–0.**

An interesting pendant to the above game is Przepiorka–Nimzowitsch, Kecskemet, 1927: **1. P—Q4, N—KB3; 2. N—KB3, P—K3; 3. P—B4, P—QN3; 4. N—B3, B—N2; 5. Q—B2, B—N5; 6. P—QR3, B × N +; 7. Q × B, P—Q3; 8. P—KN3, QN—Q2; 9. B—N2, Q—K2; 10. 0—0, 0—0** (reaching the same position as Uhlmann–Larsen); **11. P—QN4, N—K5; 12. Q—B2, P—KB4; 13. N—N5, QN—B3; 14. N × N** (better 14. P—B3), **14. ... B × N; 15. B × B, N × B; 16. P—B3, N—B3; 17. B—N2, R—B2; 18. QR—B1** (correct was 18. R—B2), **18. ... QR—KB1; 19. Q—Q3, P—KR4‡; 20. P—K4?.** (Walking straight into an ambush. Why on earth did Black mass his artillery on the KB file if not to prevent White's P—K4?) **P × P; 21. P × P, N—N5; 22. P—R3, N—B7; 23. Q—K2, N × P +; 24. K—R1, Q—N4; 25. R × R, R × R; 26. Q—N2, N—B7 +; 27. K—N1, Q—K6. 0–1.**

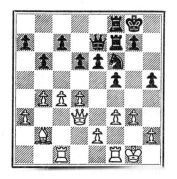

In connection with the 'modern' variation (4. P—K3, 0—0; 5. N—B3, P—Q4; 6. B—Q3, P—B4; 7. 0—0), it is very interesting to compare Réti–Nimzowitsch, Berlin, 1928, see below, with Geller–Petrosian, Amsterdam, 1956, which continued 7. ... N—B3; **8. P—QR3, B × N; 9. P × B, Q—B2; 10. Q—B2, N—QR4; 11. BP × P, P—B5; 12. B—K2, P × P; 13. N—Q2, B—N5; 14. B × B, N × B; 15. P—N3, P—B4; 16. R—N1, N—QB3?** (correct was 16. ... P—QN3, e.g. 17. R—K1, QR—K1 with the threat 18. ... P—B5, or 17. P—QR4, QR—K1; 18. B—R3, R—B3; 19. KR—K1, Q—B2; 20. N—B1, R/3—K3 with a perfect blockade of White's expansion possibilities in the centre); **17. P—QR4, Q—Q2; 18. B—R3, KR—K1; 19. KR—K1, P—QN3; 20. R—K2, Q—K3; 21. R/1—K1, Q—R3; 22. N—B1, Q—R4; 23. P—B3!, N—B3; 24. N—Q2, R—K3; 25. P—K4,** White has overcome the blockade and goes on to win.

Here is the prototype game:

RÉTI–NIMZOWITSCH, Berlin, 1928

1. P—Q4, N—KB3; 2. P—QB4, P—K3; 3. N—QB3, B—N5; 4. Q—B2, P—Q4; 5. P—K3, P—B4; 6. N—B3, N—B3; 7. P—QR3, B × N +; 8. P × B, P—QN3; 9. B—Q3, 0—0; 10. P × QP,

KP×P; **11. 0—0, P—B5!; 12. B—
K2, B—N5!; 13. R—K1, B—R4; 14.
N—Q2, B—N3** (even stronger than
... B×B); **15. Q—Q1, P—QN4;
16. P—B3, P—QR4?!‡** (Prophylaxis
was called for here, rather than pro-
vocation, therefore 16. ... R—K1!
Now White lifts the blockade by
means of a pawn sacrifice to gain
scope for his bishops); **17. P—K4!,
P×P; 18. N×KP** (18. P×P?, N×
QP!), **18. ... B×N; 19. P×B,**
N×KP; **20. Q—B2, P—B4** (threatening ... N×QP again); **21.
B—B3, Q—B3; 22. R—N1, P—N5; 23. BP×P?** (23. RP×P!,
P×P; **24.** B×N, P×B; **25.** B—K3! would keep White above
water), **23. ... Q×P+; 24. B—K3, Q—Q6; 25. Q×Q, P×Q;
26. P—N5, N—K4** (Nimzowitsch has the knight pair, so he is
content); **27. B×N** (well, he did have the knight pair), **27. ...
P×B; 28. B—Q4, N—B5; 29. R×P, N×P; 30. R—K7!, R—B5!;
31. B—K5!** (not 31. R×P+, K—B1; 32. R—KB1, R×R+; 33.
K×R, P—Q7; 34. K—K2, P—Q8=Q+; 35. K×Q, R—Q1
winning), **31. ... N×R; 32. B×R, R—Q1; 33. P—N6.** (The
best chance. If 33. R—K1 then ... P—Q7; 34. R—Q1, P—
R5; 35. P—N6, P—R6; 36. P—N7, P—R7; 37. B—K5, R—
N1!; 38. B×R, P—R8 and wins, since White's B cannot retreat
in view of ... Q—R2+/×P—Nimzowitsch.) **33. ... P—Q7;
34. B×P, N×B; 35. P—N7, R—KB1** (threatens mate and therefore gives him a vital tempo. Without this tempo White would
have excellent drawing chances by means of R—QB7—B8);
**36. P—R3, N—B5; 37. R—K6, P—R5; 38. R—QR6, N—K4;
39. R×P, R—N1; 40. R—QN4, K—B2; 41. K—R2, K—K2;
42. R—KR4, P—R3; 43. R—QN4, N—B2; 44. R—N4, P—N4;
45. R—K4+, K—B3; 46. R—QN4, N—Q3; 47. P—R4, R×P;
48. P×P+, P×P; 49. R—QR4, R—N6; 50. P—N3, N—B4;
51. P—N4, N—R5; 52. R—R5, R—QB6; 53. R—R8, K—K4;
54. R—KB8, K—K5; 55. R—B7, R—Q6; 56. R—B8, N—N3;
57. R—B5, R—Q4. 0–1.**

(12) *Flank Openings*

Nimzowitsch made a number of important contributions to the
theory of these openings. 1. P—QN3 is dealt with separately, here
we deal with the English and the Réti. In *Chess Praxis* Nimzowitsch
has something to say which could well serve as a motto for Larsen's
preoccupation with his rooks' pawns—which Nimzowitsch shared,

especially moves of the KRP early in the game.* He wrote: 'To glance at the wings with the centre in mind is the deepest sense of positional play.'

(A) (i) ENGLISH: **1. P—QB4.** Nimzowitsch often used the English, sometimes with P—KN3, and sometimes with P—K3, hoping to transpose into a reversed Sicilian—see, for example, Nimzowitsch–Spielmann, Carlsbad, 1929 (page 229). It is interesting to note here a comment that Larsen makes in his book of his games: 'I became a devotee of the Najdorf Variation ... in 1951. Afterwards I even began to play openings like 1. P—QB4, P—K4; 2. P—Q3, N—KB3; 3. P—QR3!? hoping for 3. ... P—Q4; 4. P×P, N×P; 5. N—KB3, N—QB3; 6. P—K4 the dear variation with a tempo extra.' Nimzowitsch–Norman-Hansen, 1923, opened with **1. P—QB4, P—K4; 2. P—QR3, N—KB3; 3. N—QB3, P—Q4; 4. P×P, N×P.**

Nimzowitsch's main contribution to the English was the Dresden blockade formation with pawns on c4, d3 and e4, or, for Black, c5, d6 and e5. He was very proud of this idea which looked weakening but was not (a rudimentary form of this blockade system is to be found in some games by Staunton, but we do not know if Nimzowitsch was aware of Staunton's games).

Nimzowitsch himself says of this idea: 'As early as 1924 I had tried, after the moves 1. P—KB4, P—QB4; 2. P—K4, N—QB3; 3. P—Q3, P—KN3, the move 4. P—QB4, whose motif I visualised as a blockade spanning half the board, and ... I made the following note: "Since this move is not inspired by the hope of preventing, or even of making ... P—Q4 more difficult, a special explanation is needed. Black wishes to build up the configuration PK3, PQ4. This done, he will consider the extension of his attacking formation on the Q wing, i.e. by ... N—Q5 when opportunity offers, in order, after N×N, P×N, to bring pressure in the QB file on White's P—QB2. The text move is made to forestall this possible extension of play on the Q wing. The hole at Q4 does not seem to be a serious matter." ... To this problem I was ever seeking to bring out new sides, and so it came that, as Black in Dresden, 1926, after the moves 1. P—K4, P—QB4; 2. N—KB3, N—QB3; 3. N—QB3 I ventured the move 3. ... P—K4, which at that time caused a huge sensation.' In connection with this the reader might also like to refer to Nimzowitsch–Rubinstein, Dresden, 1926 (page 2), which (by demonstrating that the backward White QP is not weak) was one of the factors which helped to give birth to the Boleslavsky Sicilian (1. P—K4, P—QB4; 2. N—KB3, N—QB3; 3. P—Q4, P×P; 4. N×P, N—B3; 5. N—B3, P—Q3; 6. B—K2, P—K4).

---

* For similar play with the QRP see his games as Black from the 1934 Match versus Stahlberg.

The influence of Nimzowitsch's extensive writings concerning the Dresden blockade can perhaps be traced in the Botvinnik systems of the English. Some modern examples of this influence are: Botvinnik–Geller, U.S.S.R. Team Championship, 1966, which opened with **1. P—QB4, P—KN3; 2. P—KN3, B—N2; 3. B—N2, P—K4; 4. N—QB3, P—Q3; 5. P—Q3, N—K2; 6. P—K4, 0—0; 7. KN—K2, QN—B3; 8. 0—0, B—K3; 9. N—Q5.** Botvinnik–Petrosian, U.S.S.R. Team Championship, 1966, varied with **8. ... P—B4; 9. N—Q5.** Keene–Kagan, Skopje, 1972, went **1. N—KB3, P—QB4; 2. P—KN3, P—KN3; 3. B—N2, B—N2; 4. 0—0, P—K4; 5. P—B4, N—K2; 6. N—B3, QN—B3; 7. P—Q3, 0—0; 8. R—N1, P—Q3; 9. P—QR3, P—QR4!; 10. B—Q2, P—KR3?!** and it was later errors on Black's part, not his pawn formation, which led to his downfall.*

An example of Nimzowitsch's treatment is Nimzowitsch– Sämisch, Dresden, 1926: **1. P—QB4, P—K4; 2. N—QB3, N—KB3; 3. N—B3, N—B3; 4. P—K4, B—N5; 5. P—Q3, P—Q3; 6. P—KN3, B—N5** (Nimzowitsch–Mieses, Hanover, 1926, varied with **6. ... B—QB4; 7. B—N2, N—KN5; 8. 0—0, P—B4; 9. N—Q5, P—KR3?; 10. P×P, B×P; 11. N—R4, B—K3; 12. N—N6, R—KN1; 13. P—KR3, N—B3; 14. B—K3, B×N; 15. P×B, N—Q5; 16. P—B4, Q—Q2; 17. P—QN4, B—N3; 18. P×P, P×P; 19. N×P, Q—K2; 20. N—B4** with a clearly won position). **7. B—K2** (With Nimzowitsch the move P—KN3 did not necessarily promise a fianchettoed KB.) **7. ... P—KR3; 8. B—K3, B×N+; 9. P×B, Q—Q2; 10. Q—B2, 0—0; 11. Q—Q2, N—R2; 12. P—KR3!, B×P; 13. N—N1, B—N5; 14. P—B3, B—K3; 15. P—Q4, P×P; 16. P×P, P—Q4; 17. BP×P, B×P; 18. P×B, Q×P; 19. R—Q1, KR—K1; 20. K—B2, N—B3; 21. R—R4, N—K2; 22. B—Q3, N—B4; 23. B×N, Q×B; 24. K—N2, R—K2; 25. B—B2, QR—K1; 26. R—B4, Q—N3; 27. P—Q5, R—K4; 28. R—Q4, R—Q1; 29. Q—R5, N—R4; 30. Q×BP, QR—K1; 31. P—Q6.** 1–0. There also exists a little known Alekhine game on similar lines, but Alekhine did not give it much publicity—in fact he did not even publish it in his collections of best games—Black–Tarrasch, Vienna, 1922: 1. P—QB4, P—K4; 2. N—QB3, N—QB3; 3. P—KN3, P—KN3; 4. B—N2, B—N2; 5. P—Q3, KN—K2; 6. P—B4, P—Q3; 7. N—B3, 0—0; 8. 0—0, P—KR3; 9. P—K4, P—B4; 10. N—Q5 (1–0 57).

(ii) **1. P—QB4, P—K4; 2. N—QB3, N—QB3; 3. N—B3, N—B3; 4. P—K4, B—B4; 5. N×P.‡** This sequence was invented by Nimzowitsch, and made its appearance in the game Nimzowitsch–

---

* Also well playable is 10. ... R—N1.

Yates, Dresden, 1926. See also the
game Nimzowitsch–Réti, Berlin, 1928
(page 215). This line has also had
its fair share of success in modern
times, for example Botvinnik–Keres,
U.S.S.R. Team Championship, 1966:
**4. P—KN3, B—B4; 5. N × P,‡ B ×
P + ; 6. K × B, N × N; 7. P—K4**
(transposing into the Nimzowitsch
scheme), **P—B4; 8. P—Q3, P—Q3;
9. P—KR3, P—KR4; 10. B—K2,
N—R2; 11. K—N2, P—R5; 12. P—**

**KN4, N—N4; 13. B—K3, B—Q2; 14. Q—Q2, N—K3; 15. P—N4,
P—QN3; 16. QR—QN1, B—B3; 17. KR—KB1, B—N2; 18. K—
N1, N—B3; 19. N—Q5, N/B3—Q5; 20. B—Q1, P—B3; 21. K—
R2** (preparing P—KN5), **21. ... B—B3; 22. P—QR4, P—R4?!;
23. P × RP, P × P; 24. Q—KB2, R—QR2; 25. P—N5, 0—0; 26.
P—N6, P—B4?** (26. ... B—K1; 27. Q—KN2, P—B4; 28. P × P,
N × P; 29. Q—K4 was more stubborn); **27. R—N8!** 1–0. The queen
is deflected from the defence of the KRP.

(B) Réti: **1. N—KB3.** Nimzowitsch made two serious contributions to this line; one was at Dresden, 1926 (again! which tournament
seems to have been one of Nimzowitsch's creative peaks), when he
played **1. ... P—QB4!**, a line that is now very popular, and followed
it up with ... P—Q3 and ... P—K4 all according to plan; the other
significant contribution was in his game (as Black) against Kashdan
at Bled, 1931: **1. ... P—Q4; 2. P—B4, P × P; 3. N—R3, P—
QB4; 4. P—KN3, N—QB3; 5. N × P, P—B3; 6. B—N2, P—
K4** (this set-up has been widely regarded as a Botvinnik invention);
**7. P—Q3, B—K3; 8. 0—0, N—K2; 9. KN—Q2, N—Q4; 10.
N—K4, B—K2; 11. N—K3, Q—Q2** with a reversed 'Maroczy
Bind'.

Concerning the 'Bind' formation from White's side Nimzowitsch
also had something to say: Nimzowitsch–Capablanca, Carlsbad,
1929—**1. P—QB4, N—KB3; 2. N—QB3, P—B4; 3. N—B3,
N—B3; 4. P—Q4, P × P; 5. N × P, P—KN3; 6. P—K4, B—N2;
7. N—B2, 0—0; 8. B—K2, P—Q3; 9. 0—0, N—Q2; 10. B—K3,
N—B4; 11. N—Q4, B—Q2; 12. Q—Q2, R—B1; 13. QR—Q1,
R—K1; 14. K—R1, Q—R4; 15. P—B3** (P—B4!?), **N—K3!;
16. N—N3, Q—N5; 17. Q—B2, N—R4; 18. N × N, Q × N** (a5);
**19. R—Q5, N—B4; 20. B—Q2, Q—B2; 21. B—K1, N—K3;
22. P—QN3, N—Q5; 23. Q—Q2, N × B; 24. Q × N, P—QR3;
25. P—QR4, P—QN4; 26. RP × P, B × N; 27. B × B, P × P;
28. Q—Q2, P × P; 29. Q—R6, P—B3; 30. R—KN5!** ½–½ (30. ...

P×P; 31. R×P+, P×R; 32. Q×P+, K—R1; 33. Q—R6+ = not 32. ... K—B1?; 33. B—Q2!).

Portisch–Gheorghiu, Teesside, 1972, varied from this with: **11. ... N×N?!; 12. B×N, B—K3; 13. B×B, K×B; 14. Q—Q4+, P—B3; 15. QR—Q1?, P—QR4** = (although White eventually won the game), better was 15. P—QN4! 7. N—B2 in the 'Bind' formation has become a great favourite with Portisch.

(13) 1. *P—QN3*

This is all the rage nowadays as a result of Larsen's success with it. Larsen's games with this line are often very close to the Nimzowitsch originals, for example Larsen–Wade, Teesside, 1972, will bear comparison with any of Nimzowitsch's efforts:

1. P—QN3, P—Q4; 2. B—N2, P—QB4; 3. P—K3, N—KB3; 4. B—N5+, B—Q2; 5. B×B+, QN×B; 6. N—KB3, P—K3; 7. P—B4, B—K2; 8. 0—0, 0—0; 9. Q—K2, P—QR3; 10. N—B3, Q—R4; 11. P×P, P×P; 12. P—Q4, QR—B1; 13. P×P, N×P; 14. N—Q4!, N—K3; 15. N—B5!, B—R6; 16. QR—B1, R—B2; 17. N—QR4!, B×B; 18. Q×B, P—QN4; 19. N—B5!, Q—N3; 20. P—QN4, N×N; 21. R×N, R×R; 22. P×R, Q—K3; 23. N—Q4, Q—K4; 24. Q—R3, N—N5; 25. N—B3, Q—B2; 26. R—B1, P—QR4; 27. Q—Q3, P—N5; 28. P—B6, N—B3; 29. N—Q4, P—R4; 30. Q—B5, Q—B1; 31. P—B7, P—QR5; 32. Q×Q, R×Q; 33. N—B5. 1–0.

Another modern game, which really is pure Nimzowitsch, is Fischer–Mecking, Palma, 1970: **1. P—QN3, P—Q4; 2. B—N2, P—QB4; 3. N—KB3, N—QB3; 4. P—K3, N—B3; 5. B—N5, B—Q2; 6. 0—0, P—K3; 7. P—Q3, B—K2; 8. B/5×N, B×B; 9. N—K5, R—QB1; 10. N—Q2, 0—0; 11. P—KB4, N—Q2; 12. Q—N4!, N×N; 13. B×N, B—B3; 14. R—B3, Q—K2** (only now does the game leave the rails of 1927 theory! For 14. ...

B×B, which Alekhine regarded as best, see Nimzowitsch–Spielmann below): **15. R/1—KB1, P—QR4; 16. R—N3, B×B; 17. P×B, P—B4; 18. P×Pe.p., R×P;‡ 19. Q×NP+!, Q×Q; 20. R×R, Q×R/6; 21. P×Q, R—K1; 22. P—KN4, P—R5; 23. N—B3, P×P; 24. RP×P, K—N2; 25. P—N5, P—K4; 26. N—R4, B—Q2; 27. R—Q6, B—K3; 28. K—B2, K—B2; 29. R—N6, R—K2; 30. P—K4, P×P; 31. P×P, P—B5;**

32. P—QN4, B—N5; 33. K—K3, R—Q2; 34. P—N6 +, K—B1; 35. P × P, R × P; 36. N—N6 +, K—K1; 37. N × P, B—B1; 38. N × P, K—Q1; 39. N—Q6, R—N2; 40. K—B2, K—B2; 41. N × B, K × N; 42. R—Q6. 1–0.

NIMZOWITSCH–SPIELMANN, New York, 1927

12. Q—N4! 'This "brutal" move and, in fact, the whole plan of throwing the heavy pieces into the assault on the K side occurred only because the variation: **12. ... P—B4?; 13. Q × NP + !, K × Q; 14. N × B dis. +, B—B3; 15. N × Q, B × B; 16. N × P +** seemed to mitigate the "brutality" to a significant extent' (Nimzowitsch). **12. ... N × N; 13. B × N** (13. P × N?!, B—N4!—Alekhine in the tournament book), **13. ...B—B3; 14. R—B3, B × B; 15. P × B, Q—B2** (16. ... Q—R4; 17. R—N3 and N—B3 ±); **16. Q—R5, P—KR3** (16. ... P—B4?; 17. P × Pe.p., R × P; 18. R × R, P × R; 19. Q—N4 +; 16. ... B—K1!; 17. R—R3, P—KR3; 18. N—B3, P—B4); **17. QR—KB1, P—KN3.** (17. ... B—K1; 18. R—N3, P—B4; 19. Q × RP, Q × P; 20. Q—B4!, Q—B3; 21. N—B3 ±—dark square control!); **18. Q × RP, Q × P; 19. R—B6, Q—R4** (the only defence against R—B3—KR3); **20. Q × Q, P × Q; 21. N—B3, R—B2; 22. R—R6, P—B3; 23. N—R4, B—K1, 24. R/6 × BP, R × R; 25. R × R, R—K2; 26. K—B2, K—N2; 27. R—B4, B—Q2; 28. K—K2?** (28. K—K1! cuts out the possibility of ... B—N5 +), **28. ... P—K4!; 29. R—B5, R—K1** (now R × RP is impossible, so Black's resistance can continue); **30. R—B2, P—K5; 31. R—B4, R—K4; 32. K—Q2, P—N4; 33. P—N3, B—R6; 34. P—Q4, P × P; 35. P × P, R—N4; 36. P—B3, P—R4; 37. R—B2, P—R5; 38. K—K3, P—R6; 39. R—B2, B—B8; 40. R—B1, B—Q6; 41. N—N2, R—B4; 42. N—B4, K—B2; 43. R—Q1, K—K2?; 44. N × B, P × N; 45. P—QN4, K—Q3; 46. K × P, R—B7; 47. R—Q2, R—B6 + ; 48. K—B2, K—K3; 49. R—K2 +, K—Q3; 50. K—N3, R—Q6; 51. R—K5, P—R5; 52. P × P, R—R6; 53. R—R5, K—B3; 54. R—R6 +, K—B2; 55. P—R5.** 1–0. Black could still have held up the winning process for some time with 43. ... B—B7; 44. R—KN1, P—R5, although White should triumph eventually after 45. P—KN4.

Nimzowitsch often prefaced the move P—QN3 with 1. N—KB3. A modern player who shares this tendency is Ulf Andersson, e.g. Andersson–Tatai, Palma, 1971: **1. N—KB3, P—Q4; 2. P—QN3, P—QB4; 3. P—K3, N—QB3; 4. B—N5!** (obtaining a Nimzoindian with colours reversed as in the previous example), **4. ... B—Q2; 5. 0–0, P—K3; 6. B—N2, KN—K2; 7. P—B4, P—QR3; 8. B × N, B × B; 9. N—K5, Q—B2; 10. P—Q3, R—Q1; 11. Q—K2,**

P—B3; 12. N×B, N×N; 13. P×P, R×P; 14. N—B3, R—Q1;
15. N—K4, Q—B2; 16. QR—B1, N—N5; 17. B—R3, P—B4;
18. N—N5, Q—B3; 19. B×N, P×B; 20. P—B4, P—R3;
21. N—B3, B—Q3; 22. P—K4, P×P; 23. P×P, B×P; 24. P—K5,
Q—B4; 25. R—B7, 0—0; 26. P—N3, Q—N5; 27. R—B4, P—QN4;
28. R—K4, R—Q4; 29. K—R1, R×P; 30. N×R. 1–0.

A Nimzowitsch example, effectively a reversed Dutch defence, is
Nimzowitsch–Buerger, London, 1927: 1. P—QN3, N—KB3;
2. B—N2, P—K3; 3. P—KB4, P—Q4; 4. N—KB3, B—K2;
5. P—K3, QN—Q2; 6. B—Q3, N—K5; 7. N—K5, 0—0; 8. 0—0,
N×N; 9. KB×N, N—Q2; 10. B—KB3, B—B3; 11. N—B3, P—B4;
12. Q—K1, P—QN3; 13. P—KN4, B—R3; 14. P—Q3, P—Q5?!
(better 14. ... R—B1 with an eventual ... P—B5 in mind);
15. N—K4, R—B1; 16. N×B+, N×N; 17. P—K4, P—K4;
18. P—B5, P—R3; 19. Q—N3, R—K1; 20. P—KR4, N—R2;
21. B—B1, P—B3; 22. R—B2, R—B2; 23. R—N2, Q—K2;
24. Q—R3, R—B3; 25. B—Q2, R—Q1; 26. K—R1, R/Q1—Q3;
27. P—R4, B—B1; 28. QR—KN1, P—R3; 29. R—R2, K—R1;
30. P—N5, BP×P; 31. P×P, P—N4; 32. P×NP, P×NP;
33. Q—R4, P—B5; 34. P×RP, Q×Q; 35. P×P+. 1–0.

(14) *Various Experiments*

Nimzowitsch had a great love for experimental opening play, often,
it seemed, only for its own sake. Sometimes it appeared as if he just
wanted to show how much he could get away with!

There follow some examples of Nimzowitsch's more far-fetched,
at times even absurd, ideas:

(a) NIMZOWITSCH–MIESES, Göteborg, 1920

1. P—QB4, P—KB4; 2. P—QN3, P—K4; 3. N—QB3, N—KB3;
4. B—N2, P—Q4; 5. P×P, N×P; 6. P—N3, N×N; 7. P×N?!,
B—Q3; 8. B—N2, N—B3; 9. Q—Q5, Q—K2; 10. P—K4, B—K3;

11. Q—N5, 0—0; 12. Q×NP, B—
Q2; 13. Q—R6, QR—N1; 14. N—
B3, N—N5! (Nimzowitsch's original
conception boomerangs); 15. P×N,
B×P+; 16. N—Q2, B—N4; 17.
Q×P, B×N+; 18. K×B, Q—Q3+;
19. K—B2, B—Q6+; 20. K—B3
(this king march is by no means
voluntary), 20. ... R—N3!; 21. Q—
R5, Q—Q5+; 22. K—Q2, Q×P+;
23. K×B, R—Q1+‡; 24. Q—Q5+,
R×Q+; 25. P×R, P—K5+; 26.

K—B3, Q—K6 + ; 27. K—B2, Q—Q6 + ; 28. K—B1, R—N4; 29.
B—QR3, R × QP; 30. B—B1, Q—K6 + ; 31. K—B2, R—Q7 + ;
32. K—N1, R—Q8 + . 0–1.

(b) Sämisch–Nimzowitsch, Carlsbad, 1923

1. P—Q4, N—KB3; 2. P—QB4, P—QN3; 3. N—QB3, B—N2;
4. Q—B2 and now Nimzowitsch played ... N—B3?! and even went
on to win. 5. P—Q5, N—QN5; 6. Q—Q1, P—QR4; 7. P—K4,
P—K4; 8. P—KN3, P—N3; 9. B—N2, B—N2; 10. KN—K2, 0—0;
11. 0—0, P—Q3; 12. P—B4, P × P; 13. P × P, R—K1; 14. N—N3,
N—Q2. Provocation followed by restraint. Black won on move 72
after many ups and downs.

(c) Maroczy–Nimzowitsch, San Remo, 1930

1. P—K4, N—QB3; 2. N—QB3, P—K3; 3. P—Q4, B—N5;
4. N—B3, P—Q3!?; 5. B—KB4, KN—K2; 6. B—K2, B × N + ;
7. P × B, 0—0; 8. 0—0, N—N3; 9. B—K3, Q—K2; 10. R—K1,
R—Q2; 11. Q—B1, P—N3; 12. N—Q2, P—K4; 13. B—Q3,
Q—B3; 14. N—N3, P—KR3; 15. P—QR4, P—QR4; 16. B—QN5,
QR—K1; 17. P—B3, N—N1; 18. B—KB1, B—B3; 19. P—QB4,
P × P; 20. N × P(d4), B—N2; 21. N—N5, N—R3; 22. B—Q4,
Q—Q1; 23. Q—Q2, N—N5; 24. B—B3, N—R3; 25. B—Q4,
B—B3 (Black has a good position but it is difficult to break through);
26. QR—Q1, R—K2 (restraining the White KP); 27. Q—B2,
KR—K1; 28. Q—N3, R—K3; 29. K—R1, Q—K2; 30. B—B2,
N—N5; 31. P—B3, N—R3; 32. N—Q4, B × RP (the exchange
sacrifice is a good try, but it still fails to give Black a clear advantage);
33. R—R1, B—Q2; 34. N × R, Q × N; 35. P—B5!, N × P;
36. B × N, NP × B; 37. R × P, Q—B3; 38. R—QB1, P—R4. ½–½.

(d) Treybal–Nimzowitsch, Baden-Baden, 1925

1. P—K4, N—QB3; 2. N—KB3, P—KN3; 3. P—Q4, B—N2;
4. N—QB3, P—Q3 (an ancestor of the Pirc/Modern defence);
5. B—K3, N—R3 ('Up to this point Black's opening could only be
described as unfavourable, but this move is suicide. You can only
play like this in a simultaneous display'); 6. P—KR3, P—B4 ('The
unsound point of the previous move'); 7. P—Q5, P × P?; 8. N × P,
B—B4?? ('Even after 8. ... N—QN1 which is relatively best,
Black's position is without consolation'); 9. P × N, P × P ('For on
9. ... B × N there would follow 10. B × N, B × B; 11. Q—Q4, or
10. ... B × N; 11. Q × B, B × B; 12. P × P and 13. B—N5 + ');
10. B—Q3, Q—N1; 11. 0—0, Q × P; 12. Q—Q2, N—B2;
13. Q—R5, N—K4 ('Black makes what he can of the position, but
you simply cannot hand a piece to a master player'); 14. N × N,

Q×N; 15. Q—R4, B—Q2; 16. QR—Q1, 0—0; 17. KR—K1,
P—K3; 18. N—N3, Q—B3; 19. Q—R5, Q—Q1; 20. R—N1,
P—K4; 21. B—QR6, P—Q4; 22. B—B5, R—B2; 23. B—N7,
R—N1; 24. Q×RP, Q—K1; 25. B×P. 1–0. [Comments by
Nimzowitsch]

(e) SÄMISCH–NIMZOWITSCH, Baden-Baden, 1925

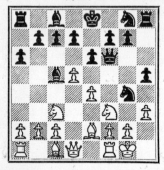

1. P—Q4, N—QB3; 2. P—Q5, N—
K4 (extreme provocation!); 3. P—
K4, P—K3; 4. N—KB3, Q—B3?!;
5. B—K2, B—B4; 6. N—B3, P—
QR3; 7. 0—0, N—N5?!; 8. P—KR3,
P—KR4‡; 9. B—KN5, Q—N3; 10.
P×P, BP×P; 11. Q—Q2, B—K2;
12. B—KB4, P—K4; 13. B×P, P—
Q3; 14. B—KB4, B—Q2; 15. P—
K5! and White went on to win.
Contrary to popular belief Nimzo-
witsch did not always beat Sämisch!

CONCLUSION

Harry Golombek once wrote of 'Romantic players' (and he classed
Nimzowitsch as a 'Romantic') that they were 'innovators, not so
much of variations, but of ideas'.

I certainly think this is true of Nimzowitsch's influence on modern
chess theory, where so many of the original strategic ideas stem from
Nimzowitsch himself while, in an alarmingly large number of cases,
the actual variations we still employ were elaborated by the arch-
realist Alekhine.

Take, for example, 2. ... N—KB3 in the Sicilian. This is virtually
untouched now, but without the intellectual ancestry provided by
this variation Alekhine's defence (which is now extremely popular)
might never have come into being.

Or the so-called Panov–Botvinnik attack in the Caro Kann.
Nimzowitsch used this against Alekhine at Bled, 1931, and then
Alekhine himself became its most enthusiastic practitioner. Why on
earth we call it the Panov–Botvinnik I shall never understand!

In the English opening Nimzowitsch was the most eloquent
propagandist for the systems with White pawns on QB4 and K4, yet
the actual variations now in mode stem more from Alekhine's game
versus Tarrasch (q.v.).

In the Nimzowitsch Defence to the QP itself we can now see
Nimzowitsch's ideas at work both in the 'modern system' and the
Hübner variation but perhaps the only variation, as such, to survive

intact into modern tournament practice from the 1920s came from the game E. Rabinovitch–Alekhine, Moscow, 1920: **1. P—Q4, N—KB3; 2. N—KB3, P—QN3; 3. P—B4, P—K3** (observe the rapidity with which Alekhine had assimilated the new ideas); **4. N—B3, B—N2; 5. P—K3, B—N5; 6. Q—B2, N—K5; 7. B—Q3, P—KB4; 8. 0—0, B ×N; 9. P × B, 0—0; 10. N—Q2, Q—R5!; 11. P—B3, N × N; 12. B × N, N—B3** and this precise sequence, which was dimly sired in Nimzowitsch's games from St. Petersburg, 1914, has actually been employed in contemporary practice by Larsen, Fischer and Botvinnik.

CHAPTER V

THE DUALITY OF NIMZOWITSCH

Du bist dir nur des einen Triebs bewusst;
O lerne nie den andern kennen!
Zwei Seelen wohnen, ach! in meiner Brust,
Die eine will sich von der andern trennen;
Goethe: Faust Part 1*

All chessmasters (and not just masters) have personal styles and highly individual methods of approaching identical problems. Of course, in certain situations, all strong players will do identical things (e.g. 'White to play and win', will usually elicit the same response from any good player) but it is those cases where the element of choice crops up that concern us here. Style, and examination of the questions arising from it, can afford a fascinating point of departure for a discussion of the play of the great masters. Even one's choice of opening can go a long way to determining the nature of a style.

All this may sound rather vague and naturally, when dealing with such terms, there is a great danger of descending into meaningless generalisations. However, if we bear in mind the possible presence of such dangers, I feel that we are now in a position to discuss what I believe to lie at the very heart of Nimzowitsch's chess style, and this is the duality already mentioned. In Nimzowitsch's games we observe a strange tension between the desire to restrain the opponent's possibilities (prevention or prophylaxis) and the urge to provoke the opponent into a sharp and bitter struggle: by doing something outrageous, or apparently unplayable, or by running grave risks of a positional, or tactical, variety. In other words, with Nimzowitsch, we see a powerful awareness of the presence of the opponent as someone who must be restrained or provoked rather than the preoccupation with one's own positive plans which one associates with other great masters, such as Alekhine, Bogoljubow, Tal or Fischer. I associate the direct, positive action of an Alekhine,

---

* By this one passion you are quite possessed—
You'd best admit no other to a share.
Two souls, alas, are housed within my breast,
And each will wrestle for the mastery there.

or a Fischer, with a homogeneous, harmonious unity of chess style as opposed to the dualism and indirection which pervades Nimzowitsch. (Elsewhere I have equated these two Nimzowitschian poles in modern chess with Korchnoi—the apostle of heroic defence*—and Petrosian—the High Priest of prophylaxis.)

These twin poles of Nimzowitsch's style can be exemplified here in concrete fashion by two miniature games (although there are further examples throughout this volume); in one Nimzowitsch (according to his own published theories) concentrates on the absolute minimisation of his opponent's possibilities. This is the so-called 'Immortal Zugzwang Game'. I prefer to see it as an example of total paralysis of the opposition; the ultimate expression of prophylaxis, where the opponent's possibilities are reduced to that degree above zero required to avoid stalemate. The other game, equally well known, is an example of a deliberately pursued maximisation of the opponent's possibilities; in this case for material gain, but examples will recur in this book where this maximisation occurs for other than material reasons.

There is an objection to my theory which you might voice, namely: that Nimzowitsch's win is against a good master player (Sämisch), while his loss is to the mighty world champion (Alekhine). In answer to this I would point out that Nimzowitsch did not always defeat Sämisch in their games, and when he did it was rarely in such drastic fashion. This game is merely an extreme example of a particular trend in Nimzowitsch's play. Likewise with the Alekhine game, which is also a case taken to its absolute. Nimzowitsch beat Alekhine on several occasions and, not infrequently, a high degree of provocation was involved in his victory.

(i) SÄMISCH–NIMZOWITSCH, Copenhagen, 1923. *Queen's Indian Defence*

1. P—Q4, N—KB3; 2. P—QB4, P—K3; 3. N—KB3, P—QN3; 4. P—KN3, B—N2; 5. B—N2, B—K2; 6. N—B3, 0—0; 7. 0—0, P—Q4; 8. N—K5, P—B3; 9. P × P (9. P—K4! is much stronger. e.g. ... P × BP; 10. N × P/c4, B—R3; 11. P—N3, P—QN4; 12. N—K3, P—N5; 13. N—K2, B × N; 14. Q × B, Q × P; 15. B—N2, excellent compensation), **9. ... BP × P; 10. B—B4, P—QR3!; 11. R—B1, P—QN4; 12. Q—N3, N—B3; 13. N × N, B × N; 14. P—KR3, Q—Q2; 15. K—R2, N—R4; 16. B—Q2, P—B4; 17. Q— Q1, P—N5; 18. N—N1, B—QN4; 19. R—N1, B—Q3; 20. P— K4, BP × P!** (sacrificing a piece to paralyse the entire White position); **21. Q × N, R × P; 22. Q—N5, QR—KB1; 23. K—R1, R/1—B4;**

---

* Cf. Chapter 6, section 9, of *Chess Praxis.*

24. Q—K3, B—Q6; 25. QR—K1, P—R3!‡ White resigns.

As can readily be seen White has no moves left at all that do not lead to disaster. A most remarkable finish. Nimzowitsch was to write of this game: 'May my dear colleague Sämisch not take it amiss that I seize every opportunity to publish this game, which is known in Denmark as the Immortal Zugzwang Game. I have no choice, for, in its sacrificial spirit, which yet denies the attack in any conventional sense, this game is just as characteristic for our own time as the Immortal Sacrificial Game was for the age of Anderssen. Nowadays we sacrifice for the sake of prophylaxis, or in order to introduce a blockade, or to decrease the dynamic potential of the opposing forces, not, however, in the interests of a brutal act of violence. Brutality is out of date!'

(ii) ALEKHINE–NIMZOWITSCH, Bled, 1931. *French Defence*

1. P—K4, P—K3; 2. P—Q4, P—Q4; 3. N—QB3, B—N5; 4. N—K2, P × P (an interesting Russian idea is 4. ... N—K2; 5. P—QR3, B—R4; 6. P—QN4, B—N3; 7. P—K5, P—QR4! with good counterplay); **5. P—QR3, B × N +** (... B—K2 is more circumspect); **6. N × B, P—KB4** (heroic defence but most perilous in this case. Nimzowitsch decides to cling at all costs to his extra material. 6. ... N—QB3 is much 'better'). **7. P—B3** (a game Sir George Thomas–Nimzowitsch, Marienbad, 1925, went: 7. B—KB4, N—KB3; 8. P—KB3, 0—0; 9. P × P, N × P; 10. N × N, P × N; 11. Q—Q2, N—Q2; 12. B—K2, P—B4 and Black maintained his extra material into the endgame and this eventually brought him victory, in spite of White's bishops and the precarious nature of Black's booty), **7. ... P × P; 8. Q × P, Q × P** (absolutely consistent with the heroic defence syndrome); **9. Q—N3, N—KB3; 10. Q × NP, Q—K4 +?** (... R—N1!; 11. Q × BP, N—B3—Alekhine—and Black can fight on); **11. B—K2, R—N1; 12. Q—R6, R—N3; 13. Q—R4, B—Q2; 14. B—N5, B—B3; 15. 0—0—0, B × P; 16. KR—K1, B—K5; 17. B—R5, N × B; 18. R—Q8 +, K—B2; 19. Q × N.** 'Nimzowitsch quite rightly resigned here, as there are no more decent moves for Black—even 19. ... K—N2 would lose the Q after 20. N × B, P × N; 21. B—R6 + ! This was, I believe, the shortest defeat in his career' (Alekhine).

From this game we can see just how double-edged an attribute the second 'passion' could be.

Granted, then, the existence of this Nimzowitschian duality, what, we might ask, is its effect? Well, I see its major effect as an influence exerted over Nimzowitsch's mode of combination, which is highly individualistic, and, at times, almost mystical. I tend to regard many of Nimzowitsch's combinations as 'ambushes' rather than as the organic exploitation of conventional resources—be it in never so brilliant a manner—which we normally term a 'combination'.

Of course the word 'ambush' really means nothing more than an elaborate trap, in common parlance, but in this context I am attempting to imbue it with the significance of a novel technical term extending beyond its normal associations. In other words, what Nimzowitsch, in many cases, would describe as a 'combination', I would describe as an 'ambush', and I would not mean 'trap!'

I think that it is only possible to get at the precise meaning of this term by reference to concrete examples, and I would draw your special attention to two games by Nimzowitsch from this collection in which he defeats the great masters, Rubinstein (Marienbad, 1925) and Alekhine (Semmering, 1926) by means of the 'ambush'. One could alternatively describe the 'ambush' as a defensive or preventive combination, in that Nimzowitsch, in both cases, organises a deep refutation of a course of action which the opponent is under no compulsion to adopt. The combination only works by virtue of the opponent's activity, yet, at the same time, notably in the Rubinstein game, Nimzowitsch takes measures to deter his opponent from adopting any other course to the fatal one actually chosen.

Before moving on to the main body of games I invite you to examine the following game plus two highly pertinent notes from Nimzowitsch himself. Remember that Schlechter had formed a very definite plan for victory which consisted of these three stages: (i) Opening of the KR file; (ii) establishment of a pawn chain d5/e4/f3/g4 to clamp down on any Black counterplay, and (iii) an overwhelming assault in the KR file against Black's helpless K side.

In view of this the climax of Nimzowitsch's preventive combination (32. ... R—R1) is all the more remarkable.

SCHLECHTER–NIMZOWITSCH, Carlsbad, 1907. *Ruy Lopez*
1. P—K4, P—K4; 2. N—KB3, N—QB3; 3. B—N5, P—QR3;
4. B—R4, N—B3; 5. N—B3, B—N5; 6. N—Q5, B—K2; 7. O—O,
O—O; 8. R—K1, P—Q3; 9. N × N +, B × N; 10. P—B3, P—R3;
11. P—KR3, N—K2; 12. P—Q4, N—N3; 13. B—K3, K—R2;
14. Q—Q2, B—K3; 15. B—B2, Q—K2; 16. P—Q5, B—Q2;
17. K—R2, N—R1; 18. N—N1, P—KN4; 19. P—KN3, N—N3;
20. Q—Q1, B—N2; 21. Q—B3, P—QR4; 22. N—K2, B—N4;

23. P—QR4, B—Q2; 24. R—R1. Nimzowitsch wrote at this point:
'With this move White plans to break through eventually with
P—R4, e.g.: 24. ... P—N3; 25. P—R4, P×P; 26. P×P, N×P;
27. Q—R5, P—KB4; 28. K—N1, etc. But Black discovers a move,
which not only has a high preventive value, but which also has the
attribute of driving the opponent into quick action.' **24. ... Q—K1!;
25. P—R4, Q—B1; 26. B—Q3, B—N5; 27. Q—N2, P×P; 28. P—
B3, P—R6; 29. Q—B1, P—KB4!; 30. P×B, P×KP; 31. Q×P,
P×B; 32. B×P, R—R1!‡** White resigns.

Nimzowitsch again: 'The fact that the preventive move 24. ...
Q—K1 contains a threat at the same time by no means detracts from
its purity in a prophylactic sense. It illustrates a very definite form of
prophylaxis in which part of the plan is to precipitate the opponent
into action.' Had Black played 29. ... B—Q2 then 30. P—KN4 and
Q×RP would have decided the game in White's favour (murderous
attack in KR file).

With this remarkable example of an ambush the way is opened for
an examination of Nimzowitsch's creative achievements extending
over a tournament career of thirty years.

CHAPTER VI

SELECTED GAMES

GAMES, 1904–1906

First Steps

Many of the games that follow are discussed by Nimzowitsch in his autobiography

COBURG, 1904 (Hauptturnier A)

		1	2	3	4	5	6	7	8	9	10	11	12	13	14	15	16	17	
1	Neumann	–	1	1	½	½	½	1	1	1	½	½	1	1	1	1	1	1	13½
2	Vidmar	0	–	1	1	1	1	½	½	1	½	1	1	1	1	1	1	1	13½
3	Duras	0	0	–	1	1	0	1	1	½	1	1	1	1	1	1	1	1	12½
4	Spielmann	½	0	0	–	1	1	1	½	1	0	1	1	1	1	1	1	1	12
5	Lange	½	0	0	0	–	0	1	1	1	1	1	1	½	1	1	1	1	11
6	Nimzowitsch	½	0	1	0	1	–	0	½	1	1	1	1	½	1	0	1	1	10½
7	Gregory	0	½	0	0	0	1	–	0	½	1	½	1	1	1	1	1	1	9½
8	Post	0	½	0	½	0	½	1	–	½	1	1	½	1	0	1	1	1	9½
9	Möwig	0	0	½	0	0	0	½	½	–	1	0	1	1	1	1	1	1	8½
10	Cohn, E.	½	½	0	1	0	0	0	0	0	–	1	1	½	0	1	1	1	7½
11	v. Balla	½	0	0	0	0	0	½	0	1	0	–	0	½	1	1	1	1	6½
12	Hilse	0	0	0	0	0	0	0	½	0	0	1	–	0	1	1	1	½	5
13	Johner	0	0	0	0	½	½	0	0	0	½	½	1	–	½	1	0	½	5
14	Nyholm	0	0	0	0	0	0	0	1	0	1	0	0	½	–	0	1	1	4½
15	Kaegbein	0	0	0	0	0	1	0	0	0	0	0	0	0	1	–	½	1	3½
16	Schneider	0	0	0	0	0	0	0	0	0	0	0	0	1	0	½	–	1	2½
17	Rausch	0	0	0	0	0	0	0	0	0	0	0	½	½	0	0	0	–	1

VIENNA, 1905

		1	2	3	4	5	6	7	8	9	10	
1	Schlechter	—	1½	1½	½1	½½	11	11	½0	11	½½	13
2	Wolf	0½	—	1½	00	11	½½	1½	½1	11	11	12
3	Löwy	0½	0½	—	01	½1	½½	1½	11	½½	1½	10½
4	Perlis	½0	11	10	—	0½	1½	½½	½½	10	11	10½
5	Fleischmann	½½	00	½0	1½	—	10	11	01	00	11	9
6	Nimzowitsch	00	½½	½½	0½	01	—	0½	½1	½½	½1	8
7	Vidmar	00	0½	0½	½½	00	1½	—	1½	½1	½0	7
8	Albin	½1	½0	00	½½	10	½0	0½	—	½1	½0	7
9	Neumann	00	00	½½	01	11	½½	½0	½0	—	01	7
10	v. Balla	½½	00	0½	00	00	½0	½1	½1	10	—	6

BARMEN—(B Group), August 12–31, 1905

	1	2	3	4	5	6	7	8	9	10	11	12	13	14	15	16	17	18	
1 Fleischmann	—	½	0	1	1	1	1	½	1	½	0	1	½	1	1	1	1	1	13
2 Swiderski	½	—	1	1	0	1	1	1	1	0	½	1	0	0	1	1	1	1	12
3 W. Cohn	1	0	—	½	½	1	½	½	½	1	0	1	1	1	0	1	1	1	11½
4 Fahrni	0	0	½	—	½	0	1	0	1	½	1	1	1	½	1	½	1	1	10½
5 Neumann	0	1	½	½	—	0	0	1	0	½	½	1	1	1	½	1	1	1	10½
6 Perlis	0	0	0	1	1	—	½	0	1	1	1	0	1	1	1	1	1	0	10½
7 Caro	0	0	½	0	1	½	—	½	½	½	1	½	1	0	1	½	1	1	9½
8 Reggio	½	0	½	1	0	1	½	—	0	0	1	½	1	½	½	½	1	1	9½
9 Kopa	0	0	½	0	1	0	½	1	—	½	1	1	0	½	1	½	½	1	9
10 Lee	½	1	0	½	½	0	½	1	½	—	1	½	0	0	½	½	½	1	8½
11 Spielmann	1	½	1	0	½	0	0	0	0	0	—	1	0	1	1	1	½	1	8½
12 Leussen	0	0	0	0	0	1	½	½	0	½	0	—	1	1	1	½	1	1	8
13 Post	½	1	0	0	0	0	0	0	1	1	1	0	—	½	½	½	1	1	8
14 Przepiorka	0	1	0	½	0	0	1	½	½	1	0	0	½	—	½	½	½	½	7
15 Nimzowitsch	0	0	1	0	½	0	0	½	0	½	0	0	½	½	—	½	1	1	6
16 Schwan	0	0	0	½	0	0	½	½	½	½	0	½	½	½	½	—	½	1	6
17 J. W. Baird	0	0	0	0	0	0	0	0	½	½	½	0	0	½	0	½	—	1	3½
18 Petterson	0	0	0	0	0	1	0	0	0	0	0	0	0	½	0	0	0	—	1½

MUNICH, 1906

	1	2	3	4	5	6	
1 Nimzowitsch	—	½1	11	½1	½1	11	8½
2 Spielmann	½0	—	01	01	11	11	6½
3 E. Cohn	00	10	—	01	10	11	5
4 Przepiorka	½0	10	10	—	0½	11	5
5 Elyashov	½0	00	01	1½	—	11	5
6 Kürschner	00	00	00	00	00	—	0

NIMZOWITSCH–HILSE, Coburg, 1904. *Vienna Game*

1. P—K4, P—K4; 2. N—QB3, N—QB3; 3. B—B4, B—B4; 4. P—Q3, P—Q3; 5. P—B4. (Nimzowitsch rapidly abandoned such rustic openings as this. They never appear in his later years.) **5. ... N—B3; 6. P—B5, P—KR3; 7. P—KN4, N—QR4; 8. Q—B3, N×B; 9. P×N, P—B3; 10. B—Q2, P—R3; 11. 0—0—0, P—QN4; 12. KN—K2, B—N2; 13. P—KR4, Q—K2; 14. P—N5, N—Q2; 15. N—N3, P—B3; 16. B—K3, NP×P; 17. Q—R5+, K—Q1; 18. B×B, N×B; 19. Q—K2, K—K1; 20. P×BP, P×P; 21. Q×P, P—QR4; 22. Q—K2, K—Q2; 23. R—R2, QR—KN1; 24. Q—K3, K—B2; 25. R/2—Q2, R—Q1; 26. N—R5, Q—B2; 27. N—N3, P—R4; 28. R—N2, QR—KN1?** (Allowing a brilliant sacrifice **28. ... KR—N1** would have been safe enough.) **29. R×P!, K×R** (**29. ... R×N; 30. Q×N, R×R; 31. N—N5+, K—B1; 32. R×P+, B×R; 33. N—Q6+, + –** Schlechter); **30. R—Q2+, K—B2; 31. Q×N, K—N1** (**31. ... R×N; 32. N—N5+**); **32. Q—Q6+, K—R1; 33. N/N3—K2, R—Q1; 34. Q—B5, R×R; 35. Q×P+, K—N1; 36. K×R, Q—Q2+; 37. K—B1, R—Q1; 38. P—N4, Q—QB2; 39. Q—B5, R—N1; 40. P—R4, Q—Q1; 41. P—N5, P×P; 42. Q×P, K—R1; 43. Q—B5, R—N2** (**43. ... R—N5!**); **44. K—N2, K—N1; 45. N—B1, R—QB2; 46. Q—N5, K—B1; 47. N—N3, Q—Q2; 48. Q—K2, Q—B2; 49. N—N5, R—Q2; 50. N—B5‡, R—Q1; 51. N—K6, R—Q2; 52. Q—B4+, K—N1; 53. N—B5, R—K2** (**53. ... Q×Q; 54. N×R+, K—R/or B1; 55. N—N6+, + –**); **54. Q×Q, R×Q; 55. N—Q6, R—N2; 56. N/5×B, R—N5; 57. N—B5, R×RP; 58. N—Q3, R—N5; 59. N—K8, R×P; 60. N×BP, R×P; 61. N×RP, P—K5** (**61. ... R—N5; 62. N×P, R—N4; 63. N—N7, R×N; 64. P—B6, R—N2+; 65. K—**

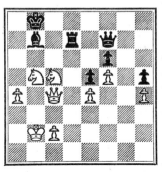

B1 + –); **62. P—B6, R—R4; 63. P—B7, R—KB4; 64. N—K5, P—K6; 65. N—N3. 1–0.**

Nimzowitsch's inspired handling of his queen plus knight(s) in this game from his very first tournament is a portent of his more mature efforts in the same genre, e.g. versus Spielmann, Stockholm, 1920 (Nimzowitsch: Black), versus Wendel and versus Bogoljubow, San Remo, 1930.

The first encounter between Nimzowitsch and Tarrasch:

TARRASCH–NIMZOWITSCH, Nuremburg, 1904. *Q. P. Tchigorin's Defence*

The notes to this game are by Nimzowitsch, translated from Russian

'An historic struggle'

1. P—Q4	P—Q4		4. P—K3	P—K3
2. P—QB4	N—QB3		5. N—B3	B × N
3. N—KB3	B—N5			

Quite possibly a bad move, but bearing in mind what follows—what a beautiful challenge! 'I couldn't care less about the theory of lost tempi!' that is what this move says.

Black does not fear to spare White the move P—KR3 since he wants to know whether White will recapture on f3 with Q or pawn.

6. Q × B
After the recapture with the pawn White's centre would forfeit much of its expansion potential.

6. ...   N/3—K2
So the pursuit of the 'primitive' (i.e. mate) appealed to my eighteen-year-old point of view. In fact Black achieves a good position by novel means and what arose from my revolutionary logic was the transposition from one opening variation to another. (Tchigorin to Stonewall. R.D.K.)

7. B—Q3	P—QB3		9. B—Q2	N—KB3
8. 0—0	P—KB4			

By playing ... Q—Q2 ... followed by ... N—R3 ... N—N3 and ... B—Q3 Black could, in my opinion, have achieved a satisfactory Stonewall set-up.

After the text Black is faced with a sea of troubles.

Position after 16. B—B3, QR—KN1

10. P × P! BP × P
Here I adhered too closely to my blockading principles. Now I would play ... KP × P with the idea: 11. B × P, N × B; 12. Q × N, B—Q3 and so on. Black would continue by developing his Q and QR on the K file which would place severe obstacles in the path of White's conversion of his extra pawn. It was at this point that Tarrasch made use of his own 'stratagem' (cf. page 13).

11. QR—B1 P—KN4

In the style of youth!

12. Q—N3	**K—B2**		**15. N—K2**	**Q—N3**
13. P—B3	**N—B3**		**16. B—B3**	**QR—KN1‡**
14. Q ×P	**B—K2**			

Black has succeeded in working up some attack and it is not easy for White to capitalise on his extra pawn, partly because the presence of the Black Q on b6 makes it more difficult for White to play P—K4. It is worth considering whether White's position is as good as Tarrasch thought it was at move 10.

17. Q—R4	**R—N3**	**18. Q—R3?**	

He should have played N—B4.

18. ... B—B1!

A quiet move with the double threat of ... B—R3 and ... R—R3.

19. N—B4	**R—R3**		**24. Q—K3**	**P—K4!**
20. Q—N3	**B—Q3**		**25. BP ×P**	**P—B5**
21. Q—B2	**R—KN1**		**26. Q—Q2**	**N ×QP**
22. P—KN3	**B ×N**		**27. K—N2!**	
23. P × B	**N – KR4**			

White must not fall for 27. B—N6 + in view of ... Q ×B!; 28. Q ×N, P ×P; 29. Q ×P +, K—K1!; 30. Q—N5 +, Q—B3. In his turn Black should avoid (27. B—N6 +) 27. ... R/3 × B; 28. B ×N, N ×P; 29. P ×N, R ×P +; 30. K—B2, R—N7 +; 31. K—K1, R ×Q; 32. B ×Q, R/1—N7; 33. R—B2, P ×B; 34. R—B7 + and White wins.

27. ... N ×NP!?

A mistake typical of my play at that time. I had in mind a deep combination but, all the same, I failed to appreciate that my own K was vulnerable. The most accurate continuation was 27. ... P ×P, which secures the win without difficulty, e.g. 27. ... P ×P; 28. P—KR3, Q—K3 (threatening to sacrifice the Q on h3); 29. R—KR1, Q ×P; 30. Q ×R, N—B5 +; 31. K—B1, P—N7 + and mate in two moves.

28. Q ×P +	**N/6—B4 dis. +**	
29. K—R1	**R ×P +!?‡**	

The point. Unfortunately this combination is not sound.

30. K × R
If Q × R then Black obtains perpetual check with ... N—N6 +.

30. ... Q—N3   **31. Q—N4**
Tarrasch overlooks the resource 31. P—K6 +, K × P; 32. B × N +, N × B; 33. KR—K1 +, K—Q2; 34. Q—KN4 and wins, thanks to the pin on the knight.

31. ...	**Q—R3 +**	**35. K—R1**	**N—N6 +**
32. Q—R3	**Q—B5 +**	**36. K—N2**	**N × R dis. +**
33. K—R1	**N—N6 +**	**37. K × N**	**Q × R +**
34. K—N2	**N/6—B4 dis. +**	**38. B—K1**	

(Black has won the exchange as a result of his remarkable combination but White retains many threats against the exposed Black K. Therefore Nimzowitsch returns the exchange to keep the initiative in his own hands. R.D.K.)

38. ... R—N8 + !   **40. B—B1 Q × P**
39. K × R Q × B +
Already Black could force a draw with ... N—K7 +.

41. Q × P + Q—N2 + ?
Black should not have decentralised his superbly placed queen in this fashion. He could have played ... K—B1 and if 42. K—B2 then ... N—B4. After the text White exploits the weakness of the dark squares, but in those days I gave no thought to such refinements.

42. Q × Q + K × Q
Here my opponent declined my offer of a draw, and the game produced an ending which was difficult in any case but especially so for a youth.

43. K—B2 K—B3   **44. K—K3 N—K3**
... N—B3! was better.

45. P—B4
He should have played B—R3.

45. ...	**N—Q1!**	**51. P—B5**	**N—K4**
46. B—N2	**K—K3**	**52. B—N5**	**K × P**
47. K—Q4	**N—B3 +**	**53. K × P**	**N—B2**
48. K—B5	**N—K2**	**54. B—Q7 +**	**K—B3**
49. B—R3 +	**K—B3**	**55. B—B8**	**N—K4!**
50. B—Q7	**N—N3**		

Intending the counter-manœuvre ... N—Q6 and if in reply P—N3 then ... N—N5 +.

56. P—N4 N—Q6
Even in its dying moments the game is still of dramatic interest. Black can now force a draw.

57. P—R3, P—N3; **58.** B—R6, N—K8; **59.** P—R4, N—B7; **60.** P—N5, K—K2; **61.** K—B6, K—Q1; **62.** K—N7, N—Q5; **63.** K × P, K—B2; **64.** B—N7, N—N6; **65.** B—B3, N—B4; **66.** P—R5, P × P; **67.** P—N6 +, K—Q3; **68.** B—Q1, K—B3; **69.** B—R4 +, K—Q3; **70.** B—K8, K—Q4; **71.** K—R8, P—R5. Draw agreed.

H. WOLF–NIMZOWITSCH, Vienna, 1905. *Ruy Lopez, Schliemann Defence*

1. P—K4, P—K4; **2.** N—KB3, N—QB3; **3.** B—N5, P—B4!?; **4.** P—Q3, N—B3; **5.** Q—K2, B—B4; **6.** N—B3, N—Q5; **7.** N × N, B × N; **8.** B—QB4, P—B5; **9.** P—KN3, P—B6; **10.** Q × P, P—Q4; **11.** P × P (11. N × P!), **11.** ... 0—0; **12.** Q—K2, B—N5; **13.** P—B3, N—K5!!; **14.** P × B (14 QP × N, B × P; 15. Q—B1 looks like an improvement), **14.** ... N × N; **15.** P × N, B × P + ; **16.** B— Q2, B × R; **17.** P—B3, P—QN4; **18.** B—N3, P—QR4?; **19.** P— Q6 +, K—R1; **20.** B—Q5, R—R3? (... R—QN1); **21.** P—N5, Q × QP; **22.** B—K4, Q—B4; **23.** R—B1, R × R + ; **24.** Q × R, B × P; **25.** Q—B5, P—N3; **26.** Q—QB8 +, K—N2; **27.** Q × R, B × B + ; **28.** K × B, Q—KB7 + ; **29.** K—B3, Q—Q5 + ; **30.** K—B2, Q—B4 + . ½–½.

NIMZOWITSCH–ALBIN, Vienna, 1905. *Alekhine's Defence (?)* (*Alekhine was thirteen years old at the time*)

1. P—K4, N—KB3; **2.** P—K5, N—N1?! (a misinterpretation, although the move has also been played by Petrosian; he lost as well!); **3.** P—Q4, P—Q4; **4.** B—Q3, P—K3; **5.** N—K2, N—QB3; **6.** P—QB3, N/1—K2; **7.** B—KN5, Q—Q2; **8.** N—Q2, N—N3; **9.** 0—0, B—K2; **10.** P—KB4, Q—Q1; **11.** N—B3, P—KR3; **12.** B × B, QN × B; **13.** Q—Q2, P—QB3; **14.** N—N3, P—KR4; **15.** P— B5! (Black's development has been much too eccentric and inefficient to cope with this breakthrough), **15.** ... P × P; **16.** N—N5, P—B5; **17.** R × P!, N × R; **18.** Q × N, B—K3; **19.** R—KB1, Q—N3 (19 ... Q—B2; 20. N × BP, R—KB1; 21. N—Q6 +, K—Q2; 22. Q × R, R × Q; 23. R × R, Q—N3; 24. R—QN8 + - Nimzowitsch); **20.** N—B5, N × N; **21.** B × N, Q—B2 (21 ... 0—0—0; 22. N × P!); **22.** B × B, P × B; **23.** N × P, Q—K2; **24.** Q—B5, K—Q2; **25.** N— B8 + +, K—B2; **26.** N—N6, Q—K1; **27.** N × R, Q × N; **28.** Q— K6, K—N3; **29.** Q—K7, Q—R3; **30.** Q—B5 +, K—R3; **31.** P— QN4, P—QN4 (or 31. ... P—QN3; 32. P—N5 +, P × P; 33. Q— R3 +, K—N2; 34. R—B7 +, K—B3; 35. P—R3!, P—R5!; 36. K— R1! + - Nimzowitsch); **32.** P—KR3, P—R5; **33.** K—R1, Q—K3; **34.** R—B7, Q—R3; **35.** P—R4, Q—K3; **36.** P—R5, Q—K1; **37.** R × P +, R × R; **38.** Q—N6. Mate.

Nimzowitsch–Spielmann. From their match at Munich, 1905.
Scotch Game

1. P—K4, P—K4; 2. N—KB3, N—QB3; 3. P—Q4, P×P; 4.
N×P, N—B3; 5. N—QB3, B—N5; 6. N×N, NP×N; 7. B—Q3,
P—Q4; 8. P×P, P×P; 9. 0—0, 0—0; 10. B—KN5, P—B3; 11.
N—K2, B—Q3; 12. N—Q4, B—Q2; 13. Q—B3, B—K4; 14. N—
B5!, Q—B2; 15. QR—K1, QR—K1; 16. P—B3, B×N; 17. Q×B,
P—N3; 18. Q—B3, N—R4; 19. B—KR6, N—N2; 20. K—R1,
P—KB4; 21. R—K2, R—B2; 22. R/1—K1, R/2—K2; 23. B—KN5,
R—K3; 24. P—B4, Q—Q3; 25. P×P, P×P (Nimzowitsch now
exploits his bishops to harry Black's rooks and to batter Black's QP);
26. B—N5, R—N1; 27. B—QR4, B×P (a clever win of a pawn, but
it doesn't help him at all; Black's pawns are weak and, in addition,
his king is exposed); 28. B—N3, R—N4!; 29. R—Q1, B—B3; 30.
B—KB4, Q—R3; 31. R×R, N×R; 32. B×P, Q—N3; 33. B—R6,
K—R1; 34. B×N (clearing a path for the Q invasion which follows),
34. ... Q×B; 35. Q—R8+, Q—N1; 36. Q×P, R—N1; 37. P—
KR3, R—R1; 38. Q—N6, B—K4; 39. P—B4, B—N2; 40. B×B+,
K×B; 41. R—Q7+, K—R3; 42. Q—KB6. 1–0. An attractive game.

Nimzowitsch–Forgacs,* Barmen, 1905. *Scotch Game*
The attack that failed

1. P—K4, P—K4; 2. N—KB3, N—QB3; 3. P—Q4, P×P; 4.
N×P, N—KB3; 5. N—QB3, B—N5; 6. N×N, NP×N; 7. B—Q3,
P—Q4; 8. P×P, P×P; 9. 0—0, 0—0; 10. B—KN5, P—B3; 11.
N—K2, B—N5; 12. P—KB3, B—R4; 13. N—N3, B—N3; 14. P—
KB4, B×B; 15. P×B?!, R—K1; 16. P—Q4, P—KR3; 17. B—R4,
Q—Q3; 18. P—B5, N—K5; 19. Q—N4, K—R2; 20. N—R5, R—
KN1; 21. R—B3, Q—Q2; 22. B—N3. (Planning to bring the piece
round to K5 to augment the pressure against Black's KNP, but the
resultant attack proves insufficient. There was a seductive alternative
in 22. R—KR3, QR—K1; 23. B—B6, e.g. 23. ... N×B; 24.
Q×P+!, R×Q; 25. N×N+, K—R1; 26. R×P+ and mates; or
23. ... P×B; 24. Q×N! But Nimzowitsch's notes reveal that this
imaginative idea also amounts to nothing: 23. B—B6, B—B1;
24. Q—B4, P—N3! [24. ... N×B?; 25. Q×P+!]; 25. P×P+,
P×P; 26. N—N3, N×B; 27. Q×N, B—N2; 28. Q—B4, KR—B1;
29. Q—Q2, Q—N5; 30. R—Q1, Q×P+ and Black wins. White's
men huddled on the extreme K wing are quite powerless against
Black's central counter-attack), 22. ... QR—K1; 23. B—K5,
B—Q3; 24. R—KR3, B×B; 25. P×B, R×P; 26. N×P, R×N;
27. R×P+, K—N1!; 28. Q—R4, P—B3; 29. Q—R5, R—R2;

---

* Otherwise known as 'Fleischmann'.

30. Q—N6 +, K—R1; 31. R—K1, R × R; 32. Q × R +, K—N1; 33. R—K3, Q × P. 0–1.

SPIELMANN–NIMZOWITSCH, Barmen, 1905. *Vienna Gambit*

Nimzowitsch learns about doubled pawns, the hard way

1. P—K4, P—K4; 2. N—QB3, B—B4; 3. P—B4, P—Q3; 4. N—B3, N—KB3; 5. B—B4, N—B3; 6. P—Q3, B—K3; 7. B—N5, P—QR3; 8. B × N +, P × B; 9. P—B5, B—B1; 10. B—N5, Q—Q2; 11. B × N, P × B; 12. Q—Q2, B—N2; 13. N—K2, P—KR4; 14. N—R4, 0—0—0; 15. 0—0—0, P—Q4; 16. N—N3, B—B1; 17. K—N1, P—Q5? (17. ... B—R3!; 18. Q—K2, B—N4; 19. N—B3, B—B5. The text breaks nearly all of the rules Nimzowitsch was later to formulate concerning the correct way to handle a double-pawn complex. On top of that the move loses material); **18. Q—K2, B—R3; 19. N × P, B—N4; 20. P—KN3, P—B4; 21. N—N2, P—B5; 22. P—KR4, P—B6‡.** (The following 'combination' presents rather a pathetic spectacle.) **23. P × B, Q—R5; 24. K—R1, R × N; 25. R × R, P × P + ; 26. K—N1, B—Q4; 27. P × B, R × P; 28. R—R8 +, K—N2; 29. Q—B3, P—B3; 30. Q—R5. 1–0.**

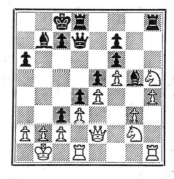

SPIELMANN–NIMZOWITSCH, Munich, 1906. *King's Gambit*

1. P—K4, P—K4; 2. P—KB4, P—Q4; 3. KP × P, P—QB3!?; 4. Q—B3 (4. N—QB3!?), **4. ... KP × P; 5. P × P, N × P; 6. B—N5, N—B3; 7. P—Q4, B—Q2; 8. N—K2, Q—N3; 9. Q—Q3, B—Q3; 10. P—B4, 0—0; 11. B × N** (11. P—B5, Q—R4 + ; 12. B—Q2, N—QN5), **11. ... B × B; 12. P—B5, B × BP; 13. P × B, Q × BP; 14. B × P, KR—K1; 15. N—B3, B × P; 16. 0—0—0, B × R; 17. R × B, QR—Q1; 18. Q—B2, N—Q4; 19. B—Q2, N—N5; 20. Q—Q1, N—Q6 + ; 21. K—N1, N—B7. 0–1.**

A pleasant enough game but in comparison with the heavyweight struggles these two were to have in the years of their grandmaster-hood it looks like a blitz or skittles encounter. Their only reversion to such habits of childhood was their game from Semmering, 1926 (q.v.).

According to my calculations Nimzowitsch and Spielmann played a total of fifty games against each other in the course of their tourna-ment and match careers of which 19 were drawn, while Nimzowitsch won 18 and Spielmann 13.

GAMES, 1907–1914, *Established Master*

OSTENDE, Master Group May, 16–June 14, 1907

	1	2	3	4	5	6	7	8	9	10	11	12	13	14	15	16	17	18	19	20	21	22	23	24	25	26	27	28	29	
1 Bernstein	–	½	0	1	½	1	1	1	1	½	1	0	1	½	½	1	1	0	½	1	1	½	1	0	1	1	1	0	1	19½
2 Rubinstein	½	–	½	1	½	0	1	1	½	½	½	1	0	½	½	½	0	1	1	1	1	½	1	½	1	1	1	1	1	19½
3 Mieses	1	½	–	1	0	½	1	0	½	1	1	0	1	1	1	1	1	1	½	0	1	1	1	1	1	0	0	0	1	19
4 Nimzowitsch	0	0	0	–	1	½	0	½	½	½	½	1	1	1	½	½	1	1	½	½	1	1	½	1	1	1	1	1	1	19
5 Fleischmann	½	½	1	0	–	½	1	0	½	½	1	½	½	1	½	1	½	1	½	1	0	½	½	1	½	1	1	1	1	18½
6 Teichmann	0	1	½	½	½	–	½	½	½	0	½	1	0	0	1	0	½	1	1	0	1	1	1	1	1	1	1	1	1	18
7 Duras	0	0	0	1	0	½	–	½	0	½	1	1	0	0	1	½	1	1	1	1	½	1	1	1	1	0	1	1	1	17½
8 Salwe	0	0	1	½	1	½	½	–	0	1	1	1	½	1	½	1	1	1	½	½	½	½	1	1	0	½	0	0	1	17
9 Marco	0	½	½	½	½	½	1	1	–	0	½	½	½	1	½	1	½	½	½	½	0	1	1	0	1	1	½	½	1	16½
10 John	½	½	0	½	½	1	½	0	1	–	½	1	½	1	½	½	½	0	½	½	½	½	½	1	0	1	1	½	1	16
11 Tartakower	0	½	0	½	0	½	0	0	½	½	–	½	½	1	1	1	1	½	½	1	1	0	½	1	1	1	1	1	0	16
12 E. Cohn	1	0	1	0	½	0	0	0	½	0	½	–	½	1	0	½	1	0	1	1	1	1	½	1	½	½	1	0	1	15
13 Znosko-Borowsky	0	1	0	0	½	1	1	½	½	½	½	½	–	0	1	0	½	1	½	1	1	½	½	½	0	½	1	1	0	15
14 Spielmann	½	½	0	0	0	1	1	0	0	0	0	0	1	–	½	0	1	½	½	1	1	1	½	0	1	1	1	1	1	15
15 Blackburne	½	½	0	½	½	0	0	½	½	½	0	1	0	½	–	1	0	1	0	0	1	1	1	1	1	1	½	1	0	14½
16 Perlis	0	½	0	½	0	1	½	0	0	½	0	½	1	1	0	–	0	0	½	1	0	0	1	1	1	1	½	1	1	13½
17 Swiderski	0	½	0	½	0	1	0	0	½	½	0	0	½	0	1	1	–	1	½	0	0	½	½	1	1	0	1	1	1	13
18 Shories	1	0	0	0	0	0	0	0	½	1	½	1	0	½	0	1	0	–	1	1	1	1	1	0	0	1	1	0	0	12½
19 Suchting	½	0	½	½	½	0	0	½	½	½	½	0	½	½	1	½	½	0	–	0	½	½	½	½	½	0	1	1	1	12½
20 Billecard	0	0	1	½	0	1	0	½	½	½	0	0	0	0	1	0	1	0	1	–	1	½	1	½	0	1	0	½	½	12
21 W. Cohn	0	0	0	0	1	0	½	½	1	½	0	0	0	0	0	1	1	0	½	0	–	1	½	1	1	½	0	1	1	12
22 Leonhardt	½	½	0	0	½	0	0	½	0	½	1	0	½	0	0	1	½	0	½	½	0	–	½	0	1	1	½	1	1	11½
23 Metger	0	0	0	½	½	0	0	0	0	½	½	½	½	½	0	0	½	0	½	0	½	½	–	½	1	1	1	1	1	11
24 von Scheve	1	½	0	0	0	0	0	0	1	0	0	0	½	1	0	0	0	1	½	½	0	1	½	–	1	0	½	1	1	11
25 Lee	0	0	0	0	½	0	0	1	0	1	0	½	1	0	0	0	0	1	½	1	0	0	0	0	–	½	1	½	1	9½
26 Shoosmith	0	0	1	0	0	0	1	½	0	0	0	½	½	0	0	0	1	0	1	0	½	0	0	1	½	–	0	1	1	9½
27 Jacob	0	0	1	0	0	0	0	1	½	0	0	0	0	0	½	½	0	0	0	1	1	½	0	½	0	1	–	0	1	8½
28 van Vliet	1	0	1	0	0	0	0	1	½	½	0	1	0	0	0	0	0	1	0	½	0	0	0	0	½	0	1	–	½	8½
29 Mortimer	0	0	0	0	0	0	0	0	0	0	1	0	1	0	1	0	0	1	0	½	0	0	0	0	0	0	0	½	–	5

CARLSBAD, August 2C–September 17, 1907

		1	2	3	4	5	6	7	8	9	10	11	12	13	14	15	16	17	18	19	20	21	
1	Rubinstein	–	½	½	0	½	½	1	1	1	½	1	1	0	1	1	1	½	1	1	1	1	15
2	Maroczy	½	–	0	½	½	½	1	½	1	½	½	½	1	1	1	½	½	1	1	1	1	14
3	Leonhardt	½	1	–	½	0	1	1	½	½	½	1	½	½	1	1	½	1	½	1	0	1	13½
4	Nimzowitsch	1	½	½	–	1	½	½	½	½	½	0	0	½	0	1	½	1	1	1	1	1	12½
5	Schlechter	½	½	1	0	–	½	½	0	0	½	½	½	½	1	1	1	1	½	1	1	1	12½
6	Vidmar	½	½	0	½	½	–	1	1	½	1	1	0	1	1	0	½	1	1	1	0	0	12
7	Duras	0	0	0	½	½	0	–	1	0	0	1	½	1	1	1	1	1	1	1	1	0	11½
8	Teichmann	0	½	½	½	1	0	0	–	1	1	½	½	1	1	½	½	½	0	½	1	1	11½
9	Salwe	0	0	½	½	1	½	1	0	–	½	0	½	0	½	1	1	1	½	1	1	½	11
10	Wolf	½	½	½	½	½	0	1	0	½	–	½	½	1	1	1	½	0	1	0	½	½	10½
11	Dus Chotimirski	0	½	0	1	½	0	0	½	1	½	–	0	1	0	1	1	1	0	0	1	1	10
12	Marshall	0	0	½	1	½	1	½	½	½	½	1	–	½	0	0	½	0	0	1	1	1	12
13	Spielmann	1	0	½	½	½	0	0	0	1	0	0	½	–	0	1	½	1	0	1	1	1	9½
14	Tartakower	0	0	0	1	0	0	0	0	½	0	1	1	1	–	0	½	0	1	1	1	1	9
15	Janowski	0	0	0	0	0	1	0	½	0	0	0	1	0	1	–	1	1	1	0	1	1	8½
16	Berger	0	½	½	½	0	½	0	½	0	½	0	½	½	½	0	–	1	1	0	½	½	7½
17	Mieses	½	½	0	0	0	0	0	½	0	1	0	1	0	1	0	0	–	1	1	1	0	7½
18	Tchigorin	0	0	½	0	½	0	0	1	½	0	1	1	1	0	0	0	0	–	1	0	1	7½
19	Olland	0	0	0	0	0	0	0	½	0	1	1	0	0	0	1	1	0	0	–	1	1	6½
20	E. Cohn	0	0	1	0	0	1	0	0	0	½	0	0	0	0	0	½	0	1	0	–	1	5
21	P. Johner	0	0	0	0	0	1	1	0	½	½	0	0	0	0	0	½	1	0	0	0	–	4½

HAMBURG, 1910

		1	2	3	4	5	6	7	8	9	10	11	12	13	14	15	16	17	
1	Schlechter	–	0	1	½	½	½	1	1	1	½	1	1	½	1	½	½	1	11½
2	Duras	1	–	1	½	½	1	1	½	0	½	1	½	1	1	0	½	1	11
3	Nimzowitsch	0	0	–	1	1	½	½	½	1	1	½	1	0	½	1	1	1	10½
4	Spielmann	½	½	0	–	0	½	½	½	1	1	½	0	1	1	1	1	1	10
5	Marshall	½	½	0	1	–	0	½	0	½	1	1	½	1	0	1	1	1	9½
6	Teichmann	½	0	½	½	1	–	½	1	½	0	½	½	1	½	½	1	1	9½
7	Alekhine	0	0	½	½	½	½	–	½	0	0	½	1	½	1	1	1	1	8½
8	Dus Chotimirski	0	½	½	½	1	0	½	–	1	0	0	1	½	0	1	1	1	8½
9	Forgacs	0	1	0	0	½	½	1	0	–	½	1	½	½	½	1	½	½	8
10	Tarrasch	½	½	0	0	0	1	1	1	½	–	½	0	½	½	1	1	0	8
11	Köhnlein	0	0	½	½	0	½	½	1	0	½	–	1	½	0	1	0	1	7
12	Leonhardt	0	½	0	1	½	½	0	0	½	1	0	–	1	1	0	0	1	7
13	Salwe	½	0	1	0	0	0	½	½	½	½	½	0		1	0	1	1	7
14	Tartakower	0	0	½	0	1	½	0	1	½	½	1	0	0	–	1	½	½	7
15	Speyer	½	1	0	0	0	½	0	0	0	0	0	1	1	0	–	1	½	5½
16	John	½	½	0	0	0	0	0	0	½	0	1	1	0	½	0	–	1	5
17	Yates	0	0	0	0	0	0	0	0	½	1	0	0	0	½	½	0	–	2½

SAN SEBASTIAN, February 19–March 17, 1911

		1	2	3	4	5	6	7	8	9	10	11	12	13	14	15	
1	Capablanca	–	0	½	½	1	½	½	1	1	½	1	½	1	½	1	9½
2	Rubinstein	1	–	½	½	½	½	½	½	½	½	1	½	½	1	1	9
3	Vidmar	½	½	–	0	½	½	½	1	½	½	1	½	1	1	1	9
4	Marshall	½	½	1	–	½	½	½	½	½	1	1	½	½	0	1	8½
5	Nimzowitsch	0	½	½	½	–	½	0	½	1	1	½	½	½	½	1	7½
6	Schlechter	½	½	½	½	½	–	½	0	½	½	1	½	½	1	½	7½
7	Tarrasch	½	½	½	½	1	½	–	1	½	0	½	½	1	0	½	7½
8	Bernstein	0	½	0	½	½	1	0	–	1	1	½	1	0	1	0	7
9	Spielmann	0	½	½	½	0	½	½	0	–	½	½	1	½	1	1	7
10	Teichmann	½	½	½	0	0	½	1	0	½	–	0	½	½	1	1	6½
11	Janowski	0	0	0	0	½	0	½	½	½	1	–	0	1	1	1	6
12	Maroczy	½	½	½	½	½	½	½	0	0	½	1	–	½	½	0	6
13	Burn	0	½	0	½	½	½	0	1	½	½	0	½	–	0	½	5
14	Duras	½	0	0	1	½	0	1	0	0	0	0	½	1	–	½	5
15	Leonhardt	0	0	0	0	0	½	½	1	0	0	0	1	½	½	–	4

CARLSBAD, August 21–September 24, 1911

	1	2	3	4	5	6	7	8	9	10	11	12	13	14	15	16	17	18	19	20	21	22	23	24	25	26	
1 Teichmann	–	1	1	1	½	1	½	1	1	½	0	1	½	½	½	1	0	½	½	1	½	1	½	1	1	1	18
2 Schlechter	0	–	½	0	½	½	½	1	½	1	0	½	1	1	1	1	1	0	½	1	1	1	½	1	1	1	17
3 Rubinstein	0	½	–	½	0	½	½	1	½	1	1	0	½	1	1	½	1	1	1	½	½	½	1	1	1	1	17
4 Rotlevi	0	1	½	–	1	1	0	0	1	0	½	1	1	0	1	1	0	1	1	1	1	0	0	1	1	1	16
5 Marshall	½	½	1	0	–	½	0	½	½	½	1	½	½	½	1	1	½	1	0	½	1	1	0	1	1	1	15½
6 Nimzowitsch	0	½	½	0	½	–	½	½	0	0	0	½	1	1	1	½	½	1	1	½	1	1	1	1	1	1	15½
7 Vidmar	½	½	½	1	1	½	–	0	½	0	1	1	½	0	1	½	1	0	0	½	½	1	1	½	1	1	15
8 Alekhine	0	0	0	1	½	½	1	–	1	0	1	0	0	1	½	1	0	½	0	1	0	1	1	1	½	1	13½
9 Tartakower	0	½	½	0	½	1	½	0	–	½	1	½	½	½	½	1	0	1	1	1	1	0	1	0	0	1	13½
10 Leonhardt	½	0	0	1	½	1	1	1	½	–	0	½	½	0	0	½	1	½	1	1	0	0	1	1	1	0	13½
11 Duras	1	1	0	½	0	1	0	0	0	1	–	0	½	1	0	0	½	1	1	½	½	1	½	1	½	1	13½
12 Spielmann	0	½	1	0	½	½	0	1	½	½	1	–	0	1	1	½	½	½	1	½	½	1	0	0	1	0	13
13 Perlis	½	0	½	0	½	0	½	1	½	½	½	1	–	½	1	½	1	1	0	½	1	0	0	0	0	1	12
14 E. Cohn	½	0	0	1	½	0	1	0	½	1	0	0	½	–	½	½	1	0	1	0	1	0	½	1	1	0	11½
15 Levenfish	½	0	0	0	0	0	0	½	½	1	1	0	0	½	–	1	1	½	½	1	½	1	1	0	1	0	11½
16 Süchting	0	0	½	0	0	½	½	0	0	½	1	½	½	½	0	–	1	1	0	0	½	1	½	1	1	1	11½
17 Burn	1	0	0	1	½	½	0	1	1	0	½	½	0	0	0	0	–	0	½	½	1	1	1	1	0	0	11
18 Salwe	½	1	0	0	0	0	1	½	0	½	0	½	0	1	½	0	1	–	1	½	½	0	½	½	1	½	11
19 P. Johner	½	½	0	0	1	0	1	1	0	0	0	0	1	0	½	1	½	0	–	1	½	0	1	1	0	0	10½
20 Kostic	0	0	½	0	½	½	½	0	0	0	½	½	½	1	0	1	½	½	0	–	½	½	1	1	0	1	10½
21 Rabinowitsch	½	0	½	0	0	0	½	1	0	1	½	½	0	0	½	½	0	½	½	½	–	1	½	0	1	1	10½
22 D. Chotimirski	0	0	½	1	0	0	0	0	1	1	0	0	1	1	0	0	0	1	1	½	0	–	1	0	0	1	10
23 Alapin	½	½	0	1	1	0	0	0	0	0	½	1	1	½	0	½	0	½	0	0	½	0	–	½	½	0	8½
24 Chajes	0	0	0	0	0	0	½	0	1	0	0	1	1	0	1	0	0	½	0	0	1	1	½	–	0	1	8½
25 Fahrni	0	0	0	0	0	0	0	½	1	0	½	0	1	0	0	0	1	0	1	1	0	1	½	1	–	0	8½
26 Jaffe	0	0	0	0	0	0	0	0	0	1	0	1	0	1	1	0	1	½	1	0	0	0	1	0	1	–	8½

SAN SEBASTIAN, February 19–March 20, 1912

	1	2	3	4	5	6	7	8	9	10	11	
1 Rubinstein	—	½1	01	½1	½½	1½	01	11	½½	½1	½	12½
2 Nimzowitsch	½0	—	01	1½	0½	11	11	½½	½½	11	½	12
3 Spielmann	10	10	—	10	1½	½1	½½	½1	½½	1½	1	12
4 Tarrasch	½0	0½	01	—	11	01	½0	½½	11	11	1	11½
5 Perlis	½½	1½	0½	00	—	1½	½1	½½	½½	1½	½	10
6 Marshall	0½	00	½0	10	0½	—	½1	1½	½½	11	1	9½
7 Duras	10	00	½½	½1	½0	½0	—	½½	½1	01	½	8½
8 Schlechter	00	½½	½0	½½	½½	0½	½½	—	½½	1½	½	8
9 Teichmann	½½	½½	½½	00	½½	½½	½0	½½	—	½½	½	8
10 Leonhardt	½0	00	0½	00	0½	00	10	0½	½½	—	1	5
11 Forgacs	½	½	0	0	½	0	½	½	½	0	—	3

ALL-RUSSIAN CHAMPIONSHIP, VILNA, September, 1912

	1	2	3	4	5	6	7	8	9	10	11	
1 Rubinstein	—	½½	1½	1½	11	11	11	00	01	½½	—	12
2 Bernstein	½½	—	1½	0½	11	00	0½	11	11	11	—	11½
3 Levitsky	0½	0½	—	½1	½½	11	0½	1½	½1	11	—	11
4 Nimzowitsch	0½	1½	½0	—	½½	½0	1½	1½	½1	11	—	10½
5 Flamberg	00	00	½½	½½	—	1½	10	½1	1½	1½	—	9
6 Alekhine	00	11	00	½1	0½	—	11	0½	01	10	—	8½
7 Levenfish	00	1½	1½	0½	01	00	—	½1	½1	½½	—	8½
8 Freymann	11	00	0½	0½	½0	1½	½0	—	½1	10	—	8
9 Alapin	10	00	½0	½0	0½	10	½0	½0	—	½1	—	6
10 Salwe	½½	00	00	00	0½	01	½½	01	½0	—	—	5
11 Rabinovich	0	½	0	—	½	0	0	0	0	½	—	can-celled

ALL-RUSSIAN CHAMPIONSHIP, ST. PETERSBURG, 1913–1914

	1	2	3	4	5	6	7	8	9	10	11	12	13	14	15	16	17	18	
1 Alekhine	–	1	1	0	1	1	½	0	1	1	1	1	1	1	1	1	0	1	13½
2 Nimzowitsch	0	–	½	½	1	1	0	1	1	1	½	1	1	1	1	1	1	1	13½
3 Flamberg	0	½	–	1	½	0	1	1	1	½	1	1	1	½	1	1	1	1	13
4 Lovtzsky	1	½	0	–	½	0	0	1	1	1	½	½	1	1	1	½	1	½	11
5 Levenfish	0	0	½	½	–	1	0	0	1	0	1	1	1	1	1	1	½	1	10½
6 Znosko-Borowsky	0	0	1	1	0	–	½	1	0	½	½	1	0	½	1	1	1	1	10
7 Smorodsky	½	1	0	1	1	½	–	½	0	½	0	1	1	0	½	1	1	½	10
8 Bogoljubow	1	0	0	0	1	0	½	–	½	½	1	0	1	1	½	½	1	1	9½
9 Evenson	0	0	0	0	0	1	1	½	–	0	½	1	1	1	0	1	1	1	9
10 Alapin	0	0	½	0	1	½	½	½	1	–	0	0	½	½	½	1	1	1	8½
11 Salwe	0	½	0	½	0	½	1	0	½	1	–	0	1	1	½	1	0	1	8½
12 Freymann	0	0	0	½	0	0	0	1	0	1	1	–	0	½	1	0	1	1	7
13 Levitsky	0	0	0	0	0	1	0	0	0	½	0	1	–	1	1	1	0	1	6½
14 Taubenhaus	0	0	½	0	0	½	1	0	0	½	0	½	0	–	0	1	1	1	6
15 Lebedev	0	0	0	0	0	0	½	½	1	½	½	0	0	1	–	0	1	0	5
16 Evtifeyev	0	0	0	½	0	0	0	½	0	0	0	1	0	0	1	–	1	½	4½
17 Gregory	1	0	0	0	½	0	0	0	0	0	1	0	1	0	0	0	–	0	3½
18 Elyashov	0	0	0	½	0	0	½	0	0	0	0	0	0	0	1	½	1	–	3½

ST. PETERSBURG, 1914

Preliminary

		1	2	3	4	5	6	7	8	9	10	11	
1	Capablanca	–	½	½	1	½	1	½	1	1	1	1	8
2	Lasker	½	–	½	½	½	0	1	½	1	1	1	6½
3	Tarrasch	½	½	–	½	½	1	½	1	1	0	1	6½
4	Alekhine	0	½	½	–	1	½	1	½	½	½	1	6
5	Marshall	½	½	½	0	–	1	½	½	1	1	½	6
6	Bernstein	0	1	0	½	0	–	½	½	½	1	1	5
7	Rubinstein	½	0	½	0	½	½	–	½	½	1	1	5
8	Nimzowitsch	0	½	0	½	½	½	½	–	0	½	1	4
9	Blackburne	0	0	0	½	0	½	½	1	–	0	1	3½
10	Janowski	0	0	1	½	0	0	0	½	1	–	½	3½
11	Gunsberg	0	0	0	0	½	0	0	0	0	½	–	1

Final

1	Lasker	6½	—	½1	11	1½	11	13½
2	Capablanca	8	½0	—	½1	10	11	13
3	Alekhine	6	00	½0	—	11	1½	10
4	Tarrasch	6½	0½	01	00	—	0½	8½
5	Marshall	6	00	00	0½	1½	—	8
			1	2	3	4	5	

NIMZOWITSCH–SALWE, Carlsbad, 1911. *French Defence*
('From first move to last this game is highly instructive; moreover, I
regard it as the first game to be played in the spirit of the new
philosophy of the centre, which I originated.' NIMZOWITSCH.)

This encounter between Nimzowitsch and Salwe (and Nimzowitsch's
tract attendant upon this game—'The surrender of the centre, a
prejudice', 1913) exerted a major influence on the whole attitude
towards central control. After his game with Salwe Nimzowitsch
wrote: 'True, pawns are best fitted for building up the centre, since
they are the most stable; on the other hand pieces stationed in the
centre can very well take the place of pawns. Moreover, the centre
can often be effectively held at long range by bishops and rooks, so
that the actual occupation of the centre by a pawn or pawns does
not necessarily mean its control.'

This, and similar statements by Nimzowitsch, provided the initial
strategic foundation for such popular contemporary defences as the
Pirc or Alekhine where Black's pieces challenge a White pawn centre.

The Salwe game is a fine illustration of the struggle between piece
control and pawn occupation of the centre. Furthermore, I think you
will agree, we will come to notice several characteristics in common
between Nimzowitsch's handling of the French Defence with 3. P—
K5 and his later treatment of the 'Nimzowitsch Attack', with regard
to the dark squares in general and e5 in particular. Up to the beginning of the 1920s 3. P—K5 in the French was, perhaps, Nimzowitsch's most trusted weapon, and he scored many victories with it.
From 1923 onwards, however, the examples become increasingly
isolated and its paramount place in Nimzowitsch's repertoire was
taken over by N—KB3 and P—QN3 systems. The parallels are there
indeed.

1. P—K4　P—K3　　　　　　**3. P—K5**
2. P—Q4　P—Q4
Creating the famous pawn-chain which earns such a profound
discussion in Chapter IX of *My System*.

3. ...　　P—QB4　　　　　　**4. P—QB3**
4. Q—N4!? was Nimzowitsch's last word on this in the 1920s.

4. ...　　N—QB3　　　　　　**6. B—Q3**
5. N—B3　Q—N3
More circumspect is 6. B—K2

6. ...　B—Q2?!
This plausible move, planning ... R—B1 and only then ...
P × P, has virtually disappeared from master praxis as a result of this

very game. However, it is not entirely extinct. Normal now is
6. ... P×P, 7. P×P and only then ... B—Q2, threatening ...
N×QP. In this case Nimzowitsch would probably have sacrificed a
move (8. B—K2, cf., page 51) rather than a pawn (8. 0—0).

7. P×P

This very good move which 'surrenders' his pawn centre, but only
in return for the possibility of control by pieces, certainly struck the
leading players of the time as odd, but we should not overlook that
(with few exceptions) they were impressed by the fact of Nimzowitsch's success with his plan. The highly orthodox Dr. Vidmar
wrote of this move in the official tournament book of Carlsbad,
1911: 'After 6. ... B—Q2 the following, ostensibly unsound,
continuation (7. P×P, etc.) is possible, which, however, gives White
a good game.'

And Vidmar was full of praise for Nimzowitsch's conduct of the
remainder of the game.

We can see from this that the degree of opposition from the
'establishment' of the chess world which Nimzowitsch had to face in
his early career has been somewhat exaggerated. In his *Hypermodern
Chess*, Reinfeld writes: 'It should be borne in mind that Nimzowitsch's play here was so revolutionary that it earned him little more
than contempt. Few critics were able to appreciate the fine points of
this game. For this move (7. P×P), one of the deepest ever played,
Nimzowitsch was roundly damned by the chess world.' Unfortunately, the facts contradict this pleasantly romantic view.

That opposition which he did have to surmount from certain
isolated but implacable quarters was probably grounded as much in
personal animosity and incompatibility as in disagreement over
theories of chess.

7. ...   B×P   8. 0—0

Hort–Andersson, Reykjavik, 1972, went: 8. Q—K2, P—QR4!
(which Salwe should have played on move 8); 9. QN—Q2, P—R5;
10. P—QN4, P×P e.p.; 11. N×P, B—R6; 12. 0—0, KN—K2;
13. B—Q2, N—N3; 14. QN—Q4, B—K2; 15. KR—K1 + =

8. ...   P—B3?!   9. P—QN4!

Serving a dual-purpose: (i) the QNP is protected with tempo,
therefore White's QB can travel to KB4 to over-protect the vital
blockade square e5; (ii) Black's KB is driven away from the support
blockade square Q4. By move 18 (see Diagram) White has a firm
grip on both of these key squares and Black's hanging central pawn
majority is absolutely crippled and immobile. ('First restrain, then
blockade and finally destroy', was the relevant Nimzowitsch
aphorism.)

9. ...   B—K2   **11. N × P   N × N**
10. B—KB4   P × P   **12. B × N   N—B3**
Or 12. ... B—KB3; 13. Q—R5 +, P—N3; 14. B × P +, P × B;
15. Q × P +, K—K2; 16. B × B +, N × B; 17. Q—N7 + (Nimzowitsch)

13. N—Q2   0—0   **14. N—B3   B—Q3**
Here is one variation, again stemming from Nimzowitsch, which
shows just how weak Black's centre really is: 14. ... B—N4;
15. B—Q4, Q—R3; 16. B × B, Q × B; 17. N—N5, Q—B3; 18. R—
K1 + −. Black could also seek to lift the blockade with 14. ... N—
N5 but after 15. B—N3 (15. B—Q4, Q—B2 threatening ...
R × N!), 15. ... B—KB3 (... B—Q3?; 16. B × P +! and N—
N5 +); 16. P—KR3, N—R3; 17. B—K5, N—B2; 18. B × B,
P × B; 19. P—B4! White is still in control, in view of Black's
weakened king position, e.g. 19. ... P—Q5?; 20. N × P! 19. ...
P × P; 20. B × BP and Black's bishop hangs, or 19. ... Q × NP;
20. P × P, P × P; 21. R—N1 with a dangerous attack.

15. Q—K2!
A question of move order: why not first 15. B—Q4?
In *My System* and its epigoni there is stated: not 15. B—Q4?,
Q—B2; 16. Q—K2, N—N5!; 17. P—KR3, P—K4! and Black frees
himself. The 'reserve blockader' (Nf3) has failed to attain its objective (e5). But is this really so? During the course of a discussion on
3. P—K5 in the French Defence the British Master George Botterill
demonstrated the following concealed possibility to me: 15. B—
Q4!?, Q—B2; 16. Q—K2, N—N5, as above, and now 17. B × P + !?,
K—R1; 18. N—K5!, B × N (also good for White is 18. ... N × N;
19. Q—R5, R—B3; 20. B—N6 +, K—N1; 21. Q—R7 +, K—B1;
22. Q—R8 +, K—K2; 23. Q × P +, R—B2; 24. B × R, N × B;
25. B—B6 +); 19. Q × N, B × B; 20. Q—R5, R—B3; 21. B—N6 +,
K—N1; 22. P × B and won easily—Botterill–Deighton, Bradford,
1965.
Of course, Black must accept the sacrifice, when he should emerge
on top, although the variations are not simple: 17. ... K × B!;
18. N—N5 +, K—N3!; 19. Q × N, R—B5; 20. Q—R3, K × N;
21. B × NP (21. B—K3 meets with a similar defence), 21. ... K—
N3! and if 22. Q—R6 +, K—B2; 23. Q—R7 then ... K—K1
seems adequate.
None of this is mentioned by Nimzowitsch, or, for that matter, by
anybody else who has annotated his Salwe game. As Botterill put it
to me—this analysis doesn't exactly upset everything written about
Nimzowitsch–Salwe. If anything it shows how much greater precision
and depth of calculation is required for deciding between 15. B—

Q4!? and 15. Q—K2! How much of that do you think Nimzowitsch saw? How much did he need to see?

15. ...   QR—B1
16. B—Q4   Q—B2
17. N—K5   B—K1
18. QR—K1‡

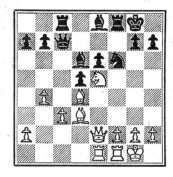

Total strangulation! White's blockade creates a most aesthetic impression. The remedy now chosen by Salwe is desperate, involving, as it does, the surrender of the bishop pair in an open position.

18. ...   B ×N

A horrible move to have to make.

19. B × B   Q—B3   21. Q—B2   R—KB2
20. B—Q4   B—Q2   22. R—K3

Bringing up reinforcements to assault Black's king's fortress.

22. ...   P—QN3   24. B × RP!
23. R—N3   K—R1

Winning a pawn and shattering the position of the enemy king. The B is immune to capture, e.g: 24. ... N × B; 25. Q—N6, K—N1; 26. B × KNP, N—B1; 27. Q—R6, N—R2; 28. B—B6 +. Observe the role played in this note by White's QB, and compare with Nimzowitsch–Wolf (page 141).

24. ...   P—K4

A typical burst of counterplay after material loss but it is of a purely temporary nature.

25. B—N6   R—K2   28. B—N5   R × P
26. R—K1   Q—Q3   29. R × R   P × R
27. B—K3   P—Q5   30. Q × P

With the superior position and an extra pawn.

30. ...   K—N1   35. R × R   K × R
31. P—QR3 K—B1   36. B—Q3   K—Q3
32. B—R4   B—K1   37. B × N   P × B
33. B—B5   Q—Q5   38. K—B1   B—B3
34. Q × Q   P × Q   39. P—KR4   Resigns

And two more examples from the same tournament to illustrate the broad strategic theme of the previous game:

(i) NIMZOWITSCH–LEVENFISH, Carlsbad, 1911. *French Defence*

With two bishops for two knights, and a central pawn majority, Black probably felt confident in the outcome of this game. But Nimzowitsch proves that the opposing centre is a liability because the squares in front of it are weak, inviting invasion by blockading knights. The bishops, locked behind the pawns, are never given a chance. Not strictly true! Nimzowitsch inadvertently allows the bishops to escape, but then proceeds to dominate them with his knights on an open board.

1. P—K4, P—K3; 2. P—Q4, P—Q4; 3. P—K5, P—QB4; 4. P—QB3, N—QB3; 5. N—B3, P—B3!?; 6. B—QN5 (naturally preparing to exchange bishops for knights), **6. ... B—Q2; 7. O—O, Q—N3** (7. ... N × KP?; 8. N × N, B × B; 9. Q—R5 +, K—K2; 10. Q—B7 +, K—Q3; 11. P × P +, K × N; 12. R—K1 +, K—B4; 13. Q—R5 +, P—N4; 14. P—N4. Mate—Nimzowitsch); **8. B × N, P × B; 9. P × KBP, N × P?** (9. ... P × BP!); **10. N—K5, B—Q3; 11. P × P, B × P; 12. B—N5, Q—Q1; 13. B × N!** (and the other one), **13. ... Q × B; 14. Q—R5 +.** (A common device in Nimzowitsch's games. The idea is to weaken Black's K side.) **14. ... P—N3; 15. Q—K2, R—Q1; 16. N—Q2, O—O; 17. QR—K1, KR—K1; 18. K—R1, B—Q3; 19. P—KB4, P—B4; 20. P—B4** (20. Q—R6!), **20. ... B—KB1; 21. P × P, B—B1** (Black gives up a pawn to smash the blockade and bring his prelates to life); **22. N—K4, Q—N2; 23. P × P** (23. P—Q6!?), **23. ... B × P; 24. Q—R6, K—R1; 25. R—Q1, B—N1; 26. P—QN3, R—Q5; 27. R × R, P × R; 28. Q—R5, R—B1; 29. R—Q1, R—B7; 30. P—KR3, Q—N2; 31. R × P, B—B4** (with serious threats, e.g. 32. R—R4, B—N3; 33. Q—K1, B—Q4; or 33. Q—R6, Q × Q; 34. R × Q and, once again, ... B—Q4 and Black penetrates to White's sensitive KN2 square); **32. Q—Q8!.** (The taming of the bishops. If now 32. ... B × R; 33. Q × B(d4), Q—N2!; 34. N—Q6 and there is no answer to 35. N—K8 accompanied by a lethal discovered check. Can a 'system' really teach you to spot variations like this one?) **32. ... B—K2; 33. Q—Q7** (what follows now is a rout), **33. ... Q—R3; 34. R—Q3, B—B1; 35. N—B7 +, B × N; 36. Q × B, R—B1; 37. R—Q7. 1–0.**

(ii) ALAPIN–NIMZOWITSCH, Carlsbad, 1911. *Proto-Modern Defence*

While still touching on the theme of the pawn centre versus piece pressure this game is also noteworthy for Vidmar's note to move 5 which reveals that by no means everyone in pre-Great War chess society regarded Nimzowitsch as a pernicious heretic.

1. P—K4, P—QB3; 2. P—QB4, P—Q3; 3. P—Q4, N—B3;
4. N—QB3, QN—Q2; 5. P—B4. (Vidmar: 'It is not good to move
all the pawns in the opening. For, in this case, the pawns no longer
provide the protective skeleton of the position but become a thin,
sensitive membrane, behind which are clustered the exposed king
and the pieces. The chain is shattered only too easily and then the
pieces have their work cut out to protect the pawns which are far
advanced and therefore weak. But White, like so many players who
only believe in the Lopez and the QP, imagines that such an irregular
opening necessarily demands acts of violence. He meets with a fine
reception from his opponent, for if anyone knows how to handle the
opening well, it is Nimzowitsch.') 5. ... P—K4; 6. N—B3, P × P;
7. Q × P, N—B4; 8. B—Q3, Q—N3; 9. B—B2, B—K2; 10. 0—0,
0—0; 11. K—R1, R—Q1; 12. R—N1, B—K3; 13. P—B5, B—QB1;
14. B—N5, N(4)—Q2; 15. Q—Q2, P—QR3; 16. P—QN3, Q—B2;
17. QR—Q1, P—QN4; 18. KR—K1, N—K4; 19. P × P, RP × P;
20. B—N1, B—N2; 21. Q—B1, Q—N3; 22. P—KR3, N × N! (the
prelude to a neat combination which leaves Black with a positionally
overwhelming game); 23. P × N, Q—B7; 24. Q—K3, Q—N6;
25. P—B4, Q × Q; 26. R × Q, P—R3; 27. B—R4, P—N5;
28. N—R4, N × P!; 29, R × N, B × B; 30. R × NP, R—R2;
31. B—K4, B—K2; 32. B—B3, P—Q4; 33. R/4—Q4, R—Q3;
34. K—R2, R—B3; 35. B—N4, B—Q3; 36. R—QB1?, P—R4!;
37. K—N3 (37. B × P, R × P; 38. B—N4, R × P and wins a piece),
37. ... P × B; 38. P × P, P—N4; 39. P × P e.p., P × P; 40. P—N5,
R—B4; 41. K—B3, R—R1; 42. N—B5, B × N; 43. R × B, R × RP.
0–1. In his own notes to this game Nimzowitsch referred to White's
centre as a 'tiger, ready to spring', and his own handling of the
opening as the 'taming' of said tiger.

NIMZOWITSCH–DUS-CHOTIMIRSKI, Carlsbad, 1911. *Sicilian Defence*

1. P—K4	P—QB4	4. N × P	N—B3
2. N—KB3	N—QB3	5. N—QB3	P—Q3
3. P—Q4	P × P	6. B—QB4	

Only rarely do we come across such a directly aggressive
opening variation employed by Nimzowitsch. Rapid development
was not one of the maestro's favourite themes in his written
works.

| 6. ... | B—Q2 | 7. B—KN5 |

In the tournament book Vidmar now suggests 7. ... Q—R4,
while modern theory prefers 7. ... P—K3; 8. N/4—N5, Q—N1
with a sharp struggle. Instead of either of these rational continuations there comes a great surprise.

7. ...   N × P?

This combination is quite incredible. How can it possibly succeed when White's development is so far superior to his own? Dus-Chotimirski, by the way, was notorious for his surprise moves and surprise results. At St. Petersburg, 1909, his final overall placing was mediocre but *en route* he defeated the joint first prize winners—Lasker and Rubinstein.

8. N × N   Q—R4 +   9. P—B3!

Could it be that Black had overlooked this, expecting only 9. B—Q2, Q—K4 regaining the piece?

9. ...   Q—K4   10. Q—K2

Also possible was the miserly 10. B—Q3 (threatening P—KB4!), N × N; 11. P × N, Q × QP when Black has only two pawns for his piece and must lose. However, Nimzowitsch's chess soul has divined a combination which he cannot resist, although it involves the return of all his plunder, and more. Dus-Chotimirski's opening play must have provoked him. We should be grateful for Nimzowitsch's grandiose decision on move 10 for 10. B—Q3 (intending to exploit the extra material) would have deprived us of the delightful combination which now follows.

10. ...   P—Q4   12. O—O—O
11. B × QP   Q × B(d5)

Intending the piquant variation: 13. N—N5, Q—K4; 14. N(4)—Q6 +, P × N; 15. N—B7. Mate.

12. ...   Q × P

Now Black is even material ahead, but it is White's turn to speak.

13. N—Q6 +   K—Q1   15. N—N7 +   K—B1
14. N × N +   P × N   16. R × B!   K × R

Alternatively Black can remove White's king rook from the board with 16. ... Q—R8 + ; 17. K—B2, Q × R when 18. N—B5 is one way to force the win. Black's king has no way of escaping from the vice-like grip of the White pieces, a grip which can be augmented, if necessary, by 19. B—B4.

17. R—Q1 +   K—B1   18. Q—K4‡

This centralisation of White's most powerful piece obliges Black to surrender his Q, lest worse befall.

18. ...   Q—R8 +

If 18. ... K × N; 19. R—Q7 +, K—N3; 20. B—K3 +, P—B 21. B × P + ! and White wins as he pleases.

19. K—B2   Q×R+
20. K×Q   K×N
21. Q—N4+

Nominally Black still enjoys a material advantage, but none of his pieces can do anything constructive. White's next few manœuvres are very fine and soon induce complete paralysis of the Black position.

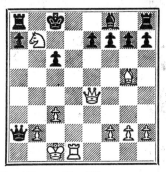

21. ...	K—B1	25. Q—R2+	K—N2
22. Q—QB4	K—N2	26. B—K3	P—B4
23. Q—N3+	K—R3	27. Q—N3+	K—B2
24. Q×P	R—B1	28. Q—K6	K—Q1

A pathetic move, but if Black seeks to develop with ... P—N3 a check on K5 costs him a rook.

29. B—B4   P—KR4

If now 29. ... P—N3; 30. Q—K5, R—KN1; 31. Q—Q5+

30. P—B4

Preparing a 'zugzwang' position which, in a minor key, fore shadows his famous victory versus Sämisch twelve years later (cf. page 81).

| 30. ... | P—R5 | 32. K—B2 | Resigns |
| 31. B—Q2 | K—B2 | | |

For if 32. ... R—R4; 33. B—B4+, K—Q1; 34. Q—B7, R—KR1; 35. Q—B5 and once Black has exhausted the irrelevant moves of his RP's he will have to shed more material—moves of the QR to QR1 or QB3 allow Q—Q5+ as does ... R—KN1. Also the king is tied to the defence of the QR and the KR to the defence of the B. Equally disastrous (i.e. fatally loosening) would be the surrender of the KP or KNP with ... P—K3 or ... P—KN3. An amusing lightweight forming a humorous contrast to Nimzowitsch's normally more sober achievements.

They have sown the wind, and they shall reap the whirlwind.
Hosea 8.7

RUBINSTEIN–NIMZOWITSCH, Last round, San Sebastian, 1912.
Old Indian Defence

At the commencement of the final round of this great tournament Nimzowitsch led the field with 12 points ahead of Rubinstein with 11½, but these two still had to meet. In view of this circumstance one might have expected a restrained approach from Nimzowitsch, attempting to keep the draw in hand—in fact one could be excused for expecting anything but what actually occurred. Nimzowitsch went straight for the throat of his mighty adversary; obviously he was not content to coast home, as a greater realist would have done. And Rubinstein was only too happy to add to the conflagration. Eventually it was Nimzowitsch who succumbed to the spirits which he personally had conjured, but the tension scarred both players, as can be seen from moves 25 and 26.

1. P—Q4 N—KB3

Already something of a sensation indicating a particularly aggressive attitude. Of course, this move is normal now but at San Sebastian it was only employed twice in the twenty games commencing 1. P—Q4.

2. P—QB4	**P—Q3***	**4. N—B3**	**P—K4**
3. N—KB3	**QN—Q2**	**5. P—K4**	**B—K2**

The text is rather passive since Black's position has little potential for aggressive (and sound) expansion. Modern theory prefers . . . P—KN3 with transposition to a King's Indian Defence.

6. B—K2	**0—0**	**9. P—QN3**	**P—B3**
7. 0—0	**R—K1**	**10. B—N2**	**N—R4?!**
8. Q—B2	**B—B1**		

In later years Nimzowitsch was to react in a highly scathing manner against this pseudo-aggressive decentralisation.** In the heat of battle, however, it must have terrified the opponent. The objectively best course, it should be added, is to exchange on d4 and then follow up with . . . N—B4 and . . . P—QR4, restraining White's KP, as in the Hanham version of Philidor's defence favoured by Nimzowitsch. Given accurate play by White the bluff attack introduced by the text should probably lose.

* In his notes to this decisive encounter from the *Berliner Lokalanzeiger* Dr. Tarrasch wrote: 'Nimzowitsch has a pronounced liking for ugly opening moves; it is fortunate that he is thoroughly refuted here by Rubinstein, whose play is always in good taste, for it would have been an absolute scandal if such unaesthetic play had been crowned with the first prize!'

Of course, Nimzowitsch was by no means overjoyed to see these remarks in print and promptly challenged Tarrasch to a theoretical duel (i.e. match) for stakes with the opening from his game versus Rubinstein. Needless to say, the good doctor tacitly declined Nimzowitsch's offer.

Nimzowitsch had his revenge many years later when he wrote in his *Chess Praxis*: 'Our feeling for what is aesthetic in chess must be anchored in thought, that is the point. He who is dazzled by outward appearances can easily come to regard as "ugly" moves which are by no means so. After all, the beauty of chess lies in the thought that goes into it.'

** Cf. *My System*, Part II, Chapter 1, section vi.

11. P—N3   N—N1
A truly remarkable method of bringing the QB into play.

12. QR—Q1   Q—B3   13. N—N1
Si duo faciunt idem. . . . The point of this retreat is to increase the pressure against Black's KP.

13. ...   B—R6   14. KR—K1   N—B5
Naturally the N is immune in view of ... Q—N3 +.

15. P × P
Inaugurating a counter-combination.

15. ...   P × P   17. B—KB1?!
16. N × P   R × N
Not best; White can decide matters here by simple chess: 17. B × R, N × B + ; 18. Q × N, Q × B; 19. R—Q8 and Black is paralysed.

17. ...   N—Q2   18. Q—Q2
The climax of Rubinstein's grand conception. Black is threatened with the loss of his entire army, but Nimzowitsch discovers some concealed resources.

18. ...   B ʌ B   20. K—N2   N—N4
19. R × B   N—R6 +   21. P—B4   Q—N3!
Not ... N × P; 22. Q × N and wins.

22. P × N
22. P × R ?, Q × P + would be ruinous for White.

22. ...   R × KP
The best chance. There are some neat alternative lines of play given by Nimzowitsch: (i) 22. ... R—K2; 23. B—R3, P—QB4; 24. N—B3 with great positional advantage to White; (ii) as above up to 23. ... Q × P + ; 24. K—N1, P—QB4; 25. R(B1)—K1; (iii) 22. ... Q × P + ; 23. K—R3, R—K2; 24. R(Q1)—K1 winning a piece.

23. Q × N   R—K7 +
24. R—B2   Q—K5 +
25. K—N1   B—B4?‡
Nimzowitsch overlooks that White can deliver checkmate by means of 26. Q × BP +, K—R1; 27. Q × NP. Mate. Apparently both players were involved in a hectic time scramble and the excitement was becoming too much for them. With this grotesque blunder Nimzowitsch fails to seize an

excellent drawing chance suggested by Mieses in the tournament book, to wit: 25. ... R × R; 26. K × R, Q—B7 + ; 27. Q—Q2, B—B4 + ; 28. K—N2, Q—K5 + ; 29. K—R3, Q—B4 +. Now 30. K—R4 would be perilous for White in view of the exposed position of his king (e.g. 30. ... P—KR3 and the molestation of the white monarch continues) while I do not see how the alternatives avoid perpetual check. Thus Nimzowitsch could have secured his very first tournament victory in a Grandmaster event. As it was he had to wait another ten years or so before he gained first prize in a tournament of similar calibre to San Sebastian. Of course, this was due in no small measure to the intervention of the Great War, which was inimical to many activities, including the organisation of international chess tournaments.

26. B—Q4?
Rubinstein misses it too! This wins indeed, but there was a quicker method available. The rest is in the nature of an anti-climax.

26. ...   B × B
27. Q × B   R—K8 +
And the game concluded: **28. R—B1, R × R + ; 29. K × R, Q—R8 + ; 30. K—B2, Q × P + ; 31. K—B3, P—B3; 32. Q—Q2, Q—R6; 33. Q—Q7, P—KB4; 34. N—B3, Q—R4 + ; 35. K—N2, Q × P; 36. Q—K6 +, K—R1; 37. N—K2, Q—KR4; 38. R—Q7, R—K1; 39. N—B4, R × Q; 40. N × Q.**

The tournament book stops here with the comment that Black resigned after a few more unimportant moves—so 1–0 and first prize to Rubinstein. Another triumph for chess in its struggle with the human mind.

In the tournament book of San Sebastian Mieses (who was a great admirer of Dr. Tarrasch) summed up the various achievements of the players and he had this to say of Nimzowitsch: 'A. Nimzowitsch's main strength does not lie in the realm of strategy but in original, often bizarre, yet always profoundly conceived manœuvres, which are difficult to refute in practical play. He is a sly tactician whose combinations sometimes contain a mischievous element. It is questionable, though, whether he will ever succeed in ridding himself of a certain nervousness which, especially in San Sebastian, made itself apparent again and again in most disturbing fashion, and from which he had to suffer less himself than did his opponents, the tournament controller and the spectators.'

LEVENFISH–NIMZOWITSCH, Vilna, 1912. *Caro Kann*
1. P—K4 P—QB3   2. P—QB4
A very old move which has become popular of late. White's idea is

to discourage 2. ... P—Q4. Here is what could happen if Black were stubbornly to proceed with his opening strategy: 2. ... P—Q4; 3. BP × P, P × P; 4. P × P, N—KB3; 5. N—QB3, N × P; 6. B—B4, N—N3; 7. B—N3, N—B3; 8. N—B3, P—N3; 9. P—QR4, P—QR4; 10. P—Q4, B—N2; 11. B—K3, N—N5; 12. P—Q5 and Black has lost ground in the centre (Markland–Bhend, Skopje, 1972). Black would have done better to play 7. ..., P—N3 with good chances of maintaining himself.

2. ... P—K3
Intending at all costs to establish a central foothold.

3 N—KB3
One testimony to the venerable antiquity of 2. P—QB4 is the twentieth game of the Staunton–St. Amant Match, Paris, 1843, which continued: 3. P—Q4, P—Q4; 4. BP × P, KP × P; 5. P × P (5. P—K5, B—B4; 6. N—K2 is recommended by Petrosian!), 5. ... P × P; 6. N—QB3, N—KB3; 7. N—B3, B—K2; 8. B—Q3, 0—0; 9. 0—0, B—KN5.

3. ...	P—Q4	5. P × P	P × P
4. KP × P	KP × P	6. B—N5 +	

The modern treatment of this position, which guarantees White a slight initiative, is: 6. N—B3, N—KB3; 7. B—N5 +, N—B3; 8. 0—0, B—K2; 9. N—K5, B—Q2; 10. P—Q4, 0—0; 11. B—N5 as in game I of the Hübner–Petrosian Candidates' Match, Seville, 1971. The early development of White's QN to c3 (putting immediate pressure on Black's QP) would prevent the elastic development of his K side forces chosen here by Nimzowitsch (... B—Q3 and ... KN—K2).

6. ...	N—B3	7. 0—0?!

It was still not too late for 7. N—B3, which would probably have transposed into the previous note.

7. ... B—Q3!
Very good. Now that this move is possible Black can develop his KN on K2 and repulse any pinning attempt by White's QB (B—KN5) with ... P—KB3.

8. P—Q4
The symmetrical pawn-structure that has arisen does not mean that Nimzowitsch was playing for a draw. We have only to examine Nimzowitsch's numerous victories as Black in the Exchange Variations of the French Defence to appreciate this fact. There is even a chapter in *Chess Praxis* on the 'asymmetrical handling of symmetrical variations'.

8. ...   **KN—K2**   **10. QB—R4   0—0**
9. B—N5   P—B3   **11. QN—Q2**

A move with a slightly defensive orientation which proves that something must have already gone wrong for White. After the natural 11. N—B3 White feared ... B—KN5 with pressure against d4, while the preventive measure 11. P—KR3 would allow ... N—B4!∓ and White's QB runs out of squares.

11. ...   **B—KN5**   **12. B × N?!**

A very strange move which is based on the pursuit of a tactical chimaera. After 12. ... P × B; 13. R—B1 White has play against Black's backward QBP, whilst the recapture ...

12. ...   **N × B**
allows ...

13. Q—N3
... forking two pawns.

13. ...   **B—N5**
An adequate defence, for the moment.

14. N—K5
Here it is! The point of White's manœuvre commencing 12. B × N. Black is threatened on all sides and the plausible 14. ... B × N; 15. N × B, P—KN4; 16. B—N3, P—B4 fails to 17. Q × NP, Q—B1 (17. ... N—R4?; 18. N—R6 +, K—R1; 19. B—K5 +); 18. B— K5!! (planning N—R6 mate), 18. ... N × B; 19. Q × Q, and N × N, with an extra pawn. Having seen through this pretty trap Nimzowitsch resolves to sacrifice his QNP in the interests of disorganising the hostile base.

14. ...   **N × N**   **16. Q × P**
15. Q × B   N—Q6!

Events have now passed out of White's control. He can no longer act, only react.

16. ...   **B—K7**   **17. KR—N1**

'Saving the exchange, but at the cost of a very serious dislocation of his position' (Tartakower).

17. ...   **R—B1**

'Does not this centralisation, carried through right into the heart of the hostile position, strike one as humorous?' (Nimzowitsch).

18. N—B1   P—N4

With White's army driven literally into one cramped corner of the board and with Black pieces dominating the centre Nimzowitsch now

proceeds to launch a vigorous attack against White's king, which has
hitherto avoided injury.

19. B—N3   P—B4
20. B—K5   R—KB2
21. Q—R6   P—B5‡
Announcing the horrible threat of
... P—B6 and if P—KN3 ...
N × B − +. If White halts the advance
of Black's KBP with 22. P—B3 then
... R—B7 is decisive. 22. P—B3,
R—B7 (threatening ... N × B); 23.
Q—R3, N × B; 24. P × N, Q—N3 + ;
25. K—R1, Q—B7 − +.

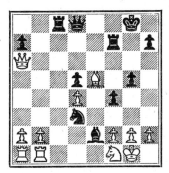

In a way it is a great shame that
Levenfish avoided this. The situation after 22. P—B3, R—B7 is
picturesque.

22. R—K1
Sacrificing the exchange fails to bring relief, but the attempt is
quite comprehensible.

22. ...   N × R   23. Q × R
He hopes for 23. ... N—B7; 24. R—Q1 with a pawn for the
exchange and counterplay to come in the shape of Q—R5, but now
Nimzowitsch discovers a blow quite in keeping with his ruthless and
powerful conduct of the game up to this point.

23. ...   N × P!
An unpleasant surprise for White. Black maintains his extra
material and, in addition, wrenches the attack back into his own
grasp.

24. N—Q2   N—R5   26. K—R1   P—N5
25. N—B3   N—N3
A couple of hammer strokes finish White off.

27. N—Q2   Q—Q2   29. P—KR3   P—N6
28. R—KN1   R—B7
Which caused White to abdicate on the spot. Levenfish had had
enough of the battering. I find this one of Nimzowitsch's most
impressive games.

ALEKHINE–NIMZOWITSCH, St. Petersburg, 1914.* *French Defence*
Second game of the play-off for the Championship of all the Russias.

* Very early in 1914 and therefore possibly 1913 according to the old Julian
calendar. Alekhine gives it as January, 1914, Nimzowitsch as 1913.

E

1. P—K4	**P—K3**	**3. N—QB3**	**N—KB3**
2. P—Q4	**P—Q4**	**4. P × P**	

This rather tame course was probably dictated by the score in the match so far, which was 1–0 to Alekhine. A draw in the second game would have clinched the tie-break in Alekhine's favour.

4. ... N × P

Provocative, but in view of the score Nimzowitsch had to avoid clear and simple positions. In a way it is strange that Alekhine, given his intention to employ an exchange variation at all, did not resort to P × P on move 3.

5. N—B3	**P—QN3**
6. B—N5 +	**P—B3**
7. B—Q3	**B—K2**
8. 0—0	**N—Q2**
9. N × N	**BP × N**
10. Q—K2	**0—0**
11. B—KB4	**B—N2**
12. P—B3	**B—KB3**
13. KR—K1	**Q—K2‡**

White has built up an excellent position and he could now have increased his advantage by occupying the outpost square e5, for example: 14. N—K5, N × N; 15. B × N, B × B; 16. Q × B and White will follow up with P—KB4. The move he actually chooses seems illogical, in that White effects the exchange of his powerful KB for Black's rather feeble QB.

14. B—QR6?!	**B × B**	**16. Q—N5**	**Q—N2**
15. Q × B	**N—N1**	**17. R—K3**	**N—B3**

White still retains a plus on the K side in view of his possibility of concentrating superior force in that sector. In order to create counterplay one would have expected Nimzowitsch to set in motion a minority attack by means of ... P—QN4 ... P—QR4, etc., but instead he undertakes nothing in any positive sense. He seems content to adopt a purely defensive attitude and to lure his opponent into ostensibly powerful but potentially weakening aggressive gestures. Since Alekhine only needed a draw from this game Nimzowitsch's policy of provocation represented a subtle psychological ploy. Had Nimzowitsch, on the other hand, made an immediate attempt to exploit what positive resources his position did contain, then Alekhine would have been forewarned and would have been able to adopt a neutralising policy before it became too late. As it was, Alekhine thought he had all the time in the world at his disposal and, when the counter-attack did finally set in, his defensive reserves were seriously depleted.

At the time, of course, Nimzowitsch had no idea that he was 'foredoomed' to win. His provocation strategy could equally have ended in total disaster and a crushing 2–0 victory for his rival in the play-off match!

18. Q—Q3	P—N3		21. QR—K1	Q—B2
19. B—R6	B—N2		22. P—KR4	
20. B × B	K × B			

The Grande Armée sets off for Moscow (Nimzowitsch's king). Alekhine has tired of the simplification involved in his 4th and 14th moves.

22. ...	QR—K1		26. P—KN3	Q—B3
23. P—R5	Q—B5		27. Q—K3	R—Q1
24. N—K5	N × N		28. K—N2	R/2—Q2
25. R × N	R—K2		29. R—KR1	K—B1

The beginning of a strategic king march. Nimzowitsch realises that his K side will soon be unfit for royal habitation and his monarch flees to political asylum on the opposite wing. One can only speculate concerning the extent to which Alekhine felt himself provoked by the sight of his opponent's king wandering around in the centre of the board.

30. R—R4	K—K1		32. R—KB4
31. Q—R6	K—K2		

Naturally White cannot capture the KRP since he would shed his Q to ... R—KR1. Nevertheless White's position still makes an imposing impression on the unbiased observer.

32. ...   Q—R1

By no means the first, or the last, time that Nimzowitsch was to play such a move. The point is to prevent the invasion of his position by the White Q.

33. R—K1   R—QB1
34. R—KR1

Threatening P × P and thus inducing Black's outlandish response.

34. ...	Q—N1!
35. Q—N5 +	K—Q3‡

Who would believe that Alekhine could lose such a position? It looks as if Black is fighting for his very survival rather than hoping for victory.

36. Q—K5+ K—B3   37. P—R4?

Just the sort of vain attacking gesture for which Nimzowitsch must have been praying. White later comes to regret this rash advance which does not increase his attacking prospects one whit.

37. ... K—N2

The completion of a remarkable journey, and under enemy fire, from g8 to b7.

38. R—R1	**Q—R1**		**41. Q—K2**	**P—QR3**
39. R—B6	**Q—Q1**		**42. Q—K3**	**Q—N2**
40. R—B3	**Q—R1**		**43. P—R6?!**	

White wants to exploit the diagonal outpost at g7 by occupying it with his Q but the idea is double-edged in the extreme and it might have been preferable to open the KR file. After the phase of provocation from Nimzowitsch there now follows some prophylaxis (to draw the sting from Q—N7) before he embarks on the counterattack. Black already possesses the initiative (believe it or not) as a result of White's indiscretions with both his rook pawns.

43. ...	**Q—B1**		**45. R—B6**	**Q—B1**
44. Q—K5	**Q—R1**		**46. R—R1**	

Preparing for Q—N7 and if Black exchanges queens White's R will already exert unpleasant pressure against Black's KRP.

46. ... Q—Q1   47. R—B4 R—B5!

The first sign of genuine activity from Black that we have so far witnessed in this game. Quite unexpectedly White is thrown on to the defensive, for if 48. Q—N7, P—B4!; 49. Q—K5, R × RP; 50. Q × KP, R—K2; 51. Q—B6, Q—Q2 and Black controls all the open files.

48. R—R1

The beginning of the retreat from Moscow.

48. ... R—B3   49. R—B6

If now Q—N7 Black has ... P—B4; 50. Q—K5, Q—N4; 51. R—R1, R—K2 followed, once again, by ... R—B5.

49. ... Q—QN1

In a pure R + P ending White would experience great difficulty in defending his Q side against a much belated minority attack.

50. Q—K3 R—K2

Creating the threat of ... P—K4 at some later date.

51. Q—B3 Q—K1   52. P—KN4?

This further weakening advance must be incorrect. Is it possible that Alekhine had completely misjudged the position and was suffering from the delusion that he was still forcing matters?

52. ... Q—Q2

Masterly inactivity from Nimzowitsch. Perhaps Alekhine will wreck his own position entirely and thus obviate the necessity for Black to intervene in the proceedings at all.

53. R—K1 R—B2   54. P—N3

Also unpalatable is 54. R—QR1, R—B5; 55. Q—Q1. After the move of the text White's pawn formation begins to look like a sponge.

54. ... K—R2   55. P—N5

This only makes things worse. On g5 the pawn is even more exposed to attack than it was on g4.

55. ... Q—Q3!

Planning the decisive infiltration which will pin down White's forces to defence of the porous Q wing.

56. Q—Q3 Q—R6   59. Q—Q3 Q R6
57. Q—B2 Q—N5   60. R—QN1
58. R—QB1 Q—Q3

In answer to Q—B2 at this point Nimzowitsch would have played ... R—B3 followed by ... R/2—B2.

60. ... Q—R7   61. R—B3 P—K4!

Announcing a glorious counter-attack which swiftly gathers momentum and sweeps White's shattered position from the board. As a point of accuracy Black is not lured into a premature conversion of his positional plus into material spoils by means of ... R × P? when White would obtain some play with 62. Q × R, Q × R; 63. Q—B8.

62. R—K3

62. P × P is impossible in view of the weakness of the KNP, e.g. ... R × KP; 63. R—N3, R—KB4; 64. Q—B1, P—Q5; 65. P × P, R—B7 − +. The rapid convergence in this line of all Black's major pieces at the f2 point is quite startling.

62. ... P—K5

A decisive gain of terrain. As so often when a counter-attack does materialise after a prolonged period of defence the erstwhile aggressors seem totally enervated and unable to co-ordinate any sort of resistance.

63. Q—Q1

The retreat continues,

63. ... P—B4‡

Threatening to smother White with ... P—B5, so the capture *en passant* is forced when Black can utilise the KB file for his own dark designs.

64.	P × P e.p.	R—B2
65.	R—R1	Q—N7
66.	R—N1	Q—R6
67.	P—QB4	R × KBP
68.	P × P	R/2—B2
69.	R—K2	Q—Q3
70.	Q—B2	Q × P
71.	K—B1	P—K6

The Beresina, and on this occasion there are no survivors.

| 72. | R × P | Q—R8 + | | 74. | K—Q3 | Q—Q4 |
| 73. | K—K2 | R × P + | | 75. | Q—B8 | R—Q2 |

White resigns.

(The carnage is dreadful: 76. R—K4, R—B6 + ; 77. K—Q2, Q—N4 + ; 78. K—B2, Q—N7 +.)

This protracted war of attrition against a future world champion is one of Nimzowitsch's most typical and most imposing achievements.

Appendix to Alekhine–Nimzowitsch: The strategic King March in the middlegame

The preceding game provides an excellent illustration of a theme that appears frequently in Nimzowitsch's play: the K march. That is not to say that Nimzowitsch exercised a monopoly over this strategic device, but I would claim that it characterises Nimzowitsch's games more than those of other masters of his day, precisely because the qualities we associate with such marches are prophylaxis, provocation and psychological warfare of a rather indirect and tortuous variety.

Let us examine the motives for the king march in the Alekhine game: (i) Mind-blowing provocation. It can be most disconcerting to see your opponent's king (his most vulnerable piece) wandering at will across large sections of the board when you are in no position to impede its progress or otherwise molest it. (ii) As a pre-emptive defence mechanism: the king vacates a threatened wing and seeks more hospitable climes. (iii) As a portent of aggressive action on the vacated wing itself. In this game Nimzowitsch envisaged an eventual advance of his K side pawns and the presence of his own king would obviously have handicapped the advance.

Nimzowitsch once wrote: 'Ich liebe die Königspromenaden', which meant that he liked to take his kings for walks. There follow some examples of this liking from Nimzowitsch's career. In each of them the motives are more specific than in the all-embracing Alekhine example given above.

(a) E. COHN–NIMZOWITSCH, Carlsbad, 1911.
Position after 68. ... K/R3—N2

The game continued: **69. R—B2, K—B2; 70. K—R2, K—K2; 71. R—K2, Q—B8; 72. Q—B2, K—Q2; 73. R—K1, Q—B3; 74. K—N2, R—N5; 75. R—KB1, Q—B2; 76. Q—B3, K—B1; 77. Q—B2, K—N1; 78. K—R3, K—R2; 79. R—KN1, Q—Q2; 80. K—R2, Q—Q3; 81. K—R3, Q—QB3; 82. R—K1, Q—K3; 83. K—R2, Q—K5; 84. K—R3, Q—K3; 85. K—R2, Q—K2; 86. K—R3, Q—K5; 87. R—KN1, Q—K3; 88. K—R2, R—K5; 89. R—QB1.** White

cracks at last. Nimzowitsch's strange play appears to have disturbed his opponent's psychological balance and Cohn collapses abruptly. **89. ... R×KP; 90. Q—B4, R—K7+** and Black won without further difficulty. Nimzowitsch: 'It may be that the Logos of the win does not stand out with the desirable clarity but one thing is certain: the difficulties with which the defender had to contend were such that that the question of conceding a draw (advocated by the tournament book) simply could not arise.'

Dr. Euwe also had something to say about this game in his monumental work on the middlegame: 'Nimzowitsch was the only chess master who ever carried out a systematic investigation into the subject of manœuvring. The ideas of Nimzowitsch are so fundamental that he must be considered the greatest pioneer of all in this domain—but ... can the methods he employs here really be classified as manœuvring or is he merely marking time?'

Nimzowitsch felt an undeniable attraction for such 'manœuvring' procedures ('lavieren' or 'tacking'* in his original German) whereas Capablanca, a more lucid player all round than Nimzowitsch, manœuvred only when absolutely necessary, according to Dr. Euwe.

* Cf. also page 277.

(b) CARL NILSSON–NIMZOWITSCH, Eskilstuna, 1921 (as part of a simultaneous display given by Nimzowitsch over thirty-four boards)

Position after 19. K/N1—R1:

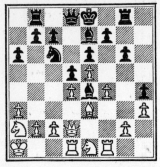

19. ... K—Q2!; 20. R—KN1, K—B1; 21. N—B1, P—N3; 22. P—QN4, P—R4; 23. P—B3, P × P; 24. BP × P, R—KR1; 25. K—N2, K—N2; 26. N—R2, P—KN4. The K stroll has energised Black's whole position. Not only does he possess strong threats against White's K (Black's 25th move threatened ... R × P!), but he is also in a position to seize the initiative on the opposite wing. 27. P × P, B × KNP; 28. P—N4, P × P e.p.; 29. R × P, B × B; 30. R × B, Q—R5; 31. Q—B3, N—R2; 32. R—QB1, Q—B7 + ; 33. K—N3, N—N4; 34. Q—B6 +, K—B1; 35. Q × N, Q × R +. White resigns.

(c) NIMZOWITSCH–ASZTALOS, Bled, 1931. *English opening*
A paradigm case of reason (iii).
1. P—QB4, N—KB3; 2. N—QB3, P—B4; 3. P—KN3, N—B3; 4. B—N2, P—K3; 5. N—R3, B—K2; 6. P—Q3, P—Q3; 7. 0—0, 0—0; 8. N—B4, P—QR3; 9. P—N3, Q—B2; 10. P—K3, R—N1; 11. P—QR4, P—QN3; 12. P—Q4, N—QN5; 13. B—QR3, B—N2; 14. P—Q5, P—K4; 15. N—Q3. Removing Black's only aggressively posted piece. The dominating factor in the game from now on is White's massive control of space in a situation where Black has precious few possibilities of organising any sort of disruptive thrust. (We all know that a cramped position of itself is not necessarily an evil.) 15. ... N × N; 16. Q × N, QR—K1; 17. QR—K1, N—Q2; 18. P—K4, B—KB3; 19. B—B1, R—K2; 20. B—Q2, R/1—K1; 21. R—R1. To induce the petrification of the Q side whereafter White can turn his undivided attention to Black's K. 21. ... P—QR4; 22. QR—K1, Q—Q1; 23. P—R4, N—B1; 24. Q—B3, B—R3; 25. B—R3, R—R2; 26. K—N2, B—K2; 27. R—KR1, R/2—R1; 28. N—Q1, R—R2; 29. N—K3, R—R1; 30. R/K1—KN1, R—R2; 31. K—B1. The king sets off. Really this is to be seen as a prophylactic measure against a possible Black counter-attack on the K side after White has opened lines in that sector. 31. ... Q—N1; 32. K—K1, B—Q1; 33. K—Q1, B—K2; 34. K—B2, Q—B2; 35. B—B3, R/1—R1; 36. Q—K2, Q—Q1; 37. P—B4, P—B3;

38. B—K6 + !‡, N × B; 39. P × N, B—N2; 40. Q—Q3, Q—K1; 41. P—B5, B—B3; 42. P—KN4, K—R1; 43. R—N3, R—N1; 44. R/1—KN1, R/2—N2; 45. B—Q2. Minimisation of Black's possibilities. In the case of ... P—QN4 (which is desperate anyway), White would play 46. BP × P, B × P; 47. P × B, R × P; 48. N—B4 and the aggressive R on g3 also serves to defend White's QNP. **45. ... R—**

Q1; 46. N—Q1, R/2—N1; 47. N— B3, R/Q1—B1; 48. Q—K2, R—N2; 49. P—N5, R—Q1; 50. P—N6, B—B1. There is no salvation in the blocking move ... P—R3 since White would sacrifice a piece with 51. B × P, P × B; 52. P— N7 +, K—N1; 53. R—N6 followed by Q—R5 and the barricades fall. **51. P × P, K × P; 52. R—N6.** Black resigns.

I have already drawn attention to the influence exerted over Petrosian by Nimzowitsch's writings (via his trainer Ebralidze) and, since I am also concerned in this volume to analyse the effects of Nimzowitsch's teachings on subsequent generations, it does not seem out of place to quote an example of a strategic K march by Petrosian in a manner that conforms entirely to the Nimzowitschian precedents. The position is given below, Black to move.

DIEZ DEL CORRAL–PETROSIAN, Palma, 1969

22. ... K—B1. Fleeing the menaced wing. **23. Q—N5, K—K1; 24. QR— QB1, K—Q2; 25. P—R5, P × P; 26. R × P, R—KN1; 27. R—R7, K—B1; 28. Q—R4, Q—N3; 29. R—R8, R × R; 30. Q × R +, K—N2; 31. Q— KB8, R—B1; 32. Q—Q6, Q—K1; 33. P—R4, R—Q1; 34. Q—R3, Q— K2; 35. Q—B3, R—QB1; 36. B—Q2, P—KN4!** As so often the corollary to the vacation of a wing is an advance in that very area. The king march is

not only an escape along the lines of a scorched earth policy (the invading army crashes through but then finds that there is nothing worthwhile left to attack), but also the prelude to an increase in energy over the whole board. **37. Q—B2, P—B5!; 38. P × P, P × P; 39. B × P, R—N1 +; 40. B—N3, N × QP; 41. Q—B3, N—K7; 42. Q—B6 +, K—N1; 43. R—K1, N—B5 +; 44. K—B1, N—Q6;**

45. R—N1, Q—KB2; 46. Q—Q6 +, K—N2; 47. K—K2, R—QB1!; 48. P—R5, R—B7 + ; 49. K—B1, N × BP. White now sacrificed his rook futilely on QN6 and resigned on move 55.

Before we leave the subject of the K march I think a distinction should be drawn between the strategic variety, with which we have here been concerned, and the tactical variety which we associate with Steinitz ('The king is a strong piece', etc.) and which tends to occur at an earlier stage of the game. Here is one example which I hope will clear up any confusion:

STEINITZ–PAULSEN (L.), Baden-Baden, 1870

1. P—K4, P—K4; 2. N—QB3, N—QB3; 3. P—B4, P × P; 4. P—Q4?!, Q—R5 + ; 5. K—K2; P—Q3; 6. N—B3, B—N5; 7. B × P, 0—0—0; 8. K—K3 (lending protection to his central pawns!?), 8. ... Q—R4; 9. B—K2, Q—R4; 10. P—QR3, B × N; 11. K × B, Q—R4 + ; 12. K—K3; Steinitz won on move 36.

For a further striking example of a K march in the *middlegame* I would refer the reader to Petrosian–Unzicker, Hamburg, 1960, which can be found in Peter Clarke's *Petrosian's Best Games of Chess*.

GAMES, 1915–1924

The Intervention of Reality & Progress towards Recovery

The Great War, the Russian Revolution and their Aftermath

GOTHENBURG, August 1–22, 1920

	1	2	3	4	5	6	7	8	9	10	11	12	13	14	
1 Reti	–	0	1	1	½	1	1	½	½	½	1	½	1	1	9½
2 Rubinstein	1	–	0	1	0	½	1	1	½	½	1	1	½	1	9
3 Bogoljubow	0	1	–	0	0	1	0	1	1	1	0	1	1	1	8
4 Kostic	0	0	1	–	0	½	½	½	½	½	1	1	1	1	7½
5 Mieses	½	1	1	1	–	½	0	0	0	½	½	1	½	1	7½
6 Tartakower	0	½	0	½	½	–	1	½	1	½	1	½	1	½	7½
7 Tarrasch	0	0	1	½	1	0	–	½	½	1	1	½	1	½	7½
8 Maroczy	½	0	0	½	1	½	½	–	0	½	½	½	1	½	6
9 Marco	½	½	0	½	1	0	½	1	–	½	0	0	½	½	5½
10 Breyer	½	½	0	½	½	½	0	½	½	–	1	½	½	0	5½
11 Spielmann	0	0	1	0	½	0	0	½	1	0	–	½	1	½	5
12 Nimzowitsch	½	0	0	0	0	½	½	½	1	½	½	–	0	½	4½
13 Möller	0	½	0	0	½	0	0	0	½	½	0	1	–	1	4
14 Selesniew	0	0	0	0	0	½	½	½	½	1	½	½	0	–	4

STOCKHOLM, October–November, 1920

	1	2	3	4	5	6	7	8	
1 Bogoljubow	—	1½	10	11	11	11	11	11	12½
2 Nimzowitsch	0½	—	11	11	11	11	11	½1	12
3 Olson	01	00	—	0½	0½	11	11	11	8
4 Spielmann	00	00	1½	—	01	01	10	11	6½
5 Wendel	00	00	1½	10	—	10	1½	11	6
6 Jacobsen	00	00	00	10	01	—	0½	1½	5½
7 Nyholm	00	00	00	01	1½	1½	—	1½	4
8 Svanberg	00	½0	00	00	00	00	0½	—	1½

COPENHAGEN, March 3–14, 1923

	1	2	3	4	5	6	
1 Nimzowitsch	—	11	½1	½1	11	½1	8
2 Sämisch	00	—	½0	1½	1½	1½	6
3 Tartakower	½0	½0	—	1½	11	11	6
4 Spielmann	½0	0½	0½	—	½0	11	5½
5 Jacobsen	00	0½	00	½0	—	1½	3
6 Möller	½0	0½	00	00	0½	—	1½

CARLSBAD, April 28–May 20, 1923

	1	2	3	4	5	6	7	8	9	10	11	12	13	14	15	16	17	18	
1 Alekhine	–	1	1	1	½	½	0	0	½	½	1	1	1	1	½	1	1	0	11½
2 Bogoljubow	0	–	½	½	0	1	1	½	½	1	1	1	0	½	1	1	1	1	11½
3 Maroczy	0	½	–	1	½	½	½	1	½	½	½	½	½	1	1	1	1	1	11½
4 Grünfeld	0	½	0	–	½	1	1	½	½	1	½	½	1	½	½	½	1	1	10½
5 Réti	½	1	½	½	–	½	½	1	1	1	½	1	1	0	½	1	0	0	10½
6 Nimzowitsch	½	0	½	0	½	–	0	1	½	1	1	1	1	1	1	0	0	1	10
7 Treybal	1	0	½	0	½	1	–	0	½	½	½	½	1	½	½	1	1	1	10
8 Yates	1	½	0	½	0	0	1	–	½	½	1	½	0	1	1	½	½	1	9½
9 Teichmann	½	½	½	½	0	½	½	½	–	½	0	½	½	½	½	1	1	1	9
10 Tartakower	½	0	½	0	0	0	½	½	½	–	½	½	½	½	1	1	1	1	8½
11 Tarrasch	0	0	½	½	½	0	½	0	1	½	–	0	1	1	½	1	1	0	8
12 Rubinstein	0	0	½	½	0	0	½	½	½	½	1	–	0	0	1	1	½	1	7½
13 J. Bernstein	0	1	½	0	0	0	0	1	½	½	0	1	–	½	0	1	1	0	7
14 Wolf	0	½	0	½	1	0	½	0	½	½	0	1	½	–	0	½	0	1	6½
15 Sämisch	½	0	0	½	½	0	½	0	½	0	½	0	1	1	–	0	1	0	6
16 Thomas	0	0	0	½	0	1	0	½	0	0	0	0	0	½	1	–	1	1	5½
17 Chajes	0	0	0	0	1	1	0	½	0	0	0	½	0	1	0	0	–	1	5
18 Spielmann	1	0	0	0	1	0	0	0	0	0	1	0	1	0	1	0	0	–	5

COPENHAGEN, Nordic Championship, 1924

	1	2	3	4	5	6	7	8	9	10	11	
1 Nimzowitsch	–	1	1	1	1	1	1	½	1	1	1	9½
2 P. Johner	0	–	½	1	½	1	1	1	1	1	1	8
3 Nilsson	0	½	–	1	1	1	1	0	1	0	1	6½
4 Krause	0	0	0	–	½	0	1	0	1	1	1	4½
5 Kinch	0	½	0	½	–	1	0	½	0	1	1	4½
6 Olson	0	0	0	1	0	–	½	½	1	½	1	4½
7 Lövenborg	0	0	0	0	1	½	–	1	0	1	1	4½
8 Berndtson	½	0	1	1	½	½	0	–	0	½	½	4½
9 Brinckmann	0	0	0	0	1	0	1	1	–	0	1	4
10 Kier	0	0	1	0	0	½	0	½	1	–	½	3½
11 Giersing	0	0	0	0	0	0	0	½	0	½	–	1

The worst result of Nimzowitsch's mature chess career came at Gothenburg, 1920. Not that his games were lacking in combativeness or in brilliant ideas—the trouble stemmed from the deprivations of the war years and Nimzowitsch's subsequent flight from Riga to Scandinavia. At Gothenburg Nimzowitsch simply lacked the power to carry through his profound strategic achievements to the victorious conclusions which they so richly merited. In *Chess Praxis* he wrote: 'At that time I was still suffering from the effects of the psychic oppression of the fearful post-war period which I, as just one of many victims, had recently lived through.'

His games against Breyer and Réti (who took first prize in the tournament) convey the gravity of Nimzowitsch's plight.

RÉTI–NIMZOWITSCH. Gothenburg, 1920. *Q.P. Opening*
1. P—Q4, P—Q4; 2. P—QB4, P—QB3; 3. P—K3, N—B3; 4. N—QB3, Q—N3; 5. B—Q3, B—N5; 6. Q—R4?!, P—K3; 7. P—B5, Q—B2; 8. P—QN4, QN—Q2; 9. P—B4, B—K2; 10. N—B3, B×N!; 11. P×B, N—R4; 12. B—Q2, 0—0; 13. N—K2, P—B4; 14. N—N3, N/4—B3; 15. 0—0—0. (If 15. 0—0, K—R1!; 16. K—R1, R—KN1 preparing ... P—KN4 with good chances for Black. In view of this Réti rejects all thought of caution and plays for a storm against Black's king.) 15. ... P—QN3; 16. Q—B2, P—QR4; 17. QR—N1, RP×P; 18. B×BP, P×B; 19. N×P, R—B2; 20. N—R6+, K—B1; 21. N×R, K×N; 22. P—K4, NP×P; 23. P—K5, P×P!. (The point. This exchange offer breaks the force of White's attack and leaves the initiative firmly in Black's hands. Of course, any retreat of the KN on move 23, allowing 24. Q×RP, would result in speedy defeat for Black.) 24. P×N, N×P; 25. R—N2, Q—Q3; 26. KR—N1, B—B1; 27. P—KR4, R—R6; 28. P—R5, P—N6;

29. Q—N2, P×P‡; 30. Q—N7+, Q—Q2; 31. Q×Q+, N×Q−+; 32. K—N2, N—N3; 33. K—R1, R×P? (33. ... P—B4!−+); 34. K×P, N—B5; 35. B—B1, K—B3; 36. R—Q1, B—R6; 37. B×B, R×B+; 38. K—N1, R—N6+; 39. K—R2, R—R6+; 40. K—N1, N—K6; 41. R—N3, P—B4; 42. R—Q2, R—R3; 43. R—QN2, R—K3? (43. ... P—B5!−+); 44. R—N7, N—B4; 45. R—QR3, P—B5; 46. R—R8, R—

K8+; 47. K—R2, R—K7+; 48. K—N1, P—Q6?? (48. ... N—K2!−+); 49. R—B8+!=, K—K3; 50. R—N6+, K—K2;

51. R × N, R—K8 + ; **52.** K—N2, P—Q7; **53.** R × P, P—Q8 = Q;
54. R—N7 +, K—K1; **55.** R—N8 +, K—K2; **56.** R—N7 +, K—B3;
57. R—N6 +. ½–½.

NIMZOWITSCH–BREYER. Gothenburg, 1920. *Ruy Lopez*
(by transposition)

Once again Nimzowitsch gives up the exchange for a winning
position, but then his concentration and stamina fade, with lamen-
table results.

1. P—K4, P—K4; **2.** N—KB3, N—QB3; **3.** N—B3, N—B3;
4. B—N5, P—Q3; **5.** P—Q4, B—Q2; **6.** B × N, B × B; **7.** Q—
Q3, N—Q2; **8.** P—Q5, N—B4; **9.** Q—B4, B—Q2; **10.** P—QN4,
N—R3 (Black's KN!); **11.** B—K3, B—K2; **12.** 0—0, 0—0; **13.** P—
QR4, K—R1; **14.** N—QN5, Q—N1 (14. ... P—N3!?; 15. N ×
RP, P—KB4; 16. N—QN5, P—B5); **15.** P—B3, P—R3; **16.** N—
Q2, P—N4; **17.** KR—K1, P—KB4; **18.** P × P, B × P; **19.** N—B1.
(Is it too fanciful to discern the germs of the modern light-square
strategy against the King's Indian Defence in Nimzowitsch's
treatment of this position?) **19.** ... B—N3; **20.** N—N3, B—B3;
21. P—B3, B—N2; **22.** R—R2!? (22. R—K2! K—R2; 23. P—R4,
P—B3; 24. P × BP, QNP × P; 25. P—KR5! + - —Nimzowitsch),
22. ... B—B2; **23.** N—K4, P—B3; **24.** N/5 × QP, B × P; **25.** Q—
K2, B × R; **26.** Q × B, Q—B2; **27.** P—N5, P × P; **28.** P × P, N—
N1; **29.** Q—K6, P—R3; **30.** P—R4, RP × P; **31.** P × P, R—R3;
32. R—Q1, Q—B5; **33.** Q × Q, P × Q; **34.** P × P, B—B3; **35.** R—
N1, P—N3; **36.** B × P, N—Q2; **37.** B—K3, B—R5; **38.** N × P (38.
R—N7! + -), **38.** ... N—B3; **39.** N × N, B × N; **40.** N—Q2. ('Also
here White could win by direct attack: 40. R—N7! White
plays—a manifestation of depression!—too few direct attacks.'—
Nimzowitsch in *Chess Praxis.*) **40.** ... R—KN1; **41.** N—K4, B—
R5; **42.** K—R2, R—R7; **43.** B—Q2, B—N6 + = ; **44.** K—R3, B—
B5; **45.** N—B6, R—KB1; **46.** B × B, P × B; **47.** R—N6, R—R8;
48. K—N4, R—KN8; **49.** K × P, R × P; **50.** K—B5, R—KR7;
51. K—N6, R—N7 + ; **52.** N—N4, R—N6; **53.** R—N7, R/6 × P;
54. R—R7 +, K—N1; **55.** R—QB7, K—R1; **56.** P—B4, R—N1 + ;
57. R—N7. ½–½.

One game relieved the general gloom of Nimzowitsch's performance at Gothenburg and that was his brilliancy against Marco
(Black). Ironically the opening was Nimzowitsch's beloved Philidor,
but this time he had changed sides.

1. P—K4, P—K4; **2.** N—KB3, P—Q3; **3.** P—Q4, N—Q2; **4.** B—
QB4, P—QB3; **5.** P—QR4, B—K2; **6.** N—B3, KN—B3; **7.** 0—0,
P—KR3; **8.** P—QN3, Q—B2; **9.** B—N2, N—B1. He had no choice

but to abandon his plan (which consisted of ... P—KN4 and
... N—N3) and play ... 0—0. After the text Nimzowitsch unleashes
a combinative hurricane of unusual violence. **10. P × P, P × P;
11. N × P!!, Q × N; 12. N—Q5.** The point. Black cannot capture on
b2 in view of N—B7. Mate. **12. ... Q—Q3.** (Or 12. ... Q—N1;
13. N × B, K × N; 14. B—R3 +, K—K1; 15. B—Q6 checkmating
Black's queen.) Variations in which Nimzowitsch mates the opposing
Q abound in his games, for example versus Mieses at Kissingen,
1928 (page 138), or in the opening of his game versus Bogoljubow,
San Remo, 1930 (page 242), or versus Mannheimer, Frankfurt,
1930 (page 37). **13. B—R3, P × N.** This gives Black three pieces for
Q + P, but Marco's position is so disorganised that he has no hope of
offering effective resistance. The alternative was worse, though:
13. ... P—B4; 14. P—K5, Q × P; 15. R—K1, N—K5; 16. R × N,
Q × KR; 17. N—B7. Mate (Nimzowitsch). **14. B × Q, P × B;
15. B × B, K × B; 16. P—K5, N/3—Q2; 17. Q—Q6 +, K—Q1;
18. P—B4, P—QR4; 19. P—B5, R—R3; 20. Q—Q5, K—K2;
21. Q × BP, R—QB3; 22. Q Q5, P—R4; 23. Q × P, KR—R3;
24. QR—K1, P—QN3; 25. Q—Q2, K—Q1; 26. Q—Q5, R × P;
27. P—K6, P × P; 28. P × P, N × P; 29. R × N, B—N2; 30. R—
B8 +** and Marco resigned.

SPIELMANN–NIMZOWITSCH. Stockholm, 1920.
KP Nimzowitsch Defence

1. P—K4 N—QB3
Nimzowitsch's own patent defence to 1. P—K4. It has some
points in common with Alekhine's defence (1. P—K4, N—KB3)
but it poses a less immediate challenge to White's centre.

2. P—Q4
2. N—KB3 allows 2. ... P—K4 which is, in a way, a moral
defeat for both players!

2. ... P—Q4!
The pure, Nimzowitschian interpretation of this defence which
normally leads to intricate pawn-chain play. On the rare occasions
when this defence is employed in contemporary chess 2. ... P—K4
tends to be preferred.

3. P—K5
One might have expected the more fluid 3. N—QB3!? from Spielmann (cf. game versus Wendel, page 137).

3. ... B—B4
An even more provocative method of handling this provocative
defence is 3. ... P—B3!?

4. N—K2?!

Better is 4. N—KB3!? The plan chosen by White diverts too many pieces from the protection of his centre (d4) and could have boomeranged seriously had Black played correctly on move 7.

4.	...	P—K3	6. P—KR4	P—KR4
5.	N—N3	B—N3	7. B—K2	B—K2?!

Inviting remarkable complications. Instead of this flank defence to White's pressure against his KRP it was possible to obtain a fine position by means of a central counter-attack, as suggested later by Nimzowitsch: thus 7. ... N—N5!; 8. N—R3, P—QB4; 9. P—QB3, N—QB3 and White's centre is in danger of collapse, e.g. 10. N × P, B × N; 11. B × B, P × P; 12. P × P, B—N5 + ; 13. K—B1, B × N; 14. P × B, P—KN3; 15. B—K2, R × P; 16. R × R, Q × R threatening mate and the QP.

Nimzowitsch's ideas in the opening phase of this game were to reappear in slightly amended form in some games by Soviet Grandmasters forty years further on: for example—Spassky–Bronstein, U.S.S.R. Championship, 1961, opened as follows: **1. P—K4, P—QB3; 2. P—Q4, P—Q4; 3. P—K5, B—B4; 4. P—KR4, P—KR4; 5. N—K2, P—K3; 6. N—N3, B—N3** (Tal-Botvinnik, 14th game, World Championship Match, 1961, varied with: 6. ... P—KN3; 7. N × B, NP × N; 8. P—QB4, P—B4! the reply to 8. B—K2 would have been ... P—QB4!; 9. P—QB3, P × P; 10. P × P, N—QB3; 11. B × P, Q—N3 with a good game for Black); **7. N—Q2, P—QB4; 8. P × P, KB × P; 9. N—N3, Q—N3; 10. N × B, Q × N; 11. P—QB3, N—QB3; 12. B—K3, Q—R4; 13. B—K2, KN—K2; 14. 0—0, N × P; 15. B × KRP, B × B; 16. N × B, 0—0—0** with an eventual draw. Surely there are parallels here in the particular attitude to the centre adopted by Black in answer to White's thrust with the KRP.

8. B × P	B × B	11. R × R	B × R
9. N × B	P—KN3	12. Q—Q3	
10. N—B4	R × P		

A trap of a lower order. If Black should play the heedless 12. ... B—N4? (intending ... B × N, leaving himself with the knight pair against White's N plus bad bishop) then 13. N × KP!, P × N; 14. Q × P + would lead to total ruin for him.

12. ... KN—K2!!

An ambush!? Surely Black must now lose material?

13. P—KN3 N—B4

13. ... B—N4 would lose to the old trap 14. N × KP, so the text is forced. The remarkable move, then, was Black's 12th which

prepared this combination. White could decline Black's 'passive' sacrifice with 14. P—QB3, allowing ... B—N4 at last, but why should he?

Is it obvious that Black obtains anything concrete for his sacrificed piece?

14. P × B   N/4 × QP

So far the compensation amounts to one pawn, but more is to come, since the foundations of White's pawn centre have been destroyed. The threats at the moment (positively crude in comparison with the enchanting variations based on the power of his centralised knight pair which Nimzowitsch soon conjures up) are (i) 15. ... N—N5; 16. Q × N, N × P + and (ii) 15. ... N × KP; 16. Q × N, N—B6 + .

15. N—QR3   Q × P

Rejecting the possibility of entering an endgame where he would possess three pawns for a piece: 15. ... N × KP; 16. Q—R3, N(5)—B6 + ; 17. K—B1, Q × P. In this case it would certainly be Black who would be justified in playing for a win. However, Nimzowitsch had observed a variation of truly shattering beauty and he could not resist the temptation to play for its actualisation on the board.

16. Q—R3   Q—N4?!

It was still possible to steer for an ending which promised every chance of victory (16. ... Q × Q; 17. N × Q, N × KP; 18. B—B4, N/4—B6 + and ... P—K4). With the text (which is actually a trap of very high order operating within the general framework of the ambush inaugurated by his 12th move) Nimzowitsch subordinates his desire for the accumulation of points to his desire for the creation of beauty. 16. ... Q—N4?! is a move stamped clearly with the Romantic spirit in contradistinction to the Realistic 16. ... Q × Q.

17. B—K3?

A plausible move which, however, loses spectacularly. The line conceived by Nimzowitsch ran as follows: 17. Q—R8 +, K—Q2; 18. Q × R (this part of the combination is reminiscent of the Anderssen–Kieseritsky 'Immortal Game'), 18. ... Q—N8 + ; 19. K—Q2, Q × P + ; 20. K—B3, N—N6! and wins. That there exists a dual solution in 20. ... N—B6 (as was pointed out after the game) was experienced by Nimzowitsch as a source of aesthetic regret.

After 20. ... N—N6‡ Nimzowitsch's own notes stop and my reconstruction of his winning process is as follows: (i) 21. RP × N,

Q—Q5. Mate. (ii) 21. BP × N, Q—Q5 + ; 22. K—B2, N—N5 + ; 23. K—N1, Q—K5 + . (iii) 21. N—Q3, Q—Q5 + ; 22. K × N, N—R4. Mate. (iv) 21. N—N5, Q—K8 + ; 22. K—Q3, N—B4. Mate; or 22. B—Q2, Q × B + ; 23. K × N, Q—N5. Mate. (v) 21. K × N, Q—N3 + ; 22. N—N5 (22. K—B3, Q—Q5 + ; 23. K—N3, Q—N5. Mate), Q × N + ; 23. K—B3, Q—B5 + ; 24. K—Q2, Q × N + . (va) 25. K—Q3, Q—K5 + ; 26. K—Q2, N × P; 27. Q × RP, N—B6 + ; 28. K—B3, Q—QB5. Mate; if in this line 27. K—B3, P—Q5 + ; 28. K—N3, Q—Q4 + ; 29. K—R3 (29. K—R4, P—N4 + or 29. P—B4, P × P e.p. + ; 30. K × P, Q—Q6 + ; 31. K—N4, N—B3 + ; 32. K—B5, P—N3. Mate; or 32. K—R4, P—N4. Mate), N—B5 + ; 30. K—N4, P—R4 + ; 31. K—R4, P—N4 + . (vb) 25. K—K1, Q—K5 + ; 26. K—B2, N—Q5; 27. B—R6, Q—B6 + ; 28. K—N1, N—K7 + ; 29. K—R2, Q—B7 + and mate next move. (30. K—R1, N—N6 mate). (vc) 25. K—K2, Q—K5 + ; 26. B—K3, P—Q5 with more than enough for the exchange.

But there is a flaw in this conception, and that is why a Realist would have contented himself with 16. ... Q × Q, preferring to retain the possibility of 16. ... Q—N4 for his annotations. The flaw goes like this: 17. N—Q3!, Q—N8 + ; 18. K—Q2, N × KP?; 19. N × N, Q × P + with inadequate compensation, or 18. ... K—Q2?; 19. N—B5 + , K—K2; 20. Q—R4 + , K—K1; 21. Q—R8 + , K—K2; 22. Q—B6 + and P—QB3. This refutation was given by Nimzowitsch in his notes, but we have no indication as to when he spotted the strength of 17. N—Q3!—before or after he played ... Q—N4?! In my opinion Black should play quietly with 17. ... 0—0—0! when his prospects are still not bad. He is ahead in development with two pawns for a piece and with White somewhat tied up.

The 17th move chosen by White allows a superb display of pyrotechnics to break out which must have thrilled the spectators.

17. ...   Q—N8 +   18. Q—B1

Or 18. K—Q2, Q × R; 19. Q—R8 + , K—Q2; 20. Q × R, Q × NP! winning.

18. ...   N—B6 +   20. K—Q2   N—B6 +
19. K—K2   N/6—Q5 +   21. K—K2   N/3—Q5 +
No draw.

22. K—Q3?

The losing error. It was essential to eliminate one of the knights with 22. B × N. Admittedly the continuation: 22. ... N × B + ; 23. K—Q3, Q—N4!; 24. K × N, Q × N + ; 25. K—Q3, P—QB4 is unpleasant for White, but it was obligatory to continue thus if White wanted to resist.

22. ...	**Q—N4**	**24. R—KB1**	**0—0—0‡**
23. Q—R3	**Q × P**		

Now that Black has completed his development White is helpless. This position should be preserved for the benefit of posterity with a ...‡

25. P—N3	**P—QN4**
26. N × QNP	**Q—K5 +**
27. K—B3	**Q × P +**
28. K—N4	**P—B4 +**

White resigns.

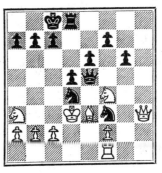

I must confess that the above game by Nimzowitsch exercises a deep fascination for me and I have almost certainly played it over more times than any other game by Nimzowitsch. The ramifications of the combination commencing on his 12th move have the artificiality and contrivance of a composed problem, and the rare beauty which is sometimes captured by a problem, yet this game is also possessed of a further dimension—it is a struggle, which a problem most emphatically is not. Nimzowitsch's thoughts here were not just an intellectual exercise, they were an integral part of a conflict with the mind of another man.

WENDEL–NIMZOWITSCH, Stockholm, 1921 (Match Game?)
KP Nimzowitsch Defence

1. P—K4	**N—QB3**	**3. N—QB3**
2. P—Q4	**P—Q4**	

One of the sharpest methods of combatting Nimzowitsch's special defence. With this move White offers a pawn sacrifice in order to destroy Black's strong point on d5. In this case Nimzowitsch accepts the challenge.

3. ...   **P × P**

The alternative is the stolid refusal to give ground 3. ... P—K3. Later in the 1920s Nimzowitsch gained many victories with this move, one of which is sufficiently amusing to merit reproduction here: Mieses–Nimzowitsch, Kissingen, 1928: **3.** ...   **P—K3;**

4. P × P (P—K5!), P × P; 5. B—K3, B—KB4; 6. B—Q3, KN—K2; 7. KN—K2, N—N5; 8. B × B, N × B; 9. B—B4, P—KN4; 10. B— Q2, B—K2; 11. Q—B1, P—KB3; 12. N—Q1, N—B3; 13. P—QB3, N—R5; 14. N—K3, Q—Q2; 15. Q—B2, P—B4; 16. P—KB4, 0—0—0; 17. 0—0—0, KR—B1; 18. QR—B1, QR—K1; 19. P × P,

B × P; 20. N—KB4, N—K2; 21. K— N1, B × N; 22. R × B, N/2—N3; 23, R—B2, P—B5; 24. N—Q1, Q—N5; 25. B—B1, N—B4; 26. R/1—B1 N—Q3; 27. P—KR3, Q—N4; 28. R—K2, R—K5; 29. R/2—B2, R/1— K1; 30. Q—Q3, N—B4; 31. R—N1, N—N6; 32. B—Q2, Q—B4; 33. P— R3, Q—K3; 34. K—R1, Q—QB3; 35. Q—B3, P—KR4; 36. K—R2, Q—N4 (completing the encirclement); **37. K—R1, N—R5‡** check mate, but to White's queen rather than his king!

The methodical restriction and minimisation of White's opportunities, eventually leading to a helpless paralysis on the part of the opposing army, stamps the above as a close relative to the 'immortal Zugzwang Game' versus Sämisch.

4. P—Q5   N—K4

For 4. ... N—N1 consult the theoretical survey, page 43. I once reached the position after 4. ... N—K4 and my opponent (White) replied 5. N × P?! The continuation was eccentric: 5. ... N—KB3; 6. N × N +, KP × N; 7. P—KB4, N—N3; 8. B—N5 +, B—Q2; 9. Q—K2 +, B—K2; 10. P—KR4, P—QR3; 11. B × B +, Q × B; 12. P—R5, N—B1; 13. P—QB4, 0—0—0; 14. B—K3, B—N5 +; 15. K—B2, P—KN4; 16. P—R3, R—K1; 17. Q—Q3, P × P; 18. B × P, B—B4 +; 19. K—N3, R—N1 +; 20. K—R2, Q—N5. Black later blundered and lost but this position is by no means bad for him.

5. B—KB4!   N—N3   6. B—N3   P—QR3?!

Black naturally has to prevent N—N5 and the obvious way to achieve this is 6. ... P—KB4 (note that 6. ... P—K4 fails to 7. P × P e.p., B × P; 8. N—N5!) but Nimzowitsch then feared 7. P—KR4, P—B5; 8. P—R5 (Boleslavsky gives 8. B—R2!), 8. ... P × B; 9. P × N, P × P +; 10. K × P which looks anything but clear to me. However, in view of Boleslavsky's improvement on move 8 for White the entire sequence with 7. ... P—B5 seems suspect.

But that is not the end of this question. During the British Championship Congress, 1972, I observed a game played between two boys in the Under-16 Tournament which bears testimony to the attraction which some of Nimzowitsch's virtually unanalysed, tactically complex ideas can exert over young players. The junior game (those involved were M. Goldschmidt and C. Crouch) which I noticed reached the position after 7. P—KR4 and then Black played 7. ... P—K4!? The game continued: 8. P—R5 (if 8. P × P e.p. I presume that Black must reply ... Q × Q + ; 9. R × Q, B—N5 when he will shed his QBP in return for White's KP), 8. ... P—B5 (we have, in effect, reached Nimzowitsch's line above but with 8. ... P—K4 substituted for 8. ... P × B. The point of Crouch's move-order is that he avoids Boleslavsky's 8. B—R2); 9. P × N, P × B; 10. R × P?, P × P + ; 11. K × P, R × R; 12. P × R, Q—R5 + and Black must win in short order. Does this resuscitate 6. ... P—KB4? White's play can obviously be improved at move 10, e.g. 10. BP × P or 10. N × P. Probably the latter of these moves is the more convincing and therein may lie the answer to Black's ingenious innovation.

7. P—B3?!
Much stronger is Boleslavsky's 7. B—QB4!, N—B3; 8. Q—K2, D—D4; 9. 0 0 0 ı ₁ White's choice in the game permits Nimzo-witsch to return his extra pawn for a lasting initiative.

7. ...	P—KB4!	9. B—B2	P—K4
8. P × P	P—B5	10. N—B3	

10. P × P e.p.? B × P would give Black a splendid development and leave White with a weak KP.

10. ... B—Q3
'A move dictated by the law of the blockade (passed and semi-passed pawns must be blockaded)' (Nimzowitsch). Nimzowitsch regarded this position as approximately level and considered that White's next few moves should have been B—Q3/0—0 and N—K2, followed by the activation of his left wing majority (P—QB4—B5). As it is, White fails to spot this plan and indulges, instead, in a series of highly artificial manœuvres. Nimzowitsch exploits the respite to restrain White's Q side advance for good and Wendel then finds that he has no counterplay anywhere.

11. P—KR4? P—N4
The first step in the restraint of P—QB4, etc.

12. P—R5	N—B1	14. B—K2	P—N5
13. B—R4	Q—Q2	15. N—QN1	N—B3

Threatening White's KP and KRP. White has but one method of avoiding material loss.

16. B × N

Unpleasant but forced. After this exchange Black's centre is strengthened and he is given the open KN file as a free gift in which to operate against White's weak KNP. On top of this the absence of White's QB leaves him woefully exposed on the dark squares. From now on White is reduced to meeting Black's threats and can form no positive schemes of his own.

16. ...	P × B		20. R—R3	Q—N1
17. N/1—Q2	Q—N2		21. N—R4	N—B4
18. K—B1	N—Q2		22. R—R1	R—N1
19. P—R6	Q—N6		23. P—B3?!	

A weird reaction to Black's last move, which was obviously conceived as a prophylactic measure against 23. P—B3. Black now seizes the QN file in addition to his other treasures.

23. ...	P × P		26. N—B4	B—Q2
24. P × P	Q—N6		27. N × B +	P × N
25. Q—B2	R—N1		28. B—B3‡	

In control of all the open lines and all the dark squares and with White's units strewn at random around the perimeters of the battlefield Black has an obviously winning position. The positional way to victory, pointed out by Nimzowitsch, was 28. ... K—Q1, e.g. 29. N—B5, B × N; 30. P × B (threatening R—R3); 30. ... R—K1; 31. R—R3, Q—N1! and White's position is an unco-ordinated shambles.

But, as so often, Nimzowitsch espies a combination which leads even more rapidly to the desired goal. And, as we might expect, this combination is laced with problem moves. It almost looks like a constructed situation rather than a game continuation. Black to play and win; it is certainly worthwhile trying to find Nimzowitsch's beautiful win yourself before inspecting the remainder of the game.

28. ...	B—N4 +
29. P—B4	B × P +
30. Q × B	R—N7
31. B—K2	R—KN5
32. Q—B1	

32. R—R3 looks like an adequate defence, but then comes the brilliant stroke R × N!, e.g. 33. R × Q, R—R8 + ; 34. K—B2, P × R + ; 35. K × P, R × R; 'Black wins the QRP and then decides the game in his favour by a direct attack with the

rooks. Do not overlook that passed Black QRP lurking in the background' (Nimzowitsch).

32. ...   R × N   34. K × R   Q × P +
33. R × R   R × B!

As in his game versus Spielmann from Stockholm, 1920, Nimzowitsch harries the whole White army with his Q and N. Meanwhile, the White KR will not run away.

35. K—Q1   Q—B8 +   36. K—Q2

Or 36. K—B2, Q—Q6 + ; 37. K—N2, N—R5 with a 'problem mate' (Nimzowitsch).

36. ...   Q—Q6 +   38. K—B1   Q × R
37. K—K1   Q—N6 +

With the shelter of his K completely swept away White is hopelessly lost. Black's material investment amounts to a mere exchange and he will soon annex some more of White's pawns.

39. K—N1   Q—N6 +   41. K—N1   N × P
40. K—R1   Q—R6 +   42. Q—B6 +

Taking a circuitous route to the defence of the White K.

42. ...   K—R2   45. Q—N2   Q—K6 +
43. Q—B7 +   K—N3   46. K—R2   N—B7
44. Q—N7 +   K—R4   47. R—KB1

Or 47. R—KN1, Q—K7 and White has no checks (Nimzowitsch).

47. ...   N—N5 +   49. R—KN1   P—B4
48. K—R1   P—K5

White is so tied up that the only danger Black has to avoid is an accidental stalemate.

50. P—R4   K × P   52. R—N1   P—B6
51. P—R5   K—N4   53. Q—N2   P—B7

White resigns.

NIMZOWITSCH–H. WOLF, Carlsbad, 1923. *Nimzowitsch Attack*
1. N—KB3

In our own eclectic age (as regards chess ideas) such an initial move hardly requires any explanation, but in 1923 1. N—KB3, when adopted by a respectable master player, was still something quite out of the ordinary, although it very rapidly became commonplace. 1923 was a key year for the general practical adoption of those theoretical ideas (known as hypermodern) which had challenged the hegemony of the classical* theories elaborated by (*inter alios*) Dr. Tarrasch.

* The term used by Nimzowitsch was 'pseudo-classical'.

The areas of dispute between the so-called classical and hyper-modern masters were manifold and complex but this game does illustrate one of the points at contention: by and large classical dogma held that control of the centre derived from occupation by pawns. In many cases this is obviously a correct view; but the hyper-moderns (Réti, Nimzowitsch, Breyer, Grünfeld and sometimes Alekhine) enriched the concept of central control by stating that it could equally well derive from observation by pieces, and the particular opening systems newly designed to test this belief (Réti's opening, 1. P—KN3, the English opening and the Nimzowitsch Attack) were rooted in the empirical demonstration of successful central control by pieces alone provided by Nimzowitsch's famous victory versus Salwe from Carlsbad, 1911 (page 104), which actually commenced with a more orthodox début. That this revolutionary game was played in 1911 is of significance and, apropos the struggle between the classicists and the hypermoderns, I would like to suggest here that the real battle took place, not hand to hand in the 1920s, but at long range. The classical broadsides emanating from Dr. Tarrasch, etc., were fired before the First World War (cf. p. 112 for Tarrasch's strictures on Nimzowitsch's opening play versus Rubin-stein at San Sebastian, 1912) at a time when the great classical masters monopolised the most highly-respected organs of the chess press and before they had properly grasped that there was a genuine alternative to their own teachings.

By the mid-1920s, however, the real theoretical battle was already more than half won by the hypermoderns and nobody (apart from some isolated and feeble rearguard actions by, e.g., Rubinstein or Teichmann, who referred to Réti's opening as the 'stupid double hole variation') questioned the validity of the hypermodern concepts as a worthwhile contribution to our understanding of chess. What could be more 'hypermodern' than Alekhine's defence? Yet Tarrasch himself played it on at least two occasions and Rubinstein also used it, while Capablanca became a devotee of the English and Réti systems after his loss to Réti in 1924. Tarrasch even played Réti's opening, as in his game (as White) versus Alekhine from Semmering, 1926: 1. N—KB3(!), P—Q4; 2. P—B4, P—Q5; 3. P—QN4, P—QB4; 4. B—N2, P—KN3; 5. P—K3, B—N2; 6. P × BP, P—K4; 7. P × P, P × P; 8. P—Q3, N—QR3; 9. QN—Q2, N × P; 10. N—N3, N—K3; 11. P—N3, N—K2; 12. B—N2, 0—0; 13. 0—0, N—B3. In fact there was no real resistance. As soon as the hyper-modern ideas were introduced and seen to work they won rapid general acceptance. The polemic campaign conducted by the vic-torious hypermoderns, themselves now in control of the chess media, was directed against a monster that had, in fact, only been rampant before the First War. *Chess Praxis* was published in 1928 and contains a chapter titled: 'The triumph (or victory march) of the ugly and bizarre moves'. This is a sarcastic reference to something Tarrasch wrote in 1911 about Nimzowitsch's game with Capablanca from San Sebastian which commenced (Nimzowitsch: White) 1. P—K4, P—K3; 2. P—Q3, whereupon the good Doctor wrote: 'Nimzowitsch is one of the most talented of the youngest generation of masters and he is possessed of a pronounced personal style. Only, he does have a penchant for peculiar, bizarre, indeed ugly moves in the opening, with which he does certainly succeed now and again [as for example versus Teichmann], but which here bring about his defeat in the face of quite simple methods of counter-play from the opponent.' (*My System*, game 40.)

Note how the words 'ugly' and 'bizarre' still hurt after an interval of seventeen years. Nimzowitsch, now in a position of strength apropos the media, seems to be exacting his revenge.

He specifically denies this in *Chess Praxis*: 'But we do not wish to "square accounts", the formalistic school of pseudo-classicism is dead and you cannot beat a dead man. If in the following pages we record a few value judgements from that time the object is not to "square accounts" but is purely one of technical interest.'

But is this really so? Elsewhere we quote at length from Nimzowitsch's Russian language booklet: 'How I became a Grandmaster' (1929) and there Nimzowitsch, in his treatment of Tarrasch, certainly looks as if he wishes to 'square accounts' with an enemy whose position had previously been too well entrenched to suffer theoretical damage.

In *My System* Nimzowitsch admits that the foe had been defeated for some time—the following concerns a game he played in 1911: 'The old dogmas, such as the ossified teaching on the centre, the worship of the open game, and in general the whole formalistic conception of the game, who bothers himself today about these? The new ideas, however, those supposed byways not to be recommended to the public, these are become today highways, on which great and small move freely in the consciousness of absolute security.'

The security was so great, in fact, that virtually no attention was devoted in the 1920s to the overtly 'classical' responses (I mean, of course, the Four pawns attack and the Exchange variation) to those typically hypermodern defences: the Alekhine and the Grünfeld.

| 1. ... | P—Q4 | 3. B—N2 | P—B4 |
| 2. P—QN3 | N—KB3 | 4. P—K3 | |

The first example in this book of the Nimzowitsch Attack, which is characterised by the fianchetto of the QB, but not necessarily of the KB. In the further course of play White intends to conduct a dark square campaign along the QR1—KR8 diagonal employing the square e5 as a strong point in the attack. This play against a central square (e5) is one feature that distinguishes the Nimzowitsch Attack from Réti's Opening, where White fianchettoes both bishops and then operates specifically against the Black Pawn centre, as in one of Réti's inaugural games with this system, also from Carlsbad, 1923: (Black: Rubinstein) 1. N—KB3, P—Q4; 2. P—KN3, N—KB3; 3. B—N2, P—KN3; 4. P—B4, P—Q5; 5. P—Q3, B—N2; 6. P—QN4 and Black's pawn wedge in the centre was undermined from the flanks. The Carlsbad tournament took place from late April to mid-May, 1923, and Réti had actually played his first international game with his new system a few weeks earlier at Margate (April 4, 1923) versus Grünfeld. But Nimzowitsch had got there first! At Copenhagen (March 3-14, 1923) Nimzowitsch opened as follows against Spielmann: 1. N—KB3, N—KB3; 2. P—QN3, P—Q4; 3. B—N2, P—K3; 4. P—N3, B—Q3; 5. B—N2, QN—Q2; 6. P—B4, P—B3; 7. 0—0, 0—0 and the game ended in a draw after 34 moves. Even in 1910 Nimzowitsch was experimenting with double fianchetto systems that were reminiscent of Staunton's games sixty years previously, e.g. Hamburg, 1910, as White versus Schlechter: 1. P—QB4, P—K4; 2. P—KN3, N—KB3; 3. B—N2, B—K2; 4. N—QB3, 0—0; 5.N—B3, N—B3; 6. 0—0, P—Q3; 7. P—N3, R—K1; 8. B—N2, B—Q2; 9. P—Q4, P×P; 10. N×P, B—KB1; 11. P—K3 + =.

4. ... N—B3?!
Dubious. White can masquerade as Black quite happily in the opening, but when Black pretends to be White he is inviting difficulties. Black should have avoided the coming pin with a more circumspect course such as 4. ... P—K3.

5. B—N5 B—Q2	**7. P—Q3**
6. 0—0 P—K3	

Much stronger than 7. P—Q4 which would run counter to White's whole strategy by blocking the diagonal of the QB.

7. ... B—K2	**9. KB×N**
8. QN—Q2 0—0	

A typically Nimzowitschian voluntary exchange of bishop for knight. Here it serves to emphasise White's control of the K5 square —with his pieces!

9. ... B×B	**11. QN—B3**
10. N—K5 N—Q2	

One would have expected the automatic infliction of a doubled-pawn complex (11. N × B) from the later Nimzowitsch, but in this relatively early game he was more concerned with maintaining his grip on e5.

11. ...R—B1   12. Q—K2 N×N

Enhancing White's hold over e5, but after the challenge 12. ... P—B3; 13. N×B, R×N both 14. P—B4 and 14. P—K4 leave White with the better game.

13. N×N B—K1

An artificial move animated by a desire (which only persists for a further nine moves) to preserve his bishop pair.

14. Q—N4

With the horrible threat of 15. N—B6, breaking down in drastic fashion Black's entire lines of resistance along the a1–h8 diagonal. Black is now obliged to renounce any plans he may have harboured of dispossessing White's knight of its advanced station on e5. The alternative to the course chosen (which abandons the square forever) was 14. ... B—KB3; 15. P—KB4, but this too looks unpromising for Black.

14. ... P—B4

At least this has the merit of driving White's queen from its menacing position.

15. Q—K2 B—KB3   16. P—QB4

A good move which serves the dual purpose of restraining any advance of Black's Q side pawns (e.g. by ... P—QN4 and ... P—QB5) and of putting pressure on Black's centre.

16. ... Q—K2   17. P—B4

Conquering his K5 square permanently.

17. ... B—B2?

Hereabouts Black wastes valuable time. Now, or on move 22, it was essential to organise counterplay by means of ... P—QN4!

18. P—KR3

This innocent looking pawn move is in fact the prelude to a vicious onslaught against the Black King.

18. ... KR—Q1   19. K—R2

In anticipation of his 21st move.

19. ...   R—B2   21. R—KN1! P×P
20. R—B2 B—K1

Given that Black ought to undertake some positive action this is not a bad idea, although it cedes White a central pawn majority. However after ...

22. NP × P‡

... establishing the above-mentioned majority. It was imperative to play 22. ... P—QN4! with some counter-chances. So far Nimzowitsch has provided us with an exemplary taming of the hostile bishop pair, but now Black spoils the demonstration by surrendering one of his bishops quite gratuitously. Perhaps he was pinning his faith in the drawing potential of opposite bishop situations, but all he succeeds in doing is ceding his opponent lifelong hegemony over the dark squares—a free gift of thirty-two squares. The prelate which now arrives at e5 radiates power in all directions and is worth at least a rook.

22. ... B × N?
The decisive error.

23. B × B   R/2—Q2   24. P—N4   P × P
Or 24. ... R × P; 25. P × P with victorious threats against Black's KN2 square. Note that this variation is a logical, if exaggerated, continuation of the dark square campaign introduced by White's second move.

25. Q × P   B—N3   26. P—Q4
Eliminating the last weakness in the White camp (Pawn Q3) and announcing the triumphal advance of the central pawn majority. The reader might care to compare the winning process in this game (dark square assault against opposing KN2 square coupled with diversionary advance of central pawns) with that of Spielmann–Nimzowitsch, San Sebastian, 1911, page 57 (light square assault against opposing KN2 square in conjunction with diversionary advance of passed QRP).

26. ...	P × P	32. R × R	Q—B1
27. P × P	B—B4	33. Q—N4	B—B4
28. Q—R5	B—N3	34. Q—N2	P—KR3
29. Q—K2	R—KB1	35. R—N3	K—R2
30. R—N5	R—B4	36. P—Q5!	
31. R/2—KN2	R × R		

The long awaited penetration into enemy territory.

36. ...   R—KB2   37. P—Q6‡
With a neat threat exemplifying my note to move 26: 38. R × P +, R × R; 39. Q × R +, Q × Q; 40. B × Q, K × B; 41. P—Q7. In order

to forestall this Black is obliged to inflict on himself a further weakening
of his dark squares.

37. ...   P—KN3
38. P—B5   Q—B1
39. R—QB3

White's control of space has
reached alarming proportions. He
now intends a breakthrough based on
P—B6 which Black must prevent,
even at the price of more wounds in
his position.

39. ...   Q—B3

Bitter necessity. The newly created QBP is born into a world of
tears and misery.

40. Q × Q   P × Q   **41. P—KR4**

Black cannot seize the open file: 41. ... R—QN2; 42. R—QN3!
and if Black exchanges on b3 the QP promotes at the double.

41. ...   K—N1   **42. R—QN3**

The ending is easily won. Black's half of the opposite bishop's
'drawing mechanism' (Bf5) is locked out of play and quite useless.

42. ...	**R—Q2**	**46. K—B2**	**B—Q4**
43. R—N8 +	**K—B2**	**47. K—K3**	**B—N7**
44. R—QB8	**B—K5**	**48. K—Q4**	**B—B6**
45. K—N3	**P—KR4**	**49. B—R8**	**P—K4 +**

If Black 'passes' White has an attractive winning method in 49. ...
B—Q4; 50. K—K5, B—B6; 51. B—N7!, K × B; 52. R—B7 or
51. ... B—Q4; 52. B—R6 and then R—KB8. A triumph for the
dark squares.

50. K × P	**B—Q4**	**52. B—N5**	**K—N2**
51. B—B6	**B—B6**	**53. P—B5**	**B—N5**

Or 53. ... P × P; 54. R—B7!

54. P—B6 +   K—R2   **55. R × P   Resigns.**

In this game Nimzowitsch appears as a wizard with supernatural
influence over the dark squares which obey his every whim and
fancy. I find it quite amazing that he should not have chosen this fine
game to include in his own published collection.

SPIELMANN–NIMZOWITSCH, Carlsbad, 1923. *Caro Kann*

In his games and writings Steinitz taught that, with the centre closed,
it was possible to launch an attack on the wings, as in the following

extract from a rather old-fashioned opening: Dubois–Steinitz, London, 1862: 1. P—K4, P—K4; 2. N—KB3, N—QB3; 3. B—B4, B—B4; 4. 0—0?!, N—B3; 5. P—Q3, P—Q3; 6. B—KN5?!, P—KR3!; 7. B—R4, P—KN4; 8. B—N3, P—KR4; 9. P—KR4, B—KN5 with a virulent attack against White's king, since 10. P × P allows ... P—R5; 11. B—R2, N—R2∓.

In this game with Spielmann Nimzowitsch reinterprets this particular Steinitzian concept in the light of contemporary opening theory.

1. P—K4	P—QB3	4. P—QB3	N—QB3
2. P—Q4	P—Q4	5. B—KB4?!	B—B4!
3. P × P	P × P		

At that time an innovation. In fact, Nimzowitsch's fifth move is so strong that no one plays 5. B—KB4 any more. The point is that White now has no good developing square for his KB since B—Q3 allows the exchange of light-squared bishops. Such an exchange would react to Black's advantage in view of the pawn-structure— White's centre pawns are fixed on dark squares impeding his bishop; Black's are on light squares. Thus White's light squares in the centre could become weak, inviting Black to seize the potential outposts on c4 or e4.

Now we are wiser and we play 5. B—Q3, as in the game Fischer–Petrosian, World versus U.S.S.R. Match, 1971: 5. ... N—B3; 6. B—KB4 (only now), B—N5; 7. Q—N3, N—QR4; 8. Q—R4+, B—Q2; 9. Q—B2, P—K3; 10. N—B3, Q—N3; 11. P—QR4!, R—B1; 12. QN—Q2, N—B3; 13. Q—N1!, N—KR4; 14. B—K3, P—KR3; 15. N—K5± a demonstration of the continued vitality of the exchange Caro Kann, although Petrosian's response was rather feeble.

6. N—B3	P—K3	8. QN—Q2	P—B3
7. Q—N3	Q—Q2		

Very good. Black protects his K4 square and prepares the advance of his K side pawns. That this advance occurs with the speed and force of a mechanised 'Blitzkrieg' stems from Black's unassailable central position, and White's next move.

9. B—K2?

Nimzowitsch recommended central activity with 9. P—B4! which would have deterred Black from the ambitious course he now adopts. That way lay equality.

9. ...	P—KN4	11. P—KR3	KN—K2
10. B—N3	P—KR4	12. 0—0?	

Castling into the attack is an error reminiscent of Dubois' in the

Steinitz game (4. 0—0?!). 12. P—B4! would have succeeded in restricting Black's advantage to one of the purely positional variety, e.g. 12. ... P × P; 13. B × P, N—Q4 'with a fortified central knight?' (Nimzowitsch). After the text, on the other hand, White is crushed by the simplest of means.

12. ... B—R3‡
Threat: ... P—N5.

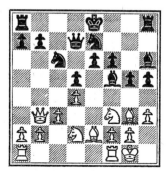

13. N—K1
A truly ghastly move to have to make.

13. ... P—N5
14. Q—Q1 B × N
Wins a pawn.

15. Q × B	**P × P**	**17. KR—K1**	**P—R5**
16. N—Q3	**P—N3**	**18. B—R2**	**K—B2!**

Here Black avoids a trap: 18. ... 0—0—0?; 19. N—B5! and B—QR6 +.

19. P—KN4 P × P e.p.   21. K—N2 B—K5 +
20. B × P   P—R7 +

Nimzowitsch was later to recommend 21. ... P—K4!; 22. P × P, B—K5 +; 23. P—B3, QR—KN1 as stronger. The move played, however, seems quite sufficient.

22. B—B3
More tenacious is P—B3.

22. ...   N—B4   24. N—B4
23. B × B   P × B
Or 24. R × P, Q—Q4!

24. ...   P—K4   26. B × N   Q—N5 +
25. N—K2   N—R5 +

and mates, e.g. 27. N—N3, Q—B6 +; 28. K—R3, R × B +; 29. K × R, R—R1 +.

A powerful game by our hero, but we must remember that the poor wreck of a master conducting the white pieces did not represent the real Spielmann. Carlsbad, 1923, was, for Spielmann, the disastrous equivalent of Göteborg, 1920, in Nimzowitsch's career. For a magnificent clash between these two great players, then both at the peak of their powers, I recommend their game from Carlsbad, 1929 (page 229).

F

NIMZOWITSCH–TARTAKOWER, Carlsbad, 1923. *Nimzowitsch Attack*

1. N—KB3	P—KB4	3. B—N2	B—N2
2. P—QN3	P—QN3	4. P—N3	B × N?!

An interesting and original idea. It looks stupid to surrender the powerful QB in this fashion, but the move does have a sound positional basis in that (a) the mobility of White's central pawns decreases after the recapture with his KP and (b) Black hopes to shut White's bishop pair out of the game by establishing a vast blockade of light-squared pawns. However, in this case the plan fails, partly because Black never succeeds in overcoming the weakening of his pawn chain created by his first move (. . . P—KB4) and partly because White's development is efficient enough to permit him a counter-attack on the very light squares Black hoped to control. So 4. ... B × N gets no applause, but that does not mean that the whole idea must be abandoned. Many players since 1923 have felt the attraction of such apparently antipositional moves as ... B × N, and it is only by constant experimentation with these ostensibly outlandish possibilities that the genuinely workable methods can be elaborated, e.g. Larsen–M. Colon, San Juan, 1969: 1. P—QN3, P—QN3; 2. B—N2, B—N2; 3. P—KB4, P—KB4; 4. P—K3, N—KB3; 5. B × N, KP × B; 6. N—KB3, B—K2; 7. N—B3, P—N3; 8. P—KR3, B—N5; 9. N—QN5, P—QR3; 10. QN—Q4, N—B3; 11. N × N, B × N; 12. B—Q3, Q—K2; 13. Q—K2, P—QR4; 14. P—KN4 + =.

5. P × B   P—K3   6. P—KB4

The first step towards the creation of an outpost at e5 (N—R3—B4—K5) which cannot be driven away by ... P—Q3 in view of the weakness of the KP in the open file. With his 6th move White also prepares to unleash his KB along the h1–a8 diagonal, and this is the harbinger of the light-square counter-attack mentioned in the previous note.

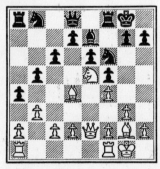

6. ...	N—KB3
7. B—N2	P—B3
8. 0—0	B—K2
9. Q—K2	0—0
10. N—R3	P—QR4

There is no other way of developing the QN in as much as ... P—QN4 fails to N × P.

11. N—B4	P—R5
12. B—Q4	P—QN4
13. N—K5‡	

Both sides have achieved pretty much what they wanted: Black has manufactured his light-square blockade while White has established an outpost at K5 (Nimzowitsch insisted in his own notes that this was an outpost in the a1–h8 diagonal rather than an outpost in the K file). However, Black's next move seems wrong, since it only serves to encourage phase two of White's strategy—the light-square counter-attack.

13. ... N—Q4?!
13. ... N—R3 is more sensible, when Nimzowitsch intended KR—K1, confidently increasing the pressure, rather than N × BP, obtaining several pawns for a piece.

14. P—B4   NP × P   15. P × BP   N—N5
'In the understandable desire to take advantage of the N's short sojourn in a central position (d5), according to the motto—"via the centre into enemy land". The scheme, however, proves disastrous. But with passive play (. . . N—B2) an ultimate breakthrough by P—Q4—Q5 would have been decisive' (Nimzowitsch).

16. B—QB3   P—R6
If 16. ... N/1—R3; 17. P—QR3 traps a N. The text precludes this unpleasant possibility.

17. P—Q4   N/1—R3   19. P—B5!
18. QR—N1   R—N1
Tactical circumstances sometimes require that strategic plans should be modified. White abandons his light-square campaign (which consisted in playing P—Q5) and even gives away an attractive central light square (d5) because he has seen that he can win Black's N by severing its lines of communication!

19. ...   B—B3   21. BP × B
20. R—N3   B × N
White's N had to be eliminated for otherwise Black's Q could not have come to the aid of her far-flung N.

21. ...   Q—R4
Black's pieces are drawn to the place of their ruin as if by the charm of a powerful lodestone, but Black had no alternative to ... Q—R4 if he wished to save his QRP.

22. KR—N1
The frontal pin.

22. ...   R—N2
23. Q—Q2
The diagonal pin.

Position after 24. B—B1

23. ... KR—N1   **24. B—B1**

The global pin.

It is surprising that Black has any moves at all, but Tartakower finds a sly way to play on.

24. ... Q—B2!   **25. B × N(b4)**

The most clear-cut. White ends up with two rooks, a bishop and some attack for the Queen.

25. ... N × B; 26. R × N, Q—R4; 27. R × R, Q × Q; 28. R × R +, K—B2; 29. B—B4, Q × QP; 30. B—N3, Q × QBP; 31. R—N7, Q × KP; 32. R × P +, K—B3; 33. R/1—Q1, P—B4; 34. R/7—Q6, Q—B6; 35. R × P +, K—N4; 36. R—K3, Q—N5; 37. R—QB1, P—KB5; 38. R—K5 +, K—R3; 39. R/5 × BP and White delivered mate on move 48.

A game which contains some ideas (from both players) that are refreshingly out of the ordinary.

World Championship Candidate

BADEN-BADEN, April 15–May 14, 1925

	1	2	3	4	5	6	7	8	9	10	11	12	13	14	15	16	17	18	19	20	21	
1 Alekhine	–	½	1	½	1	½	1	½	1	½	1	½	1	½	1	½	1	1	1	1	1	16
2 Rubinstein	½	–	½	½	½	0	½	½	½	1	½	1	1	1	1	1	½	1	1	1	1	14½
3 Sämisch	0	½	–	1	0	½	½	½	1	½	1	1	1	½	1	½	0	1	1	1	1	13½
4 Bogoljubow	½	½	0	–	0	1	0	0	1	1	1	1	1	½	0	1	½	1	1	1	1	13
5 Marshall	0	½	1	1	–	½	1	½	½	½	0	½	½	½	½	½	1	1	½	1	1	12½
6 Tartakower	½	1	½	0	½	–	½	½	1	½	½	½	½	½	1	1	½	½	1	½	1	12½
7 Rabinowitsch	0	½	½	1	0	½	–	½	0	½	½	1	½	1	½	1	1	1	½	½	1	12
8 Grünfeld	½	½	½	1	½	½	½	–	½	0	0	½	1	1	0	½	1	0	1	1	1	11½
9 Nimzowitsch	0	½	0	0	½	0	1	½	–	½	1	½	0	1	½	1	½	1	1	½	1	11
10 Torre	½	0	½	0	½	½	½	1	½	–	½	½	0	0	1	½	½	½	1	1	1	10½
11 Réti	0	½	0	0	1	½	½	1	0	½	–	1	½	1	½	½	½	0	1	0	1	10
12 Spielmann	½	0	0	0	½	½	0	½	½	½	0	–	½	1	1	1	0	1	½	1	1	10
13 Treybal	0	0	0	0	½	½	½	0	1	1	½	½	–	1	0	½	½	1	1	½	1	10
14 Carls	½	0	½	½	½	½	0	0	0	1	0	0	0	–	0	1	1	½	1	1	1	9
15 Yates	0	0	0	1	½	0	½	1	½	0	½	0	1	1	–	0	0	0	1	0	1	8
16 Rosselli	½	0	½	0	½	0	0	½	0	½	½	0	½	0	1	–	1	1	0	½	½	7½
17 Tarrasch	0	½	1	½	0	½	0	0	½	½	½	1	½	0	1	0	–	½	0	0	½	7½
18 Colle	0	0	0	0	0	½	0	1	0	½	1	0	0	½	1	0	½	–	0	1	1	7
19 Mieses	0	0	0	0	½	0	½	0	0	0	0	½	0	0	0	1	1	1	–	1	1	6½
20 Thomas	0	0	0	0	0	½	½	0	½	0	1	0	½	0	1	½	1	0	0	–	½	6
21 te Kolste	0	0	0	0	0	0	0	0	0	0	0	0	0	0	0	½	½	0	0	½	–	1½

MARIENBAD, May 21–June 8, 1925

	1	2	3	4	5	6	7	8	9	10	11	12	13	14	15	16	
1 Rubinstein	–	0	½	½	½	1	1	½	1	0	1	1	1	1	1	1	11
2 Nimzowitsch	1	–	0	½	1	½	½	1	½	1	1	½	1	1	1	½	11
3 Marshall	½	1	–	½	½	½	½	½	1	1	½	½	1	½	½	1	10
4 Torre	½	½	½	–	1	½	0	1	1	1	½	1	½	½	½	1	10
5 Réti	½	0	½	0	–	0	1	0	½	1	1	1	1	1	1	1	9½
6 Tartakower	0	½	½	½	1	–	0	1	1	½	½	½	½	1	1	1	9½
7 Spielmann	0	½	½	1	0	1	–	0	½	½	½	0	1	1	1	1	8½
8 Grünfeld	½	0	½	0	1	0	1	–	1	½	½	½	½	½	½	1	8
9 Yates	0	½	0	0	½	0	½	0	–	1	½	1	½	½	1	1	7
10 Opocensky	1	0	0	0	0	½	½	½	0	–	½	0	½	1	1	1	6½
11 Thomas	0	0	½	½	0	½	½	½	½	½	–	0	1	½	1	0	6
12 Przepiorka	0	½	½	0	0	½	1	½	0	1	1	–	1	0	0	0	6
13 Janowski	0	0	0	½	0	½	0	½	½	½	0	0	–	1	1	1	5½
14 Sämisch	0	0	½	½	0	0	0	½	½	0	½	1	0	–	1	1	5½
15 Michell	0	0	½	½	0	0	0	½	0	0	0	1	0	0	–	1	3½
16 Haida	0	½	0	0	0	0	0	0	0	0	1	1	0	0	0	–	2½

BRESLAU, July 19–August 1; 1925

	1	2	3	4	5	6	7	8	9	10	11	12	
1 Bogoljubow	–	1	½	0	1	1	1	1	1	1	1	1	9½
2 Nimzowitsch	0	–	½	½	½	0	1	1	1	1	1	1	7½
3 Rubinstein	½	½	–	½	½	1	½	1	0	½	1	1	7
4 Wagner	1	½	½	–	1	½	0	0	1	½	1	1	7
5 Grünfeld	0	½	½	0	–	½	½	½	1	½	1	1	6
6 Réti	0	1	0	½	½	–	1	0	1	½	½	1	6
7 Becker	0	0	½	1	½	0	–	½	1	1	1	½	6
8 Sämisch	0	0	0	1	½	1	½	–	0	½	½	1	5
9 von Gottschall	0	0	1	0	0	0	0	1	–	1	0	1	4
10 Tarrasch	0	0	½	½	½	½	0	½	0	–	0	1	3½
11 Blümich	0	0	0	0	0	½	0	½	1	1	–	0	3
12 Moritz	0	0	0	0	0	0	½	0	0	0	1	–	1½

SEMMERING, March 7–29, 1926

	1	2	3	4	5	6	7	8	9	10	11	12	13	14	15	16	17	18	
1 Spielmann	–	½	1	1	1	0	½	½	1	1	1	1	1	½	1	½	½	1	13
2 Alekhine	½	–	0	0	1	1	1	1	1	½	1	½	1	0	1	1	1	1	12½
3 Vidmar	0	1	–	1	1	½	0	1	½	1	1	½	1	1	½	1	½	½	12
4 Nimzowitsch	0	1	0	–	½	1	½	1	0	1	½	1	1	1	½	½	1	1	11½
5 Tartakower	0	0	0	½	–	½	1	0	1	1	1	1	½	1	1	1	1	1	11½
6 Rubinstein	1	0	½	0	½	–	½	1	1	0	½	0	1	½	1	½	1	1	10
7 Tarrasch	½	0	1	½	0	½	–	1	0	0	0	1	½	1	1	1	1	1	10
8 Réti	½	0	0	0	1	0	0	–	1	1	1	0	½	1	1	½	1	1	9½
9 Grünfeld	0	0	½	1	0	0	1	0	–	0	½	½	1	1	1	1	½	1	9
10 Janowski	0	½	0	0	0	1	1	0	1	–	½	0	½	0	1	1	1	1	8½
11 Treybal	0	0	0	½	0	½	1	0	½	½	–	1	1	1	0	1	½	½	8
12 Vajda	0	½	½	0	0	1	0	1	½	1	0	–	0	½	½	½	½	1	7½
13 Yates	0	0	0	0	½	0	½	½	0	½	0	1	–	½	½	1	1	1	7
14 Gilg	½	1	0	0	0	½	0	0	0	1	0	½	½	–	½	0	½	1	6
15 Kmoch	0	0	½	½	0	0	0	0	0	0	1	½	½	½	–	1	½	1	6
16 Davidson	½	0	0	½	0	½	0	½	0	0	0	½	0	1	0	–	1	1	5½
17 Michel	½	0	½	0	0	0	0	0	½	0	½	½	0	½	½	0	–	1	4½
18 Rosselli	0	0	½	0	0	0	0	0	0	0	½	0	0	0	0	0	0	–	1

DRESDEN, April 4–14, 1926

	1	2	3	4	5	6	7	8	9	10	
1 Nimzowitsch	–	½	1	1	1	1	1	1	1	1	8½
2 Alekhine	½	–	1	1	½	½	1	½	1	1	7
3 Rubinstein	0	0	–	½	1	1	1	1	1	1	6½
4 Tartakower	0	0	½	–	½	1	½	½	1	1	5
5 von Holzhausen	0	½	0	½	–	0	1	1	0	1	4
6 P. Johner	0	½	0	0	1	–	1	0	0	1	3½
7 Sämisch	0	0	0	½	0	0	–	1	½	1	3
8 Yates	0	½	0	½	0	1	0	–	1	0	3
9 Blümich	0	0	0	0	1	1	½	0	–	0	2½
10 L. Steiner	0	0	0	0	0	0	0	1	1	–	2

HANOVER, 1926

	1	2	3	4	5	6	7	8	
1 Nimzowitsch	–	½	1	1	1	1	1	1	6½
2 Rubinstein	½	–	1	1	½	1	1	1	6
3 von Holzhausen	0	0	–	1	½	1	1	½	4
4 Mieses	0	0	0	–	½	1	1	½	3
5 Sämisch	0	½	½	½	–	0	1	½	3
6 Antze	0	0	0	0	1	–	½	1	2½
7 v. Gottschall	0	0	0	0	0	½	–	1	1½
8 Duhm	0	0	½	½	½	0	0	–	1½

NEW YORK, CANDIDATES' TOURNAMENT,
February 19–March 25, 1927

(The winner—or second place if Capablanca won—would challenge Capablanca
for the World Championship)

	1	2	3	4	5	6	
1 Capablanca	——	1½½½	1½1½	½½1½	½½1½	11½1	14
2 Alekhine	0½½½	——	½01½	½½½½	1½½1	½1½1	11½
3 Nimzowitsch	0½0½	½10½	——	100½	11½½	1½½1	10½
4 Vidmar	½½0½	½½½½	011½	——	½½½½	½01½	10
5 Spielmann	½½0½	0½½0	00½½	½½½½	——	½½1½	8
6 Marshall	00½0	½0½0	0½½0	½10½	½½0½	——	6

BERLIN, May, 1927

		1	2	3	4	5	6	7	8	9	10	
1	Brinckmann	–	0	1	½	1	1	1	½	½	1	6½
2	Nimzowitsch	1	–	0	½	1	1	0	½	1	1	6
3	Bogoljubow	0	1	–	0	½	½	1	1	1	1	6
4	Sämisch	½	½	1	–	½	1	0	1	½	1	6
5	Ahues	0	0	½	½	–	½	1	1	½	1	5
6	Enoch	0	0	½	0	½	–	½	1	1	1	4½
7	List	0	1	0	1	0	½	–	1	1	0	4½
8	Mieses	½	½	0	0	0	0	0	–	½	1	2½
9	Schweinburg	½	0	0	½	½	0	0	½	–	½	2½
10	Elstner	0	0	0	0	0	0	1	0	½	–	1½

COPENHAGEN, 1927

1	Maroczy	4
2	Nimzowitsch	3½
3	Ruben	3½
4	Andersen	2
5	Norman-Hansen	2
6	Petersen	0

KECSKEMET, June 25–July 14, 1927

	1	2	3	4	5	6	7	8	9	10	11	12	13	14	15	16	17	18	19	20	
1 Alekhine	—	½	½	1½	½1	½	½	½½	1	.	1	1	.	.	.	1	.	1	.	1	12
2 Nimzowitsch	½	—	½0	½	1	½1	½1	1	.	1	.	.	½	1	½	.	1	.	1	.	11½
3 L. Steiner	½	½1	—	0	½	1½	½½	½	.	1	.	.	1	1	1	.	1	.	1.	.	11½
4 Asztalos	0½	½	1	—	½½	½	0	½½	½	.	1	1	.	.	.	1	.	½	.	1	9½
5 Kmoch	½0	0	½	½½	—	½	½	½½	½	.	½	1	.	.	.	1	.	½	.	1	8½
6 Vajda	½	½0	0½	½	½	—	1½	1	.	½	.	.	½	1	1	.	½	.	.	.	8½
7 Ahues	½	½0	½½	1	½	0½	—	½	.	½	.	.	½	.	1	.	1	.	1	.	8½
8 Gilg	½½	0	½	½½	½½	0	½	—	½	.	½	½	.	.	.	1	.	1	.	½	8
9 Tartakower	0	.	.	½	½	.	.	½	—	½	½½	½1	1	1	½	0½	.	1	.	1	9½
10 Grünfeld	.	0	0	.	.	½	½	.	½	—	½	½	1½	½1	½½	½	½	.	1	.	8½
11 Takacs	0	.	.	0	½	.	.	½	½½	½	—	10	0	1	1	½½	.	1	.	½	8
12 Yates	0	.	.	0	0	.	.	½	½0	½	01	—	1	½	1	01	.	1	.	1	8
13 Berndtsson	.	½	0	.	.	½	½	.	0	0½	1	0	—	01	01	1	½	.	½	.	7
14 Vukovic	.	0	0	.	.	0	1	.	0	½0	0	½	10	—	01	1	0	.	1	.	6
15 Colle	.	½	0	.	.	0	0	.	½	½½	0	0	10	10	—	0	1	.	1	.	6
16 Brinckmann	0	.	.	0	0	.	.	0	1½	½	½½	10	0	0	1	—	0	0	.	1	6
17 Przepiorka	.	0	0	.	.	½	0	.	.	½	.	.	½	1	0	.	—	.	0	.	2½
18 Müller	0	.	.	½	½	.	.	0	0	.	0	0	.	.	.	1	0	—	.	½	2½
19 Szekely	.	0	0	.	.	1	0	.	.	0	.	.	½	0	0	.	1	.	—	.	2½
20 Sarkozy	0	.	.	0	0	.	.	½	0	.	½	0	.	.	.	0	.	½	.	—	1½

LONDON, July 18–30, 1927

	1	2	3	4	5	6	7	8	9	10	11	12	
1 Nimzowitsch	–	1	0	½	1	½	0	1	1	1	1	1	8
2 Tartakower	0	–	½	½	1	1	1	½	½	1	1	1	8
3 Marshall	1	½	–	½	½	½	½	1	1	1	½	½	7½
4 Vidmar	½	½	½	–	1	0	0	1	1	½	1	1	7
5 Bogoljubow	0	0	½	0	–	1	1	½	½	1	1	1	6½
6 Réti	½	0	½	1	0	–	1	½	1	0	½	½	5½
7 Winter	1	0	½	1	0	0	–	½	1	1	½	0	5½
8 Colle	0	½	0	0	½	½	½	–	½	0	1	1	4½
9 Buerger	0	½	0	0	½	0	0	½	–	1	0	1	3½
10 Thomas	0	0	0	½	0	1	0	1	0	–	1	0	3½
11 Yates	0	0	½	0	0	½	½	0	1	0	–	1	3½
12 Fairhurst	0	0	½	0	0	½	1	0	0	1	0	–	3

NIENDORF, 1927

	1	2	3	4	5	6	7	8	
1 Nimzowitsch	–	½	½	1	½	1	1	1	5½
2 Tartakower	½	–	½	1	½	1	1	1	5½
3 Colle	½	½	–	½	½	½	½	1	4
4 Ahues	0	0	½	–	½	½	1	1	3½
5 Kostic	½	½	½	½	–	0	1	½	3½
6 Brinckmann	0	0	½	½	1	–	0	1	3
7 Kmoch	0	0	½	0	0	1	–	½	2
8 Steiner	0	0	0	0	½	0	½	–	1

LONDON, Imperial Chess Club, October 10–24, 1927

	1	2	3	4	5	6	
1 Nimzowitsch	—	1½	1½	11	½1	11	8½
2 Yates	½0	—	½½	10	11	11	6½
3 Winter	0½	½½	—	10	11	01	5½
4 Buerger	00	01	01	—	1½	11	5½
5 Goldstein	½0	00	00	0½	—	1½	2½
6 Morrison	00	00	10	00	0½	—	1½

BERLIN, Berliner Schachgesellschaft, February, 1928

		1	2	3	4	5	6	7	8	9	10	11	12	13	14	
1	Nimzowitsch	–	½	½	½	1	1	½	0	1	1	1	1	1	1	10
2	Bogoljubow	½	–	½	1	1	1	1	0	1	½	½	½	1	1	9½
3	Tartakower	½	½	–	1	1	½	1	0	½	½	1	½	½	½	8
4	P. Johner	½	0	0	–	½	½	½	1	1	1	1	1	½	0	7½
5	Helling	0	0	0	½	–	1	0	1	½	1	1	0	1	1	7
6	Brinckmann	0	0	½	½	0	–	1	½	½	½	1	1	½	½	6½
7	Réti	½	0	0	½	1	0	–	0	½	1	½	1	1	½	6½
8	L. Steiner	1	1	1	0	0	½	1	–	½	½	0	0	½	½	6½
9	Ahues	0	0	½	0	½	½	½	½	–	½	½	1	½	1	6
10	Sämisch	0	½	½	0	0	½	0	½	½	–	½	1	1	1	6
11	Leonhardt	0	½	0	0	0	0	½	1	½	½	–	0	1	½	4½
12	Schlage	0	½	½	0	1	0	0	1	0	0	1	–	0	½	4½
13	Stoltz	0	0	½	½	0	½	0	½	½	0	0	1	–	1	4½
14	Koch	0	0	½	1	0	½	½	½	0	0	½	½	0	–	4

KISSINGEN, August 12–25, 1928

		1	2	3	4	5	6	7	8	9	10	11	12	
1	Bogoljubow	–	0	½	1	½	1	1	½	1	1	1	½	8
2	Capablanca	1	–	½	½	½	½	1	1	½	0	½	1	7
3	Euwe	½	½	–	1	½	1	0	0	1	½	½	1	6½
4	Rubinstein	0	½	0	–	1	½	½	1	1	½	½	1	6½
5	Nimzowitsch	½	½	½	0	–	½	½	½	0	1	1	1	6
6	Réti	0	½	0	½	½	–	½	1	½	½	1	½	5½
7	Yates	0	0	1	½	½	½	–	½	0	½	½	1	5
8	Tartakower	½	0	1	0	½	0	½	–	1	½	½	½	5
9	Marshall	0	½	0	0	1	½	1	0	–	1	½	½	5
10	Spielmann	0	1	½	½	0	½	½	½	0	–	½	½	4½
11	Tarrasch	0	½	½	½	0	0	½	½	½	½	–	½	4
12	Mieses	½	0	0	0	0	½	0	½	½	½	½	–	3

BERLIN, 'Tageblatt' Tournament, October 11–25, 1928

		1	2	3	4	5	6	7	
1	Capablanca	—	½½	½½	½½	1½	11	11	8½
2	Nimzowitsch	½½	—	½0	½½	01	11	1½	7
3	Spielmann	½½	½1	—	½0	11	½0	½½	6½
4	Tartakower	½½	½½	½1	—	00	½0	1½	5½
5	Rubinstein	0½	10	00	11	—	01	0½	5
6	Réti	00	00	½1	½1	10	—	½½	5
7	Marshall	00	0½	½½	0½	1½	½½	—	4½

COPENHAGEN, 1928

1	Nimzowitsch	4
2	Norman-Hansen	3½
3	Gemzøe	2½
4	Andersen	2
5	Ruben	1½
6	Spielmann	1½

RUBINSTEIN–NIMZOWITSCH, Marienbad, 1925
Queen's Indian Defence

1. P—Q4	N—KB3	**3.** P—KN3	P—B4
2. N—KB3	P—QN3		

The Marienbad variation, employed for the first time in this game. Black takes advantage of White's omission of P—QB4 to strike at the centre in a manner not normally available in the Q Indian. If White were to react with P—Q5 there would follow . . . B—N2; 5. P—B4, P—QN4 undermining White's central position.

4. B—N2	B—N2	**5.** P×P	

This capture away from the centre has been criticised, but possibly unfairly, since it does, at least, grant White some influence over the centre in the shape of d5. Anyway, the alternatives are hardly enticing, e.g. 5. 0—0, P×P; 6. N×P, B×B; 7. K×B, P—N3; 8. P—QB4, B—N2; 9. N—QB3, Q—B1; 10. P—N3, Q—N2+ and Black will play . . . P—Q4 with complete equality.

5. . . .	P×P	**6.** P—B4	P—N3

A most powerful deployment of the KB which is not usually open to Black in this defence.

7. P—N3	B—N2	**9.** 0—0	N—B3
8. B—N2	0—0		

Black's strategy revolves around the advance . . . P—QR4—R5, exploiting the slight exposure of White's QNP on the open QN file. The method chosen by Nimzowitsch to achieve this advance is typically complex. In a game Monticelli–Capablanca, played four years later at Barcelona, the great Cuban brought about the desired thrust in his own characteristically lucid fashion, in other words: poles apart from the manner devised by Nimzowitsch: 9. . . . P—Q3; 10. N—B3, N—K5; 11. Q—B1, N×N; 12. B×N, B×B; 13. Q×B, P—QR4; 14. KR—Q1, N—Q2; 15. Q—K3, K—N2; 16. P—KR3, N—B3; 17. P—KN4?!, P—R3, 18. N—K1, Q—B2; 19. N—Q3, B×B; 20. K×B, P—R5; 21. N—B4, KR—QN1 and Black was well on top.

In the German edition of *My System* Nimzowitsch provided a long explanatory note to his choice: 9. . . . N—B3 which, incidentally, grants us an insight into the mechanism of the ambush.

Strangely, this note failed to appear in its entirety in the English translation, so I will take this opportunity to rectify the omission.

'A normal move which, however, has a deeper meaning: one would rather have expected . . . P—Q3 followed by . . . P—QR4 . . . QN—Q2—N3 and . . . P—R5. However desirable it may be to dispose of the isolated QRP in this fashion it is still by no means advisable to announce this desire in too direct a fashion. Precisely in this, in my opinion, resides the chief fallacy of the pseudo-classical brand of strategy; I mean that the representatives of this school went to great pains to carry out, let us say, a certain advance without bearing in mind (i) that there is a thing known as the metamorphosis of advantages, that one advantage can be exchanged for another; (ii) that in many cases the opponent will voluntarily renounce a vital point of his own accord without our exerting any force in the matter at all.

'In our present case White will naturally develop his QN on c3 to hold up ... P—QR5, but will the N occupy this square for eternity? Of course not, since it is striving itself to reach the square d5, and if it were to go there the possibility of ... P—R5 would fall into our lap like a ripe fruit. In any case the N is better placed at c6 than at b6 for White is clearly planning the configuration Nc3, Qc2, Pe4. Black therefore relies on the counter-configuration Nc6, Pd6, Pe5, and ... N—Q5 thus sheltering his QP behind the N.'

10. N—B3   P—QR4
11. Q—Q2   P—Q3
12. N—K1?‡

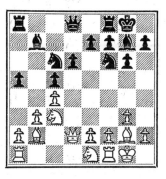

White wants to occupy the d5 square with a piece at all cost (N—K1—B2—K3—Q5), but this manœuvre consumes too much time, and it is from this point that White's difficulties commence. He had to jump into d5 at once: 12. N—Q5!, N × N; 13. B × B, K × B; 14. P × N with chances for both sides. White has prospects of advancing his central pawns and of creating play along the a1–h8 diagonal; Black has counter-chances on the Q side.

12. ...   Q—Q2   14. N—K3   B × B
13. N—B2   N—QN5!   15. K × B?

This dogmatic refusal to reroute his N away from the d5 square is probably the decisive error. Certainly White is quite lost after a further eight moves. 15. N × B was necessary for now White's K wanders into the firing line.

15. ... Q—N2 + !

Acutely embarrassing for White. If he replies 16. K—N1 then ... N—K5; 17. N × N, Q × N and White can no longer hold up ... P—R5 without inflicting a serious wound on his own position in the QN file (e.g. by P—QR4). The course actually chosen by White permits Black to introduce an annoying pin.

16. P—B3   B—R3
Nimzowitsch ironically describes this pin as 'harmless' but his KB ultimately wins the game for him by picking off an enemy N.

17. N/c3—Q1
A cumbersome move, but how else is White to break the force of the pin? Black was threatening, for example, to cause havoc with ... KR—Q1 and ... P—Q4. The text abandons of itself the protection of a4, but it contains the serious counter-threat B × N and Q × P, and if Black were to move his KN then Q—B3 would come into consideration for White.

17. ...   P—R5
Seizing the opportunity to play this thematic blow while he can. Positionally it wrecks White's Q side and White cannot as yet play B × N, P × B; 19. Q × P in view of ... P × P and the QRP is pinned.

18. P × P   KR—K1!!
A brilliant combinative move and the key to the ambush. 18. ... R × P? really would allow B × N, etc., and to retreat the KN (in the interests of preventing B × N) would release all the tension. With the text Black positively invites his opponent to play B × N, but if White does not agree he stands positionally much worse. Nimzowitsch wrote of this preventive combination: 'This purely defensive move (against the aforesaid threat B × N, etc.) is the more surprising, since, after the energetic thrust at move 17, which had been so eagerly awaited for so long, anything but a defensive move was to be expected. This amalgamation of attack and defence stamps the combination as a truly original one.'

19. B × N
Walking straight into the ambush. Rubinstein does not believe in the viability of Black's queer-looking moves.

19. ...   P × B   20. K—B2
Threatening P—B4, frustrating all Black's plans.

20. ...   P—B4!!
The point, which White presumably overlooked when he so avidly doubled Black's KBP's on move 19. Black now has two threats against which White is helpless: (i) ... P—B5, P × P ... B × P with a horrendous pin and (ii) ... B—N2—Q5 with equally disastrous effect.

21. Q × P
Releasing one pin and gaining a pawn.

21. ... B—N2   22. R—QN1 B—Q5‡
Threatening ... N—Q6 +.

23. K–N2
Meekly placing his head on the block. The only way to test Black's idea was as follows, and only in this way do we see revealed the full, profound beauty of Nimzowitsch's conception: 23. R—N3!, R—K3; 24. Q—B4, Q—K2 (threat . . . N—B7); 25. K—N2, R—K1; 26. P—QR3!, N—B7!; 27. N—Q5!, R × P + ; 28. K—R1, R × KRP + !!; 29. K × R, Q—K7 + and Black wins. If 27.

N × N Black could resort to more simple methods with ... R × P + and ... R × N threatening ... Q—K7.

After the text move White loses a piece and Black has but a few technical problems to overcome before gaining the full point.

23. ...	**B × N**	**26. R—B2**	**R × R +**
24. N × B	**R × N**	**27. Q × R**	**R × P**
25. Q × BP	**R × P +**		

27. ... Q—K2 would also have won without too many difficulties but the method chosen by Nimzowitsch is more precise.

28. P—QR3
If 28. Q—N2 then simply ... Q—B1.

28. ...	**R × P**	**31. Q × Q**	**N × Q**
29. Q—K2	**R—R1**	**32. R—QR1**	**N—B2**
30. P—B5	**Q—R3**	**33. R × R +**	**N × R**

Nimzowitsch stops here in *My System* with the comment that Black won. The concluding moves were: **34. K—B2, K—B1; 35. K—K3, K—K2; 36. K—Q4, K—K3; 37. P—B4, P—B3; 38. K—B4, N—B2.** White resigns.

NIMZOWITSCH–ALEKHINE, Semmering, 1926. *Alekhine's Defence*
I would urge the reader to play through this game from the Black side on at least one occasion.

1. P—K4 N—KB3   2. N—QB3
Indirection already. Nimzowitsch avoids the natural and good P—K5.

2. ...	P—Q4	4. P—KB4	P—K3
3. P—K5	KN—Q2	5. N—B3	

In the book of the tournament Nimzowitsch drew attention to the weird possibility 5. Q—N4, N—QB3; 6. N—B3, N—N5; 7. K—Q1 which he helpfully assessed as unclear.

5. ...	P—QB4	8. 0—0	0—0
6. P—KN3	N—QB3	9. P—Q3	N—N3
7. B—N2	B—K2	10. N—K2	P—Q5

A complicated move, quite in Alekhine's style. He plans to menace the e3 square with a knight. Alternatively, Black could have obtained a free game with no weaknesses by means of 10. ... P—B3; 11. P × P, B × P; 12. P—B3, P—K4, which is hardly an advertisement for Nimzowitsch's handling of the opening. When Alekhine does actually attempt to free his position on the K side with ... P—B3 it turns out to be an error.

11. P—KN4	P—B3?!	12. P × P	P × P

If ... B × P; 13. N—N3, P—K4; 14. P—B5 with obvious advantage to White, who has a mobile K side pawn majority and the superb e4 square for his knight. So Black has little choice but to loosen his king's defences by recapturing with the pawn.

13. N—N3	N—Q4	15. N—R4	
14. Q—K2	B—Q3		

Threatening a complete blockade of the Black position with B × N and N—B5.

15. ...	N/3—K2	16. B—Q2	

Instead of this Nimzowitsch later recommended the sharp N—R5, N—N3; 17. B × N followed by N—B5.

16. ... Q—B2
17. Q—B2 P—B5!
18. P × P N—K6!‡
Bringing the White attack to a standstill at the, very temporary, cost of a pawn.

19. B × N
Of course White cannot tolerate the continued presence of the hostile knight in his camp.

19. ... P × B
20. Q—B3

The pawn is immune on account of ... B—B4. It is clear that White will eventually surround the advanced Black KP and swallow it, but even then Black will obtain tremendous compensation in the shape of bishop diagonals towards White's king. Incidentally, it is better to preserve the KBP with the text move than to cover c4 with Q—K2, allowing ... B × P.

20. ...	Q × P	23. P—B3	Q—N3
21. N—K4	B—B2	24. K—R1	N—Q4?
22. P—N3	Q—Q5	25. P—B5	

Missing a good opportunity in 25. P—N5! e.g. ... P—B4; 26. Q—R5!, P × N; 27. B × P, R—B2; 28. P—N6, and White wins by direct attack. In view of this Black would have done better with the developing move 24. ... B—Q2.

25. ...	N—B5	27. B—B1	
26. KR—Q1	K—R1		

In the interests of containing Black's passed pawn White is obliged to indulge in some unpleasant contortions. Black could have tried ... P—K7!? on the previous move.

27. ...	P × P	29. R—K1	B—Q2
28. P × P	B—K4		

Heading for a post on the c6–h1 diagonal, along which White is notably exposed, with no pawn cover and a variety of poorly protected pieces which can be pinned to his king. Alekhine now proceeds to gather momentum for the final combinative assault against White's 'weakened position' and I strongly suspect that almost any other master but Nimzowitsch would have succumbed to the onslaught which Alekhine unleashes.

30. R × P

Material consolation, at least, but this also opens the b6–g1 diagonal for Black's pieces.

30. ...	B—B3	31. QR—K1	N—Q4

With the benefit of hindsight we can say that ... QR—Q1 would have been better, but with the text Alekhine is preparing what must have seemed to him at the time a devastating combinational blow.

32. R—Q3

Black now had to play a consolidating move, such as ... R—KN1, abandoning thoughts of immediate victory. What he plays in the game looks like the kiss of death for White, but Nimzowitsch's play over the last few moves has been expressly designed to parry this most attractive of courses chosen by his opponent.

32. ... N × P‡

Is this the end? If now 33. R × N (which Alekhine surely expected)

there would follow ... B × R; 34. Q × B, Q—B7 and White can resign. But White has a 'truly startling counter-combination at his disposal' (Nimzowitsch).

33. N—N6 + !!
Black falls victim to a grand ambush. It looks almost as if this combination had no 'right' to be in the position at all, especially considering White's next amazing move.

33. ...   P × N   34. Q—N4!!
A piece to the bad, and with a large section of his army tied up by an embarrassing pin, White can still afford to play a quiet move and win. 34. P × P gets nowhere after ... K—N2; 35. Q—R3, R—R1.

34. ...   R—B2?
White threatens mate with R—R3 + and Alekhine fails to adjust to the altered situation. Nimzowitsch suggested as a superior defence: 34. ... R—KN1, e.g. 35. P × P, K—N2; 36. R—Q7 +, B × R; 37. Q × B +, K × P; 38. B—Q3, K—R3; 39. Q—R3 +, K—N2; 40. R—N1 +, Q × R + and White's win is a long way off.

35. R—R3 +   K—N2
Or ... R—R2; 36. R × R +, K × R; 37. Q × P +, K—R1; 38. Q—R6 +, K—N1; 39. B—B4 +, B—Q4; 40. R—KN1 + -.

36. B—B4
Another quiet move, this time to break the pin. If Black replies with ... P—N4 there would follow the beautiful variation: 37. R—R7 + !, K × R; 38. Q—R5 +, K—N2; 39. Q × R +, K—R1; 40. Q—R5 +, K—N2; 41. Q—N6 + and mates.

36. ...   B—Q4
37. P × P   N × N
38. P × R dis. +   K—B1‡
39. R × N
Quite sufficient, but a more fitting conclusion would have been 39. Q—N8 +, K—K2; 40. P—B8 = Q +, R × Q;   41. R—R7 +,   K—K1; 42. Q × B.

39. ...   B × R +
40. Q × B

Ironically White has reconquered the very central light squares along which he seemed so threatened just a few moves back. Black loses now because his own king can find no shelter against White's light-square attack!

40. ... K—K2   **41. P—B8 = Q +**

A queen sacrifice?

41. ... R × Q   **42. Q—Q5 Q—Q3**

Losing a piece, but 42. ... Q—B3 (hoping for some sympathy from the light-square diagonal which was once his dearest friend) would be worse after 43. R—R7 +, K—K1; 44. B—N5.

The game concluded: **43. Q × P +, K—Q1; 44. R—Q3, B—Q5; 45. Q—K4, R—K1; 46. R × B.** Black resigns.

Rarely can the mature Alekhine have suffered such a crushing defeat!

NIMZOWITSCH–RUBINSTEIN, Semmering, 1926. *Nimzowitsch Attack*

1. N—KB3 P—Q4   **2. P—QN3 P—QB4**

Such a move can hardly be castigated as an error, but it does nothing to hinder White's intention of playing B—QN5 × QN which enhances his control of the square e5. 2. ... N—KB3 would have been more elastic.

3. B—N2

Theory states that this move is doubtful after 3. ... P—B3, but in that case, surely, White can continue: 4. P—K3, P—K4; 5. B—N5 +, N—B3; 6. 0—0, B—Q3; 7. P—B4, with good chances.

3. ... N—QB3?!

3. ... N—KB3 would have been less demanding.

4.	P—K3	N—B3
5.	B—N5	B—Q2
6.	0—0	P—K3
7.	P—Q3	B—K2
8.	QN—Q2	0—0
9.	B × QN	B × B
10.	N—K5‡	

We have seen all this before, cf. page 144. Wolf here played 10. ... N—Q2. Rubinstein, on the other hand, is by no means inclined to part so lightly with the bishop pair. The position after 10. N—K5 can be interpreted by White in two essentially different ways: (i) the NK5 can be exchanged at the first opportunity for a Black minor piece in order to de-obstruct the action of the QB along the a1–h8 diagonal. White will then exploit the mobility of his central pawns by massing his pieces in the centre and playing P—K4. This was the course favoured by Nimzowitsch in his games from Semmering, 1926. Or (ii) White can play for a direct attack on Black's king by maintaining a piece on K5 and following up with moves like Q—N4—R5 and R—KB3—N3—KR3. This was the method subsequently favoured by Nimzowitsch and by Fischer! (Cf. theoretical survey, page 74.)

10. ... B—K1

Nimzowitsch (White) against Rosselli del Turco, also from Semmering, diverged from the above with: 10. ... R—B1; 11. P—KB4, N—K1; 12. P—K4, P×P; 13. P×P, N—B3; 14. Q—K2, Q—B2; 15. QR—Q1, KR—Q1; 16. P—QR4, P—QN3; 17. P—B5, P×P; 18. P×P, B—KB1; 19. N—N4, N×N; 20. Q×N, K—R1; 21. P—B6+ = and 1–0 in 57.

11. P—KB4 N—Q2

By transposition (the game actually commenced 1. P—QN3) Nimzowitsch–Sämisch, Carlsbad, 1929, continued: 11. ... Q—B2; 12. R—B3, N—Q2; 13. R—N3, P—KN3 (13. ... P—B3?; 14. Q—N4!); 14. Q—N4, B—KB3; 15. N/2—B3, B—N2; 16. R—R3, P—B4; 17. Q—R4, N—B3; 18. N—N5, P—KR4; 19. N×KP, Q—K2; 20. N×B!, Q×N; 21. R—N3, N—N5; 22. Q—N5, N×N; 23. B×N, Q—R2; 24. P—B4, B—B2; 25. Q×BP, P×P; 26. NP×P, KR—K1; 27. Q—K4, QR—Q1; 28. P—Q4, P×P; 29. P×P, K—B1; 30. Q×QNP, R—K2; 31. Q—N4. 1–0.

12. N×N

Nimzowitsch's analysis of the alternative 12. Q—N4!? deserves a mention: 12. ... N×N; 13. P×N, Q—R4; 14. R—B2 (preparing N—B1—N3—R5), 14. ... Q—N5; 15. P—K4, B—QB3; 16. P—QR3, Q—R4; 17. P×P, B×P (17. ... P×P; 18. P—K6, P—B3; 19. N—B3 threatening N—R4—B5); 18. N—B1, Q—B2 (18. ... P—QN4; 19. P—QR4!); 19. N—K3, P—QN4 ('the typical counterchance: ... P—QB5 must be realised, even at the cost of a pawn'— Nimzowitsch—cf. also Black's 29th move breakthrough in the text of Nimzowitsch–Rubinstein itself); 20. N×B, P×N; 21. P—K6, P—B3; 22. QR—KB1, K—R1; 23. R—B3 (—KR3)+ –.

12. ... Q×N   13. P—K4 P—B3

A muffling device to oppose the activity of White's QB. Furthermore, with his QB on f7 (covering the c4 square) Black is building up fire-power for the eventual advance ... P—QB4—B5.

14. Q—B3   B—B2   15. P—QR4

Hoping to clamp down on ... P—QN4 ... P—QB5, etc. However, as Nimzowitsch states, there is, in the long run, no adequate
preventative remedy against this advance, unless he wants to follow
up with the highly negative piece of prophylaxis: R—R2 and KR—
QR1; but this would effectively eradicate White's chances on the K
side and in the centre.

15. ...   P—QN3

Not 15. ... P—QR3?; 16. P—R5!

16. QR—K1

Also possible, according to Nimzowitsch, was 16. P—KN4 followed by P—KR4 and P—N5. He actually adopted a similar procedure (as Black) against Vidmar the following year in the New York
Candidates' Tournament. [1. P—Q4, N—KB3; 2. N—KB3, P—K3;
3. P—B4, B—N5 + ; 4. B—Q2, Q—K2; 5. N—B3, 0—0; 6. P—K3,
P—Q3; 7. B—K2, P—QN3; 8. 0—0, B—N2; 9. Q—B2, QN—Q2;
10. QR—Q1, B × QN; 11. B × B, N—K5; 12. B—K1, P—KB4;
13. Q—N3, P—B4; 14. N—Q2, N × N; 15. R × N, P—K4;
16. P × KP, QP × P; 17. P—B3, P—KN4! and 0–1 in 29.]

16. ...   P—QR3

Announcing his imminent intention of playing ... P—QN4.

17. P—B5   QP × P?!

Alternatives that came into consideration were 17. ... KR—K1!?
and 17. ... P—Q5!? Not, however, 17. ... KP × P?; 18. P × QP!
(threat: P—B4), ... B × P; 19. R × B! + −

18. Q × P   P—K4   19. R—K3?!

Hurling his rook into the fray along the third rank, but this move
is probably not best. White has created a beautiful strongpoint on e4
but he now fails to utilise this advantage in the proper manner. It was
necessary to establish a knight on this square, rather than the vulnerable Q, hence the correct course was: 19. Q—KR4, P—QN4;
20. N—K4, P—B5; 21. NP × P, NP × P; 22. R—K3, threatening
23. R—R3, 22. ... P—R3; 23. R—N3 with a dangerous attack
against the cramped quarters of the Black king. During the game
Nimzowitsch was possibly seduced by the tactical possibility which
actually occurred, and his conduct of the attack over the next few
moves proceeds in cavalier fashion, with little regard for the defence
of his extreme left wing.

19. ...   P—QN4   20. R—N3

Threat: 21. Q—N4, P—N3; 22. P × P, winning a piece.

20. ... K—R1!   **21. N—B3**

Once again White should have played to establish his N on the wonderful K4 square: 21. Q—KN4, P—N3; 22. N→K4, with a promising attack. The text throws this possibility overboard permanently.

21. ... P × P?

Overhasty. Rubinstein clearly expected an automatic recapture on a4, leaving White with shattered pawns; he must have overlooked the following beautiful stroke. 21. ... B—Q3 was imperative.

22. N × P! Q—K1

The only move. If 22. ... P × P White delivers mate with a pretty Q sacrifice: 23. Q × KP, B—B3; 24. Q × B, P × Q; 25. B × P. Mate.

23. Q—KN4 R—KN1‡

Cramped quarters indeed.

24. N × B + ?

Probably played very quickly in the knowledge that the subsequent capture of Black's front QRP must win. However, with the text Nimzowitsch misses a neat win pointed out by K. Emmerich in Kagan's magazine: 24. N—N6 + !, B × N; 25. P × B, P—R3; 26. R—R3, Q—KB1; 27. Q—N5!, P—R6; 28. B × P!

(Emmerich gave a much slower win commencing B—R1. 28. B × P was found by Alfred Christensen and published in the Danish magazine in 1937—according to B. Nielsen's work on Nimzowitsch in Danish), 28. ... B × B; 29. R × B, P—R7; 30. R × Q, P—R8 = Q + ; 31. R—B1 and Black cannot ward off the R sacrifice on h6. Oddly enough, Nimzowitsch even remained oblivious to this possibility in his published notes to the game in *Chess Praxis* and elsewhere. Chess blindness?!

With such a tremendous concentration of force directly facing Black's king, it is only to be expected that a combinative solution exists.

24. ...	Q × N	27. Q—N6	P—R3
25. Q × RP	Q—Q4	28. R—K1	Q—Q2
26. Q—KN4	B—Q1	29. R—K6	

An impractical decision. After 29. R—K4 ('mit absoluter Brettbeherrschung'—Nimzowitsch) Rubinstein might have taken the hint and resigned. The text plans a brilliant finish, but Nimzowitsch was so upset by Black's next surprise move that he panicked and gave up the idea.

29. ... P—B5!

Rubinstein finds a very good unsettling try. Actually, as Nimzowitsch later pointed out, White can now force the win with 30. R × BP, B × R; 31. B × B, P × B; 32. Q × RP +, Q—R2; 33. Q × P +, R—N2; 34. R—N6, P × NP; 35. P × P, K—N1; 36. R—R6, R—KB2; 37. Q—N5 +, R—N2; 38. Q—B4 (or 38. Q—R5) + - but, in time trouble, White abandons the whole project.

30. NP × P?   QR—N1   32. R—K1
31. B—B3   R—N8 +
Home again.

32. ...   B—N3 + ?
32. ... R × R + ; 33. B × R, Q—R5 was a slight improvement. The B check weakens the defences of the f6 pawn.

33. K—B1   R × R +   34. B × R   Q—R5
Black has obtained decided counter-attacking chances to make up for the loss of two pawns. White's task is complicated by the fact that his major pieces cannot return easily to the defence of his Q side, therefore he 'defends' by throwing them into a final assault against Black's king.

35. R—R3!   R—KB1
If 35. ... R—K1 White can break Black's attack and gain five pawns for the exchange by means of 36. R × P +, P × R; 37. Q × RP +, K—N1; 38. Q—N6 +, K—R1; 39. Q × P + and Q × B.

36. B—B3   B—Q1
Black feels a pressing need to reprotect his KBP, but by this stage his only chance lay in counter-attack. Nimzowitsch gave: 36. ... Q × P/c2; 37. R × P +, P × R; 38. Q × RP +, K—N1; 39. Q—N6 +, K—R1; 40. B × P +, R × B; 41. Q × R +, K—N1; 42. Q × B, Q × QP + and White still has to overcome various technical difficulties.

37. B—Q2   Q × P/c2   39. K—K2   Q—B7 +
38. B × P!   Q—N8 +   40. K—K3
White absolutely refuses to discover check. In fact 40. B—Q2 + might spoil everything after 40. ... K—N1; 41. R—R7, R—B2 threatening ... R—K2 +.

40. ...   **B—N3** +

Or 40. ... Q—B8 + ;   41. K—K4, Q—K8 + ;   42. R—K3, Q—R5 + ; 43. K—Q5, P × B; 44. R—R3! + –.

41. K—K4   Q—K7 +

42. R—K3‡ Resigns.

A highly amusing final position.

Not a very accurate game, but full of ideas and brilliant touches. The brilliancy manqué and subsequent see-saw struggle are typical of Nimzowitsch, as we shall observe more closely from the preamble to his game versus Bogoljubow from San Remo, 1930.

SPIELMANN–NIMZOWITSCH, Semmering, 1926. *Greco Counter-Gambit* We witness here an impressive example of Nimzowitsch's uncompromising approach to tournament chess and also of his courage, for it took courage indeed to adopt the hazardous Greco against so dangerous an adept of the sacrificial, open game as Spielmann, especially when first prize in the tournament depended on the result.

1. P—K4   P—K4   3. N × P

2. N—KB3   P—KB4!?

Of late 3. B—B4 has grown in popularity, but this book is no place for an exhaustive analysis of the modern refinements of such confused and confusing tactical lines. Suffice it to mention that the text is a sensible method of maintaining a small plus for White.

3. ...   Q—B3

3. ... N—QB3 ?! is sometimes played here, inviting 4. Q—R5 +, P—N3; 5. N × NP, N—B3, when the situation is far from clear. Stronger, however, is the simple 4. N × N! and Black will have no compensation for his pawn.

4. P—Q4   P—Q3   6. N—B3

5. N—B4   P × P

As on might expect, Spielmann opts for a developing move rather than the hyper-subtle 6. N—K3, which was Nimzowitsch's own recommendation in this position, introduced in his brilliancy versus Behting, played at Riga in 1919, which continued: 6. N—K3 (the 'Blockading knight' Nimzowitsch wrote of this move: 'Even if all the rest of the world play here 6. N—B3, I yet hold my move N—K3 to be more correct, and this for reasons based on the "system"'), 6. ... P—B3 (or 6. ... N—B3; 7. P—Q5, N—K4; 8. N—B3;

Q—N3; 9. Q—Q4, N—KB3; 10. N—N5); **7. B—B4, P—Q4;
8. B—N3, B—K3; 9. P—QB4, Q—B2; 10. Q—K2, N—B3;
11. 0—0, B—QN5; 12. B—Q2, B × B; 13. N × B, 0—0; 14. P—B4,
P × QBP; 15. N/2 × BP, Q—K2; 16. P—B5, B—Q4; 17. N × B,
P × N; 18. N—K3, Q—Q2; 19. N × P!, N × N; 20. Q × P, R—Q1;
21. P—B6!, P × P** (21. ... N—B3; 22. P—B7 +, K—B1; 23. Q × P);
**22. R—B5, K—R1; 23. R × N, R—K1; 24. R × Q, R × Q; 25. R—
Q8 +, K—N2; 26. R—N8 +, K—R3; 27. R—KB1.** 1-0.

We can only speculate concerning the line Nimzowitsch would
have adopted had Spielmann chosen to play 6. N—K3 against its
inventor.

6. ...   Q—N3   7. P—Q5?!

White decides to surround Black's KP, but, as a result, Black
streaks past him in the matter of mobilisation. 7. P—B3 is more
dynamic.

**7. ...   N—KB3   9. Q—Q4   0—0
8. B—K3   B—K2   10. N—Q2**

Perhaps White had anticipated a Black defence of the KP by
10. ... B—B4, when 11. P—KR3, P—KR4; 12. 0—0—0 followed
by B—K2 and P—KN4 would leave White on top. Instead, Nimzowitsch willingly sacrifices the pawn in the interests of seizing the
initiative.

**10. ...   P—B4!   12. Q—B4 +   K—R1
11. P × P e.p.   N × P   13. 0—0—0**

White cannot capture the KP as yet in view of the defence . . .
P—Q4.

13. ...   B—N5   14. P—B3   P—Q4!

The feeble 14. ... P × P; 15. P × P, B—B4 would react in White's
favour after 16. R—N1.

15. N × QP

White has no choice.

**15. ...   N × N   17. P × P   QR—B1?
16. Q × N/5   P × P**

One slip and the whole of Black's good work is spoiled. The text,
threatening, as it does, ... N—N5 looks most fearsome, but it
grants White a vital tempo which he turns to account by launching a
counter-offensive in the KN file. Two superior possibilities, suggested
by Tartakower, are (i) the alarming: 17. ... Q × P + ; 18. K × Q,
N—N5 + ; 19. K—N1, N × Q with a good position for Black, and
(ii) the cunning: 17. ... N—N5; 18. Q—N3, P—QR4! with the
threat of . . . P—R5.

18. B—Q3

A sure way to lose was 18. P × B?, N—N5; 19. Q—K4, R × P + ;
20. K—N1, R × N with evil intentions against both members of the
White Royal Family.

18. ...	**B—KB4**	**20. Q—B4**
19. B × B	**R × B**	

The defence just holds, since White can co-ordinate his forces with
continual gains of tempo. Here White pins Black's N, while the
White queen's flight on the following turn obliges the retreat of her
sable counterpart.

20. ...	**P—N4**
21. Q—KN4	**Q—B2**
22. KR—N1	**N—N5**
23. P—B3	**N × P +**
24. K—N1	**P—N5‡**

The concentration of hostile force
in the vicinity of White's king suggests
that Black will arrive first, but with
his next move White heralds his own
attack, and this packs the greater
punch.

25. B—Q4	**B—N4**	**30. N—Q6**	**Q × KBP**
26. P—QB4	**P—N6**	**31. B × P +**	**K—N1**
27. N—K4	**Q—N3**	**32. B—K5 dis. +**	**K—B1**
28. Q × B!	**R × Q**	**33. R—B5 +**	**Resigns.**
29. R × R	**Q—B2**		

Nimzowitsch's decision in this game to abandon the style of
gradually unfolding aggression we normally associate with his post-
war strategic formulations represents a throw-back to his youth,
when his tactical flair predominated over any nascent awareness of
strategic principles. Whatever the explanation, Nimzowitsch never
again grappled with Spielmann on the latter's home ground (i.e.
gambit territory). In their subsequent clashes Nimzowitsch preferred
to involve Spielmann in protracted wars of attrition stemming from
closed openings.

Dynamic Chess by R. N. Coles is a book I much admire and which
I can recommend to any student of the development of ideas in chess.
But I have one complaint: in my opinion the author has not been
entirely fair in his assessment of Nimzowitsch. For example, 'Nimzo-
witsch worked out a complete theory of what he termed the
"Blockade", the essence of which was that preventative measures

could and should be taken against hostile expansion, in other words, hostile dynamic possibilities, before one's own attack was launched.'

'The idea of reducing one's opponent's dynamism rather than increasing one's own was much more negative than Breyer's view of the matter, and it possibly explains why Nimzowitsch never quite reached the heights of success attained by more dynamic players.'

But in this judgement Coles overlooked the duality which we have already touched on that exists at the heart of Nimzowitsch's attitude to the art of chess. Not only do we find in Nimzowitsch the elements of prophylaxis, prevention and paralysis, but also provocation to a high degree, the maximisation of the opponent's possibilities plus deliberately assumed postures of 'heroic defence' and invitations issued to the adversary to engage in bitter, obscure and dubious battle, such as the brevity between Alekhine (White) and Nimzowitsch from Vilna, 1912: **1. P—Q4, N—KB3; 2. N—KB3, P—Q3; 3. B—N5, B—B4; 4. B×N, KP×B; 5. QN—Q2, N—Q2; 6. P—K4, B—N5; 7. B—K2, B—K2; 8. N—R4, B×B; 9. Q×B, 0—0; 10. N—B5, K—R1; 11. Q—N4, R—KN1; 12. 0—0—0, B—B1; 13. N—B4, Q—K1; 14. R—Q3, P—KN3; 15. R—KN3, Q—K3; 16. P—Q5, Q—K1, 17. N/4—K3, N—K4; 18. Q—R4, P×N; 19. R—R3, P—KR3; 20. Q×BP+, K—R2; 21. P—KB4, N—N3; 22. N×P, Q×P; 23. Q×P+, K—R1; 24. Q—B6+, K—R2.** ½–½.

Or the following game between the same opponents in which the struggle reached such intensity that it did not come to a halt with Alekhine's resignation—which obviously terminated the game as such—but continued in the combatants' own notes—(Nimzowitsch in *Chess Praxis* and Alekhine in the tournament book of New York, 1927).

NIMZOWITSCH–ALEKHINE, New York, 1927. *Nimzowitsch Attack*
Notes marked (N) are by Nimzowitsch, those marked (A) by Alekhine. Author's intervention is denoted by (RDK).

**1. N—KB3 N—KB3   3. P—N3
2. P—QN3 P—Q3**

So, the purest *hypermodernerei*. In this game it would certainly have brought White no laurels if his opponent had not over-estimated his position and imagined that such a set-up could be refuted by virtually any means. (A)

3. ... P—K4   4. P—B4

'Bizarre!' He does not fear ... P—K5. Anybody else would have chosen 4. P—Q3. (N)

4. ... P—K5

This dark-square weakening move sows the seeds of all his future difficulties. (N)

This move is justified, since White is as good as forced to play his knight to the edge of the board. After 5. N—Q4, P—Q4!; 6. P × P, Q × P; 7. P—K3, Q—K4 his position would inspire anything but confidence. (A)

5. N—R4! (N)

So g2 was not destined for the B, thirsting for a fianchetto, but as a haven for the 'bizarre' knight. (N)

5. ... P—Q4

Leads to a not entirely unexceptionable excursion by the Q, but by this stage there was hardly anything better. (N)

Quieter, and likewise good, was 5. ... B—K2. The immediate clearance in the centre is, however, more consequent. (A)

6. P × P   Q × P

Correct was 6. ... N × P whereby, with the simplest of means, the unsound nature of the opposing dispositions would have been exposed. If then 7. Q—B2, B—K2!; 8. Q × KP, 0—0 with unpleasant threats, e.g. 9. B—QN2, R—K1; 10. B—N2, N—N5! followed by ... B—B1. In that case the ... 'double-hole' opening would once again have been reduced *ad absurdum*. (A)

7. N—B3   Q—B3! (N)

If ... Q—K4 then 8. P—B4 is unpleasant. The text has the advantage at least of forcing the following weakening of the opponent's light squares. (A)

8. P—K3

Permanently renouncing the possibility of a fianchetto. (N) After 8. N—N2 I had intended ... P—K6!, e.g. 9. BP × P, B—R6; 10. R—KN1, N—N5. (A)

8. ... P—QR3

More consistent would have been 8. ... B—N5 continuing 9. Q × B!, N × Q; 10. B—N5, N—B3; 11. B—N2, P—QR3; 12. B × Q +, N × B; 13. N—K2, N—KN5; 14. P—B3, P × P; 15. N × P, 0—0—0 + =. This variation provides an insight into Black's defensive resources: he evidently does have some counter-play on the light squares, and if he plays his none too numerous trumps correctly, he has the chance of neutralising White's pressure on the dark squares. The continuation selected by Alekhine makes the task of defence more onerous without, as yet, rendering it hopeless. (N)

It would not have been at all advisable to permit the exchange of

queens (8. ... B—N5; 9. Q×B, etc.) in view of the exposed situation of Black's central pawn and the possibility of invasion by
White's knight via f5. But the preventive move of the text, which
grants White a vital development tempo, is a clear proof that the
capture with the Q on move 6 had more dark than bright sides. (A)

9. B—QN2	B—N5	11. N×B	N/1—Q2
10. B—K2	B×B	12. R—QB1	Q—N3

Thereafter Black is at a disadvantage and has to struggle for
equality. Black should have played 12. ... N—B4; 13. O—O,
Q—Q2; 14. B×N, P×B leading to a position with reciprocal strong
and weak points. The outcome of such a position could hardly be
predicted. (A)

13. O—O

Here Nimzowitsch recommends a very obscure attacking line:
13. Q—B2, N—B4; 14. O—O, N—Q6; 15. B×N, Q or P×B;
16. N—B4, but he does not bother to analyse the complications.
Presumably the idea is to meet 15. ... N×R with 16. Q×KP+
and 16. ... N×R with 17. N—Q5, N—K7; 18. K—R1 followed
by N×P+. (RDK)

13. ... B—Q3	14. P—B3

Also 14. P—Q3 comes into consideration. The sharp text move
leads to complications of an unfathomable nature from which Black
finally emerges with sufficient positional equivalent for his sacrificed
material. (A)

14. ... B—K4!(?) (N)

The introductory move to the interesting sacrificial combination
which follows. Unsatisfactory in any case was 14. ... P×P;
15. R×KBP, N—K4; 16. B×N, B×B; 17. P—Q4, B—Q3;
18. N—B3 and P—K4+. (A)

Exceptionally interesting! He wishes at all costs to occupy light-
squared terrain (d3). But what does the Logos of the game say to
this? Well, he adopts a sceptical attitude to the whole affair. Where-
fore should the light squares suddenly develop the capacity to
eclipse the dark squares? After Black's lapse on the 8th move his
dark-square weakness had become chronic. White has made no
mistake (for 13. O—O was certainly no error); it follows that Black's
violent, if ingenious, attempt needs must be in some way unsound.
(N)

15. B×B	N×B	16. P×P	N—Q6

A necessary consequence of his 14th move. 16. N×KP was
obviously insufficient on account of 17. Q—B2. (A)

17. R—QB3 0—0—0   **18. Q—N1! (A)**
Now Black is forced to invest more in the business. (A)

18. ...   **N × P!‡ (A)**
No *coup d'état* without a sacrifice. (N)

There was another combination available to Black, but White would have been able to refute it by returning the material for a winning attack: 18. ... N—B4; 19. P—Q3, N—R5; 20. P × N, Q × P + ; 21. K—R1!, Q × N; 22. R/1—B1, R—Q2; 23. Q—N6, N—K1; 24. R—QN1, N—Q3; 25. Q—R7 + −. (A)

19. R × N   **N × QP**   **21. Q—B5 +**   **K—N1**
20. R × R +   **R × R**   **22. R—K1**

22. R—B1 also came into consideration. (N)

Up to now White has been playing forced moves, but now he has a choice once again and it's by no means clear that he selects the best move. If doubt could indeed be cast on Black's positional sacrifice, now was the time to do it by 22. R—B1, Q × P + ; 23. Q—B2, but even in that case Black would not be entirely without chances after 23. ... Q—K2!; 24. N—B5, Q—K4, etc. (A)

22. ...   **Q × P +**   **24. N—B4 Q—QB6**
23. Q—B2 Q—Q6

Black could have retained good drawing chances with 24. ... Q—B7. What would that prove? That the *coup d'état* was sound? Or that dark squares and light squares can assume power at will? No, nothing of the kind. For, in the first place, the draw after 24. ... Q—B7 is by no means assured, and secondly it remains to be demonstrated that White could not have improved on his play at some point, perhaps at move 22; thirdly there are, unfortunately, many positions in which a clearly demonstrable superiority does not suffice to win the game. Victory by baring should still count! (N)*

Only after this inaccurate move does White come to effective counter-play. Black could have obtained a fully viable game by threatening White's QRP with 24. ... Q—B7; e.g.

(i) 25. R—K2, Q × RP; 26. K—N2, P—KN4; 27. N—B3, P × N; 28. N × N, P × P; 29. P × P, Q—R4! and the Q arrives

---

* 'baring'—antiquated rule that a player can win by taking all of his opponent's pieces and leaving him with a bare king. Thus K and N versus K is + −. (RDK)

at d5 with tempo when it will no longer be difficult for Black to force a favourable ending.

(ii) 25. N—B3, N × N + ; 26. Q × N, Q × RP once again with full compensation for the sacrificed piece. (A)

25. R—K3! (A)
Black has overlooked the force of this fine defensive move and now comes in *angustis*. (A)

25. ...   Q—B8 +
There follows a bitter struggle. White wins, but only after many hours of the most stubborn contest. (N)

26. K—N2	Q—B3 +		30. N—B2	P—KB4
27. N—B3	P—KN4		31. R—K2	Q—QB4
28. N—Q3	N × N		32. N—Q3	Q—Q5
29. Q × N	Q—B7 +		33. N—K5	P—B5! (A)

Over the last few moves Black has done everything possible. The following *pawn* exchange obviously signifies an increase in his prospects of a draw. (A)

34. N—B4   P × P (?) (A)
Black had to preface this with ... P—B1 (threat ... P—N5), or ... R—N1, for every exchange of *pieces* is obviously to White's advantage. (A)

35. R—Q2	Q—R1		37. P × P	Q—Q5
36. R × R +	Q × R			

In the long run Black cannot avoid the Q exchange. If Black's Q leaves the Q file (and Black doesn't have many moves at his disposal), then White can provoke new weaknesses with N—R5. (A)

38. Q—B8 +	K—R2		40. K × Q	P—KR4
39. Q—B2	Q × Q +			

40. ... P—N4 offered the last practical chance. But this was move 40. ... (A)

41. K—K3‡
The sealed move. (N)

41. ...   P—B4
The main variation is 41. ... P—N4; 42. N—Q2, P—R5; 43. P—KN4, P—R6; 44. K—B3, P—B4; 45. N—K4, P—B5; 46. P—N4, K—N3; 47. K—N3, K—B3; 48. N × P, P—B6; 49. N—B3 + —. (N)

On 41. .... P—N4 White would have won as follows: 42. N—Q2, P—R5; 43. P—KN4, P—B4; 44. N—K4, P—R6; 45. K—B3, P—B5; 46. P×P, P×P; 47. K—N3, K—N3; 48. K×P, K—R4; 49. K—N3, K—N5; 50. K—B3, K—R6; 51. K—K3, K×P; 52. K—Q4, K—N6; 53. N—B5 +, etc. (A)

42. P—R4	P—N4	45. N—K4	P—R5
43. P×P	P×P	46. P—KN4	P—R6
44. N—Q2	K—N3	47. K—B3	P—N5

A last ingenious flicker of life before darkness sets in. (N)

| 48. N×NP | P—B5 | 49. N—K4 | P×P |

Or 49. .... P—B6; 50. N—B2—Q3. (N)

50. P—N5	P—N7	54. P—N7	K—Q6
51. N—Q2	K—B4	55. P—N8 = Q	K×N
52. P—N6	P—R7	56. Q—R2	K—B7
53. K—N2	K—Q5	57. Q—B4	Black resigns.

A great fighting game. (N)

Nimzowitsch's conduct of this game is to be regarded less as an example of positional hypermodernism than as a display of heroic defence in action. But such an indirect method of conducting the struggle (*à la* Korchnoy nowadays, perhaps) is not to everyone's taste. As Nimzowitsch himself was to write of the contemporary general attitude to such apparently discordant games:

'People still shy away in fear from a mark of attack in their own camp and a decidedly formalistic conception of "defence" still seems to be the order of the day. The timid concern for pin-headed "correctness" of moves and the anxious avoidance of untrodden paths and particularly the fear of the "colossal" (of anything on the grand scale)—how vividly does all this recall the long-dead pseudo-classical epoch!'

And even today do such games gain the publicity they deserve?

A Question of Brilliance

(This game was awarded the 3rd Schönheitspreis at New York behind 1 Capablanca–Spielmann and 2 Alekhine–Marshall.)

NIMZOWITSCH–MARSHALL, New York, 1927. *Modern Benoni*

| 1. P—QB4 | N—KB3 | 3. N—KB3 | P—B4 |
| 2. P—Q4 | P—K3 | | |

'Marshall permitted himself a few extravagances in the openings at New York; an unfortunate affair in a top class tournament' (!) (Nimzowitsch).

The Modern Benoni, introduced with this move, is now considered highly respectable and is often employed by (for example) Fischer, Tal and Matulović. White gains a central preponderance, more or less by force, but Black disposes over dynamic counter-chances in the shape of his Q side pawn majority and the powerful diagonal of his KB (a1–h8), plus the pressure he can exert in the half-open K file against White's centre.

4. P—Q5
The only testing reply. 4. P—KN3 is exposed as very feeble after 4. ... P × P; 5. N × P, B—N5 + ; 6. B—Q2, B—K2!

4. ... P—Q3
Normal now would be 4. ... P × P; 5. P × P, P—Q3. The move of the text was favoured by Marshall, although only as a method of transposition. At this point we might have expected from Marshall the violent Blumenfeld Gambit, which had recently been revived in a game by Spielmann (Black: Kmoch, Semmering, 1926): 4. ... P—QN4; 5. B—N5, P × QP; 6. P × QP, P—KR3; 7. B × N (Spielmann himself recommended 7. B—B4, P—Q3; 8. P—K4, P—QR3; 9. P—QR4, P—N5; 10. QN—Q2), 7. ... Q × B; 8. Q—B2, P—Q3; 9. P—K4, P—R3; 10. P—QR4, P—N5; 11. QN—Q2 (now we prefer 11. KN—Q2!, B—K2; 12. N—B4, N—Q2; 13. N/1—Q2±), 11. ... B—N5; 12. B—K2, N—Q2; 13. 0—0, B—K2; 14. K—R1, B × N; 15. B × B, N—K4; 16. B—K2, P—N4; 17. P—KN3, P—KR4! – +.

5. N—B3 P × P   6. P × P P—KN3
Reaching the conventional Modern Benoni position. It says a lot for Marshall that he was prepared to champion this defence at New York in spite of the criticism levelled at him by all the pundits.

7. N—Q2
Heading for the impressive blockading square QB4. In an earlier round Capablanca had played against Marshall 7. P—KN3 when there ensued: 7. ... B—N2; 8. B—N2, 0—0; 9. 0—0, R—K1; 10. N—Q2, N/1—Q2; 11. P—KR3, N—N3; 12. P—QR4, B—Q2; 13. P—R5, N—B1; 14. N—B4, Q—B2; 15. P—K4, P—QN4 and Black had a satisfactory position.

7. ... QN—Q2
For many years theory was to regard this move as an error, preferring 7. ... B—N2, e.g. 8. N—B4, 0—0; 9. B—B4 (or 9. B—N5, Q—Q2!), 9. ... N—K1 when Black drums up counterplay either with the ultra-sharp ... B × N and ... P—QN4 or the steady ... P—N3 ... B—QR3 and ... QB × N, reducing the pressure against d6.

However, this opinion had to be revised when Fischer, in the footsteps of his illustrious compatriot, Marshall, chose 7. ... QN—Q2 against Spassky in their 1972 World Championship Match (cf. theoretical survey, page 62).

8. N—B4

A more cunning way of playing to reach the position which actually arises after move 10 of this game is 8. P—K4, B—N2; 9. B—Q3 (9. N—B4?, Q—K2!) ... 0—0; 10. N—B4, N—N3 (... Q—K2; 11. B—B4! which was previously unplayable in view of ... N × KP); 11. N—K3.

8. ... N—N3   9. P—K4 B—N2?

A slip. Perhaps Marshall simply failed to consider White's next move. Black should seek relief by means of 9. ... N × N!; 10. B × N, B—N2; 11. 0—0, 0—0; 12. B—B4, P—QR3; 13. P—QR4, N—R4 =, Gligorić–Trifunović, Yugoslav Championship, 1957.

10. N—K3!

A very fine strategic retreat. White plans P—QR4—R5 and then renewed equine occupation of c4 with pressure against Black's position in general (and his QP in particular) which it would be impossible to neutralise. Black could not reply to P—QR4 with ... P—QR4 since this would give away all the Q side light squares, especially b5.

10. ...   0—0
11. B—Q3‡ N—R4!?

The plan inaugurated by the text has come in for a lot of unwarranted criticism. Marshall's idea is not just to deliver mate on h2 but to create dark-square counter-play for his minor pieces. The real mistake comes on move 16. I should point out something else that speaks for the American Grandmaster's choice of 11th move: there is a dearth of good alternatives! (Cf. my theoretical survey, page 62, where 11. ... R—K1 comes horribly to grief.)

12. 0—0   B—K4   14. P—R5 N—Q2
13. P—QR4 N—KB5 15. N—B4

White must surrender his useful KB but in return he hopes to eliminate his Black opposite number, which is the bulwark of the dark-squared defences of Black's king. 15. B—B2 is less good:

15. ... Q—R5; 16. P—KN3, Q—R6; 17. P × N, B × P; 18. N—N4, N—K4! with complications not unfavourable to Black.

15. ... ˙N × B   16. Q × N   P—B4?

This undermining of the White centre looks very promising, but Nimzowitsch demonstrates conclusively that it is too loosening. Black absolutely had to preserve his KB and this was possible: 16. ... B—Q5! when the tactical point 17. N × P?, N—K4! comes to Black's rescue. ... N—K4! is also the reply to 17. B—B4 or to 17. B—K3. Note, however, that the attempt to withdraw Black's useful KB to the less exposed KN2 square fails badly: 16. ... B—N2?; 17. B—B4, N—K4; 18. N × N, P × N; 19. B—K3 with unanswerable pressure against Black's QBP.

After 16. ... B—Q5 White has many ways of preserving his advantage (e.g. 17. B—B4, N—K4; 18. B × N, P × B; 19. N—N5) but it would be an advantage of by no means decisive proportions. After the text, on the other hand, Nimzowitsch creates a winning combination of a rare artistry.

17. P × P   R × P   18. P—B4

Taking away e5 from Black's N so that Black is now forced to part with his KB. In compensation Black obtains counter-chances against White's QP, but that eventuality had been foreseen by Nimzowitsch.

In the English translation of *My System* we read the note: 'The prelude to a complicated attacking operation which was the more unexpected since N—K4 gave a good game without any effort. But for once I wanted to go in for a combination.'

The final sentence, however, distorts Nimzowitsch's meaning. The original German ran: *Aber ich wollte nun einmal Kombinieren.* This should be translated as: 'The point is, I wanted to play a combination', or 'The fact is I wanted to combine.' Since the combination lies at the very basis of Nimzowitsch's attitude to chess this is what we would expect and the official translation of *My System* betrays a misunderstanding of the Nimzowitschian spirit at this point. He was always playing combinations, although his combinative ideas were of a mysterious and rarefied nature which, perhaps, we do not always associate with the normal run of combinations: his combinations were almost ascetic in comparison with the more robust and sensual variety we associate with Alekhine. There is not even the excuse that the 'for once' is intended as an ironic aside because *nun einmal* simply has nothing to do with 'once'. It is a stock phrase which implies: 'this is a fact, isn't it?'

18. ...   B—Q5 +

An obligatory move. Black must force the QB to block the e3 square. If instead 18. ... B × N? then 19. P × B!, N—B3; 20. N—K3, R—R4; 21. P—B4 followed by B—N2 + −. Relatively better is 20. ... P—B5 but Black's QBP becomes very weak in that case.

19. B—K3 B × N

19. ... B × B + ; 20. N × B is obviously hopeless for Black.

20. Q × B

Less good now is 20. P × B, N—B3 since White does not have N—K3 at his disposal.

20. ... N—B3

Or 20. ... R × QP; 21. Q—N3, K—N2; 22. B—Q2 intending B—B3 + emphasising the absence of Black's KB. If 21. ... N—B3 then 22. P—B5 goes back into the game continuation.

21. Q—N3‡

In my early contact with *My System* I found the combination played by Nimzowitsch in this game particularly difficult to grasp, possibly because of its nature rather than as a result of the complexity of its variations. In my early youth I was accustomed to seeing combinations where the attacker forced material on to the defender and then crushed him by direct attack, and not to situations where the attacker invited his opponent to accept material. (The Capablanca–Spielmann and Alekhine–Marshall games which are discussed later are of the first and more usual combinative variety.)

In this position White's QP is *en prise* in a number of different ways and if it is captured White will obtain some compensation in terms of diagonal pins against Black's king. But what if it is not captured? What if Black just declines the invitation? Surely there is no compulsion to take White's QP, the more so since Black is well entrenched on the light squares and White has no immediate threats. If anything, the QB on K3 seems to get in the way of White's attack.

Yet there is a compulsion to accept because Black is, most strangely, devoid of positive alternatives. A possible continuation, given that Black has decided never to remove the QP, could be: 21. ... Q—B2; 22. QR—K1, B—Q2; 23. B—Q2 (the energising retreat!), 23. ... R—K1; 24. R × R +, B × R; 25. B—B3, N—K5; 26. R—K1 and Black's situation is precarious.

Just as Rubinstein was at Marienbad, 1925, so Marshall is here invited to undertake a positive course to which, it transpires, he has no productive alternative, and which apparently is not all that unpromising, but which Nimzowitsch's subsequent subtle play reveals as ruinous.

Nimzowitsch's 21. Q—N3 in this game is in the same class as his 18. ... KR—K1 versus Rubinstein (cf. p. 164). 21. Q—N3 both prevents 21. ... N/R × QP while virtually ordering Black to play one of the moves, just as 18. ... KR—K1 prevented 19. B × N whilst leaving Rubinstein with no good alternatives.

I do not always agree with Fred Reinfeld, but sometimes he does say something constructive. His note to 18. ... KR—K1 in the Rubinstein game reads like this: 'One of the very finest moves ever played by Nimzowitsch. It establishes a kind of Zugzwang over the whole board. . . .' Well, this note, as you can see, could equally be applied to 21. Q—N3 in Nimzowitsch's game versus Marshall.

21. ... R × QP

If 21. ... N × P Nimzowitsch gave 22. QR—K1! threatening B—Q2 and the doubling of rooks in the K file. 22. ... B—K3 would fail to 23. B × P! It is remarkable to see just how helpless Black is after 22. QR—K1. He can hardly move a single piece.

22. P—B5!

The dark squares come to life.

22. ... P × P

22. ... B × P; 23. B—N5, R—Q6; 24. Q × P is highly unpleasant for Black who cannot evict White's Q (... R—N1) in view of 25. B × N! + −.

23. B—N5

Nimzowitsch: 'This move contains an original point which the prize judges probably failed to appreciate, otherwise they would have awarded this game the 1st Schönheitspreis (beauty prize) rather than the 3rd. If 23. ... B—K3 then 24. Q × P, R—B1; 25. QR—K1! and the B must give up the protection of one of the two rooks when 26. B × N wins the one that has been abandoned.' Black is now so tied up by the pins that he decides to sacrifice the exchange. Actually there was little else he could do.

23. ...	R—Q5	26. Q × R	K—N2
24. N—N6 dis +	P—B5	27. QR—K1	P × P
25. Q—QB3	P × N		

Black has adequate material compensation for the exchange, but there is a small matter of mobility differential to be overcome.

28. R—K8‡

Nimzowitsch again, this time even more bitterly: 'Rather crude but easily comprehensible. . . . This sort of thing is what the prize judges usually esteem most highly, while they grope with eyes firmly closed past the more original points.'

28. ...	Q × R
29. Q × N +	K—N1
30. B—R6	Resigns.

And the interesting postscript to this is that Alekhine (who won the second beauty prize) also believed (and wrote) that he should have won the first prize—cf. Alekhine's concluding comment to his game versus Marshall in the New York tournament book: 'This game was declared by the umpire (Mr. C. Mayer) to be the most beautiful of the tournament, but it nevertheless received only the 2nd special prize because the "quality" of the Capablanca–Spielmann game was supposed to be of a higher level.'

Capablanca, of course, said nothing.

Well, the reader may judge for himself, since I now append the bare scores of the other two games. Each one is typical in its way: Nimzowitsch's mystical pawn sacrifice above, Capablanca's sacrifice of a piece to crown a positional attack and Alekhine's sacrifice of a piece to deliver mate. Don't be misled in your own judgements by the fact that Capablanca and Alekhine both sacrificed a piece while Nimzowitsch only gave up pawns. At this level of chess a deficit of 2 pawns would lose just as surely as a deficit of a piece if the combination turned out to be not quite sound.

Don't forget also to take into account the quality of the losers' resistance as well as the victors' ideas.

(i) Capablanca–Spielmann. Awarded 1st prize

1. P—Q4, P—Q4; 2. N—KB3, P—K3; 3. P—B4, N—Q2;
4. N—B3, KN—B3; 5. B—N5, B—N5; 6. P × P, P × P; 7. Q—R4,
B × N + ; 8. P × B, 0—0; 9. P—K3, P—B4; 10. B—Q3, P—B5;
11. B—B2, Q—K2; 12. 0—0, P—QR3; 13. KR—K1, Q—K3;
14. N—Q2, P—QN4; 15. Q—R5, N—K5; 16. N × N, P × N;
17. P—QR4, Q—Q4; 18. P × P!, Q × B; 19. B × P, R—N1;
20. P × P, R—N4; 21. Q—B7, N—N3; 22. P—R7, B—R6;
23. KR—N1, R × R + ; 24. R × R, P—B4; 25. B—B3, P—B5;
26. P × P. 1–0.

(ii) Alekhine–Marshall. Awarded 2nd prize
1. P—Q4, N—KB3; 2. P—QB4, P—K3; 3. N—KB3, N—K5?!;
4. N/3—Q2, B—N5; 5. Q—B2, P—Q4; 6. N—QB3, P—KB4;
7. N/2 × N, BP × N; 8. B—B4, 0—0; 9. P—K3, P—B3; 10. B—K2,
N—Q2; 11. P—QR3, B—K2; 12. 0—0, B—N4; 13. P—B3,
B × B; 14. P × B, R × P; 15. P × P(e4), R × R + ; 16. R × R, P—K4;
17. Q—Q2, P—B4; 18. P × KP, P—Q5; 19. Q—B4!; P × N;
20. Q—B7 +, K—R1; 21. P × P!, Q—N1; 22. Q—K7, P—KR3;
23. B—R5, P—R4; 24. P—K6, P—KN3; 25. P × N, B × P;
26. R—Q7. 1–0.

In the following game Nimzowitsch turns to a baroque opening
variation which leads him, first, into difficulties and subsequently
into an objectively losing position. So, Nimzowitsch 'ought' to have
lost, but let us not forget that Nimzowitsch was not playing with his
eyes closed—the attack was just as arduous to conduct as was the
defence. There was a good deal of provocation in Nimzowitsch's
handling of this game.

SPIELMANN–NIMZOWITSCH, New York, 1927
KP Nimzowitsch Defence

1. P—K4 N—QB3   2. N—KB3 P—K3
'The odds-giving style'.* Black could, of course, play 2. ...
P—K4 in perfect safety, but he prefers to create difficulties, both for
himself and his opponent, with the obscure move of the text.

3. P—Q4 P—Q4   4. P—K5
Transposing to a version of the French Defence where Black will
experience problems in undermining White's centre by means of
... P—QB4.

4. ... P—QN3
'Since Black cannot make any progress without ... P—QB4 I
would try here 4. ... N—R4!? and only after 5. P—B3 would I
continue with ... P—QN3' (Alekhine).

5. P—B3 QN—K2!?
The start of a rather artificial manœuvre designed to seize control
of the f5 square. Black seems to have abandoned all respect for the
hallowed clichés concerning development.

6. B—Q3 P—QR4
Hoping to exchange his light-squared bishop, but White forestalls
this.

---

* Nimzowitsch's quotation from *My System* continues: '. . . to use Dr.
Lasker's expression. Lasker means by this that one chooses a variation which one
considers inferior, with the idea of setting the opponent a difficult problem.'

7. Q—K2   N—B4   9. N—N5   P—N3?
8. P—KR4   P—KR4

'Black's position could, perhaps, have withstood the eccentricities committed so far, since they did not create any irreparable weaknesses in his own camp. However, this frightful weakening of f6— given the absence of any stable and effective strong-points for his own pieces—transforms his situation into a hopeless one' (Alekhine).

Nimzowitsch later recommended 9. ... KN—K2 as a superior alternative, e.g. 10. N—Q2, P—B4, and 11. N—B1 is impossible since the QP hangs.

10. N—Q2   KN—K2

And not ... N × RP?; 11. B—N5 +, but 10. ... P—B4 looks stronger.

11. N—B1

Protecting his KN3 and thus preparing to force the withdrawal of Black's N by means of P—B3 and P—KN4. If Nimzowitsch's plan was to restrain White's K side pawns it has clearly been a failure.

11. ...   P—B4   12. P—B3   P—B5

Or 12. ... P × P; 13. P—KN4!, P × NP; 14. KBP × P, N × P; 15. Q—KB2 winning outright. The advance of the text is characteristic of Nimzowitsch in that he renounces the attack against the frontal area of the White pawn-chain, preferring to transfer his onslaught to the base (c3 and b2).

Furthermore the struggle in this game has clearly been sub-divided into two theatres of war* by the very nature of the pawn-chain. 12. ... P—B5 ensures that Black will retain a valuable spatial advantage on the Q side if White fails to burst through on the opposite wing.

White must have realised that his advantage (and he does have the advantage) was by no means of a permanent nature, in view of Black's Q side prospects, but depended entirely on an accurate

exploitation of a powerful, but temporary, initiative in one sector of the board. Such situations are fraught with tension for the players and certainly create an atmosphere conducive to the perpetration of creative blunders.

13. B—B2   P—N4
14. P—KN4   N—N2‡

A fianchetto of his QN on his KN2 square!

* Cf. *My System*, Chapter IX.

15. N—N3   N—B3
And that is the KN. Black has played six moves out of fifteen with his knights and not yet touched any of his other pieces.

16. Q—N2   B—K2
On 16. ... R—QR2 Alekhine gives: 17. P × P, N × RP; 18. N × N, R × N; 19. N × BP, R × N; 20. B × P, R × RP; 21. B × R +, K × B; 22. R—KN1 + —. This variation is typical of the myriad attractive possibilities that must have been clamouring for Spielmann's attention at this stage of the game.

17. P × P   P × P
17. ... N × RP is positionally correct but tactically faulty: 18. N × N, R × N; 19. N × BP and Black can resign.

18. R—KN1
'From here on, indeed, several roads lead to Rome, and it is really bad luck for Spielmann that he fell upon virtually the only sequence which, instead of taking him to the Eternal City, led him directly into Hell' (Alekhine). 18. N—R7 would have been very strong, with the threat of 19. N—B6 +, B × N; 20. P × B, Q × P; 21. B—N5 neatly trapping Black's Q. If in reply 18. ... B × P then 19. R × B!, Q × R; 20. B—N5 is still decisive. But Spielmann wants to win with a grand combination.

18. ...   QR—R2   19. N × BP!?
And here it is. The text should, in fact, win, but the correct follow-up is not easy to find. Alekhine gives the preparatory 19. K—K2! which maintains the option of sacrificing on KB7, while eliminating any counterplay (e.g. checks on h4).

19. ...   K × N   20. N × P?
The provocation—not to mention the exhausting practical calculation of the variations of the seductive post-sacrifice alternatives—has disturbed Spielmann's judgement. Alekhine mentions four plausible alternatives which White had to analyse: (i) 20. B—N6 +, (ii) 20. N—K4, (iii) 20. N—B5, and (iv) 20. N—K2. The strongest of these is 20. N—K2, e.g. 20. ... B × P +; 21. K—Q1, K—N1; 22. N—B4, R—KB2; 23. N—N6, B—K2; 24. N × R, K × N; 25. Q—N6! and wins.

20. ...   B × P +   22. B—N6 +   K—K2
21. K—K2   N × N   23. B × N   K—Q2!
Spielmann had overlooked this, expecting only 23. ... R × B; 24. Q—N7 +, K—K1; 25. Q—N6 + which is most unpleasant for Black. After the text it is Black who is winning, although he still has to survive a whirlwind invasion of his position. Quite a triumph for

heroic defence, although one must sympathise with poor Spielmann, who had the win within his grasp but a few moves previously.

24. Q—N7 +   B—K2   25. B—B7

Threatening 26. B × P +, K × B; 27. Q—N4 +, K—B2; 28. Q—N6 +, K—B1; 29. B—R6 + and mate, but this is parried easily enough by the resumption of the Black king's march to the hinterland.

25. ...   R—R7 +   27. B—B4   R × P
26. K—Q1   K—B2

The base of White's pawn-chain falls in a highly unexpected manner.

28. Q—R7   K—N3   31. B—N6   R—N7
29. R—N8   Q—B2   32. Q—R1
30. Q—R8   N—Q1‡

Once White is compelled to retreat the end is in sight.

32. ...   R × B

Over the next few moves Black cashes in his material plus in return for a decisive initiative.

33. R × R   P—N5
34. R—N7   Q—B3
35. Q—R8   Q—R5 +
36. K—K1   N—B3!
37. Q × B   B—R5 +
38. B—N3

Or 38. R—N3, Q—B7 with annihilating effect.

38. ...   R × R   39. B × B

Re-establishing material equality.

39. ...   Q—B7!

Avoiding the trap 39. ... R—N8 +; 40. K—B2, R × R; 41. B—Q8 + !, N × B; 42. Q × N + when White secures perpetual check.

40. B—Q8 +   N × B   41. Q—N8 +   N—N2

White resigns. In this case 41. Q × N +, K—N2! is quite hopeless. Black threatens mate and the rook, while the RKN2 defends the Black king from checks.

Those notes to this game mentioned as stemming from Alekhine I have translated from his tournament book, in German, of New York, 1927.

NIMZOWITSCH–KMOCH, Kecskemet, 1927. *Bird's Opening*
1. P—KB4

Nimzowitsch experimented with this opening move at Kecskemet in several games but it never became a great favourite with him. On those occasions when he did resort to P—KB4 it was normally in conjunction with the fianchetto of the QB. Amongst contemporary Grandmasters Larsen is the only notable supporter of 1. P—KB4.

1. ... P—Q4

Probably the most sensible reply which prevents the formation of a White centre with 2. P—K4 and prepares to transpose into a Dutch Defence with reversed colours. We will never know, unfortunately, what Nimzowitsch had in mind against the From Gambit 1. ... P—K4!?; 2. P × P, P—Q3.

2. N—KB3   N—KB3   3. P—K3   B—N5

It seems to me an inflexible procedure to give up the QB at so early a stage of the game. I would have preferred here 3. ... P—KN3, e.g. 4. B—K2, B—N2; 5. 0—0, 0—0 when Black retains the option of fianchettoing his QB or of playing it to KN5 under more favourable circumstances, i.e. in a situation where White can no longer recapture on f3 with his queen and no longer has the possibility of 0—0—0 at his disposal.

Kmoch conducts the whole opening as if bishops were anathema to him, and exchanges his bishops for enemy knights at every available opportunity. Perhaps he was aware of Nimzowitsch's predilection for the knight, the more complex of the two minor pieces, and therefore decided as a matter of policy to 'saddle' him with the bishop pair.

4. P—KR3   B × N   6. N—B3   P—K3
5. Q × B   QN—Q2   7 P—KN4!

This space-gaining idea was not a new one for Nimzowitsch and it is worthwhile to quote here the analogous opening of Nimzowitsch's game with Grünfeld (who commanded the Black pieces) from Marienbad, 1925: 1. P—K3, N—KB3; 2. P—KB4, P—Q4; 3. N—KB3, B—N5; 4. P—QN3, QN—Q2; 5. B—N2, P—K3; 6. P—B4, B—K2; 7. P—KR3, B × N; 8. Q × B, 0—0; 9. P—KN4!, N—K5; 10. P—N5, P—QB3; 11. P—Q3, Q—R4 +; 12. K—K2, N—Q3; 13. B—B3, Q—N3; 14. P—KR4, N—KB4; 15. B—R3, P—Q5; 16. B × N, QP × B; 17. B × P + (17. B—R3!?, P—B7; 18. N—Q2, B—R6 is also a reasonable sacrificial possibility), 17. ... K × B; 18. N × P, Q—R4; 19. N—K4 with two good pawns for a piece. After many vicissitudes Nimzowitsch won on move 45. The influence of Nimzowitsch's original strategy in this game can be traced in

Planinc–Hartoch, Wijk aan Zee, 1973: 1. P—QN3, P—Q4; 2. B—N2, B—N5; 3. P—KR3, B—R4; 4. N—KB3, N—Q2; 5. P—K3, P—QB3; 6. P—Q3, B × N; 7. Q × B, KN—B3; 8. P—KN4, P—K4; 9. P—N5, N—KN1; 10. P—KR4, B—N5 + ; 11. K—K2!, N—K2; 12. B—KR3 ± .

7. ... B—N5
Consistent at least.

8. P—N5 B × N	**10. P—Q3 N—Q3**
9. NP × B N—K5	

Or 10. ... N × BP; 11. B—QN2 regaining the pawn with much the better game.

11. P—B4 P—QB3
Strategically correct in that Black seeks to blot White's bishops out of the game.

12. P—K4?
White wants to open up the position for his bishops at all costs, therefore he does not object to the resulting isolation of his QBP's. However, the text is oversharp and White should have contented himself with 12. B—K2, intending P—K4 at a later date.

12. ... P × KP
13. P × P P—KB4?‡
The point of this move is to bring his Q to the f5 square with pressure against White's KBP, but it turns out that White's KBP is by no means essential to the economy of his war effort and can therefore be abandoned. The disastrous side-effect of ... P—KB4 is to create a horrible weakness at e6, upon which Nimzowitsch is quick to seize. 13. ... Q—B2, keeping the position closed and protecting the NQ3, was relatively better, although White still stands well after 14. B—QN2. Best of all, though, was 13. ... N—B4! threatening White's KP and in addition 14. ... N × BP and ... Q—Q5. This would have exposed the defects of 12. P—K4.

14. P × P Q—R4 +	**16. 0—0—0 0—0—0**
15. B—Q2 Q × BP	

16. ... 0—0 would be unhealthy after 17. P—KR4 followed by B—Q3 or B—R3.

17. B—B3

The bishops go to work. This move embodies a dual threat against Black's NQ3 and his KNP, so the reply is virtually forced.

17. ...	**N—K1**	**20. Q × Q**	**R × Q**
18. P—KR4!	**R—B1**	**21. B × KP**	
19. B—R3	**Q × KBP +**		

Black is already quite lost and Nimzowitsch despatches him with a few swift strokes. Now that Black's central pawns have been swept away (partly Black's own doing—13. ... P—KB4?) there remains no barricade to hinder the deadly mechanism of the bishop pair on the open board.

After 21. B × KP White is bound to pick up one of Black's two sickly K side pawns and then the advance of the majority (White KNP and KRP) will cost Black material.

21. ...	**N—B2**	**22. B—R3**	**R × BP**

And not 22. ... R × RP?; 23. B × N + picking up the stray rook.

23. B × P	**N—Q4**	**24. P—R5**	**K—B2**

To unpin, not that it benefits him at all.

25. P—N6!	**P × P**	**26. B × N**	**P × P**

Sheer desperation. Black could just as well resign here. If he recaptures on Q2 (26. ... R × B/; 26. ... K × B), then 27. P—R6! is decisive. **27. B—K6, P—R5; 28. B—K5 +, K—N3; 29. B—Q4 +, K—N4; 30. R × P, P—B4; 31. B—B2.** Black now allows himself a final jest before capitulation: **31. ... R × P + ; 32. K × R, N—K6 + ; 33. B × N!** Black resigns.

We do not normally think of Nimzowitsch as a great artist with the bishop pair. Usually, and there are examples *passim* in this volume, we can see Nimzowitsch at the head of a cavalry charge directed against the hostile clergy. In *My System* he does indeed pay lip-service to the convention of the bishop pair (why does nobody ever talk about the knight pair?) yet the doubts are there: 'The two bishops are, in the hands of a skilful fighter, a terrible weapon, yet I confess that for a moment I dallied with the blasphemous thought of omitting them from any detailed examination in my book.' And from a further comment he lets slip it's clear which side Nimzowitsch is really on: 'Nevertheless, the reader has naturally the right to expect that I should enlighten him, as far as I can, on the dangers in which a pair of enemy bishops may involve him.' 'Enemy bishops'! 'We' over-protect, 'we' restrain, 'we' blockade and 'we' even defend heroically (i.e. 'we' provoke the enemy) but it is the enemy who has the bishop pair in his oily grasp. And, sure enough, the two classic examples of bishops beating knights chosen by Nimzowitsch to illustrate the 'two bishops' theme are famous wins by the arch-demon of pseudo-classicism himself—Dr. Tarrasch. Nimzowitsch must have experienced a profound sympathy for Kmoch after the conclusion of their game above.

NIMZOWITSCH–MORRISON, London, Imperial Chess Club, 1927
Nimzowitsch Attack (transposing to King's Indian Defence)

1. P—QN3 P—KN3

After Nimzowitsch's numerous successes between 1923 and 1927 against opponents who reacted dogmatically to 1. P—QN3 (or 1. N—KB3 and 2. P—QN3) with 1. ... P—Q4 and 2. ... P—QB4 the defence (viewed as an abstract entity) began to realise that it was probably more advisable to play ... P—Q3 rather than ... P—Q4. This way Black could exert some kind of counter-grip on the e5 square and blunt the power of White's QB in general. As a result of this new strategic insight novel methods were evolved for Black to escape from the stereotyped attempts to impose a White structure on a Black position which we saw coming to grief in Nimzowitsch's games versus Wolf, Rosselli del Turco, Rubinstein (Semmering, 1926) and Spielmann (New York, 1927).

At the great London International Tournament, just preceding the double-round event in which the present game was played, Winter (as Black) surprised Nimzowitsch with (1. P—QN3) **1. ... P—K4; 2. B—N2, P—KB3!?** when there followed: **3. P—K4** (3. P—QB4!?), **3. ... B—B4** (3. ... P—B3; 4. P—KB4, P×P; 5. N—KR3, Q—K2; 6. N—B3, P—Q4; 7. N×BP, P—Q5; 8. N/3—K2, Q×P; 9. B×P+ =, Larsen–Martinez, San Juan, 1969); **4. B—B4, N—K2; 5. Q—R5+, P—N3; 6. Q—B3, QN—B3; 7. N—K2, R—B1; 8. P—KN4, P—B4!; 9. NP×P, P—Q4; 10. P×QP, R×P; 11. Q—K4, N—N5; 12. N/1—B3, B×P+; 13. K—Q1, P—B3; 14. P×P, P×P; 15. B—R3, N/2—Q4,** and Black eventually won.

A further example of new methods (this time going disastrously wrong) can be seen in Nimzowitsch's encounter with the Swiss Master Dr. H. Joss from Zürich, 1934. This game was, in fact, the last one to be won by Nimzowitsch in a great international tournament, so it is of some historical, as well as intrinsic, interest: White: Nimzowitsch–Black: Joss: **1. N—KB3, N—KB3; 2. P—QN3, P—QN3; 3. P—N3, B—N2; 4. B—QN2, P—Q3; 5. B—N2, QN—Q2; 6. 0—0, P—N3; 7. P—B4, B—N2; 8. N—B3, N—K5; 9. Q—B2, N×N; 10. B×N, B×B; 11. Q×B, 0—0; 12. KR—K1, N—B3** (Alekhine suggested ... P—K3 and ... Q—B3 to contest the dark squares); **13. P—Q4, P—K3; 14. P—QN4, Q—K2** (... N—K5! and ... P—KB4); **15. P—QR4, KR—B1; 16. P—R5, P—QR3;**

17. KR—QB1, N—Q2; 18. Q—K3 (hovering like a vulture over the dark squares around the enemy king), **18. ... P×P; 19. R×P, P—QB4; 20. NP×P, P×P; 21. P—Q5, R—K1; 22. R—N1, QR—N1; 23. P×P, P×P; 24. N—K5, B×B; 25. R×R, N×R; 26. K×B, Q—N2+; 27. P—B3, R—QB1; 28. N—N4, Q—B3; 29. Q—K5, P—R4; 30. N—B6+, K—B2; 31. N—K4, N—Q2; 32. N—Q6+, K—K2; 33. N×R+, Q×N; 34. Q—N7+, K—Q3; 35. Q×P, N—K4; 36. Q—N1.** 1–0. An elegant victory.

2. B—N2   N—KB3   4. B—N2   P—Q3
3. P—N3   B—N2   5. P—Q4
Nimzowitsch is not going to allow ... P—K4 without a struggle. On 5. ... P—K4 he intended 6. P×P, N—N5; 7. N—QB3, N×KP; 8. Q—Q2, a method which later found favour with Olafsson and Smyslov.

5. ...   0—0   6. P—QB4   N—B3
When the history of the King's Indian Defence eventually comes to be written we will discover the full significance of the contribution to its development made by the British masters of the 1920s. The text, apparently a very modern idea, was employed repeatedly by, for example, Yates. However, in reply to the displacement P—Q5 these early pioneers invariably preferred to retreat the QN to its original square (b8) rather than advance it to QR4, which is the modern interpretation introduced by the Argentine Grandmaster Oscar Panno in the middle 1950s.

7. P—Q5   N—N1?
Excessively negative. Here ... N—QR4 was possible, e.g. 8. B—QB3, P—B4; 9. Q—Q2, P—N3, and White dare not double Black's QRPs since the surrender of his QB would imbue Black's KB with super-human strength along the a1–h8 diagonal.

8. N—QB3   QN—Q2   10. N—QR4
9. N—B3   P—QR4
An eccentric method of preventing the blockading move ... N—B4 and one which looks rather strange to modern eyes. However, the move is well motivated since the simple 10. 0—0 could land White in difficulties after 10. ... N—B4, with the threat of ... P—R5, P—QN4 ... P—R6! and ... QN—K5. In other words: 10. N—QR4 is a decentralisation of the instructive variety.

10. ...   P—K4
In order to break the diagonal of White's QB, but Nimzowitsch will have none of that.

| 11. P × P e.p. | P × P | | 13. N—K1 |
| 12. 0—0 | Q—K2 | | |

The N takes a trip to Q5.

13. ...   P—K4

Renewing the diagonal obstruction but weakening the light squares d5 and e4. However, this move will be necessary in the long run if Black is going to develop his Q side pieces.

| 14. N—B2 | K—R1 | | 15. P—K4 | N—R4 |

Making way for the other N so that Black can develop his QB. Note how White's isolated N on QR4 impedes the whole process of enemy Q side mobilisation by forbidding the squares b6 and c5 to Black's QN.

16. N—K3	N/2—B3
17. N—Q5	N × N
18. KP × N‡	

Also attractive was 18. BP × N with subsequent pressure in the QB file against c7. The capture of the text announces a more ambitious plan involving a direct attack against Black's king. The key to this attack is the erosion of Black's KP, after which White's dark-squared bishop will develop ferocious activity on the long diagonal.

| 18. ...   B—Q2 | | 19. N—B3 | N—B3 |

More active was 19. ...P—R5; 20. P × P, R—R4, although Nimzowitsch still adjudged the position after 21. N—N5, KR—R1; 22. Q—N3 as slightly in White's favour.

20. P—QR4

Confident of his prospects in the centre and on the K side, Nimzowitsch seals up the Q wing. Nevertheless, he does retain the useful QN5 square for his N with this move, so operations on the left flank cannot be entirely ruled out of White's battle campaign.

20. ...   B—N5?

At this point it was essential to bring up the reserves (... QR—K1) in order to lend increased support to (i) the Black KP and (ii) the sensitive hinterland (square e6). Omission of this precaution accounts for much of Black's coming woe.

| 21. P—B3 | B—Q2 | | 22. Q—Q2 | P—N3 |

If 22. ... QR—K1; 23. N—N5! forcing the unpleasant ...
B × N.

23. QR—K1
Piling up on the KP.

23. ... Q—Q1
Now after 23. ... QR—K1; 24. P—B4 Black could not avoid the
threatened exchange KBP × KP when he would eventually be
saddled with a weak isolated pawn on the open K file. With the text
he is able to answer P—B4 with ... P × P, thus precluding the infliction of structural weaknesses on his pawn formation. However,
23. ... Q—Q1 involves the undesirable side-effect of shutting his Q
side pieces out of the game for a further four moves.

24. P—B4
The diagonal is re-opened by force.

24. ... P × P
25. R × P
In contrast with Black's scattered units White's concentration of
central force is superb. White's position is one of those that create an
impression of optical beauty just as much as intellectual beauty.
Indeed, 'the beauty of a move lies in the thought behind it!' (Nimzowitsch). But Nimzowitsch was by no means insensitive to the possibilities of optical beauty on the chess board.

25. ... B—B4
25. ... B—B4 has two points: (a) it seeks to block the fatal KB
file and (b) it makes way for the Q to go to Q2 so that the sadly
neglected QR can enter the lists at e8. But not 25. ... B—R3?;
26. N—K4 + −. This opportunity crops up on four separate
occasions and the fourth time round Black can no longer resist the
temptation to snap at the exchange.

26. N—N5
A good move. The knight centralises at Q4 whence it menaces the
square e6 and the Bf5.

26. ... Q—Q2
Or 26. ... B—R3; 27. P—KN4, B × P; 28. R × N!, B × Q;
29. R × R double mate.

27. N—Q4   QR—K1
At last, but now White creates an irreparable weakness on f5. If
here 27. ... B—R3 there would follow 28. N—K6, R—B2;
29. P—KN4!

28. N × B   P × N

If Black first exchanges rooks White wins by force: 28. ...
R × R + ; 29. Q × R, P × N; 30. Q—K6!, Q × Q; 31. P × Q, N—R4;
32. P—K7, R—K1; 33. R × P, B × B; 34. R—B8 + .

29. R/1—KB1!

White stubbornly refuses to acknowledge that ... B—R3 is a
threat.

29. ...   B—R3

Why not? He will certainly lose anyway with 'normal' moves,
since the KBP can hardly be defended for any length of time.

30. B—KR3   Q—K2
31. B—Q4
To stop ... Q—K6 + .

31. ...   B × R
32. Q × B   Q—K5
33. Q—Q2   P—B4?‡

This results in the decentralisation
of Black's Q followed by instant loss
of the game. The only chance was the
appeasement offer 33. ... R—K4 to
dam the fatal dark-square diagonal.
But even in that case White wins
easily after 34. B × R and the annexation of the KBP.

34. P × P e.p.   Q × P   35. Q—R6
Decisive. With Black's Q on K5 this could have been prevented.

35. ...   P—Q4   36. B × BP
Threatening Q × P. Mate.

36. ...   R—B2   37. B × RP
Demolition.

37. ...   R × B   38. B × N +   Black resigns.
And the irony of the situation is that White dealt the final blow
with the very piece which Black's whole strategy was designed to
neutralise: the QB operating on the a1–h8 diagonal.

BOGOLJUBOW–NIMZOWITSCH, Bad Kissingen, 1928
Nimzo-Indian Defence

1. P—Q4   N—KB3   3. N—QB3   B—N5
2. P—QB4   P—K3   4. Q—B2   B × N + ?!
Premature, to say the least, but Nimzowitsch played this three
times at Kissingen!

5. P × B?!

Such nonchalance. Why, then, did he play 4. Q—B2? The natural move is, of course, 5. Q × B, as played by Tartakower and Rubinstein in their games against Nimzowitsch. After the text Black's fourth move is justified.

5. ... P—Q3 6. N—B3

It would have been more appropriate to play 6. P—K4, 7. B—Q3, and then follow up with N—K2 and P—B4.

6. ... Q—K2

It is interesting to compare the opening of this game with that of the clash between the same players from Carlsbad the following year (page 223). In their later game Nimzowitsch omitted ... Q—K2 and developed his QN on QB3 rather than Q2. This later method certainly represented a significant improvement over his treatment of the position in their present encounter.

7. P—N3 P—QN3 9. 0—0 QN—Q2
8. B—N2 B—N2 10. P—QR4

A good move which provokes the defensive reaction ... P—QR4 from Black, thus hindering the intended ... P—QB4 (in view of the weakness of Black's QNP) which would have been a useful link in the blockade of White's doubled pawns. In the tournament book Tartakower recommends 10. N—K1, but why should White voluntarily renounce his bishop pair? Interestingly enough, Nimzowitsch had been involved in a similar sequence against Colle at London the previous year (1927), but in that game Nimzowitsch had been White! (1. P—Q4, N—KB3; 2. N—KB3, P—K3; 3. P—B4, P—QN3; 4. P—KN3, B—N2; 5. B—N2, B—N5 +; 6. N—B3?!, 0—0; 7. 0—0, B × N; 8. P × B, P—Q3; 9. P—QR4, P—QR4; 10. B—QR3, QN—Q2; 11. N—Q2, B × B; 12. K × B, P—K4; 13. P—K4, R—K1; 14. P—B3, N—B1; 15. R—B2, 1–0 78, although Black spurned several draws.)

It seems that Nimzowitsch's interest in doubled-pawn complexes was both scientific and partisan in that he was prepared to experiment with them as well as against them.

10. ... B—K5

Criticised by Tartakower who gives 10. ... 0—0 '!'; 11. P—R5, KR—B1 followed by ... P—QB4. But how should Black meet 12. P—Q5!? with the threat of P—R6? If 12. ... KP × P; 13. P—R6, B—B3; 14. N—Q4 is highly unpleasant for Black. His best reply is the blockading 12. ... N—B4, with good chances.

11. Q—N3 P—QR4 12. KB—R3

Planning to chase away Black's bishop with consequent gains in time and space. The knight must be 'unpinned' before this is possible.

12. ... 0—0

Surely 12. ... B × N comes into consideration here. Nimzowitsch suggested 12. ... B—B4 = (13. B—N2, B—K5, etc.), or 13. B × B?, P × B; 14. Q—N5, 0—0; 15. R—K1, Q—K5; 16. N—Q2, Q—B7! = +.

13. N—Q2   B—N2   15. P—K4
14. P—B3   P—K4

All according to plan. White's centre is now a great force, the more so since Black has been unable to organise any pressure against the doubled pawns. White's long-term strategic threat is to improve the placing of his knight by means of the manœuvre: N—B1—K3—Q5, but before carrying out this threat he masses his heavy pieces in the centre. The next phase of the game, played powerfully, easily and on broad lines by White, illustrates just how dangerous a player Bogoljubow could be. Let us not forget that Bogoljubow won the first prize at Kissingen, a whole point ahead of Capablanca.

15. ... QR—K1

As a counter to White's central designs Black plans an advance on the K side.

16. R—K1   K—R1   18. B—KN2   B—N2
17. N—B1   B—B1

Not so much a tacit offer of a draw as a recognition that he will have to answer the invasion N—Q5 with ... B × N.

19. N—K3   N—R4
20. R—R2!   P—N3‡
21. R/2—K2 P—KB4
22. N—Q5   B × N
23. KP × B

Opening up an intense bombardment (hitherto concealed by White's KP) against e5.

23. ... P—KN4?!

Provoking a sharp struggle. At this point Tartakower proposed the positional pawn sacrifice 23. ... P—B5!? (to gain control of the KB file and some dark squares), e.g. 24. P—N4, N/4—B3; 25. B × P, N—R4! (25. ... N × NP; 26. B—N3); 26. B—Q2, N—B5; 27. B × N, R × B followed by ... Q—KB2 and R/1—KB1.

24. Q—N5	P—B5	27. B × N	NP × B
25. B—KR3	N/2—B3	28. P × P	
26. P × BP	N/4 × P		

Stronger 28. B—K6! to prevent Black's next move. After the text Nimzowitsch succeeds in conjuring up adequate counterplay.

28. ... R—KN1 + !   29. K—R1

The tactics commence. If 29. K—B2, N × P! and ... Q—R5 + ; or 29. K—B1, P × P; 30. B—K6, Q—N2!; 31. B × R, R × B; 32. R—B2, P—K5!; 33. P × P, P—B6 winning.

29. ... P × P   30. B—K6

To give up his rooks for Q and pawn would be a disastrous idea. After 30. R × P?, Q × R; 31. R × Q, R × R White's KR1 square becomes a sarcophagus for his own king in view of the possibility of ... R—K8.

30. ... R—N4   31. P—B5

'!!' from Tartakower. The point of this move is to shut Black's Q out of play (there were unpleasant possibilities of invasion by means of ... Q—R6 in the air), while simultaneously shattering Black's Q side pawns. It seems that the text must lead to the capture both of Black's KP and his QRP. If White seeks to distrain upon Black's KP at once with 31. R × P, R × R; 32. R × R then 32. ... Q—R6! guarantees Black ample recourse.

31. ... P × P   32. P—B4‡

Once again White avoids 32. R × P on account of 32. ... R × R; 33. R × R, N × P! Now d5 is adequately protected and White has also opened up the long dark diagonal, thus permitting Q—N2, increasing the pressure against Black's KP. On top of all this Black still has problems with his QRP, though probably that was the very least of his worries. In spite of the mounting threats Nimzowitsch succeeds in saving himself by virtue of a series of problem moves, which indicate in no uncertain fashion his acute facility for exploiting concealed tactical resources.

The diagram position might be set as a problem or study, with the caption: Black to play and draw.

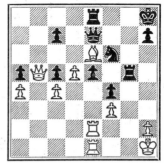

32. ... P—B3!!

A move which truly deserves the twin exclamation marks. If now 33. Q × P (QB6) there would follow:

33. ... P—K5! (expanding pawns); 34. P × P, R—K4 and Black's threat of ... P—B6 combined with the offside position of White's Q grant him a vehement attack, e.g. 35. Q—N5, P—B6; 36. R—KB2 (or 36. R—QB2, N × KP; 37. Q—N2, Q—KN2; 38. R—KN1, N—N6 + !; 39. P × N, R—R4 + ; 40. R—R2, Q × Q − +), N × KP; 37. R × P, N—B7 + or 35. B—B5, P—B6; 36. P—Q6 (36. R—K3, P—B7 and ... R × B), Q—KN2; 37. P—Q7, P × R; 38. P × R = Q +, R × Q; 39. R × P, R—KN1; 40. Q × P, N × P! (threatening Q—R8 +); 41. Q—K3, N—B6; 42. R—Q2, Q—N2 + and wins. If 42. R—QN2, N—Q8 wins.

33. Q—N2
A retreat, but powerful none the less. However, Black's previous move now enables him to undermine the supports of White's QP in such a way as to create a variety of neat pinning motifs in the K file.

| 33. ... | P × P | 35. R × P R ; R |
| 34. P × P | Q—Q3 | 36. Q × R |

In reply to 36. R × R Nimzowitsch had pre ?a td a most beautiful variation: 36. ... R—QN1; 37. Q—B3. It—N6!; 38. Q × R (or 38. Q—K1 when the pursuit continues with. ... R—N8), Q × R and Black, with centralised Q and N against Q and B, holds some positional advantage.

| 36. ... | Q × Q | 37. R × Q P—B5 |

And not 37. ... N × P?; 38. R × N, R × B; 39. R × P.

38. R—N5!
Other moves lose for White: 38. R—B5, P—B6; 39. R × P, P—B7; 40. R—B4, N × P! − +.

38. ...	P—B6	42. R × P	R—Q5
39. R—N1	R—Q1	43. K—N2	K—N2
40. R—QB1	N × P	44. K—R3	R × P
41. B × N	R × B	45. K—N4	Draw agreed.

Black's extra pawn is symbolic. It is of no use for winning purposes since White's pieces are well placed and Black's rook is tied to the defence of his own scattered QR and KB pawns.

A superb duel between two outstanding fighters.

This game took place in round three of the tournament. In the same round Capablanca and Rubinstein played a routine draw and, as his concluding comment to this game in the tournament book, Tartakower wrote: 'After this game Capablanca spoke once again of the encroaching draw-death (*Remistod*) in chess.'

CAPABLANCA–NIMZOWITSCH, Kissingen, 1928 (penultimate round)
Nimzo-Indian Defence

1. P—Q4	N—KB3	3. N—QB3	B—N5
2. P—QB4	P—K3	4. Q—B2	P—Q4(!)

Unlucky Capablanca. In his other games from Kissingen Nimzowitsch handicapped himself at this stage with the eccentric 4. ...
B × N + ?!

5. B—N5?!

A dubious gambit. Modern practice favours either 5. P—QR3,
which leads to immense complications after 5. ... B × N + ;
6. Q × B, N—K5, or 5. P × P, as in the first game of the 1963
Petrosian–Botvinnik World Championship Match, which continued:
5. ... P × P; 6. B—N5, P—KR3; 7. B × N, Q × B; 8. P—QR3,
B × N + ; 9. Q × B, P—B3; 10. P—K3, 0—0; 11. N—K2, R—K1!;
12. N—N3, P—KN3; 13. P—B3, P—KR4, with a fine game for
Black.

5. ...   P × P!

A bold and successful stroke which has put 5. B—N5 out of
operation, as far as opening theory is concerned. Nimzowitsch
recognises that White cannot regain his pawn and must, therefore,
continue in gambit style, which was not, perhaps, quite in accordance
with Capablanca's more serene tastes.

6. N—B3	P—N4	8. B × N	P × B
7. P—QR4	P—B3		

Planning to parry 9. P × P, P × P; 10. Q—K4 with ... Q—Q4,
but Alekhine demonstrated that the apparently disastrous 8. ...
Q × B is also feasible: 8. ... Q × B; 9. P × P, P × P; 10. Q—K4,
Q—N3!; 11. Q × R, Q—B7 and Black has a powerful attack, e.g.
12. Q × N, 0—0; 13. N—Q2, Q × NP; 14. R—N1, Q × N
(c3); 15. R × B, Q—B8 mate, or 14. Q × RP, B × N; 15. R—Q1,
P—K4, threatening ... B—KB4—B7. Black could also take a draw
with 15. ... B × N + ; 16. R × B, Q—B8 + and ... Q—B6 +, if he
so desired.

This suggestion is a remarkable illustration of the resources concealed on the chessboard.

9. P—KN3	P—QR3	10. B—N2	R—R2?!

It would have been more effective to employ the simple defence:
10. ... B—N2; 11. 0—0, N—Q2 followed by ... R—QN1. The
move of the text is ingenious, but somewhat artificial.

11. 0—0	R—Q2	13. Q—R6	B × N
12. Q—B1	0—0		

It is unfortunate that Black has to surrender his wonderful bishop, but White's QN is much too dangerous a piece to be reprieved. If, for example, Black should play the unsuspecting 13. ... K—R1 (intending ... R—N1 and ... B—B1—N2 with full consolidation), Capablanca planned the beautiful variation 14. N—K4, B—K2; 15. N/3—N5!, P × N; 16. N—B6, B × N; 17. B—K4 and Q × RP. Mate.

14. P × B   K—R1   15. N—Q2

Envisaging a change of front the N heads for the left flank, where it is soon joined by further detachments of the White army. 15. P—K4, with P—K5 in the air, was also possible.

15. ... P—KB4‡

To prevent N—K4.

16. KR—N1?

The aforementioned switch of front. However, if White does have any compensation for his pawn it surely lies on the K side and in the centre, but emphatically not on the Q side, where Black holds the superiority. The illogicality of White's 16th move struck Alekhine who recommended the dynamic blow 16. P—K4! as an improvement, giving 16. ... BP × P; 17. N × P, P—B3; 18. N—B5, R—KN2; 19. KR—K1. 'With sufficient positional compensation for the gambit pawn.' In the tournament book Tartakower also considered 16. P—K4 but dismissed it as follows: 16. ... P—K4 '!'; 17. KP × P, R—Q3; 18. Q—R5, P × QP; 19. N—K4, P × BP; 20. N—N5, P—R3; 21. N × P +, R × N; 22. Q × R, B—Q2, 'and Black's strong pawn mass should provide adequate compensation for the exchange'. But this we do not believe. After 22. ... B—Q2 all of White's pieces are in active play, while Black's N has no moves at all. In addition, Black's K is open to the winds, as can be seen from: 23. P × P, BP × P (23. ... RP × P permits the intervention of White's QR); 24. KR—K1, N—B3; 25. B—Q5, R—B3; 26. R—K8 +, Q × R; 27. Q × R +, K—R2; 28. Q × BP, threatening 29. R—K1 and P—B6 or 29. R × P. White must win.

In view of this Black would have been obliged to rely on Alekhine's line above in reply to 16. P—K4! leading to a struggle with mutual chances.

16. ... P—K4   17. N—B3?

It is noteworthy that Capablanca absolutely refuses to plunge into the beckoning complications until it is, objectively speaking, much too late to do him any good. Only when his position is beyond good and evil does he condescend to involve himself in a hand to hand fight. The required course here was 17. N × P!, P × QP; 18. P × QP, R × P; 19. N—K5, R—Q3; 20. Q—B4: unclear, another line which stems from Alekhine.

17. ...   R—Q3   18. Q—K3

Now, in reply to 18. Q—R5, the exchange sacrifice mentioned in the note to White's 16th move becomes more plausible: 18. ... P × QP!; 19. N—N5, P—R3; 20. N × P +, R × N; 21. Q × R, P × P and, in contrast to the similar position analysed previously, Black holds the advantage. White has no passed KBP, no control of the K file and no method of challenging Black's grip on the only open line (Q file).

18. ...   P—K5   20. P—N4
19. N—Q2   N—Q2

With ... N—B3—Q4 in the offing it is clear that White is faced with a calamity of no mean proportion, unless he can confuse the issue. White has psychology on his side in that Nimzowitsch, for the very first time in his chess career, has obtained a clearly decisive position against Capablanca. We can, therefore, sympathise with Black's nervous plight, which presumably became more acute as Capablanca, in clear contravention of his previous policy, started to seek complications.

20. ...   N—B3   21. P × BP   B × P?!

Strong, but not murderous. Alekhine gave 21. ... N—Q4!; 22. Q—R3 (22. Q × P, N × P - + or 22. Q—N3, R—N1), 22. ... N—B5; 23. Q—K3, Q—N4; 24. Q × P, B × P and it is all over. Just imagine, by playing 21. ... N—Q4 Nimzowitsch could virtually have forced Capablanca's resignation in another three moves or so, thus winning a miniature game (twenty-five moves or less) against the Cuban genius, and with Black!

22. Q—B4   Q—Q2   23. B × P

Or 23. N × KP, B × N; 24. B × B, R—N1 +, winning easily.

23. ...   N × B   25. N—N3
24. N × N   R—N3 +

There is no choice but to give up the exchange. If 25. K—R1, Q—Q4; 26. P—B3, R—K1 - +.

25. ...   B × R   27. P—B3   Q—KN2?
26. R × B   P—KB4

In furious time trouble Nimzowitsch falters. Better was 27. ...
Q—Q3; 28. Q×Q, R×Q; 29. P—K4, BP×P; 30. BP×P,
R—B6 – +.

28. K—B2 Q—B3 **29. P×P (!)**
'White captures precisely at that moment when Black has no time
to examine both possibilities of recapture' (Alekhine).

29. ... BP×P?
The wrong one, which gratuitously grants White a gigantic
passed QP.

30. R—Q1 K—N1?
Reaching the time-control. Simpler was 30. ... Q—Q3! which
should still win. (Time-control at Kissingen: thirty moves in two hours.)

31. P—Q5 Q×P?
The final blunder. 31. ... Q—Q3 was essential, and Black still has
winning chances. As we know, the blockade of all passed and semi-
passed pawns is an integral part of the System, but in the smoke of
battle system can be driven completely from one's mind by more
urgent and irrational considerations. After the text Capablanca
exploits his resources in brilliant fashion to achieve salvation.

32. P—Q6 Q—B3 **34. N×P!**
33. P—Q7 P—B6
'The dance on a volcano!' (Tartakower).

34. ... P—B7 **35. R—Q6 Q—Q1**
A blockade less illustrious by far than that mentioned in the note
to move 31. If 35. ... Q×R; 36. N×Q, R×Q; 37. P—Q8=Q+,
R—B1; 38. Q—B7, R×N; 39. Q×BP, with a probable draw,
according to Tartakower. On the whole I think Black did well to
avoid this variation.

36. Q—K5!‡
Threatening R×R+ and Q—N7
mate.

36. ... R×N
Or 36. ... R—N7+; 37. K×R,
Q—N4+; 38. K—B2, P—B8=Q;
39. Q—Q5+ =.

37. R×R+! P×R
38. Q—K8+ R—B1
39. Q×P+
Drawn by perpetual check.

A game in which Nimzowitsch's nerves got the better of his talent. Surely the annihilating blow 21. ... N—Q4! would never have escaped his attention in a blitz game or a simultaneous display, but, over the board, against the invincible Capablanca ...

A strange game this in the way that it splits up into two clearly defined phases. In the first phase (up to move 21) the deep ideas and combative spirit all emanate from Nimzowitsch, and Capablanca's moves hardly seem to have any effect on the game at all. From moves 22–39 this situation is reversed entirely and it is Capablanca who produces brilliant variations and fights a sparkling rearguard action, while Nimzowitsch scarcely bothers to intervene in the proceedings.

I wonder how Capablanca felt about the *Remistod im Schach* after this hair-raising experience?

NIMZOWITSCH–RUBINSTEIN, Berlin, *Berliner Tageblatt* Tournament, 1928. *Nimzowitsch Attack*. (Notes by Nimzowitsch, translated from Danish)

1. N—KB3

Certainly the most solid move, whereas moves such as 1. P—K4 and 1. P—Q4 are both 'committal' and 'compromising'. And, moreover, it was my intention to play as solidly as possible. To play solidly means: I. *Not to give yourself the slightest vulnerable point* (*Blottelse*). II. *Not to allow the opponent to encroach upon one's position.* In particular the first programme is immensely hard to carry out; it requires not only great watchfulness, but also exact knowledge of the character and nature of a vulnerable point. Thus it is not enough to avoid *visible* weaknesses, such as undefended (i.e. not defended by any pawn) pawns or ordinary breaches in the position with forces dispersed and open lines for the enemy.

No, one also has to strive against the *primary* dangers, which can cause the creation of a vulnerable point.

Now follow the course of the game, and you will see what is meant by this.

1. ... P—Q4   2. P—QN3 B—B4

Positionally the most correct method of development consists of the following strategic advance: 2. ... P—QB4!; 3. B—N2, N—KB3; 4. P—K3, P—K3! (not 4. ... N—B3 because of 5. B—N5 with unpleasantness for Black); 5. N—K5, QN—Q2; 6. B—N5, B—Q3; 7. N×N, B×N; 8. B×B+, Q×B; 9. B×N, P×B, and Black has a solid position with a mobile pawn-mass.

3. B—N2 P—K3   4. P—N3 P—KR3

In order to avoid the exchange of the bishop after Nh4, etc.

5. B—N2   N—Q2   7. P—Q3
6. 0—0   KN—B3
There is the plan of P—K4 (after the necessary preparations).

7. ...   B—K2   8. P—K3
Obviously the natural preparation for P—K4 consisted in the
moves 8. QN–Q2 and 9. R—K1. But this preparation would have
led to a vulnerable point in White's position, for a reason which
appears from the note to White's 11th move. Besides, it shall here be
remarked, White must reckon with the advance a7–a5 (after the
consolidating move c7–c6). Such attacks on the outermost flank are
extremely efficacious, but of course only on the condition that the
attacker's central position is ironclad. But there can hardly be
imagined a stronger central position than that which arises after
c7–c6. Thus White must continuously be ready to neutralise the
advance a7–a5.

8. ...   0—0   10. K—R1!
9. Q—K2   P—B3
White *waits* to develop the knight, because in some variations he
counts on its development to c3. E.g. now in case 10. ... P—QR4
comes, then 11. P—QR4, and if 11. ... P—QN4, then 12. P × P,
P × P and now 13. N—B3!.

10. ...   P—QR4   11. P—QR4!
'So it is made clear'! Let us now consider, that instead of P—K3
and Q—K2 the moves QN—Q2 and R—K1 had been made. In this
case Black could now have played 11. ... B—QN5, and White
would not have had anything better than 12. P—B3. But that would
have meant a weakening of the whole anatomy of the pawn-
formation. Now, on the other hand, 11. ... B—QN5 would be
ineffectual.

11. ...   N—B4   13. P—KB4
12. N—Q4   B—R2
The white pawn-formation makes a very reliable impression.
Think, on the other hand, how weak it would have been, if White
had been tempted into c2–c4, e.g. on the 7th move. It is often just
as important to know which pawn move one should forgo, as to
find out which pawn should go forward.

13. ...   KN—Q2   14. N—Q2
After White has given the knight the sum total of the opportunities
that it could be given (he held the choice between Nd2 and Nc3 open
between moves 6–8), he can now with a good conscience let the horse
make a decision.

14. ... Q—B2!
Not 14. ... P—K4, e.g. 15. P×P, N×KP; 16. N—B5, B×N;
17. R×B, N—N3; 18. QR—KB1, and White has good chances.

15. P—K4‡
The advance is carried out, without it being possible to see a shadow of weakness in White's position. Now, by the way, the meaning of 10. K—R1! becomes clear: the diagonal b6–g1 was 'safeguarded'.

15. ... P×P

Otherwise comes e4–e5 with encroachment.

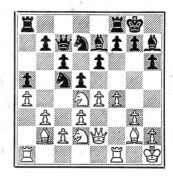

16. N(Q2)×P   N×N   17. P×N
White passes over 17. B × N to avoid the continuation ... B—B3 with certain unpleasantnesses in the diagonal f6–b2. But this watchfulness was not strictly necessary, e.g. 17. B × N, B—B3; 18. B × B +, K × B; 19. B—R3!, KR—K1 (bad is 19. ... P—QB4 because of 20. Q—K4 +, K—N1; 21. N—N5, Q—B3; 22. QR—K1); 20. QR—K1, B × N; 21. Q—K4 +, K—N1; 22. Q × B, QR—Q1, and White's position is preferable. Also on other moves (instead of ... B—B3) White retains a good game—e.g. 17. B × N, B × B; 18. Q × B, N—B4; 19. Q—K3, B—B3; 20. B—R3, Q—Q3; 21. N—B3.
It therefore looks as if 17. B × N could very well have been played.

17. ... P—K4!
A good move. But White is well prepared; no wonder, since his position is, as stated, very compact.

18. N—B3!
Not 18. N—B5? because of 18. ... B × N; 19. P × B, B—B3 with a solid strongpoint in the centre at e5.

18. ... P × P   19. P × P   KR—K1
The pawn on f4 is poisoned (19. ... Q × P; 20. N—K5! winning a piece).

20. P—K5
White's 'compactness' depends now on how the square f5 fares: if Black is in a position to make f5 into a *blockading base* (*Blokeringsbasis*), from there to get control of the neighbouring white squares, then the 'compactness' is about to go amiss. But if White should be

able to wrest f5 from the enemy's hands, then the compactness stays unaffected. White has in the meantime rightly seen that the latter is the case.

20. ... N—B4   21. N—Q4 N—K3
The fight for f5 begins!

22. QR—Q1 N × N   24. B—K4 B × B
23. B × N   B—KB4
If 24. ... Q—B1, then 25. Q—Q3!

25. Q × B QR—Q1   26. P—K6
Very good was 26. R—KN1, e.g. 26. ... P—QB4; 27. B—B3, R × R; 28. R × R, R—Q1; 29. R—Q5! (centralisation), R × R; 30. Q × R, Q—Q1; 31. Q × Q +, B × Q; 32. K—N2. Or (26. R—KN1) B—B1; 27. QR—KB1, Q—Q2?; 28. B—N6, Q—Q4; 29. Q × Q, R × Q; 30. R—Q1 with clear advantage for White. The move chosen in the game has great advantages, but also certain small faults.

26. ... B—B1   27. B—K5
Although this bishop move leads to a beautiful finish I am no longer convinced of its excellence: with the best defence Black could actually have avoided the 'finish'. The objective, both chess-strategical and chess-psychological, analysis of the move shows that the motives for the move not only consisted in combinative and positional (= centralisation) considerations, but were also dictated by a certain master-pattern (= habit), namely by the wish to 'fill the vacuum' which arose after the pawn's 'departure'. (This manœuvre I call 'filling in' (*Plombering*) in my book *My System*.)

But was the 'filling in' here necessary, or could f4–f5!? not have been played instead?

Let us look at that: 27. P—B5, P—B4; 28. B—B3!, P × P; 29. P × P, P—QN3, and now follows QR—K1: the pawn at e6 looks to be both capable of survival and dangerous. The diagnosis is therefore 'good for White'.

27. ...   Q—B1?
Hitherto Rubinstein has defended his game in an entirely capital manner, but now he commits a mistake which enables a quick decision. The correct move was 27. ... Q—K2, e.g. 28. R × R!, Q × R (bad is 28. ... R × R because of 29. P—B5, P × P; 30. P—B6; Q—KB2; 31. R—KN1, etc.); 29. P × P +, K × P; 30. P—B4, and White's advantage (centralisation) is only slight. Now, on the other hand, follows an elegant catastrophe!

28. P—B5!   P × P
29. P—B6   R × R
30. P—B7 +   K—R1
31. R × R   R—Q1
32. Q—N6!!‡ Resigns.
After 32. ... R × R + ; 33. K—
N2, R—Q7 + ; 34. K—R3 the threat
of mate on h6 cannot be parried.

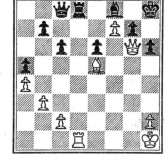

Author's Note: This is the first of
seven games translated exclusively for
this volume from Nimzowitsch's
original Danish by George Botterill and his wife (*née* Birgitte
Vibeke Egan Transø). It is worthwhile recording here some comments on Nimzowitsch's originals made to me by the translating
team: 'Reflection on Nimzowitsch's theories convinces us that one
of their principal functions is to provide an apparatus by means
of which each game can be turned into a drama—more than that,
into a morality play—in which Nimzowitsch becomes a very special
character: an almost invincible crusader, an embodiment of all
sapient virtues. In other words, annotating a game is an "ego-
trip" for Nimzowitsch.'

Two Imaginative Endgames

In his games with Marshall and Réti from the Grandmaster Tournament at Berlin in 1928 Nimzowitsch rapidly established winning
positions, but in both cases he faltered. We will deal elsewhere with
the subject of the 'path to victory infested with thorns'. In these two
games the full point could be obtained only after some refined end-
play on Nimzowitsch's part.

I have decided, therefore, to give the full scores of these games but,
so to speak, to skip over the phases preceding the endings themselves. The final and most gripping moments of these games are
annotated by Nimzowitsch himself, whose notes I have rescued (and
translated) from the comparative obscurity of *Kagans Neueste
Schachnachrichten* for Nov.–Dec., 1928.

(I) MARSHALL–NIMZOWITSCH, Berlin, 1928 ('Tageblatt')
Wagner Gambit

1. P—Q4, P—K3; 2. N—KB3, N—KB3; 3. B—N5, P—B4;
4. P—K4?!, P × P; 5. P—K5, P—KR3; 6. B—R4, P—KN4;
7. B—N3 (7 P × N, P × B; 8. Q × P, N—B3; 9. Q × KRP, Q—N3!
intending ... P—Q4 ... P—K4 ... B—K3 ... 0—0—0. Black
certainly has enough for pawn), 7. ... N—R4; 8. Q × P, N—QB3;

H

9. Q—K4, B—N2; 10. B—N5, Q—B2; 11. B × N, Q × B; 12. Q—
K2, Q—B4; 13. 0—0, N × B; 14. RP × N, P—N5; 15. N/3—Q2,
Q × KP; 16. Q × P, Q × QNP; 17. P—QB3, 0—0; 18. N—N3,
Q—B7; 19. KR—B1, Q—N3; 20. Q—K2, P—Q4∓; 21. N/1—
Q2, P—N3; 22. P—R4, B—Q2; 23. P—R5, KR—B1; 24. P × P,
P × P; 25. R × R, R × R; 26. N—B3, Q—K5; 27. Q—N2, Q—QB5;
28. N(N3)—Q4, P—K4; 29. N—B2, R—QB1; 30. N—K3, Q—B4;
31. R—Q1, B—K3; 32. Q—Q2, Q × P? (32. ... P—K5!);
33. Q × Q, R × Q; 34. N × QP, R—N6 (... B × N!? and ...
P—K5!?); 35. N—B7, B—B5; 36. R—Q8 +, K—R2; 37. R—K8,
R—N8 + ; 38. K—R2, R—N7; 39. K—N1, R—K7; 40. N—R4,
R—B7; 41. R—QN8, P—N4; 42. N—K8, P—K5; 43. N × B,
K × N; 44. N—B5 +, K—B3; 45. N—Q6, R—K7; 46. R—N7,
K—K4; 47. N × NP (47. N × BP + ?, B × N; 48. R × B, R—
K8 + - +), 47. ... R—N7; 48. N—Q6, R × R; 49. N × R‡. And
now, from this position, where most of his advantage has evaporated,
Nimzowitsch still succeeds in extracting the win.

From this point to the end of the
game Nimzowitsch is our guide: 'This
ending naturally centres around the
trapping of the knight; but how to
approach it? The knight is much
more mobile than one would believe
at first glance. Two moves are still
necessary to ensnare it: the king
must first move to Q4 (to prevent
escape at White's QB5) and the
bishop must move to QR7 for otherwise the confined knight will cross
its path as it thrashes its way out,
e.g. 49. ... K—Q4; 50. N—Q8!, K—Q3; 51. N—N7 + but if
now 51. ... K—B3; 52. N—R5 + and the bishop loses his life!
The problem appears to be insoluble after that. Considering the
great initiative the knight conceals in itself (or does anyone believe
it is going to stand still!?), it appears highly improbable, even
impossible, that Black can find time for the necessary improvement
of his retiary. However, the problem is soluble.

With the exclusive examination of the knight's situation the
analysis of the position is not exhausted; how does the pawn structure stand? When considered in such a way, White's position reveals
new weaknesses. The doubled pawns are unpleasant in a pure pawn
ending and so we now try resolutely to force out the knight with a
resulting exchange of minor pieces.

49. ... K—Q4; 50. N—Q8!, K—Q3; 51. N—N7 +, K—B3;

52. N—R5 +, K—N4. If now 53. N × B, K × N, White in fact gets a
lost pawn ending, e.g. 54. K—B1, K—Q6; 55. K—K1 (... K—Q7
was threatened), 55. ... P—R4; 56. K—Q1, P—K6; 57. P × P,
K × P; 58. K—K1, K—K5; 59. K—B2, K—B4; 60. K—B3,
K—N4 and wins.

But after 52. N—R5 +, K—N4 White doesn't exchange but plays
once again 53. N—N7 and the knight still enjoys untroubled health.
And now to the point; the solution is: 49. ... K—Q4!; 50. N—
Q8!, K—Q3; 51. N—N7 +, K—B3; 52. N—R5 +, K—Q4!!
Through the devious manœuvre K—Q4—Q3—QB3—Q4 Black has
enticed the knight from N7 to R5 and if White now returns with
53. N—N7, then the tempo move 53. ... B—R7 is suddenly there!
In the game after

49. ... K—Q4
White played the weaker

50. K—R2	B—R7!	57. K—N3	K—B4
51. P—N4	P—B3!	58. K—R4	B—B2
52. K—N3	K—B3	59. P—B4	K—Q3
53. N—R5 +	K—N3	60. P—N5	RP × P +
54. K—B4	K × N	61. P × P	P—B4
55. K × P	B—K3	62. P—N6	B—K3
56. K—B4	K—N5		

Not 62. ... B × P?; 63. K—N5 followed by P—N4.

63. K—N5	K—K4	64. K—R6	K—B3!

After 64. ... K—B5!; 65. K—R5!, K—N6; 66. K—N5, P—
B5; 67. P—N7, B—N1; 68. K—B5, B—R2 + ; 69. K—N5 the
game would be drawn.

65. P—N3
No better are 65. P—N7, B—N1; 65. K—R7, K—N4 or 65. K—
R5, K—N2.

65. ...	B—Q2	68. K—R5	B—B1!
66. K—R5	K—N2	69. K—N5	B—Q2
67. K—N5	B—K3	70. K—R5	K—B3!

Of course not 70. ... B—K1; 71. K—N5, B × P??; 72. P—N4.

71. K—R6	B—K1!	72. P—N7	B—B2

White resigns.

(II) NIMZOWITSCH–RÉTI, Berlin, 1928 ('Tageblatt'). *English Opening*
1. P—QB4, P—K4; 2. N—QB3, N—KB3; 3. N—B3, N—B3;
4. P—K4 (the Dresden Variation), 4. ... B—B4; 5. N × P, N × N;

6. P—Q4, B—Q3? (6. ... B—N5!; 7. P × N, N × P; 8. Q—B2,
B × N + ; 9. P × B, N—B4; 10. B—R3, Q—K2 with a fully playable
position, Nimzowitsch–Gemzøe, Copenhagen, 1933); **7. P—B5!,
B × P; 8. P × N, N—KN1; 9. Q—N4+ - , K—B1; 10. Q—N3,
N—K2; 11. B—QB4, N—N3; 12. P—B4, Q—R5; 13. N—Q5,
P—QB3; 14. B—K3!, P—Q3; 15. B × B, Q × Q + ; 16. P × Q,
P × B; 17. N—K3, P—N4; 18. B—K2, K—K2; 19. O—O—O!,
N—B1; 20. N—B5+, B × N; 21. P × B, N—Q2; 22. R—Q6,
QR—QB1; 23. P—KN4, P—KR3; 24. B—B3, P—B5!; 25. B × P,
N—B4; 26. B × P, KR—Q1; 27. R × R??** (time-trouble; there was
an easy win by means of 27. KR—Q1, N—Q6 + ; 28. K—N1,
R × R; 29. P × R +, K × P; 30. B × P + -), **27. ... R × R; 28. R—
Q1** (28. B × P, R—Q5), **28. ... N—Q6 + ; 29. K—N1, R—QN1;
30. P—R4, P—R3; 31. B × RP, N × NP; 32. R—Q4, N × P + ;
33. K—B2, R—N7 + ; 34. K—B1, R × P; 35. R × P, N—N3;
36. R—B7 +, K—B1; 37. R—N7, N—Q4; 38. B—B4, R—N8 + !;
39. K—N2?** (39. . K—Q2!, R—N7 + ; 40. K—K1), **39. ... R—
N7 + ; 40. K—R3, R—N6 + ; 41. K—R4, R × P** (Réti defends himself most resourcefully and it seems as if he must draw); **42. B × N,
R × P + ; 43. K—N5, R × P; 44. K—B6, R × P‡** and we reach the
critical position. Over to Nimzo-
witsch now—'White to play and
win'. First there occurred:

45. R × P +   K—K1
46. R—R7!

The sealed move. In order to
comprehend White's reason for
sparing the life of Black's KNP we
must first recall the 'Philidor
position' and the 'Szen position' and
grasp the differences that exist
between them.

(i) The Philidor position. White to play and win.
(White: Kd6, Rg1, Bd5; Black: Kd8, Re7)

(ii) The Szen position. White cannot win.
(White: Kd6, Rg1, Bd5; Black: Ke8, Rf2)

The positions already differ optically in the positioning of the
kings. In the Philidor position their majesties face each other, while
in the Szen position they are at a squint. We need to demonstrate the
Philidor solution before it is possible to understand the extremely
complicated endgame (yet one all the richer for that) which stands
before us.

The Philidor solution is:
1. R—N8 +, R—K1; 2. R—N7, R—K7 (the safest square for the R, and safer, in any case, as we shall see, than the 1st or 3rd ranks); **3. R—KR7** (waiting), **3. ... R—K8** (Zugzwang forces him to go to K8 or K6); **4. R—QN7, R—QB8!** (4. ... K—B1?; 5. R—QR7, R—QN8; 6. R—R7, K—N1; 7. R—R8 +, K—R2; 8. R—R8 +, K—N3; 9. R—N8 +, + –); **5. B—N3!, K—B1** (for 5. ... R—B6 see A); **6. R—N4!, K—Q1; 7. R—KB4, R—K8** (7. ... K—B1?; 8. B—Q5, K—N1; 9. R—QR4); **8. B—R4, K—B1; 9 R—QN4 + –** (A), or 5. ... R—B6; 6. B—K6, R—Q6 +; 7. B—Q5, R—QB6; 8. R—Q7 +!, K—B1 (8. ... K—K1; 9. R—KN7 + –); 9. R—KB7, K—N1; 10. R—N7 +, K—B1; 11. R—N4, K—Q1; 12. B—B4! + –.

In general we can say Black loses in Philidor's position because his king is short of moves and the R can therefore be brought into Zugzwang situations.

None of this applies to Szen's position (ii), e.g. **1. R—N8 +, R—B1; 2. R—N7, R—B7; 3. R—KR7, K—B1**, and for this reason the defensive potential here is considerably greater than in Philidor's position.

Now that we are *au fait* with the classic fundamentals of R and B versus R endings we can return with a clear conscience to my game with Réti:

46. ... R—K8?

Unfortunately this leads to a subsidiary variation. The main line of my analysis occurs after 46. ... K—B1; 47. K—Q6, R—K1.‡

The solution was as follows:
1. R—Q7!!, P—R4!. R moves or a move of the KNP lose even more rapidly, e.g. 1. ... R—K8; 2. R—B7 +, K—K1; 3. R—B2, K—Q1 (3. ... R—Q8; 4. R—QR2, K—B1; 5. R—R8 mate); 4. R—B8 +, R—K1; 5. R—B7, R—K7; 6. R × P and wins the KRP as well without giving Black the opportunity to escape from Philidor's position into Szen's. Or (1. R—Q7) 1. ... R—N1; 2. R—B7, K—K1; 3. R—B2, R—Q1 +; 4. K—K6, R—B1; 5. R—B7, R—B8; 6. K—Q6, if now 6. ... R—B1; 7. R × P, R—Q1 +; 8. K—K5, K—B1; 9. R—KR7 followed by 10. K—B6 and mate; or 6. ... R—K8; 7. R—B2, K—Q1; 8. R—B8 +, R—K1; 9. R—B7 transposing into the Philidor. Finally 6. ... P—N4; 7. R—B6, R—Q8; 8. R—K6 +, K—Q1

(... K—B1?, R—KN6 and mate); 9. R × P attaining the Philidor again.

That deals with the Black R moves on move 1. The only course we have not yet examined is 1. ... P—N4 and then White wins with 2. R—KR7, R—K8 (2. ... R—Q1 + ; 3. K—K5 and 4. K—B6); 3. R—B7 +, K—K1; 4. R—B6, R—Q8; 5. R—K6 + !, K—Q1; 6. R × P with the Philidor again.

After this we can see that 1. ... P—R4 really is the best possible defence.

Now there follows some tempo play. 2. R—B7 +, K—N1; 3. R—K7 + (not 3. R—B5 +, K—R2; 4. B—B7, P—N3), 3. ... K—B1; 4. R—Q7 and now Black must make a move, 4. ... P—R5. R moves or a move of the KNP would lose in the same way as before so Black has nothing left to do but rush his KRP down the board. 5. R—B7 +, K—N1; 6. R—K7 + (6. R—B4 + ?, K—R2; 7. B—B7, P—N4!), 6. ... K—B1; 7. R—Q7, P—R6; 8. R—B7 +, K—N1; 9. R—B3 +, K—R2; 10. B—B7, and wins Black's R.

All that remains to do now (after this exposition of the main line) is to register the actual conclusion of the game, which my analysis regarded as a sub-variation:

47. K—Q6	K—B1	49. R—B2!	K—Q1
48. R—B7 +	K—K1		

The curse of the KNP allows Black's K no rest: 49. ... R—Q8; 50. R—QR2, K—B1; 51. R—R8. Mate.

50. R—B8 +	R—K1	51. R—B7

The spirit of Philidor rises gradually from the grave.

51. ...	R—K8	54. R × P	R—K1
52. R × P	R—K7	55. R—R7	
53. R—KR7	R—K8		

And there he is, good old Philidor, as large as life before our eyes.

55. ...	K—B1

After the normal defensive move 55. ... R—K7 White would have ground out his Philidor.

56. R—B7 + ?

An unnecessary finesse. Faster was 56. R—QR7, R—Q1; 57. K—B6, K—N1; 58. R—R1, R—B1; 59. K—N6.

56. ...	K—N1	59. K—B6	R—K1
57. R—N7 +	K—B1	60. R—QR4	K—N1
58. R—N4	R—Q1 +	61. K—N6	

If 61. K—Q7?, R—Q1 + !

61. ... K—B1

Or 61. ... R—K3 + ; 62. B—B6. With the text move the ingenious study composer Réti hopes for 62. R—R8 +, K—Q2; 63. B—B6 +, K—Q3; 64. R × R??

62. B—B6 Black resigns.

A testimony to Nimzowitsch's prowess in the endgame in his mature years is that these practical endings (plus their variations) could be entered for endgame study competitions with an outstanding chance of success.

GAMES, 1929–1931

The Crown Prince

CARLSBAD, 1929

	1	2	3	4	5	6	7	8	9	10	11	12	13	14	15	16	17	18	19	20	21	22	
1 Nimzowitsch	–	½	1	½	½	1	1	1	½	½	1	½	½	1	½	1	0	1	½	1	½	1	15
2 Capablanca	½	–	0	½	1	½	½	½	½	½	1	1	1	½	1	0	1	1	1	1	½	1	14½
3 Spielmann	0	1	–	0	½	½	½	½	1	0	½	1	1	½	1	1	½	1	1	1	1	1	14½
4 Rubinstein	½	½	1	–	½	½	½	½	1	1	1	½	½	½	1	½	½	1	½	0	½	1	13½
5 Becker	½	0	½	½	–	1	1	1	0	0	1	½	½	½	½	½	1	½	1	1	½	0	12
6 Euwe	0	½	½	½	0	–	0	½	½	1	½	1	½	½	1	½	½	1	½	½	1	1	12
7 Vidmar	0	½	½	½	0	1	–	½	½	½	½	1	½	1	0	½	½	0	1	1	1	1	12
8 Bogoljubow	0	½	½	½	0	½	½	–	½	½	½	1	0	0	1	1	1	0	½	1	1	1	11½
9 Grünfeld	½	½	0	0	1	½	½	½	–	½	½	0	1	½	½	0	1	½	1	½	1	½	11
10 Canal	½	½	1	0	1	0	½	½	½	–	1	0	0	½	½	½	0	1	0	½	1	1	10½
11 Mattison	0	0	½	0	0	½	½	½	½	0	–	1	1	1	0	1	1	1	½	0	½	1	10½
12 Colle	½	0	0	½	½	0	0	0	1	1	0	–	1	½	1	½	1	0	½	0	1	1	10
13 Maroczy	½	0	0	½	½	½	½	1	0	1	0	0	–	½	0	0	1	½	1	1	½	1	10
14 Tartakower	0	½	½	½	½	½	0	1	½	½	0	½	½	–	½	½	½	½	½	½	½	1	10
15 Treybal	½	0	0	0	½	0	1	0	½	½	1	0	1	½	–	½	½	0	1	1	½	1	10
16 Sämisch	0	1	0	½	½	½	½	0	1	½	0	½	1	½	½	–	½	0	½	½	1	0	9½
17 Yates	1	0	½	½	0	½	½	0	0	1	0	0	0	½	½	½	–	1	½	½	1	1	9½
18 P. Johner	0	0	0	0	½	0	1	1	½	0	0	1	½	½	1	1	0	–	½	0	½	1	9
19 Marshall	½	0	0	½	0	½	0	½	0	1	½	½	0	½	0	½	½	½	–	1	1	1	9
20 Gilg	0	0	0	1	0	½	0	0	½	½	1	1	0	½	0	½	½	1	0	–	½	½	8
21 Thomas	½	½	0	½	½	0	0	0	0	0	½	0	½	½	½	0	0	½	0	½	–	1	6
22 Miss Menchik	0	0	0	0	1	0	0	0	½	0	0	0	0	0	0	1	0	0	0	½	0	–	3

SAN REMO, January 15–February 4, 1930

		1	2	3	4	5	6	7	8	9	10	11	12	13	14	15	16	
1	Alekhine	–	1	1	½	1	1	½	1	1	1	1	1	1	1	1	1	14
2	Nimzowitsch	0	–	0	1	½	1	½	½	½	½	1	1	1	1	1	1	10½
3	Rubinstein	0	1	–	0	1	½	0	1	½	1	1	0	1	1	1	1	10
4	Bogoljubow	½	0	1	–	½	0	1	½	1	1	0	1	1	0	1	1	9½
5	Yates	0	½	0	½	–	½	1	1	½	0	0	1	1	1	1	1	9
6	Ahues	0	0	½	1	½	–	1	½	1	0	0	½	1	1	½	1	8½
7	Spielmann	½	½	1	0	0	0	–	½	½	½	1	1	½	1	1	0	8
8	Vidmar	0	½	0	½	0	½	½	–	½	½	1	1	½	1	½	1	8
9	Maroczy	0	½	½	0	½	0	½	½	–	½	½	½	½	1	1	1	7½
10	Tartakower	0	½	0	0	1	1	½	½	½	–	0	0	1	½	1	1	7½
11	Colle	0	0	0	1	1	1	0	0	½	1	–	0	½	1	0	½	6½
12	Kmoch	0	0	1	0	0	½	0	0	½	1	1	–	½	0	1	1	6½
13	Araiza	0	0	0	0	0	0	½	½	½	0	½	½	–	½	½	1	4½
14	Monticelli	0	0	0	1	0	0	0	0	0	½	0	1	½	–	½	½	4
15	Grau	0	0	0	0	0	½	0	½	0	0	1	0	½	½	–	½	3½
16	Romih	0	0	0	0	0	0	1	0	0	0	½	0	0	½	½	–	2½

LIÈGE, August, 1930

		1	2	3	4	5	6	7	8	9	10	11	12	
1	Tartakower	–	1	½	½	½	½	1	½	1	1	1	1	8½
2	Sultan Khan	0	–	1	1	0	0	0	½	1	1	1	1	6½
3	Ahues	½	0	–	½	½	1	½	1	½	0	1	½	6
4	Colle	½	0	½	–	0	1	1	0	1	½	1	½	6
5	Nimzowitsch	½	1	½	1	–	½	½	½	½	0	0	1	6
6	Thomas	½	1	0	0	½	–	0	1	½	1	½	½	5½
7	Przepiorka	0	1	½	0	½	1	–	0	1	½	½	½	5½
8	Rubinstein	½	½	0	1	½	0	1	–	0	0	½	1	5
9	Weenink	0	0	½	0	½	½	0	1	–	1	½	1	5
10	Marshall	0	0	1	½	1	0	½	1	0	–	0	½	4½
11	Soultanbeieff	0	0	0	0	1	½	½	½	½	1	–	0	4
12	Pleci	0	0	½	½	0	½	½	0	0	½	1	–	3½

FRANKFURT, September 8–18, 1930

		1	2	3	4	5	6	7	8	9	10	11	12	
1	Nimzowitsch	–	½	1	1	1	0	1	1	1	1	1	1	9½
2	Kashdan	½	–	½	½	1	1	½	1	1	1	1	1	9
3	Ahues	0	½	–	½	1	½	½	½	½	1	1	1	7
4	List	0	½	½	–	½	½	1	½	1	1	1	½	7
5	Colle	0	0	0	½	–	1	0	1	1	1	1	1	6½
6	Przepiorka	1	0	½	½	0	–	1	½	0	½	1	1	6
7	Pirc	0	½	½	0	1	0	–	½	½	½	1	1	5½
8	Sämisch	0	0	½	½	0	½	½	–	½	1	1	½	5
9	Mieses	0	0	½	0	0	1	½	½	–	0	1	½	4
10	Sir G. Thomas	0	0	0	0	0	½	½	0	1	–	0	1	3
11	Mannheimer	0	0	0	0	0	0	0	0	0	1	–	1	2
12	Orbach	0	0	0	½	0	0	0	½	½	0	0	–	1½

WINTERTHUR, April 12–18, 1931

		1	2	3	4	5	6	7	8	9	
1	Nimzowitsch	–	½	1	1	1	1	1	1	1	7½
2	H. Johner	½	–	½	½	1	1	0	1	1	5½
3	Joss	0	½	–	½	½	½	½	1	½	4
4	Naegeli	0	½	½	–	0	0	1	1	1	4
5	Zimmermann	0	0	½	1	–	1	0	1	½	4
6	Henneberger	0	0	½	1	0	–	1	0	1	3½
7	Grigorieff	0	1	½	0	1	0	–	½	0	3
8	Voellmy	0	0	0	0	0	1	½	–	1	2½
9	Gygli	0	0	½	0	½	0	1	0	–	2

BLED (VELDES), August 23–September 20, 1931

		1	2	3	4	5	6	7	8	9	10	11	12	13	14	
1	Alekhine	—	1½	11	1½	½½	11	1½	1½	1½	½½	11	11	½½	11	20½
2	Bogoljubow	0½	—	½0	11	11	1½	0½	10	01	0½	00	11	½1	11	15
3	Nimzowitsch	00	½1	—	11	00	0½	½½	½½	½½	½1	1½	1½	11	0½	14
4	Flohr	0½	00	00	—	1½	½½	½1	10	1½	½1	11	½0	½1	½½	13½
5	Kashdan	½½	00	11	0½	—	1½	½½	00	1½	½½	10	11	½½	½½	13½
6	Stoltz	00	0½	1½	½½	0½	—	½1	11	½½	½1	½1	00	01	1½	13½
7	Vidmar	0½	1½	½½	½0	½½	½0	—	½½	11	½0	½½	½1	½1	½½	13½
8	Tartakower	0½	01	½½	01	11	00	½½	—	½0	½½	½½	11	½½	½½	13
9	Kostic	0½	10	½½	0½	0½	½½	00	½1	—	½½	½½	01	1½	11	12½
10	Spielmann	½½	1½	½0	½0	½½	½0	½1	½½	½½	—	0½	00	1½	11	12½
11	Maroczy	00	11	0½	00	01	½0	½½	½½	½½	1½	—	½1	½½	½½	12
12	Colle	00	00	0½	½1	00	11	½0	00	10	11	½0	—	½0	11	10½
13	Asztalos	½½	½0	00	½0	½½	10	½0	½½	0½	0½	½½	1½	—	0½	9½
14	Pirc	00	00	1½	½½	½½	0½	½½	½½	00	00	½½	00	1½	—	8½

BOGOLJUBOW–NIMZOWITSCH, Carlsbad, 1929
QP Nimzowitsch Defence
The following game contains very few 'variations', and when the possibility of a variation does crop up, on move 23, Nimzowitsch resolutely ignores it. The impressive quality of this game, therefore, stems not from its beautiful, hidden possibilities and alternatives but in Nimzowitsch's adherence to a clear line of strategic thought which he pursues with ruthless logic to the very close. In a sense there is no 'struggle' at all. Nimzowitsch raises his wand, pronounces the words of power and Bogoljubow's position promptly collapses.

1. P—Q4	N—KB3	3. N—QB3	B—N5
2. P—QB4	P—K3	4. N—B3	B × N +

Considerably more acceptable here than in the analogous position from their Kissingen game. In this position White is, at least, obliged to recapture on B3 with a pawn. From this point on the play against White's doubled pawns forms the leitmotif of Black's whole strategy.

5. P × B	P—QN3	6. P—KN3?!	

A more dynamic possibility resides in 6. B—N5, intending Q—B2, P—K3 and B—Q3. With the fianchetto Bogoljubow plans a repetition of their Kissingen experience (cf. page 200) but Nimzowitsch is ready with an improvement.

6. ...	B—N2	8. 0—0	R—K1 '!!'
7. B—N2	0—0		(Nimzowitsch)

'Black operates here, and in the following play, with prophylaxis and centralisation, according to his System. The mysterious rook move helps to forestall the possibility of N—Q2 and P—K4, thus: 9. N—Q2, B × B; 10. K × B, P—K4!; 11. P—K4, P × P and ... N × P follows' (Nimzowitsch).

9. R—K1	P—Q3	10. Q—B2?!	

Here Nimzowitsch suggested 10. N—Q2!, B × B; 11. K × B, P—K4; 12. P—K4, N—B3; 13. B—N2!, when Black has no clearcut method of attacking White's pawn front. Nevertheless, this position, with White's QB reduced to a miserably defensive rôle, would certainly not be to everyone's taste. We can see that it did not appeal to Bogoljubow.

With the text Bogoljubow still hopes for a transposition to their Kissingen game, where Black's QB was lured to its K5 square and then driven off with loss of time and space by means of the manœuvre:

B—KR3/N—Q2/P—KB3 and P—K4. However, in this case there is an important difference: Black still retains the option here of developing his QN on c6, covering a5. This invalidates the method of gaining the initiative on the Q side (P—QR4—QR5) chosen by Bogoljubow in the former game. Furthermore, the N on c6 exerts more influence on the centre (especially against White's QP) than did its fellow on d7 in the Kissingen encounter. Thus a timely ... P—K4 thrust by Black will cut straight across White's cumbersome regrouping strategem: B—KR3/KB1 followed by N—Q2 and P—K4.

10. ...	B—K5	12. B—B1	P—K4
11. Q—N3	N—B3		

Tempting was 12. ... N—QR4; 13. Q—R4, B—B3, but after 14. Q—N4 White's position is not yet 'organically diseased' (Nimzowitsch).

13. P × P
13. P—Q5, N—QR4 is also unattractive in view of the fact that White has been obliged to surrender control of his QB5 square (14. Q—R4, N—Q2).

13. ...	N × P	16. P—B3	B—N2
14. N × N	R × N	17. QR—Q1	
15. B—B4	R—K1		

Threatening P—B5.

17. ... N—Q2
'Now the picture is quite different: in spite of the stout central pawn and the bishop pair White's position suffers from a profound, inner decay. The doubled pawn is isolated and, after the inevitable P—K4, a rolling-up action will eventually take place in the K file (... P—KB4). On top of this White doesn't have a shred of counterplay anywhere' (Nimzowitsch).

18. P—K4	Q—B3	20. R—Q2	R—K2
19. B—N2	N—K4	21. R/1—Q1	B—B3

Consolidation directed against the possibility of P—QB5.

22. R—KB2	QR—K1	23. B—KB1	P—KR3

The 'variation' looms up: 23. ... N × P +; 24. R × N, P—KN4, but Black has no need to embark on such brigandage. Instead of this Nimzowitsch adheres resolutely to his strategy. He now plans to triple in the K file in preparation for the rolling-up move: ... P—KB4, which will annihilate White's last central bastion (PK4).

24. B—K2 K—R1
25. Q—R3 Q—K3‡
Preparations complete.

26. Q—B1 P—B4
Not 26. ... N × P??; 27. B × N,
Q × B; 28. B × RP! =

27. P × P   Q × KBP
28. Q—Q2 Q—B2
29. Q—Q4
Loses at once. 29. B × N was
loathsome, but essential.

29. ... N—N3!
Inflicting a second set of shattered pawns in the other B file.

30. B—Q3 N × B   32. P × Q R—KB1
31. Q × N   Q × Q
'Here many roads lead to home, and all these different roads,
thanks to the presence of the numerous doubled pawns, are a real
pleasure to tread, e.g. 32. ... R—K6 (instead of ... R—KB1);
33. K—N2, R × KBP; 34. R × R, R—K6; 35. R—KB1, R × B and
wins' (Nimzowitsch).

33. P—KB5 B—Q2   36. B × R   R—K1
34. R/1—Q2 B × P   37. K—B2 R—K4
35. RKB2—K2 R × R   38. R—Q5
By now it was possible to cease resistance.

**38. ... P—KN4; 39. R × R, P × R; 40. P—B5, P × P; 41. B—R6,
P—K5; 42. P—QR4, K—N2; 43. P—R5, P × P; 44. K × P, K—B3;
45. K—K3, K—K4; 46. B—B4, B—N5; 47. B—R6, P—R4;
48. B—B4, P—R5; 49. B—R6, B—Q8; 50. B—N7, P—N5.** White
resigns.

This game was distinguished with a prize 'for the best played
game' (500 crowns). The above game was played on August 2, 1929.
On September 6 of the same year Bogoljubow sat down to play the
first game of his world title match with Alekhine.

VIDMAR–NIMZOWITSCH, Carlsbad, 1929. *QP Opening*

This game marked the start of Nimzowitsch's finishing burst of
3½/4 which brought him up past Spielmann and Capablanca to take
first prize at Carlsbad. (Nimzowitsch often played much better chess
towards the close of long tournaments than at the beginning.) It
presents an example of Nimzowitsch carrying out a strategic prevention manœuvre which appears in the eyes of the self-made victim as a

tactical trap rather than as a strategically valuable prophylactic device.

| 1. P—Q4 | N—KB3 | 3. B—N5?! |
| 2. N—KB3 | P—K3 | |

An innocuous idea.

| 3. ... | P—B4 | 5. Q—B1 |
| 4. P—K3 | Q—N3! | |

Already White is losing his grip on the initiative, which should be his birthright in the opening.

| 5. ... | N—B3 | 7. B—Q3 | B—Q3 |
| 6. P—B3 | P—Q4 | 8. QN—Q2 | P × P |

Prophylaxis directed against the possibility of White's playing QP × P followed either by P—K4 or P—QN4/P—QR3 and P—QB4. At this point Vidmar has the following amusing note: 'Actually I have never quite been able to understand Nimzowitsch's play, but he was similarly disposed towards mine. The consequence of this was that, on practically every occasion when we met in tournament games, we, so to say, played straight past each other and the finishes of our games were often very odd indeed.' (Adapted from *Goldene Schachzeiten*.)

9. KP × P   KN—R4

Occupation of his KB5 will secure Black the bishop pair.

10. N—B1

This lends temporary cover to f4.

| 10. ... | P—KR3 | 12. N—N3 | N—B5 |
| 11. B—Q2 | Q—B2 | 13. B × N | |

Ceding Black the advantage of the two bishops. Undevelopment by 13. B—B1 would have been most distasteful.

| 13. ... | B × B | 14. Q—Q1 | P—KN3 |

To hem in White's knights. The text prevents N—R5.

| 15. 0—0 | P—KR4 | 16. KR—K1 | 0—0 |

It was possible to save a move on the game by playing 16. ... K—B1 intending 17. ... K—N2 but Nimzowitsch wanted to avoid the possibility of P—QB4 from White while his own king was still stranded in the centre.

17. Q—K2   K—N2

White's only (but adequate) compensation for Black's powerful bishops resides in his ability to occupy the outpost square K5 with a N, which would restore a measure of dark-square control to him.

Hence the correct course was 18. N—K5!, N × N; 19. P × N,
R—R1; 20. N—B1, B—Q2!; 21. N—Q2, QR—KB1; 22. N—B3,
P—B3 or 21. P—KN3, B—KN4; 22. N—Q2, QR—KB1; 23. N—
B3, B—K2; 24. N—Q4, B—B4 (Nimzowitsch) with chances for all
concerned.

18. QR—Q1? R—R1!

Preventing 19. N—K5 and thereby draining all dynamic potential
from the White position. If now 19. N—K5?, N × N; 20. P × N,
P—R5; 21. N—B1, R—R4 and wins the KP. This actually happens,
but out of phase.

19. N—B1 P—R5
20. N—K5?‡

Making a 'trap' out of a strategically motivated prophylactic
manœuvre. This is a ghastly blunder
for a master of Vidmar's class. We
should remark, however, that his
position was already seriously com-
promised in view of his inability to
create counterplay.

20. ... N × N
21. P × N R—R4

'Never before has a proud king's pawn been done to death in such
ignominious fashion!' (Nimzowitsch). 'In my sober view the move
18. ... R—R1 was a subtly conceived and skilfully laid trap into
which I fell, quite unwittingly' (Vidmar).

22. P—KN3 R × KP

White loses a vital pawn for which there is no tangible compensation.

23. Q—B3 R—N4   **25. BP × P B—Q3**
24. K—R1 P × P   **26. R—Q2 B—Q2**

Vidmar had escaped from lost positions against Nimzowitsch on
several previous occasions, so he plays on hopefully.

27. R—KB2 P—B4   **29. Q—K2 R—R1**
28. Q—K3 R—N5   **30. K—N1 B—B3**

Stronger, according to Nimzowitsch, was 30. ... P—Q5!;
31. P × P, B—B3; 32. N—K3, R × P +; 33. K—B1, R/6—R6 and
Black wins.

31. N—K3

White's Q would never escape alive if she captured the Black KP.

31. ... R—N4   **32. N—N2 P—B5!?**
The initial move of a grandiose conception which, however, was
not strictly necessary. 32. ... P—K4 would have won easily and
prosaically as would 32. ... B—B4, since 33. N—B4 fails to
... Q × N when White suffers from an embarrassment of pins.

33. P × P   B × P
34. K—B1   R × P
35. Q—B3   P—Q5
36. B—K4   R—KB4!?‡
'One has to admit the originality of
the combination commencing 36. ...
R—KB4: the way in which all the
White pieces must step forwards and
bow their heads to the general exchange conceived by the leader of
the Black forces has an almost
humorous effect' (Nimzowitsch).

The combination is indeed original and complex: unfortunately,
Nimzowitsch, bound up in his deep reflections, totally overlooked a
rapid method of execution, namely: 36. ... R—R8 + ; 37. K—K2,
B × B; 38. Q × B (f4), Q—B5 + ; 39. K—Q1, Q—Q6 + ; 40. Q—Q2,
Q × Q + and ... R × N with an extra piece.

'When this alternative solution was demonstrated to me after the
game I regretted not so much the fact that I had overlooked it, as the
fact that it was there at all, since thereby the otherwise flawless combination commencing 36. ... R—KB4 is shown to contain a
Schönheitsfehler' (Nimzowitsch).

37. Q—N4
Or 37. ... B × B, B—N6!

37. ...   R—R8 +   **40. B × R   Q—K4 + !**
38. K—K2   R × R +   **41. K—B1   KP × B**
39. K × R   B—N6   **42. P × P**
Or 42. Q—K2, B—QN4; 43. P—B4, Q × Q + ; 44. R × Q, B × P!,
re-pinning the recently unpinned rook (Nimzowitsch).

42. ...   B × R   **44. P × Q   B × N**
43. K × B   P × Q   **45. K × B   K—B2**
For some reason Nimzowitsch's opponents at Carlsbad (see also
games versus Spielmann and Bogoljubow) refused to resign in
absolutely hopeless endings and fought to the bitter end. Vidmar
is no exception. We all know about the diversionary role of the

pawn in K and P endings, so I shall refrain from further comment. **46. K—N3, K—K3; 47. K×P, K×P; 48. K—N5, K—K5; 49. K×P, K—Q6; 50. K—B5, K—B7; 51. P—N4, P—N4; 52. K—K5, K—B6; 53. K—Q5, K×P; 54. K—B6, P—R4; 55. K—N6, P—R5; 56. K—R6, P—R6; 57. K—N6, K—B5; 58. K—R5, P—N5; 59. K—R4, K—B6.** White resigns.

NIMZOWITSCH–SPIELMANN, Carlsbad, 1929. *English Opening*
With three rounds to go Spielmann led Nimzowitsch by ½ point, so Nimzowitsch was obliged to exert himself to the utmost to gain the full point. Their clash almost certainly decided the destination of the first prize.

1. P—K3   P—K4   3. N—KB3   P—K5?!
2. P—QB4   N—KB3
More reliable would be 3. ... P—Q3 followed by ... QN—Q2 and the fianchetto of the KB.

4. N—Q4   N—B3   5. N—N5!?
Here 5. N×N, QP×N; 6. P—Q4 is well playable but perhaps too simple an approach for this occasion—White had to create problems. It is easy to see that the game has transposed into a Nimzowitsch Sicilian with reversed colours (White has the extra move P—K3). At the tournament in Berlin the previous year the game Spielmann–Tartakower had commenced: 1. P—K4, P—QB4; 2. N—KB3, N—KB3; 3. P—K5, N—Q4; 4. N—B3, N—N5?!; 5. N—K4? and Black won. Very strong would have been the sacrifice of a pawn by means of 5. P—QR3, N/5—B3; 6. P—QN4!, P×P; 7. P×P, N×NP; 8. B—R3±.

5. ...   P—Q4
In the present case 5. ... P—QR3; 6. N/5—B3, P—QN4? would fail to 7. P×P, P×P; 8. B×P! But Black could have played 6. ... B—B4; 7. P—Q4, P×P e.p.; 8. B×P, P—Q3.

6. P×P   N×P   7. N/1—B3   N—B3
A retreat quite lacking in energy. Nimzowitsch suggested that 7. ... N×N!; 8. N×N, P—B4 would have been more appropriate —(9. B—B4?, N—K4!).

8. Q—R4   B—KB4   9. N—Q4!
This and the subsequent four moves by White form a manœuvre designed to shatter Black's pawn structure. However, since Black obtains definite counterplay on the light squares (d3 for example) and against White's QP (backward on an open file) we may assume

that Spielmann invited the position after move 13, assessing it as adequate for him.

9. ...   B—Q2   11. B—N5!
10. N × N   B × N
Now ... B × B?; 12. Q × B+ would shed a pawn for nil compensation.

11. ...   Q—Q2   12. B × B   Q × B
Black must acquiesce in the exchange of queens since his KP hangs.

13. Q × Q +   P × Q
White has a pronounced theoretical plus in the shape (or rather mis-shape) of Black's pawns, but, in compensation, Black has open lines, a certain control of space, and free play for his pieces. In other words: Black has a 'temporary' initiative while White holds the 'strategic' initiative firmly in his grasp. That Spielmann should lose from this position is less an indictment of his choice of opening, or of his attitude to the transition between opening and endgame, than an indication that he committed an error of judgement in his subsequent handling of the simplified position itself.

14. P—QN3   0—0—0
15. B—N2   B—N5
16. P—QR3   B × N
17. B × B   R—Q6‡
The effect of Black's last manœuvre (15. ... B—N5, etc.) has been to cause a slight weakening of White's Q side pawns (b3 is now unprotected). With the text Black seizes his light square birthright and prepares to intensify the pressure both laterally (against White's QNP) and frontally (against White's QP).

In the tournament book Nimzowitsch mentions the following possibilities leading to a slight White advantage: 17. ... KR—N1 (to protect his KNP in preparation for ... N—Q4); 18. B—Q4!, K—N2; 19. 0—0, N—Q4; 20. P—B3, P × P; 21. R × P + = or 19. R—QB1, N—Q4; 20. R—B4, P—KB4; 21. K—K2, P—N3; 22. KR—QB1, R—Q3 also + =.

17. ... R—Q6 was a pre-emptive move. Black clearly wanted to preserve his pressure against Q7, which would not be possible if White were allowed to play B—Q4, obstructing the Q file.

18. 0—0 . KR—Q1?

A mechanical developing move which does not fit the situation at all. Here Nimzowitsch recommended 18. ... R—N1! ('Such discreet use of rook energy is not at all usual in gambit-play, but it's absolutely indispensable if you want to win first prizes in tournaments'— Nimzowitsch), e.g.: 19. P—B3, N—Q4; 20. P × P, N × B; 21. P × N, R—B1! Nimzowitsch's note stops here without offering any evaluation of the position at all. The implication is that White stands well, but can this really be believed? I do not see that White has any chances to win at all after 21. ... R—B1! I suggest that White could do better to retain his bishop, e.g. (18. ... R—N1); 19. R—R2, N—Q4; 20. B—Q4, R × NP; 21. B × RP, K—N2; 22. B—Q4 and White's centralised B is superior to Black's N. If Black delays ... N—Q4 White could station his B on Q4, play P—QN4 and follow-up with R—QB1.

Such a configuration would still offer plenty of scope for advantageous manœuvring from White's side. Even after his actual 18th move it's not yet clear that Black is lost.

19. P—B3	N—Q4	22. P × P	P × P
20. B × P	R × QP	23. B × P	
21. B—Q4	P—KB4		

The long-ranging bishop is ideally suited to its task of annexing the widely separated sensitive points in the Black camp (a7/g7).

| 23. ... | R—Q6 | 25. B × N | |
| 24. P—QN4 | N × KP | | |

The knight has become too powerful on the sixth for its continued existence to be tolerated.

| 25. ... | R × B | 26. KR—K1 | R—QN6?! |

This looks highly attractive since it enables Black to mass his rooks on the 7th rank at the cost of a mere pawn. Hereafter, however, Nimzowitsch provides us with a superlative display of technique, in that he not only neutralises the powerful threats of his opponent but also evaluates his own slim advantage.

26. ... R/1—Q6; 27. K—B2, R × R; 28. R × R, R × P might have been a better chance of holding the game, although after 29. R × P Black's KRP is very weak.

| 27. R × P | R—Q7 | 29. R—B7! | |
| 28. R—K7 | P—R4 | | |

'A finesse: White (by the threat of R—B2) forces Black's next move which deprives him of the possibility of frontal attack against White's KNP by means of ... R—KN6 (after ... P—KR5 answered by P—KR3).'

29. ...   R/6—N7   31. P—R3 R/Q7—QB7
30. R—N7 K—N2   32. R—N5
Taking the fifth rank and menacing Black's KRP in the long term.

32. ... K—N3   33. R—KB1 P—B4
Obviously Black wants to create a passed pawn, but this move also
parries White's threat of P—KR4/R/1—B5—QB5 and R—N6.

34. R—B4!
To maintain his QNP, inasmuch as 34. P × P +, R × BP;
35. R × R, K × R; 36. R—B5 +, K—Q5; 37. R × P, P—B4, followed
by a rush of the Black passed pawn, would make a win out of the
question for White.

34. ... P—B5
35. P—R4‡
Fixing a weakness on h5.

With Black's rooks doubled on
the 7th and with a vicious Black
passed pawn already in his territory
I find it miraculous that White can
win in this position, yet the miracle
does indeed come to pass.

35. ... R—R7
Why not 35. ... P—B6? White
would then force the win with
36. R—B4, R—B8 + ; 37. K—R2, P—B7; 38. R/5—QB5 with
mechanical stoppage of the advanced pawn and the certain win of
Black's pawn c7. Less clear, however, is the voracious: 38. R × RP,
R—QR8; 39. R/5—QB5, R/8—R7! with the threat of ... P—B8
and R × P + and the exposed position of White's king still gives him
some problems to solve. From this we can see how useful it was to
bring up the White QR to the fourth rank, which manœuvre resulted
in a drastic increase of its lateral efficiency.

36. R—B6 +
Now planning to defend his KNP with this rook while leaving the
KR free to operate on the fifth rank against Black's weaknesses (h5
and c7). The KR will also be left as a sentinel on QB5 to discourage
over-ambition on the part of Black's front QBP

36. ... K—N2   37. R—N5 +
Black's K is driven back.

37. ... K—B1
If 37. ... K—R2; 38. R—R5 + followed by R—KN6 and eventually R × RP.

38. R—KN6 R—Q7

Or 38. ... R × RP, when White simply captures on h5 and then returns with his rook to the vital observation post on QB5.

39. R—QB5

Sealing Black's fate. The passed QBP is immobilised and the rear QBP is singled out as a victim.

39. ...	R/R7—B7	45. R × P	R—KR8
40. R—N7	K—N1	46. R—B5 +	K—N3
41. R/5 × BP	R × P +	47. K—N3	R—QB8
42. R × R	R—B8 +	48. K—B2	R—KR8
43. K—B2	K × R	49. K—K3	
44. R—N5	P—B6		

And not 49. R × P, R × P; 50. K—K3, K—N4; 51. K—Q3, K—R5 = .

49. ... R—R6 +

Or 49. ... R × P; 50. K—Q3, R—R6 + ; 51. K—B2 followed by R × P and K—N3.

50. K—Q4	P—B7	52. K—B3	K—N4
51. R × P	R × P +		

and White won: **53. K—N3, R—R6 + ; 54. R—B3, R—R4; 55. P—R4 +, K—N3; 56. R—N3, K—N2; 57. R—N7 +, K—N3; 58. R—N6 +, K—N2; 59. P—R5, K—R2; 60. K—R4, K—N2; 61. R—N7 +, K—N1; 62. P—R6, K—R1; 63. P—N5, K—N1; 64. R—K7, R—KN4; 65. P—N6, R—N1; 66. K—N5, R—N4 + ; 67. K—B6, R—N3 + ; 68. K—B5, R—N1; 69. K—Q6, R—Q1 + ; 70. K—K6.** Black resigns. If Black plays 70. ... K—R1; 71. K—B7 followed by 72. R—K8 is lethal—or 70. ... K—B1; 71. P—R7 or 70. ... R—KB1; 71. K—Q7 and 72. R—K8 + .

A magnificent ending of a rare type (the sustained double rook variety) which bears comparison with Nimzowitsch's 'immortal' against Lasker from Zürich, 1934. Nimzowitsch's victory in the above game was all the more praiseworthy in that Spielmann was then at the height of his powers. In the very next round the Austrian Grandmaster defeated Capablanca (for the second time in two years!), thus assuring himself of a share in second prize.

NIMZOWITSCH–TARTAKOWER, Carlsbad, 1929. *King's Indian Defence*
The 21st and last round of Carlsbad, 1929, saw Nimzowitsch and Spielmann leading with 14 points followed by Capablanca on 13½. The final pairings were: Capablanca–Maroczy, won by White with great ease; Mattison–Spielmann, which ended in a draw, and Nimzowitsch as above. In order to emerge sole victor Nimzowitsch

had to defeat Tartakower, who had lost but two games in the previous twenty rounds.

1. P—Q4　　N—KB3　　　　3. P—B3!?
2. P—QB4　P—KN3

An unusual move played specifically to avoid the Grünfeld Defence (3. N—QB3, P—Q4), but 3. ... P—Q4 is still playable, e.g. 3. ... P—Q4; 4. P × P, N × P; 5. P—K4, N—N3; 6. N—B3, B—N2; 7. B—K3, 0—0; 8. Q—Q2, N—B3; 9. 0—0—0, P—K4; 10. P—Q5, N—Q5; 11. P—B4, P—QB4; 12. BP × P, B—N5!

Of course, 3. P—B3!? is now known as 'Alekhine's anti-Grünfeld' method, since Alekhine adopted the move in his first title match versus Bogoljubow, which took place in 1929, after Carlsbad.

3. ...　　B—N2

Instead of seeking counterplay on Grünfeld lines as discussed above, Tartakower adheres strictly to a classical King's Indian set-up with ... P—Q3 and ... P—K4.

4. P—K4　P—Q3　　　　6. B—K3
5. N—B3　0—0

Transposing into what is now known as the Sämisch Variation which often witnesses long castling by White intending a K side pawn storm.

6. ...　　QN—Q2

A rather passive move which allows an interesting reply for White. Nowadays attention centres on more lively lines such as 6. ... P—K4; 7. P—Q5, P—B3 or 7. ... N—R4. Even 6. ... N—B3 (which had been played as early as 1927 at the London International Tournament by Yates against Vidmar) has turned out to be playable.

7. N—R3!?

Intending to play this piece around to Q3 to challenge the possible enemy establishment of an N on the blockading square c5. This is quite a bright idea on Nimzowitsch's part but on move 17 he abandons the plan in favour of an even more effective deployment of the knight's energies.

However, there is a slight defect to 7. N—R3 (see note to move 9) and the conventional 7. KN—K2 was an objectively stronger choice.

7. ...　　　P—K4　　　　8. P—Q5　P—QR4

Safeguarding the square c5. Over the next few moves Black becomes obsessed with the fortification of this square and overlooks a useful tactical possibility that might have freed his game.

9. N—B2   P—N3?

9. ... N—R4! was recommended by Nimzowitsch.

10. Q—Q2   N—B4?!

Once again Nimzowitsch suggested ... N—R4!, e.g. 11. P—KN4?, N—B5!; 12. B × N, P × B; 13. Q × P, N—K4 with tremendous compensation for the pawn in terms of dark-square control and active piece play. After 10. ... N—R4 I feel White's best course would be 11. N—Q3, P—KB4; 12. 0—0—0, removing his king from the danger zone with the utmost speed. The unimaginative text allows Nimzowitsch to create just the kind of position he must have been longing for in this crucial last round, I mean a blockade position where White alone has winning chances (in view of Black's lack of pawn-breaks) and Black has no active counterplay at all.

11. B—N5!

The first link in a chain of moves designed to restrain ... P—KB4 for ever. This pinning motif (in slightly different circumstances) has become one of the most popular modern methods of combatting the King's Indian Defence.

11. ...   B—Q2?

After this third error White obtains a winning grip on the position. It was better to unpin (11. ... Q—Q2).

12. P—KN4   Q—B1   14. P—R5   P × P

13. P—KR4   K—R1   15. B × N?!

White wants to keep the KR file open so 15. P × P would naturally be a mistake. However, it was possible to do this and retain the useful dark-squared bishop by means of 15. 0—0—0!, N—N1 (15. ... P × P?; 16. B × N, B × B; 17. Q—R6 + —); 16. R × P, P—B3; 17. B—K3.

15. ...   B × B   16. R × P

Leaving Black with an exposed KRP and gaping wounds on f5 and h5 which both constitute inviting blockade squares for White's knights. It is out of the question that Black will ever be able to force through ... P—KB4, so the absence of White's QB is not so important. Lasker pointed out another possibility for White which would have led by force to the exchange of queens and light-squared bishops, thus granting White an excellent ending: 16. Q—R6, B—N2; 17. Q × P(h5), P—R3; 18. P—N5, P—B4; 19. P × P e.p., R × P; 20. B—R3!, B—K1; 21. B × Q, B × Q; 22. R × B, R × B; 23. K—K2. Nimzowitsch's continuation is more ambitious. He is not satisfied with a minute positional advantage, but intends to reduce the entire Black army to a state of paralysis.

16. ... B—N2   **17. N—R1‡**

The change of plan. The knight heads for KR5 or KB5. Compare also Nimzowitsch–Rubinstein, Dresden, 1926—18. N—R1 and Schlechter–Nimzowitsch, Carlsbad, 1907—17. ... N—R1 or Mannheimer–Nimzowitsch, Frankfort, 1930—16. ... Q—R1 (pages 3, 83, 37). All instructive decentralisations of the first water!

17. ...   **P—KB3**
18. Q—R2   **P—R3**
19. N—N3   **K—R2**
20. B—K2   **R—KN1**
21. K—B2

'And not Q side castling since White also plans an eventual advance on the Q wing by means of P—R3 and P—N4. In order to achieve victory White has to combine simultaneous attacks on both wings; the Black K side alone would not present a sufficient object of attack' (Nimzowitsch).

21. ...   **R—R1**   **22. R—R4**

Making way for the N, which is the most efficacious blockading piece.

22. ...	**Q—K1**	**25. N—R5**	**Q—N3**
23. R—KN1	**B—KB1**	**26. P—B4**	**N—Q1**
24. K—N2	**N—N2**	**27. B—B3**	**N—B2**

Hoping to play ... KP × P at a favourable opportunity, followed by the establishment of the N at e5 or g5.

28. N—K2

Heading for the other blockading square—KB5.

28. ...	**B—K2**	**30. N/2—N3**	**K—B1**
29. K—R1	**K—N1**	**31. N—B5**	**R—KN1**

Unfortunately 31. ... P × P is impossible: 32. N × BP, Q—N4; 33. N—K6 +, B × N; 34. P × B, N—K4; 35. R × P and wins.

32. Q—Q2!

Opinions differ as to this position: 'As so often happens when the principles of the blockade are applied, White has succeeded in reducing Black's dynamic chances to nil, but at the same time has not greatly increased his own' (R. N. Coles, *Dynamic Chess*).

'A fine regrouping in accordance with White's strategy of extending his operations to the other flank' (Nimzowitsch).

32. ...   R—QB1   34. P—N3 K—Q1
33. R—R2 K—K1
The K flees, but a warm reception also awaits him on the Q side.

35. P—R3 R—QR1
36. Q—B1‡ B—KB1?
Loses at once.

'By continuing a non-committal
defence with some move like ...
R—QB1, Black could force White
either to try to develop an alternative attack elsewhere or admit that
he cannot break through. Instead, in
an effort to continue the flight of his
K to the Q side which began on the
29th move, he blunders away the
exchange. If it did nothing else, the
blockade theory strongly applied often made the task of the defence
so wearying that accuracy failed' (Coles).

'A blunder in a positionally lost situation' (Nimzowitsch).

The real effect of Tartakower's blunder on move 36 was to diminish
Nimzowitsch's blockading and manœuvring achievement (which is a
model of how such advantages in terrain should be exploited) in the
eyes of subsequent observers. Nimzowitsch was robbed of the
possibility of winning properly over the board (or of proving that he
could force the win at all) precisely because his preliminary psychological tactics were so successful.

Let us take a look at this position to see if Black could hold out:

(i) 36. ... R—QB1; 37. P—N4, P × NP; 38. RP × P, R—QR1;
     39. P—B5, QP × P; 40. N × B, K × N; 41. NP × P, P × P;
     42. Q × P +, N—Q3; 43. Q × P, KR—QB1; 44. Q—N6 and
     it seems to me that Black's compensation for his pawn is
     inadequate.

(ii) 36. ... Q—R2 (suggested by Tartakower, who wanted to
     follow up with ... Q—R1 and B—KB1); 37. P—N4, RP × P;
     38. RP × P, Q—R1; 39. P—B5, B—KB1; 40. P × NP, BP × P;
     41. R—QB2, R—B1; 42. R × R +, B × R; 43. Q—B6 winning
     easily. (39. ... QP × P would lead to positions similar to
     those arising from note (i).)

The way in which the control of terrain plus superior mobility
translate themselves into a mating attack in this variation lends
concrete testimony to the accuracy of Nimzowitsch's strategical vision.
The game concluded: 37. N—R4!, Q—R2; 38. N × P, Q—R1;

39. N × R, Q × N; 40. P—N5, KP × P; 41. P × P, Q—R2; 42. Q × P, B × P; 43. Q—B6 +, K—B1; 44. N—B5, B × N; 45. P × B, K—N2; 46. Q—N6, R—R1; 47. Q × Q, R × Q; 48. R—N6, K—B1; 49. P—B6, R—R1; 50. B—N4 +, K—Q1; 51. B—K6, K—K1; 52. B × N +, K × B; 53. R/2 × B. Resigns.

Thus did Nimzowitsch achieve the greatest tournament success of his chess career.

The path to victory infested with thorns*

'With the exception of Alekhine, who seems to win his games with remarkable ease, victory in a tournament game is, and will remain, a really rather painful affair. If you have to face a somewhat weaker opponent you commence your day's work by voluntarily accepting a quite cramped and difficult position. Let us not forget that the truly modern master has no fear of phantoms, especially those from the time of Tarrasch. In the Tarrasch time they all considered such cramped positions to be unplayable, but now we are a lot less strait-laced in our judgements. But back to the mechanics of winning games!

After you have consolidated your position diligently for one or two hours you fail, with amazing regularity, to grasp the correct moment for a sharp advance. It is naturally a difficult matter for the player bent on consolidation to behold the possibility of aggressive action on his part without some misgivings, since we are all well aware that any advance must create weaknesses in our own camp. Not to worry; after a few moves we make good the omission, in as far as that is at all possible. Naturally the advance no longer packs the punch it would have done had we carried it out at the correct moment, but at this point the opponent comes to our aid. The opponent is also human and the enemy initiative has disturbed his psychological equanimity. So he comes to our rescue and we obtain a clearly won position. However, we do not dare to believe in our success and creep around our opponent, as if we were beating the proverbial bush, instead of summoning up the courage to slit his throat on the spot. And then the opponent's strength revives, he gathers his forces, consolidates his mutilated position and finally marches off to counter-attack. But the counter-attack goes wrong and—at long last—we can notch up the full point.

'Many games at San Remo took such a course and I openly admit that I too was involved in games which lurched back and forth. . . . And yet I still love this thorny path to victory; it is as genuine as the

---

* Literally: 'Der Gewinn einer Turnierpartie als schmerzvolle Angelegenheit.' (This article by Nimzowitsch appeared in Kagan's magazine for June, 1930, as an introduction to Nimzowitch's games from San Remo.)

life-struggle itself, while the safe and easy method of winning, so highly prized in the time of Tarrasch, lacks any point of contact with external reality.

'Only in the imagination of the averagely talented critic (vulgo annotator) does that game exist in which a small openings mistake is exploited by the opponent and conducted to victory with merciless consistency. How on earth could this critic be in a position to discover the more or less concealed resources which are available in the position? (I mean equalising variations or lines which grant counterplay.) The critic sees nothing and discovers nothing and brims over with enthusiasm for the harmonious, flowing win just as many a schoolmaster, with rounded shoulders and a pot belly, raves with admiration about Julius Caesar. In reality, however, every game consists of at least two or three distinct waves! It would be odd indeed if anything else were the case, for chess is much too stable for its balance to be disturbed by one little error in the opening. Consider the following "Truth": "After 1. P—K4, P—K3; 2. P—Q4, P—Q4 the move 3. P—K5 must be regarded as the decisive error" (Tarrasch). Such things now belong in the realm of fairy stories.

'However, there is one special case in which a player can be destroyed "at a stroke" and this occurs when you are able to succeed in ruining your opponent psychologically. Dr. Alekhine achieved his victories at San Remo with such ease precisely because he succeeded in forcing his opponents into positions that did not suit them psychologically. But apart from this the struggle of tournament play is a difficult and protracted business.

'In its fascination and its rich variety it is a mirror of the life-struggle itself but, to a similar degree, it is exhausting and full of pain.'

Elsewhere Nimzowitsch once wrote: 'How is it to be explained that something inside me revolts against the playing of obvious moves? Perhaps we may perceive the underlying reason in the fact that I derive satisfaction from seeking to reveal the concealed meaning of a position by means of manœuvring play and therefore I do not wish to see this satisfaction curtailed by a banal, more or less fortuitous decision. Naturally, this phenomenon is played out beneath the threshold of consciousness. The waking consciousness will, of course, in each individual case, give preference to the more rapid means of deciding the game.'

BOGOLJUBOW–NIMZOWITSCH, San Remo, 1930
Q. P. Nimzowitsch Defence

| 1. P—Q4 | N—KB3 | 3. N—QB3 | B—N5 |
| 2. P—QB4 | P—K3 | 4. Q—N3 | |

This response became popular after Spielmann's victories with it at Carlsbad, 1929, and was employed frequently in the early 1930s. The broad defensive lines elaborated against 4. Q—N3 in Nimzowitsch's own games have scarcely been altered up to our own day.

| 4. ... | P—B4 | 6. N—B3 | N—K5 |
| 5. P × P | N—B3 | 7. B—Q2 | N × QBP |

Nimzowitsch seems to have been on very friendly terms with Emmanuel Lasker and he mentions in his own notes that 7. ... N × QBP was analysed by the two of them during the course of a visit paid by Nimzowitsch to the ex-world champion in Berlin just after the former's victory at Carlsbad, 1929.

Nimzowitsch also made an important contribution to the theory of the alternative 7. ... N × B, which may in fact be the superior choice at this stage: 7. ... N × B; 8. N × N and now (i) 8. ... 0—0; 9. 0—0—0, Q—R4; 10. P—QR3, B × BP; 11. P—K3, P—B4; 12. B—K2, P—QR3; 13. N—B3, P—QN4!; 14. P × P, P × P; 15. Q × NP, Q—R2 with a powerful attack for the sacrificed pawn, according to Nimzowitsch; or (ii) 8. ... B × P, 9. P—K3, P—QN3; 10. 0—0—0, B—N2; 11. N/2—K4, B—K2; 12. N—Q6 +, B × N; 13. R × B, Q—K2; 14. Q—Q1, R—Q1; 15. B—K2, 0—0; 16. B—B3, N—R4!; 17. B × B, N × B; 18. R—Q4, P—Q3; 19. K—N1, Q—B2 = , Euwe–Nimzowitsch, Zürich, 1934. A more recent example of this line as interpreted by a Soviet Grandmaster was the brilliant short game Barczay–Tal played at Miskolc, 1963. Tal varied from Nimzowitsch with 9. ... 0—0 when there followed: 10. B—K2, P—QN3; 11. 0—0, B—N2; 12. N/2—K4, R—N1! (12. ... B—K2; 13. QR—Q1 + =); 13. QR—Q1, P—B4; 14. N × B (14. N—Q6, B—R1), 14. ... P × N; 15. Q—R3, Q—K2; 16. N—N5, P—B5; 17. N—Q6, B—R1; 18. B—B3, P × P; 19. P × P, N—K4!; 20. B × B, R × R + ; 21. K × R, R × B; 22. K—N1, R—KB1; 23. Q × BP, Q—N4; 24. N—K4, Q—N5; 25. N—B2, R × N!; 26. K × R, Q—B4 + !; 27. K—K2, Q—R4 + ; 28. P—N4, Q × RP + ; 29. K—B1, Q—R8 + ; 30. K—B2, N × P + ; 31. K—N3, Q × R; 32. Q—B8 +, K—B2. 0–1.

8. Q—B2 P—B4!

In his own notes to his win against Bogoljubow Nimzowitsch suggested the alternative procedure: ... 0—0 combined with ... P—QR4, but this plan was virtually refuted in two games of Nimzowitsch's 1934 Match versus Stahlberg: (Nimzowitsch Black in both cases) game 3: 8. ... 0—0; 9. P—QR3, B × N; 10. B × B, P—QR4 (... P—B4!); 11. P—KN3, Q—K2; 12. B—N2, P—K4; 13. 0—0, P—R5; 14. N—Q2, P—Q3; 15. P—QN4, P × P e.p.; 16. N × P, B—K3; 17. KR—B1 + - ; and game 5: (as in game 3 up

to) **11. ... P—R5; 12. B—N2, P—QN3; 13. 0—0, B—N2;
14. QR—Q1, N—R4; 15. B—N4, B—K5; 16. Q—B3, N/R4—N6;
17. N—Q4, B × B; 18. K × B, KR—K1; 19. N × N, N × N; 20. R—
Q6, Q—B2; 21. KR—Q1, KR—Q1; 22. Q—B3!, QR—N1;
23. Q—N4, P—B3; 24. B—B3, K—R1; 25. Q—R4, P—K4?
(... K—N1!); 26. R × BP!, P × R; 27. Q × BP +, K—N1; 28. R—
Q6, R—KB1; 29. Q × P, R × P + ; 30. K—N1, K—B2; 31. R—
B6 +. 1–0.**
This drastic defeat was probably responsible for Nimzowitsch's
collapse in the subsequent games of the match.

9. P—K3?!
Insufficiently to the point. Nimzowitsch's notes recommend
9. P—QR3, B × N; 10. B × B, 0—0; 11. P—QN4, N—K5; 12. P—
K3, P—QN3; 13. B—Q3, N × B; 14. Q × N, B—N2, and this
was tried out by Alekhine (Black) against Stahlberg the following
year at Hamburg (1931), resulting in a crushing win for the World
Champion: 15. 0—0, N—K2; 16. B—K2, Q—K1; 17. KR—Q1,
R—Q1; 18. P—QR4?, P—B5!; 19. P—R5, P × KP; 20. Q × P,
N—B4; 21. Q—B3, P—Q3; 22. P × P, P × P; 23. N—K1, P—K4;
24. R—R7, N—Q5; 25. Q—K3, R—Q2; 26. R—R2, R/2—KB2;
27, P—B3, R—B5; 28. R—Q3, Q—R4; 29. B—B1, Q—N4;
30. R—KB2, P—R3; 31. K—R1, R × P! 0–1.
Thus do we see a typical case of Alekhine employing in practice,
and with great success, one of Nimzowitsch's theoretical suggestions.
The fallacy in all this is the assumption that White does not have
time to preserve his valuable QB; but he does. Much better is 12. B—
N2!, e.g. ... P—Q3; 13. P—N3!, P—K4; 14. B—N2, Q—K2;
15. 0—0, B—K3; 16. KR—Q1, QR—B1. Certainly this position
holds out more prospects for White than does the line suggested by
Nimzowitsch.

9. ...   0—0   11. 0—0—0
10. B—K2   P—QN3
White was scared to castle K side in view of the threatening
position of Black's QB on b7 (this is one reason why White would
have done better to play 9. P—QR3 and then fianchetto the KB in
defence of the K). That this was no idle fear can be seen from
Stahlberg–Alekhine above. With his 11th move Bogoljubow doubtless hoped to put pressure on Black's backward QP, but the position
of his king now becomes extremely insecure.

11. ...   P—QR4
Threatening all sorts of horrors, especially the artificial isolation of
White's QBP, which actually comes about in the game. Bogoljubow's

natural reply makes one suspect that he had overlooked the hidden point of Nimzowitsch's last move.

12. P—QR3   P—R5!!†
Not a deep idea, but a brilliant and original conception none the less. If now 13. P × B, N × P; 14. Q —N1, N—N6 and white is mated in broad daylight. The positional effect of ... P—R5 (since Bogoljubow is obviously not going to fall for the mate) is to cut off White's QBP from the remainder of his army.

13. N—N5 B × B +	**15. B—B3 P—Q4!**
14. N × B N—R4	**16. P × P B—R3**

White's position looks critical, e.g. 17. N—B3, B—Q6 – + or 17. N—Q4, R—B1; 18. N—B6, R × N; 19. P × R, B—Q6; 20. N—B1, N/R—N6 + and White loses his Q with check. With an ingenuity born of desperation Bogoljubow finds a way to play on.

17. N—B4!   B × N   18. P × P
With two pawns for his piece and with two of Black's major pieces under attack White retains some 'swindling' chances, as the game continuation reveals. But at precisely this point Nimzowitsch misses a brilliant forced win involving the sacrifice of his Q, which would have spared him much of his subsequent labour. The missed win goes like this: 18. ... B × N!; 19. R × Q, QR × R; 20. R—Q1 (20. P—K7, N/R—N6 + and ... B—Q6), 20. ... B × P – + or 20. ... R × R + ; 21, Q × R, B × P; 22. K—N1, R—B1; 23. Q—Q6, K—R1; 24. B—Q5, N/B—N6; 25. K—R2, B—N1!!; 26. B × B, R—B8; 27. B × N, P × B mate (Nimzowitsch). Note the rare mate by a pawn.

18. ...	**Q—B2?!**	**21. R × B**	**Q—B3**
19. B × R	**B × N**	**22. P—K7**	**Q × R**
20. B—Q5	**B × B**	**23. P × R = R(!) +**	

Observe Bogoljubow's sense of humour which has gone unsung in most sources where 23. P × R = Q + is given. Nimzowitsch, who ought to know, tells us that Bogoljubow did under-promote.

23. ...   K × R   24. R—Q1   Q—K4
Black's advantage of two N's (plus some attack) for R + P is indubitable, but the said advantage can only be converted into a win with great difficulty. In the following play Nimzowitsch operates according to his own principles of centralisation.

25. P—R3   P—R4   26. P—KN4?!

Planning to clear a line for his Q to reach h7, but the resultant loosening of White's pawns only helps Black. Nimzowitsch recommended counter-centralisation by means of K—N1 and R—Q4.

26. ...   RP×P   28. K—N1   P×P
27. P×P   N/R—N6+   29. R—N1

Bogoljubow had probably intended to play 29. Q—R7 but then noticed 29. ... Q—K5+; 30. Q×Q, N×Q, e.g. 31. R—N1, N×P; 32. R—N2, N—Q7+; 33. K—B2, N/Q7—K5; 34. P—N3, P—QN4, with paralysis. White's somewhat disjointed play at this stage could be explained by the proximity of the time control at move 30.

29. ...   Q—Q4   30. R—Q1
If 30. R×P?, Q—R8+ − +.

30. ...   Q—K5
31. R—N1   N—Q7+
32. K—B1   Q—Q4!‡

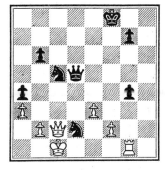

'The persistent exploitation of the central squares e5, d5 and e4 is quite in accordance with the precepts of the system' (Nimzowitsch).

33. Q—R7

Nimzowitsch: 'I had expected 33. P—N4 and analysed an elegant win against this move during the midday adjournment pause, to wit: 33. P—N4, N/B—N6+; 34. K—N2, N—B5+; 35. K—R2, N—Q5!; 36. Q×P, P—QN4!; 37. Q—R7, N—R4 dis.+; 38. K—R1, N/Q—N6+; 39. K—N1, Q—Q6+; 40. K—N2, N—B5+; 41. K—R2, Q—B7. Mate.

The N's rendered good service in this variation by driving the White K indoors while chasing the Q far away from home. But I could have spared myself all this effort if only I had chosen the immediately decisive line commencing 18. ... B×N! In that case the game would have been over long before and I would have been able to enjoy my lunch in peace. As it was I had to renounce the said lunch in magnanimous fashion in order to analyse my adjourned game.

'Just how difficult my games in this tournament were (or rather—how well I understood the task of complicating wins that stood openly there, inviting me to play them) can be seen quite clearly from the fact that in the course of the tournament I was obliged to sacrifice between six to eight lunches.

'In most of my games from San Remo I had tremendous positions (at the very least) by move 20, but then came the moment for converting the advantage into the full point and the win, but a hand's grasp away, began to recede into the distance.

'The end result is that the thorn-infested path to victory (*die schmerzvolle Art der Gewinnführung*) becomes even more thorny as a result of the renunciation of lunch and if a master already enthuses about this thorn-infested path (as I have done) then the said renunciation of his lunch will only be regarded as a thoroughly welcome intensification of the pleasure (*Genuss*) he derives from the whole process; and such is the case here. . . .'

| 33. ... | N/7—K5 | 35. K—N1 |
| 34. Q—R8 + | K—B2 | |

Or 35. R—Q1, N—N6 + ; 36. K—B2, Q—B5 + ; 37. K—N1, N/5—Q7 + (full marks for dressage); 38. R × N, Q—B8 + and mate on QR8.

35. ...   Q—Q6 +

White resigns. 36. K—R2, N—B6 + ; 37. P × N, Q—B7 + ; 38. K—R1, N—N6. Mate.

I would like to suggest that the reader compare this Q plus N attack from Nimzowitsch's mature years with his more *Sturm und Drang* effort in similar vein against Spielmann (Stockholm, 1920), page 133.

If you compare the mate in the Bogoljubow game with the mate given at the end of note (vb) to White's 17th move in the Spielmann game I think you will be pleasantly surprised by the mirror image coincidence, for in the earlier game a mate occurred with White's K on h1 and his Q on a8 while Black's mating force was Qf2 and Ng3. In this case White's mated monarch is on a1, his Q on h8 and Black's victorious army Q on c2 and Nb3.

A further example of the theme: 'the thorn-infested path to victory'.

KMOCH–NIMZOWITSCH, San Remo, 1930

Opening? (Embarrassed silence on the part of the author. I don't know whether to call it a Q-Indian or K-Indian.)

1. N—KB3	N—KB3	4. B—N2	B—KN2
2. P—B4	P—QN3	5. 0—0	
3. P—KN3	P—N3		

Or 5. N—K5, P—B3 followed by ... Q—B2 and ... P—Q3.

5. ...	0—0	8. N × N	B × N
6. N—B3	B—N2	9. P—Q5	
7. P—Q4	N—K5		

Nimzowitsch's forgotten idea for conducting this opening was revived by Portisch (as Black) in his game with Ulf Andersson from Palma, 1971: In this later game White preferred 9. B—K3 which led to his advantage after 9. ... P—Q4!?; 10. R—B1, P × P; 11. R × P, P—QB3; 12. R—B1.

Kmoch's 9th move leads to positions characteristic of the King's Indian Defence.

9. ...	P—K4!	11. N—K1	B × B
10. B—K3	P—KB4	12. N × B	P—Q3

An interesting position. Black's normal strategy would be to storm forwards on the K side with his mobile pawns, but the fact that White's KP is on K2 rather than K4 makes it more difficult for Black to fix on a target. White's normal plan would be to launch a Q side advance with P—QN4, P—QB5, etc., breaking into Black's camp at the sensitive point c7. However, the absence of White's KP from K4 also exerts an influence over White's plan of campaign in that (after P—QB5) his QP will be deprived of much of its support.

In such strategically complex positions Nimzowitsch excelled. Now many of his original ideas have been absorbed into master technique or incorporated into 'openings theory'.

13. Q—Q2 N—Q2   14. P—B3

A useful consolidating move directed against the mobility of Black's KP and KBP.

14. ... P—QR4   15. QR—N1 N—B4

Provocation. Also possible was the more solipsistic procedure ... R—B2, ... Q—KB1 followed by ... P—R3 and ... P—KN4. But Nimzowitsch prefers to encourage activity from his opponent since he correctly perceives that this very activity will ultimately be White's undoing.

16. P—N3 R—B2!

And prophylaxis! Observe the way in which Nimzowitsch guards the c7 point before it is attacked.

17. P—QR3 Q—KB1   18. KR—B1 P—R4

A device for gaining space on the K side which is now regulation in the King's Indian Defence. Given time Black will also play ... P—KN4 with an awesome array of pawns.

19. P—QN4 P × P   20. P × P N—Q2

If now 21. R—R1, to seize the QR file, then ... P—K5!; 22. B—Q4, P × P; 23. P × P, N—K4 with manifold threats. White chooses another means of aggression.

21. P—B5‡

This temporary sacrifice of a pawn looks most promising since it exposes a number of weaknesses in the Black position. However, with this move White is walking straight into a combinative ambush—it could be said that he started out on the ambush trail when he was lured into a Q side advance (with gain of tempo) by 15. .... N—B4, but what other choice did White have? Black holds the initiative on the K wing so the only alternative to Q side activity would be passive defence. Attractive though its execution might appear Nimzowitsch had prepared so efficiently for the possibility of a White Q side advance that the whole plan of carrying it through could be classed as a collective error.

21. ...	QP × P	**23.** B × N	P × B
22. P × P	N × P		

White has had to weaken his dark squares in order to shatter Black's pawns.

24. R—N5

'White seems to be in the ascendant but Black has not been marking time. In fact he has been engaged in the accumulation of attacking energy (QR file, h6–d2 diagonal, mobile pawn mass, etc., .. ,), and now emerges with a series of noxious blows which had completely escaped White's attention. We might add, by the way, that without Black's co-operation (the partly superfluous and partly provocatory ... N—B4) White would scarcely ever have been able to arrange his breakthrough with P—QB5' (Nimzowitsch).

24. ...	B—R3	**26.** P × P?	
25. P—B4	P × P		

26. N × P!, P—B5; 27. Q—Q4, Q—R6; 28. Q × P, B × N; 29. P × B and White has drawing chances in spite of the exposed position of the king. Presumably White retained his knight as a comfort for his K, but the N dies anyway, and the White KBP expires in sympathy, thus leaving the K virtually devoid of support for his dotage.

26. ... **P—B5!**

The ambush is sprung and events now develop by force. This counter-sacrifice has the effect of galvanising Black's entire army which had hitherto slumbered peacefully within the confines of the back two ranks.

27. R × P   R—R8 +   29. R/5—N1
28. R—B1   Q—R6

After 29. R × R, Q × R + Black's advantage is manifest: more secure K; B for N in an open position and better pawns (2 pawn islands to 3).

29. ...   R—R7‡
30. R—B2

Or 30. Q—K1, Q—K2; 31. P—K3, P—N4!; 32. R—R1 (32. P × P, Q × NP; 33. Q—N3, R—N2 – +), 32. ... R × R; 33. R × R, P × P; 34. P × P, Q—B4 + followed by ... Q × P with a good extra pawn (Nimzowitsch).

30. ...   R × R
31. Q × R   B × P

The final point of the combination. Black wins a pawn and bares the White K. It was also possible to play 31. ... B—B1, retaining the B for attacking purposes, when White could hardly resist successfully, so disorganised are his lines of defence (backward KP, straying QP, exposed KBP and unsheltered K).

32. N × B   Q—K6 +   33. K—N2   Q × N

An extra pawn plus the more secure position should amount to a verdict of – +, but ...

34. R—N8 +   K—R2   36. R—K8   P—R5
35. Q—B3   R—N2   37. Q—B3   Q—Q5?

37. ... Q × Q + ! followed by ... R—Q2 and ... K—R3 would have won. Now the win slips away.

38. P—K4!

Nimzowitsch admitted quite frankly in his own notes that he had forgotten that this move was legal! White's counter-attack against Black's KBP and KRP forces Nimzowitsch to start all over again.

38. ...   Q—R5   43. K—N3   P—N4
39. R—K6   R—B2   44. Q—K5   P—B5 +
40. K—R3   Q—B7   45. K—B2   Q × Q
41. Q—B4   Q—B6 +   46. R × Q   K—N3
42. K × P   Q—N2

Can Black win this position? The disappointment of not having won already, plus the fact that this position is a dead draw (after 47. P—R3), might have caused many masters to abandon the struggle and sue for peace, but there is one possibility left.

47. K—B3?
Jeopardising his game once again.

47. ... P—N5 + !
The final shot in Black's arsenal.

48. K—N2
48. K × NP, P—B6 – +

| 48. ... | R—B1 | 49. R—K7 |

The last chance was 49. R—K6 +, K—N4; 50. R—K5 + ; and 51. R—K7 with some hope left. The text loses.

49. ...	P—B6 +	54. K—N1	R—KN7 +
50. K—B2	R—KR1	55. K—R1	R—Q7
51. K—N1	R—R1	56. K—N1	R—Q8 +
52. R × P	R—R8 +	57. K—B2	R—KR8
53. K—B2	R—R7 +	58. P—Q6	

Or 58. K—N3, R—N8 + ; 59. K—B2, R—N7 + – +.

58. ... R × P +
And Black's passed pawns are the more powerful.

59. K—K3 R—K7 +
To cut off White's K.

60. K—Q3 R—K8   61. R—B2
Black wins also after 61. P—Q7, P—B7; 62. P—Q8 = Q, P—B8 = Q + ; 63. K—B2, R—B8 + ; 64. K—N2, R—N8 + ; 65. K—R2, R—R8 + ; 66. K—N2, Q—N8 + ; 67. K—B3, Q—B8 + ; 68. K—N3, R—R6 + ; 69. K—N4, Q—N7 + ; 70. K—B4, R—B6 +.

61. ... K—B2
White resigns.
After 62. R—B2, K—K3 White is completely helpless. An eventful encounter.

NIMZOWITSCH–ROMIH, San Remo, 1930. *English Opening*
(Notes to this game are by Nimzowitsch, translated from Danish)
| 1. P—QB4 P—K4 | 3. P—KN3 P—Q3 |
| 2. N—QB3 P—QB4 | 4. B—N2 |

A bishop that knows what it wants, such a bishop you can find in the dear old openings, e.g. in the variation 1. P—K4, P—K4;

2. N—KB3, N—QB3; 3. B—B4, for here the bishop stands and menaces the king. Already in the Spanish Game the threat seems to obtrude a little less sharply, as here the whole purpose is to counteract the establishment of the enemy centre. In the modern openings the situation is far worse, for there the bishops are entirely passive: they do not threaten anything, and they want nothing, save to gaze out into the distance. . . . But when the game is played to an end, then one sees with astonishment that the bishop has accomplished a great deal, both prophylactically and directly; and especially one wonders at how rich and changing such a modern bishop's destiny can be! Then the bishop of the old days can quietly go and lay itself to rest, it can no more compete with the modern bishops, than the old school (Tarrasch) can compete with the modern style of play.

| 4. ... | N—QB3 | 6. P—QR3 |
| 5. P—Q3 | P—B4 | |

Isn't the bishop modern, then?! It 'toils not itself', but lets the others work for it. Now b2-b4 will come, e.g. 7. P—QN4, P × P; 8. P × P, N × P; 9. Q—R4 +, N—QB3; *10.* B × N +, and the bishop's co-operation secures the outcome.

| 6. ... | B—Q2 | 7. P—QN4 | R—N1 |

In case of 7. ... P × P; 8. P × P, N × P; 9. B × P the a-pawn becomes weak.

8. P—N5   N—R4
Now one can see that the knight is as good as taken prisoner, and who has brought this about? The bishop on g2 has.

9. B—Q5
Many will wonder at this all too direct advance, and so I did myself during the actual encounter. I knew quite well that a slow undermining of the hostile central position (through, e.g., 9. P—B4 and 10. N—B3) would have been both the indicated and stylish course. But I thought that such a way of proceeding would take too much time, and that my opponent was not 'worth all the bother'. The reader will probably excuse this frank explanation, but one cannot silence the psychological motives of the struggle, if one wants to draw a trustworthy picture of some game or other.

| 9. ... | N—KB3 | 11. B × N | B × B |
| 10. B—N5 | B—K2 | 12. R—B1 | |

Another plan consisted in the development 12. P—K3, 13. KN—K2 and 14. P—B4.

12. ... Q—K2
13. P—K4‡
Blocking the retreat for the bishop, which now becomes 'zugtot', i.e. immobilised. Yet his position is good enough, for now castling and therewith the connection of the enemy rooks has become very difficult. That old-fashioned search for direct contact with the enemy king is in this position blended with a hypermodern flirtation with the outermost enemy queen's wing, namely with the squares c6 and b7. The direction of the attack against the last-named squares comes to bear the prime rôle later on (see the 22nd move by White).

13. ... P—KN3
... P—B5 at once came into consideration.

14. R—N1
To look after the imprisoned knight.

14. ... R—KB1
To be preferred was the manœuvre Ke8—f8—g7, in order to connect the rooks.

15. P—KR4 P—B5 **17. P—R5 NP × P!?**
16. KN—K2 B—N2
More correct was 17. ... P—N4: as Black has a piece less in play (the Na5 hardly counts), he should close the game up, rather than open it out.

18. P × P
But *not* 18. R × P, B—N5!; 19. R × RP, Q—B3 with counterplay for Black.

18. ... P × P **20. K—Q2 P—R6**
19. P—B3!! P—R5
On h3 he feels himself secure, because the bishop provides sufficient defence from d7. Now, however, follows a surprise.

21. Q—R4 P—N3 **22. B—B6!**
Faithful to the old tradition: it is indeed the recollections of childhood which finally determine one's development, and not some other, short-lived episode (such as the stay on d5)! Now the white pieces, especially the two diagonal men, stand in as modern a guise as can be wished; one could almost be tempted to say that each on its own was

misplaced, if their co-ordination did not make of them such an awe-inspiring unity.

22. ... Q—R5

I had expected 22. ... B × B; 23. P × B, B × N + ; 24. N × B, Q—QB2, whereupon a queen sacrifice was prepared, namely 25. R × RP, Q × P; 26. *Q × N!* with a winning attack (26. ... P × Q; 27. R × R +, K—B2; 28. R × P +, K—N3!; 29. R(N8)—QN7, R—KN1; 30. N—Q5, K—N4; 31. R(N7)—KB7 threatening N—K7 plus R—B5. Mate).

23. R—R2 Q—R4   24. R—N1

24. QR—R1 would also have led to a win.

24. ... B—R1

On 24. ... B × N + ; 25. N × B, Q × P would have come *N—Q5* (the knights assume the bishop's legacy!) and R—N7 with destruction.

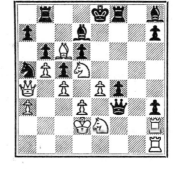

25. R(N1)—KR1   Q × P
26. N—Q5‡

The preparations are now completed, all is clear for occupation.

26. ... B—Q5   28. R(R3)—R2
27. R × P Q—B7

A last farewell to those at home before the great journey into the enemy's land begins.

28. ... Q—B6   31. R × B +   K—B1
29. R × P Q—B7*   32. N—K7 mate
30. R—K7 + K—Q1

SULTAN KHAN–NIMZOWITSCH, Liège, 1930. *Queen's Indian Defence*

1. P—Q4 N—KB3   3. N—KB3 P—QN3
2. P—QB4 P—K3   4. P—KN3 B—R3

A considerably more dynamic and 'problem-setting' move than the normal 4. ... B—N2. Nimzowitsch's innovation was subsequently borrowed by Alekhine and at the moment it numbers several Russian Grandmasters amongst its supporters—e.g. Smyslov, Bronstein, Petrosian and Keres.

* Black's 29th move is ridiculous but he loses anyway, e.g. 29. ... R—Q1; 30. N—B7. Mate; or 29. ..., B × B; 30. P × B, with the horrible threat of P—B7. Finally, 29. ..., R—B2; 30. B × B +, R × B; 31. N × B!, followed by N – B6 +. (RDK)

5. P—N3

A very natural protection of the QBP which, in addition, prepares the fianchetto of White's QB. However, the move is not best. Against 5. Q—R4, which is probably stronger, Bronstein has suggested the following active procedure: 5. ... **P—B3; 6. N—B3, P—QN4!?; 7. P × P, P × P; 8. N × P, Q—N3; 9. N—B3, B—N5; 10. B—N2, 0—0; 11. 0—0, B × N; 12. P × B, B × P,** or 9. P—K3, B—N2; 10. B—K2, B—B3! = + (Compare also theoretical section, page 63.) A dangerous line for Black is the pawn sacrifice: 5. QN—Q2, P—B4?!; 6. P—K4!, P × P; 7. P—K5, N—N1; 8. B—N2, N—QB3; 9. 0—0, B—N5; 10. Q—R4, Q—B1; 11. P—QR3, B—K2; 12. P—QN4, B—N2; 13. P—B5! with a powerful attack Gufeld–Gipslis, 37th Soviet Championship, 1969. Once again it was Bronstein who demonstrated that Black can also maintain himself satisfactorily in this line if he avoids 5. ... P—B4?! So, 5. ... **B—N5; 6. Q—B2, B—N2!; 7. B—N2, P—QR4; 8. 0—0, P—Q4; 9. N—K5, 0—0; 10. P × P, KP × P; 11. N/2—B3, N—K5; 12. B—K3, R—K1; 13. QR—B1, P—QB3; 14. KR—Q1, B—KB1; 15. N—Q3, P—B3** and Black has a very comfortable position (Portisch–Bronstein, Las Palmas, 1972).

5. ...   B—N5 +

The initial move of a counter-attack on the dark squares which forms the strategic *leit-motif* of Nimzowitsch's play until the very end of the game. Later on more direct and forceful methods were devised for Black, although it is hard to say if they represented any improvement on the Nimzowitschian scheme. Here is one example of the line handled by Smyslov (White: Uhlmann) from the Alekhine memorial tournament, Moscow, 1956: 5. ... **P—Q4; 6. B—KN2, B—N5 + ; 7. KN—Q2?** (7. B—Q2! when Smyslov intended ... B—K2), 7. ... **P—B4!; 8. QP × P, KB × P; 9. B—N2, 0—0; 10. 0—0, N—B3; 11. N—QB3, R—B1; 12. P × P?, P × P; 13. N—R4, N—Q5!; 14. N—QB3** (14. R—K1, N—B7!), 14. ... **Q—K2; 15. R—K1, N—B7!; 16. R—KB1, N × R; 17. Q × N, KR—Q1; 18. B—B3, B—R6.** 0-1.

6. B—Q2   B × B +

6. ... B—K2 followed by ... P—Q4 would transpose into Smyslov's idea above. Nimzowitsch's plan is to exchange the dark-squared bishops and then establish his central pawns on the same dark squares, thus hemming the scope of White's remaining bishop.

7. QN × B

It is more aggressive to recapture with the queen.

| 7, ... | B—N2 | 9. P × P |
| 8. B—N2 | P—B4 | |

9. 0—0, P × P; 10. N × P, B × B; 11. K × B would give Black no problems at all. Black could even consider playing more ambitiously with 11. ... Q—B1—QN2. However, aiming for equality, as above, probably represented White's most realistic course by this stage.

| 9. ... | P × P | 11. R—K1 |
| 10. 0—0 | 0—0 | |

Still angling for P—K4.

11. ...   Q—K2

Continuing his complex dark square strategy, Black will counter P—K4 by playing ... P—K4 himself, followed by ... QN—B3—Q5.

12. QR—B1

White probably expected Black to play ... P—Q4 in the near future and therefore organised potential pressure against the hanging pawns which would come into being after 12. ... P—Q4; 13. P × P, P × P.

12. ...   P—K4!

Threatening ... P—K5—K6 with total disruption. White's hand is forced.

13. P—K4   N—B3   14. N—N1

Heading for his own Q5 square. However, there is a qualitative difference in the respective equine occupations of Q5. White's N—Q5 can be met by ... B × N. Black's ... N—Q5 can be met by N × N only. After these exchanges Black will possess a dark square central pawn-wedge plus a N, while White will own a light square central pawn-wedge plus a light-squared bishop. In other words, the position, even at this stage, is tending towards an ending where Black will have the superior minor piece.

14. ...   P—Q3   15. N—B3   P—QR4

White's QNP represents an attractive target for the thrust ... P—QR4—R5. If White tries to block the position with 16. P—QR4 there would follow ... N—Q5 with possibilities of steering for the eventual rolling-up: ... P—KB4.

16. N—Q2

Nimzowitsch was full of praise for the subtle defensive manœuvre introduced by this move.

16. ...   N—Q5   17. N—B1

Also heading for Q5.

17. ...   B—B3
To lend support to ... P—R5 when the time is ripe.

18. N—K3   Q—N2   20. P × P
19. Q—Q3   P—R5
In the long run White cannot maintain his QNP at QN3. It is
better to submit to the creation of lesser weaknesses at a2
and c4.

20. ...   B × RP   22. R—N2   B—B3
21. R—N1   Q—R2   23. KR—N1   Q—B2
Threatening R—R6.

24. N—N5   Q—Q2   26. N/1—B3   P—N3
25. N—Q1   N—K1
With the ideas: ... N—N2—K3 and ... P—B4.

27. N × N   BP × N   29. P—N4
28. N—Q5   Q—R2
A rather crude method of preventing ... P—B4, which further
weakens White's dark squares. Black was better in any case but this
move does help him. After the text Black decides that the time has
come to liquidate White's N (cf. note to 14. N—N1).

29. ...   B × N   30. KP × B
After the other recapture (BP × N) Black would possess a clear,
static advantage. The capture chosen by White leads to a sharpening
of the struggle in that White now obtains potentially mobile pawns
(QBP and QP) to compensate for Black's central majority.

30. ...   N—B3   31. P—KR3
And not 31. P—N5?, N—R4!—B5.

31. ...   K—N2
A typical safety precaution. The king is more comfortable on
KN2.

32. R—N6
Threatening violence to Black's QP. If Black does not react
accurately White may even gain the upper hand.

32. ...   KR—Q1   33. R/1—N2   P—R3!
Very important. It was impossible to play 33. ... N—Q2 on
account of 34. R × P, N—B4; 35. Q—K2, R × R; 36. Q × P +,
R—B3; 37. P—N5! Hence the significance of Black's 33rd
move.

34. P—B4‡

'The crisis of the game' (Nimzo-witsch).

It seems as if White must now seize the initiative.

34. ... N—Q2!

But the dark squares come to Black's rescue. If now 35. R × P, N—B4; 36. Q—K2, P—K5! (36. ... R × R?; 37. Q × P + and P—N5 as before) 37. R × R, R × R and White's passed pawns are heavily blockaded (by a dark-squared army corps) while both of Black's aspire to the proverbial Field Marshal's baton. 38. B × P? would lose at once to ... R—K1.

35. R/6—N5 P × P?

Time-trouble! Black could win at once by means of 35. ... N—B4!; 36. Q—N1, N—R5 followed by ... N—B6 or 36. Q—K2, P—K5. After this slip Black retains a positional plus, but he can no longer count on rapid victory.

36. R—Q2 N—K4 38. R × Q P—B6?!
37. Q × QP Q × Q +

More accurate was 38. ... R × P; 39. R × P, R—QB7 threatening ... R—QR1—R7.

39. B—B1 R—R5.

Nimzowitsch did not want to grant counter-chances after 39. ... R × P; 40. P—B5.

40. R—Q2 N—Q2 42. R—N3 R/1—QR1
41. K—B2 R—R6 43. R × P N—B4

Black has even lost a pawn but he still retains the advantage in view of his dark square grip and the paralysing effect exerted by his rook along the 6th rank.

44. R × R R × R 45. K—N2 P—B4

Creating a dangerous passed pawn. A further factor in favour of Black is the mobility of his king in comparison with the limited freedom of movement enjoyed by his White counterpart.

46. P × P P × P 47. K—N1

47. B—K2! The move played is, if anything, counter-productive

47. ... K—B3 49. R—K2 K—B4
48. R—QN2 P—B5 50. R—K8 P—B6

White's bishop has no moves and mating threats loom up.

51. R—KR8   K—N4   53. R × P
52. R—Q8   R × P

Lifting the blockade and thereby forcing Black into immediate action. As it is, the action Black does take is of a decisive nature.

53. ...   N—K5   55. R—Q8   R—R8
54. P—R4 +   K—B5   56. R—KN8

Or 56. P—Q6, K—N6; 57. R—KN8 +, N—N4!; 58. P × N, P—B7 +.

56. ...   N—N6   59. R—KB8 +   N—B4
57. K—R2   N × B +   60. R × N +   K × R
58. K—R3   N—K6
White resigns.

COLLE–NIMZOWITSCH, Frankfurt, 1930. *QP Opening*

A game that would have fitted ideally into the scheme of *My System* had it not been played three years after Nimzowitsch's final version of his book. Both sides undertake wing diversions, but White's results only in a glorious triumph over a harmless pawn while Black's (closely supported by a powerful centralisation) enables his massed columns to smash down the KR file and deliver mate.

1. P—Q4   N—KB3   3. P—K3   B—B4
2. N—KB3   P—Q4   4. P—B4   P—K3

After 1920 it was rare for Nimzowitsch to adopt anything but his own defence to 1. P—Q4 but before the Great War he frequently resorted to such defensive systems as he employs here. One typical example was his game with Vidmar (White) from Coburg, 1904: 1. P—Q4, P—Q4; 2. N—KB3, B—N5; 3. P—K3, P—K3; 4. P—B4, B × N; 5. P × B, P—QB3; 6. Q—N3, Q—N3; 7. Q—B2, B—K2; 8. N—B3, B—B3 (a complicated method of fianchettoing the bishop); 9. R—KN1, N—K2; 10. P—B4, N—Q2; 11. P—QB5, Q—B2; 12. B—Q2, P—KR3; 13. P—KR4, P—KR4 (both 12. ... P—KR3 and 13. ... P—KR4 received '!!' from Schlechter. So much for the myth of the misunderstood genius. We can see from this that the people who counted—like Schlechter—were capable of appreciating Nimzowitsch's ideas even in his very first tournament appearance); 14. B—Q3, P—KN3; 15. R—R1, N—KB4; 16. B × N, KP × B; 17. K—K2, N—B1; 18. K—B3, N—K3; 19. Q—R4, 0—0 with an obvious advantage to Black. But Nimzowitsch promptly lost the game by sacrificing unsoundly.

5. Q—N3?!
Pointless, as the reply shows.

5. ... N—B3!   **6. P—B5**

6. Q × NP?, N—QN5! The text, however, releases all the pressures from Black's centre. It was probably better to play 6. P × P and follow with B—N5.

6. ... Q—B1   **7. B—N5 N—Q2**

With a threefold objective: (i) Black threatens to free himself with ... N—Q1 and ... P—QB3 followed eventually by ... P—K4; (ii) Black parries the immediate threat of N—K5 and (iii) prepares long-term over-protection of the important e5 square.

8. B × N

Forestalling (i) but now White loses control of the light squares.

8. ... P × B   **9. 0—0 P—N3!**

To bring his KB into contact with e5. Nimzowitsch had obviously learnt a lot from his game (as White) versus Torre, Marienbad, 1925, where the young Mexican had played the less accurate 9. ... B—K2, with an eventual draw.

10. N/1—Q2 B—N2   **11. N—R4**

White plans N × B to lessen the force of ... P—K4 (or to prevent the move altogether), but after the recapture ... KP × N Black will be more than compensated by his increased influence over e4 and his pressure in the K file in general.

11. ... Q—R3!

A typical method of augmenting light-square control which appears in several of Nimzowitsch's games. Note that Nimzowitsch avoids the automatic response ... 0—0 since he recognises that his king may be needed in the centre.

12. N × B KP × N

With several positional trumps: the K file, the square e4 and the eventual disruptive threat ... P—KB5.

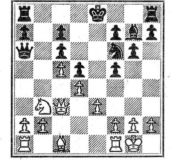

13. Q—B3 N—B3
14. N—N3‡

14. P—B3 would deny Black the use of e4 but would also leave White with a sick KP. The text commences a long-drawn-out manœuvre to molest Black's split Q side pawns.

It's interesting to examine this position for a while. If a computer were given the task of assessing the respective chances it might conclude that White stood better. After all, Black suffers from no less than two sets of doubled pawns and one isolated pawn, while White's pawns are all perfectly healthy. Yet the secret of Black's advantage lies in the fact that his 'weaknesses' are inaccessible. In fact his K side pawns are highly mobile, as we shall soon see. White's 'healthy' pawns, on the other hand, simply have no scope for expansion. A human player would also take in at a glance Black's impressive light-square control, but how does one solve the problem of explaining such intangibles to a machine possessed of 'artificial intelligence' but not of intuition?

Personally speaking, I must confess, I hope the problem is never solved!

| 14. ... | N—K5 | 16. N × Q | K—Q2! |

15. Q—R5 Q × Q

The '!' is for the foresight involved rather than for the excellence of the move itself, which is actually a forced one.

| 17. R—Q1 | KR—K1 | 19. R—Q3 |
| 18. P—KN3 | QR—N1 | |

White's diversion begins.

19. ... P—R4

And so does Black's. White should now have put up some token resistance by means of 20. P—KR4. Instead of taking this elementary precaution (although its ultimate efficacy is rather doubtful) White rushes to his perdition with the determination of a Gadarene hog.

| 20. R—R3 | P—R5 | 22. RP × P | R—KR1 |
| 21. N—N3 | P × P | 23. R × P | |

An extreme example of a decentralised diversion. Had Colle for-

gotten that it is also possible to give mate without the presence of queens on the board?

23. ... R—R6
24. N—Q2 QR—KR1
25. N—B1 P—N4‡

Threatening the slow but destructive: ... P—N5, ... N—N4—B6 and ... R—R8—N8.

26. P—B3 R—R8 +
27. K—N2 N × NP!

Dies irae, dies illa
Solvet saeclum in favilla.

28. K×N R×N   29. P—R4
Optimistically setting forth on the path that leads to apotheosis.

| 29. ... | P—B5+! | 31. K—B2 | B×P+ |
| 30. P×P | R—N8+ | 32. K—K2 | R—R7+ |

White resigns.
Utter desolation. White's Q side pieces hardly moved.

NIMZOWITSCH–AHUES, Frankfurt, 1930. *Nimzowitsch Attack*

1. N—KB3	P—Q4	5. P—B4	P—B3
2. P—QN3	P—K3	6. N—B3	B—Q3
3. B—N2	N—KB3	7. Q—B2	
4. P—K3	QN—Q2		

Black has chosen an unpretentious defensive system which would blossom into something quite promising if ever he were to play ... P—K4. White's opening strategy revolves around the restraint of this advance, which restraint could have been achieved quite simply by 7. P—Q4, but Nimzowitsch insists on adopting a more complex prophylactic method. If now 7. ... P—K4; 8. P×P, P×P; 9. N—QN5, B—N1; 10. B—R3+ −.

7. ... Q—K2   8. N—Q4
A strange move intending to parry ... P—K4 with N—B5! Nimzowitsch is not at all concerned that his N should be chased away by ... P—B4 since the advance of Black's QBP to c5 would result in a weakening of the support of the Black QP which, in turn, would dilute the force of Black's eventual ... P—K4.

| 8. ... | P—QR3 | 10. 0—0 | P—B4 |
| 9. B—K2 | 0—0 | | |

Something had to be done about the annoying N.

11. N—B3 N—N3?
Protecting his QP with a piece in preparation for the long-awaited ... P—K4, but on b6 this N is seriously out of play. If instead 11. ... P×P; 12. P×P and then ... P—K4, White replies 13. P—K4! with a powerful grip on his Q5 square, for which Black has no corresponding compensation. Now we can see the effects of White's subtle 8. N—Q4, in that the vulnerability of Black's Q4 square is already causing him some problems.
The most sensible course is probably 11. ... P—QN3 followed by

... B—N2. Perhaps Black rejected this in view of 12. P × P followed by P—Q4, when it is impossible to avoid hanging pawns on c5 and d5 (or an IQP if Black prefers).

Still, the positions arising from 11. ... P—QN3 would have offered chances to both sides. After the text White seizes the initiative and maintains it relentlessly until the end of the game.

12. P—K4!

This central blow can be regarded as the positional refutation of the decentralising 11. ... N—N3? Ideally Black would now like to play 12. ... P—Q5, but this fails to 13. P—K5, P × N; 14. B × P!, B × P; 15. N × B±.

12. ... N × KP	**14. Q × P P—K4**
13. N × N P × N	

Very optimistic. Black plans ... P—B4 with a fine game, but if Black's idea were correct it would mean that his decentralisation was good while White's centralisation was weak. Nimzowitsch could never accept such a conclusion so he naturally seeks for an outright concrete refutation of Black's violent schemes.

To be fair to Ahues it should be mentioned that there is a dearth of reasonable alternatives at this point since it is difficult to develop his Q side pieces without a tortuous preliminary move such as ... R—N1 (to be followed by ... B—Q2).

15. N × P!

In order to defeat Black's idea White must offer the sacrifice of a piece. But not the other way: 15. B × P?, B × B; 16. Q × B, Q × Q; 17. N × Q, R—K1; 18. P—B4, P—B3 – +.

15. ...   R—K1

Reinforcing the pressure against the pinned N. There are two other ways of playing to win material:

(i) 15. ... B × N; 16. Q × B, Q × Q; 17. B × Q, R—K1; 18. B—B7!, R × B; 19. B × N, R × QP; 20. B × P and White has winning chances in spite of the opposite-coloured bishops (Nimzowitsch).

(ii) 15. ... P—B3; 16. B—Q3, P × N (16. ... B × N; 17. Q × P +, K—B2; 18. QR—K1 and P—B4); 17. Q × P +, K—B2; 18. Q—N6 + (18. P—B4 is also not bad), ... K—N1; 19. P—B4 when there are many ways to win, e.g. 19. ... P × P; 20. Q—R7 +, K—B2; 21. B—N6 +, K—K3; 22. Q—R3 +, or 19. ... R—B3; 20. Q—R7 +, K—B2; 21. P × P, B × P; 22. Q—R5 +.

16. P—B4   P—B3
17. B—R5‡
If now 17. B—Q3, P—N3 is an
adequate defence. It's fascinating to
see that as Black defends himself
against one threat (B—Q3) he automatically exposes himself to a blow
from a quite different quarter (B—
R5).

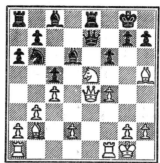

17. ...   R—B1
'!' from Nimzowitsch. Ahues'
resourceful defence obliges Nimzowitsch to reveal the full extent of
his calculations. Less testing were:

   (i) 17. ... R—Q1; 18. B—B7 +, K—R1; 19. N—N6 +, P × N;
       20. Q × KNP, B—N5; 21. QR—K1 followed by R—K3—
       R3 + and Q—R5. Mate.

   (ii) 17. P—N3; 18. B × P, P × B; 19. Q × P +, K—B1; 20. N—
       N4, B × N; 21. B × P + −.

17. ... P × N would not be much different from the game continuation.

18. P—Q3!
Black threatened ... P—N3 and ... B—B4.
White can go astray here with the plausible 18. QR—K1?, e.g.
... P—N3!; 19. B × P, P × B; 20. N × P, Q × Q; 21. R × Q, B—B4!
(Nimzowitsch).

18. ...   P × N?
At last he accepts, but in my opinion this was still premature. The
point of Nimzowitsch's previous move was to answer 18. ... P—N3
with 19. B × P, P × B; 20. N × P (20. Q × P +, Q—N2 is nothing
special for White), ... Q × Q; 21. P × Q, R—B2; 22. QR—Q1,
when he has a powerful central/K side pawn roller and superior
mobilisation in exchange for a piece. However, after 22. ... B—B2
White has no forced win available and I believe that Black's position
is capable of immense resistance. The text, on the other hand, grants
Black an actual material superiority (rather than the parity represented by B for three pawns), but since his extra piece can hardly
move it was not a course to be recommended.

19. P × P   B—B2
Or 19. ... P—N3; 20. R × R + and B × P followed by mate.

20. R × R +   Q × R
21. R—KB1   Q—Q1
Or 21. ... Q—K2; 22. R—B7, Q × R; 23. B × Q +, K × B;
24. P—Q4! (threatening P × P and P—Q5), 24. ... P × P; 25. P—
B5, N—Q2; 26. P—K6 +.

22. B—B7 +   K—R1   **23. P—K6   B × P**
If 23. ... Q—K2; 24. B × P +, K × B; 25. Q—N4 +, K—R3;
26. R—B5.

24. B × B   Q—N4   **25. R—B7**   Resigns.
I cannot help noticing a similarity in combinational motif between
this game and one won by Petrosian some twenty years later. Here
is the crucial position from the game I have in mind, Petrosian–
Pachman, Interzonal, 1952.

Black to play moved: **17. ...
B—B2** (or 17. ... P × N; 18. BP × P,
B—B2; 19. N—B6 +, K—R1;
20. N × R, Q × N; 21. P—K6 + –);
**18. N—N3, P × N; 19. N—B5, Q—
B3; 20. QP × P, P—KR4** (20. ...
Q—B1; 21. Q—N6, K—R1; 22. R—
Q3, Q—N1; 23. R—KR3, R—K3;
24. N × RP!, R × Q; 25. N—B7.
Mate); **21. Q × P, Q—B2; 22. Q—
N4, R—K3; 23. R—B3, R—N3;
24. Q × R, Q × Q; 25. N—K7 +,
K—B2; 26. N × Q, K × N; 27. P—
KN4, N—R3; 28. R—Q7, R—Q1; 29. P—B5 +, K—N4; 30. R ×
P +, K—R5; 31. P—K6, B—N3 +; 32. K—B1, R—Q8 +; 33. K—K2,
R—Q4; 34. P—B6, R—K4 +; 35. K—B1, N—B4; 36. R—B5.**
1–0. (Analysis based on that by Kotov and Yudovich in the *Soviet
School of Chess*.)
Do you think I am justified in noting any similarities? Perhaps the
parallel would have been more marked if Ahues had opted for the
toughest defence on move 18 (18. ... P—N3!).

Sir G. Thomas–Nimzowitsch, Frankfurt, 1930
Caro Kann Defence
(Notes to this game are by Nimzowitsch, translated from Danish)
1. P—K4   P—QB3   **2. N—QB3**
After the usual continuation 2. P—Q4, P—Q4; 3. N—QB3,
P × P; 4. N × P Black can play . . . B—B4. The intention behind
2. N—QB3 is, as one will soon see, to prevent this development of
the bishop.

2. ...   P—Q4   **4. N × P**
3. N—B3   P × P

Bogoljubow, for it was really he who discovered the *variation* employed in this game, has a valid point, for now 4. ... B—B4 would fail, e.g. 4. ... B—B4; 5. N—N3, B—N3; 6. P—KR4, P—KR3; 7. N—K5, B—R2; 8. Q—R5, P—KN3; 9. B—B4, P—K3; 10. Q—K2, and White stands better. But this is far from saying that 2. N—QB3 signifies a serious breach in the bastion of the Caro Kann; to be sure, ... B—B4 is cast down, but only to give way to another, more modern and more effective system of defence. See the following note!

4. ...   N—B3!

'... B—B4' is dead, '... N—B3' lives! With the usual continuation 1. P—K4, P—QB3; 2. P—Q4, P—Q4; 3. N—QB3, P × P; 4. N × P; 4. ... N—B3 is of doubtful value because of 5. N × N +. E.g. 5. ... NP × N; 6. P—QB3, B—B4; 7. N—K2 and N—N3, or 5. ... KP × N!; 6. P—QB3!, B—Q3; 7. B—Q3, 0—0; 8. Q—B2. Here, however, 5. N × N + would fail [*sic!*] against 5. ... NP × N; 6. P—QB3, *B—N5* followed by ... P—K3, ... B—Q3, ... Q—B2 and ... 0—0—0 with a solid position.

5. N—N3

Now White has not got anything at all.

5. ...   P—B4

Réti's idea.

6. P—Q4   P × P   **8. N × Q   P—QR3**
7. Q × P   Q × Q

To stop N—N5.

9. B—K2   B—N5!

To prevent the effective development of the bishop to f3. Prophylaxis is—along with centralisation and restraint (Hæmning)—the main point of the technique of consolidation! (9. ... B—N5 represents an improvement over the 9. ... P—KN3 chosen by Nimzowitsch in his game versus Ahues from San Remo earlier the same year. That previous game continued 10. 0—0, B—N2; 11. R—Q1, 0—0; 12. P—QB3, B—N5; 13. B—K3, B × B; 14. N/4 × B, R—B1; 15. R—Q2, N—B3; 16. QR—Q1, N—K4; 17. P—N3, P—QN4; 18. P—KR3, P—K3; 19. P—KB4, N—B3; 20. K—B2, P—KR4, with a very good position for Black. But White should have played 11. B—B3! with the advantage.) (RDK)

10. B—Q3!   P—K4

Not entirely consolidating! There arises, in fact, some slight weaknesses on d6 and e5, and the bishop itself on g4 comes in a way to form a weak point, because it does not find time to retreat. The first-class solid move here was 10. ... B—Q2!

11. N/Q4—B5   P—KN3   12. N—K3   QN—Q2
On 12. ... B—K3 there would follow 13. B—B4 with discomfort for Black. But now I surrender the two bishops to the opponent (unfortunately!).

13. N—K4   B—N5 +!   14. P—QB3   B—K2
To provoke P—QB3 can have its significance: the d3 square is weakened, and an eventual basis for the minority attack (=2 pawns against 3) ... b7—b5—b4 is provided.

15. N × N +   N × N   17. P—B3   N—B3
16. N × B   N × N   18. B—R6
Prevents ... 0—0—0 because of the reply B—QB4.

18. ...   B—B1   19. B × B?
This move ought to be censured: correct was 19. B—KN5, B—N2; 20. 0—0—0, and the two bishops would have continued to trouble the opponent.

19. ...   K × B   21. KR—K1   KR—K1
20. 0—0—0   K—N2   22. R—Q2   R—K2
Now the real struggle begins.

23. B—B2!
Thomas is preparing the following fine continuation: 24. R/Q2—K2, QR—K1; 25. B—R4, P—QN4; 26. B—B2 and then 27. P—QR4; the isolated b-pawn would then be hunted down (by R—Q2—Q6—QN6).
Now it rests with Black to find a yet finer counter-plan.

23. ...   P—KR4!!   24. R/Q2—K2
On 24. P—KR4 follows ... R—QB1 and ... R—B5.

24. ...   QR—K1   26. B—B2   P—R5
25. B—R4   P—QN4   27. P—R4
All according to Sir Thomas's [sic] prearranged programme. But now comes that *counterplay* he has underestimated.

27. ...   N—Q4!
But *not* 27. ... N—R4—why emerges from the note to White's 29th move.

28. P × P   P × P   29. R—Q2
On 29. R—K4 would have come 29. ... P—B4; 30. R × RP,

N—B5 and wins the exchange. With a knight on h5 instead of d5 'that doesn't work', for then, after 29. R—K4, P—B4, White simply plays 30. R—QN4! and gets the advantage.

29. ... N—B5‡

The current situation: b5 is weak, but the knight at f4 ties down White's troops. Those troops now seek freedom: White's 30th–32nd moves.

30. P—KN3	P × P
31. P × P	N—R4
32. P—KN4	

The goal is reached, but ... *

32. ...	N—B5
33. R—Q6	R—R2

Black now owns a giant knight on f4 and the a- and h-files and is therefore at a clear advantage. On the subject of these files the reader will soon hear some philosophical-critical remarks.

34. B—K4 P—N5

The minority attack!

35. P—B4

Not 35. P × P because of ... R—QN1. With the text move a king journey to b3 is planned.

35. ... R—QB1! 36. P—N3

The malicious rook! The journey Kc1—c2—b3 is now spoiled for good.

36. ... R—KR1

Now we have the two files we talked about in the note to Black's 33rd move. Both open lines are equally valuable, but their manner of creation was very different: the h-file was opened by Black, who through the menacing centralisation of the knight on f4 quite *forced* g2—g3 (... h4 × g3, h2 × g3 and the file is open). But the creation of the a-file is not of Black's doing, it arose without Black's having to exert himself at all. It was, for that matter, not White's doing either; it arose rather like a *side-effect*, which followed in the wake of another white operation, the isolating of the b-pawn.

This circumstance, that Black is operating both on the arduously conquered h-file as well as on the freely granted a-file, is a clear

---

* 32. P—KN4? is dreadfully weakening—White had to play either 32. R—N1 or 32. R—Q5. It is strange that Nimzowitsch does not castigate the error of the text in his own notes. (RDK)

demonstration that he does not suffer from that feverish activity, which is the cause of so many otherwise not untalented players quite losing their sense of perspective, and not at all being able to control events at a longer range (cf. the bird's-eye view). But that Black was able to do in the present game: he allowed the opponent to carry through his plan and worked in the meantime on his own. And when the time came, he took both the fruits of his own labours and those which his opponent had unwittingly prepared for him—both the rook's files.

37. B—N1   R—KR6   38. R—K3   P—K5!
The decisive combinative conclusion.

39. B × P
The slim chance of a draw consisted in 39. R—Q4, e.g. 39. ... P—B4; 40. NP × P, NP × P; 41. B × P.

39. ...   R—QR7   41. R—Q2
40. B—B2   R/R6—R7
Or 41. B—N1, N—K7 +.

41. ...   R—QR8 +
White resigns, since a piece is lost. One of my most difficult games in the last few years.

NIMZOWITSCH–H. JOHNER, Bern, 1931. *Nimzowitsch Attack*
(Notes to this game are by Nimzowitsch, translated from Danish)

1. N—KB3   N—KB3   3. B—N2   P—B4
2. P—QN3   P—Q4   4. P—K3   N—B3
Clearer is 4. ... P—K3, as Black then avoids the doubled pawn on c6 and c5. This doubled pawn does not necessarily have to be harmful, but it *can* become so—and therefore it is always safest to say 'No' to the whole of this interesting, but all too complicated, story.

5. B—N5   B—N5   7. P—KR3   B × N!
6. B × N +   P × B
Well played; hereby he secures tolerable conditions for the doubled pawn. On the other hand the retreat 7. ... B—R4 would lead, after P—Q3, QN—Q2 and P—KN4, to the establishment of a knight on e5, which the horrible, immobile doubled-complex at c6 and c5 would hardly be able to bear; in other words: Black aims at a certain mobility in the direction of e5 as compensation for his otherwise rather immobile pawn-formation.

8. Q × B   Q—B2   9. P—Q3   P—K3
Interesting, he offers the pawn on g7; after 10. B × N, P × B;

11. Q × BP, R—KN1; 12. Q—KB3, B—N2; 13. P—B3 the bishop would show itself to be too strong. But why not 9. ... P—K4 at once? (See the note to Black's 7th move). 9. ... P—K4 was the logical move. After the reply 10. Q—N3, N—Q2; 11. P—K4, P—B3; 12. N—B3 there follows ... N—N3 with a solid position.

| 10. | N—B3 | B—Q3 | | 12. | B × B | Q × B |
| 11. | N—R4 | B—K4 | | 13. | 0—0 | N—Q2 |

Now one can better judge the doubled pawn's bright and dark sides: the latter consist in the impossibility of obtaining its advance in a really compact manner—after ... d5–d4 there could surely always come e3–e4, and the advance ... c5–c4 is stopped for time eternal. The bright sides, on the other hand, consist in its not being easy to *force* the pawns out of their passive-defensive attitude, since at bottom that can only be accomplished through c2–c4, but in that case c4 would become useless as a square for pieces.

14. Q—K2

A manœuvre which aims at forcing d5–d4, without White at this moment having to clutch at such 'extremist' measures as c2–c4.

| 14. ... | 0—0 | | 16. | Q—R5 | KR—N1!? |
| 15. Q—Q2 | P—B4 | | | | |

This indirect defence of the bone of contention on c5 seems neither in a positional nor in a combinative sense to be dictated by the internal demands of the position: 16. ... Q—Q3 was the correct move, the rook had nothing to say on the b-file. Black thinks that 17. N × P should now cost the exchange (17. ... R—N4; 18. N × N, Q × R), but does not calculate far enough (however, that is taken care of by the opponent!). After 16. ... Q—Q3 the game would have stood equal, e.g. 17. P—QB4, P—Q5!; 18. P × P, Q × P; 19. QR—K1, P—K4; 20. R—K2, P—B5; 21. Q—B3, etc. After the text move a long and beautiful combination follows, which I consider I can count amongst my best of the last few years.

17.	N × P!!	R—N4
18.	N × N	Q × R
19.	Q—B7!‡	

Threatening Q × BP with win of the exchange.

| 19. ... | Q—B6 |
| 20. P—QR4! | |

The point! The black rook now comes to stand badly: only thereby does the planned co-operation between the Qc7 and Nd7 acquire the right degree of intensity.

20. ... R—N5
On 20. ... R—R4 comes 21. Q—Q6, R—K1; 22. N—K5 with the main threat Q—Q7.

21. N—K5
To play Q—B7+ and Q×KP with subsequent smothered mate (N—B7+, N—R6+ +, Q—N8+ and N—B7. Mate).

21. ... R—KB1
On 21. ... K—R1 there comes P—B4 and R—B3—N3 with an unparriable mating attack.

22. N×P!
With the threat of N—K7+ and win of the queen, whilst on the other hand the rook on b4 is *en prise*. Now for the first time one understands why the rook was tempted to b4 on the 20th move.

22. ... K—R1
On 22. ... Q—Q7 a whole rook is lost: 23. Q—R5!, etc.

23. Q—Q6
An amusing fork! Black resigned the game.

NIMZOWITSCH–GYGLI, Bern, 1931. *Queen's Indian Defence*
(by transposition)

1. P—QB4	P—K3	3. P—Q4	P—QN3
2. N—KB3	N—KB3	4. P—QR3!?	

Prophylaxis. White wants, in theory, to dispute the diagonal of Black's fianchettoed QB by playing P—Q5, but this move is not practicable if Black can react with the pin ... B—N5. Significantly, 4. P—QR3 has been taken up enthusiastically by Petrosian, and the variation is now known after him. I wonder how many people realise that Nimzowitsch was there first!? In what follows I shall attempt to register the fortunes of this little-explored idea of Nimzowitsch's in the context of modern theoretical developments (i.e. Petrosian's experiences with 4. P—QR3).

4. ... B—N2
The natural reply, but by no means obligatory. At Palma, 1968, Larsen, against Petrosian, varied with the bold 4. ... P—B4, when White carried out his thematic strategic advance 5. P—Q5 and gained the advantage: 5. ... P×P; 6. P×P, P—N3; 7. N—B3, B—KN2; 8. B—N5, 0—0; 9. P—K3, P—Q3; 10. N—Q2, P—KR3;

11. B—R4, N—R3; 12. B—K2, N—B2; 13. P—K4, P—QN4;
14. 0—0, Q—Q2; 15. Q—B2, R—K1; 16. KR—K1, B—N2;
17. P—KR3. White won quite rapidly with a central breakthrough.

5. N—B3   P—Q3

Best here is the direct 5. . . . P—Q4 hoping to reach positions akin
to the Q. Gambit where White's P—QR3 will be exposed as a waste
of tempo. Here are some examples: 5. . . . P—Q4; 6. P × P, N × P
(6. . . . P × P!; 7. B—N5, QN—Q2; 8. P—K3, B—K2; 9. B—Q3,
0—0; 10. 0—0, P—B4; 11. R—B1, R—K1; 12. Q—K2, P—QR3 is
more likely to suit Black's needs); 7. P—K3, B—K2; 8. B—N5 +,
P—B3; 9. B—Q3, P—QB4; 10. N × N, Q × N; 11. P × P, Q × P;
12. B—Q2, N—B3; 13. R—QB1, Q—Q3; 14. Q—B2, R—QB1;
15. 0—0, P—KR3; 16. KR—Q1, 0—0; 17. B—B3 + —, Petrosian–
Smyslov, Moscow, 1961; or 5. . . . P—Q4; 6. P—K3, QN—Q2;
7. P × P, P × P; 8. B—K2?!, B—Q3; 9. P—QN4, 0—0; 10. 0—0,
P—QR3; 11. Q—N3, Q—K2; 12. R—N1, N—K5 = +, Spassky–
Petrosian(!), World Championship, 1969.

6. P—KN3

The pure Petrosian interpretation resides in an early P—Q5, as in
Petrosian's game versus Keres from Zürich, 1961: 6. P—Q5,
B—K2, 7. P—K4, P—B3; 8. P × KP, P × P; 9. N—KN5, B—QB1;
10. P—B4, 0—0; 11. B—Q3, P—K4; 12. P—KB5, P—B4; 13. P—
KN4, N—B3; 14. N—R3, N—K1; 15. N—Q5, N—Q5; 16. 0—0;
and, although White lost, this position is not bad for him.

6. ...   QN—Q2   8. 0—0   0—0
7. B—N2   B—K2

On 8. . . . N—K5 White would play 9. N × N, B × N; 10. P—Q5!
and if . . . P—K4; 11. N × P!, B × B; 12. N—B6 or 10. . . . P × P;
11. P × P, N—B3; 12. N—Q4! + —.

9. Q—B2

Preventing the simplification that would ensue after . . . N—K5,
but the absence of the Q from her home file permits a blow aimed at
White's centre.

9. ...   P—B4   10. P—Q5

Gaining territory in the regulation fashion.

10. ...   P × P   11. N—Q2

The pin along the h1–a8 diagonal ensures the recapture of the
pawn. In the meantime the KN strives to reach c4 whence it will
radiate central energy.

11. ...   R—K1?

A stereotyped response which saddles Black with a position that is cursed with all the faults of a Benoni set-up but which has none of its redeeming features, such as a mobile Q side pawn majority or genuine pressure against White's centre.

As Nimzowitsch pointed out after the game Black should have increased the tension with 11. ... P—QN4!. On 12. N × NP, Q—N3 Black protects his QB with gain of tempo and can therefore fight for a share of the centre; the decentralising 12. P × NP hardly comes into consideration, while 12. N × QP, N × N; 13. P × N leaves Black much better off than in the game, since his Q side pawns possess a marked degree of mobility. Furthermore the exchange of one pair of minor pieces makes it easier for Black to deploy his KB on the useful long dark diagonal.

12. P—QR4
Squashing the possibility.

| 12. ... | R—N1 | 14. P—N3 | P—QR3 |
| 13. P × P | B—KB1 | 15. N—B4 | N—K4 |

The exchange of minor pieces does occur but in this case it only serves to strengthen White's stranglehold on the centre.

16. P—B4	N × N	19. B—N2	B—N2
17. P × N	B—B1	20. QR—K1	N—N5
18. P—K4	P—N3	21. N—Q1	

Black was threatening ... B—Q5 +.

21. ... B—Q2?
It must be wrong to permit the exchange of the only piece (KB) that can guard the dark squares in the vicinity of Black's king. Relatively better was the repulsive looking ... P—B3 followed by ... N—R3—B2, attempting to restrain White's P—K5. The essential thing was to retain the KB for defensive purposes. Only after Black had seen to this priority should he have tried for counterplay with ... B—Q2 and ... P—QN4.

22. B × B	K × B
23. P—R3	N—R3
24. Q—N2 + ‡	

White has a beautiful position. For better or worse Black now had to try ... P—B3, obstructing the fatal diagonal, although he probably feared P—N4—N5 in reply. Gygli's insistent refusal to create a target by playing ... P—B3 results in a much worse horror befalling him.

24. ... K—N1   25. P—N4 P—B4?

Suicide. Since White threatened P—N5 trapping his knight ... P—B3 was by now compulsory.

26. NP × P   P × P   27. R—K3

Threatening R—N3 +, to which there is no antidote.

27. ... Q—R5   28. R/1—B3 N—N5

Or ... K—B2; 29. P—K5 + —. The text amounts to resignation.

29. P × N	P × NP	31. N—B2	P—KR4
30. R—KN3	B × P	32. P—K5	

This consummation of White's strategy persuaded Black to abandon the unequal struggle. 1–0.

HENNEBERGER–NIMZOWITSCH, Winterthur, 1931. *Caro Kann*

1. P—K4	P—QB3	4. N × P	N—B3
2. P—Q4	P—Q4	5. N—N3	P—B4
3. N—QB3	P × P	6. B—N5 +?!	

Much stronger is 6. N—B3. The text weakens White's light squares (since his pawns are tending to control the central dark squares and cannot readily change their spots) and furthers Black's development

6. ...	B—Q2	8. N—B3	Q—R4 +!
7. B × B +	N/1 × B		

A far sighted plan. Nimzowitsch intends to exchange off all those White's pieces which can defend his light squares. Ideally Black is aiming to reach the ending: Black N versus White QB, and this he eventually achieves.

9. P—B3   Q—R3

White cannot tolerate the presence of the enemy Q on the powerful a6–f1 diagonal. For one thing White would have difficulty in castling if the Q were allowed to occupy its post unmolested.

10. Q—K2	Q × Q +	14. KR—K1	N—Q4
11. N × Q	R—B1	15. B—N3	P—B5
12. 0—0	P—K3	16. N—K5	N × N
13. B—B4	B—K2	17. B × N	P—B3

So, White is weak on the light squares, but why isn't Black correspondingly weak on the dark squares? Well, one reason is that Black's pawn-structure is highly elastic and it can function as a light square aggression mechanism or as a defender of the dark squares more or less at will. White's pawn formation is, to a large extent, inflexible. It exerts a minimal (static) dark square influence but has very restricted light square potential. Those light square possibilities which are open to it (P—QR4/P—KB4—B5) are not exploited by Henneberger in the subsequent course of play.

Note that Black's light square plus means that he can weaken his KP (... P—B3) to create more space for his pieces without suffering any adverse side effects.

18. B—N3   P—KN4
Covering the dark square f4 and thus hindering the relief move: N—B4.

19. P—B4   P—KR3
And not 19. ... P—N5?; 20. P—B5!, P×P; 21. R—KB1.

20. QR—Q1	**K—B2**	**22. R—KB1**	**KR—K1**
21. R—Q2	**P—N4**	**23. R—B3?**	

Positively provoking a light square blockade which is entirely in Black's interest. If Henneberger had assumed that the closure of the position which follows would only increase his prospects of keeping out the wet, he was wrong.

He had to reclaim some light square territory with: 23. P—B5 although Black stands better in any case after 23. ... B—B1; 24. P×P+, R×P; 25. R—B5, R—Q1; 26. N—B1, K—N3; 27. R/Q—KB2, R—K8+; 28. R—B1, R×R+; 29. R×R, R—K1 (Nimzowitsch).

23. ... P—KN5		**24. R—B1 P—B4**

The light squares assume threatening proportions. The e4 square beckons to a dark steed and meanwhile the White B has been reduced to a most wretched status—almost defrocked.

25. B—B2	**R—KN1**	**27. K—N2 B—Q3**
26. P—KN3	**P—KR4**	

In the picturesque German phrase used by Nimzowitsch himself, White is 'eingeschnürt'. I will leave it to your imagination to correlate the meaning with the plight of White's position.

28. R—B1   P—R5
29. R/2—Q1   R—KR1
30. R—Q2   K—K2
Black improves the position of his king.

31. R/2—B2   K—Q2
32. R—K1   R—R2‡
Hereabouts Nimzowitsch had to make up his mind about which particular breakthrough plan to choose: should he seal up the K side (... P—

R6) and turn his attention to the other wing, or should he open up both wings and seek an all embracing penetration of the White defence? It is entirely possible that Nimzowitsch opted for the less promising course at this point, since the open KR file also grants White defensive possibilities.

When one has a beautiful positional advantage of the type possessed by Nimzowitsch here there is a temptation to do absolutely nothing, simply because your position is so beautiful that you don't want to alter it in any way.

I know the feeling well, but after a while one is stricken by feelings of guilt that no positive action (in the sense of winning the game) has been undertaken for some time. One can then be seized by a sudden compulsion to act which may (as was possibly the case here) result in the selection of an over-precipitate winning procedure as a kind of extreme psychological compensation for the previous phase of prolonged narcissism.

33. R—QR1   P × P?!
The blockading idea in this case is not fully consonant with the opening of both wings.

34. P × P   P—R4   35. R/2—B1?
While prepares to rush his rooks to the KR file to ward off the hostile invasion, but the exchange of all the heavy pieces leads to a marked deterioration of White's defensive chances. He should have played 35. P—R4! (light squares), e.g. ... P—N5; 36. P × P, N × NP; 37. R—B3, N—Q4; 38. R—B2, R—QN1 with some hope left for White.

35. ...   R/1—KR1   36. R—R1
Just what Black wants. He should have played 36. B—N1 and then done nothing, although his position would have been by no means attractive.

36. ...   R × R   38. K × R   P—N5
37. R × R   R × R   39. K—N2   P—R5?!
As so often Nimzowitsch prefers the complex to the simple. Simpler here was 39. ... K—B3; 40. K—B1, K—N4; 41. K—K1, P—N6; 42. P × P, P × P; 43. K—Q2, K—B5 − + .

40. P × P   B × NP   42. B—K1!
41. K—B1   K—B3
Hoping for 42. ... N—K6 + ; 43. K—B2, N—Q8 + ; 44. K—B1, B × B; 45. K × B, N × P; 46. N—B3 with some chance of holding Black off.

42. ...   K—N4   43. N—B3 +

Allowing Black to reach his dream ending (N versus QB) but the exchange of bishops is also without prospects for White: 43. B × B, K × B; 44. K—K1, P—B6; 45. P × P, N × QBP – +.

43. ... B × N   44. P × B K—B3

Black has a colossal light-square superiority, but how is he to organise a breakthrough? The position is blocked in the extreme. However, a study-like win exists and it does not escape Nimzowitsch's attention. In Nimzowitsch's mature years hardly anything escaped his attention in simplified positions.

45. K—K2 N—B3   47. K—K2 K—Q4
46. K—K3 N—K5   48. K—K3 K—Q3
Triangulation number 1!

49. K—K2 K—B3   51. K—K2 N—Q3
50. K—K3 K—Q4
Threatening ... K—K5.

52. K—K3 N—N4   53. B—Q2
Forced.

53. ...   N—R6
54. B—B1
Also obligatory. If 54. B—K1, N—B7 + ; 55. K—Q2, N × B; 56. K × N, K—K5; 57. K—K2, P—R6.

54. ...   N—N8
55. B—N2 P—R6
56. B—R1‡
The final humiliation for the poor cleric: close confinement to the tower.

56. ... K—Q3
Triangulation number 2!

57. K—K2 K—B3   58. K—Q1
Or 58. K—K3, K—Q4, and White must give way, or if White attempts an imitation triangulation Black wins neatly: 58. K—B2, N—Q7; 59. K—K2, N—K5 or 59. K—N1 (... N—K5; 60. K—N2), 59. ... N—N6!

58. ... K—Q4   59. K—B2 K—K5
Black no longer needs his N. That might seem rather ungrateful but the N surrenders its life in the service of a higher ideal.

60. K × N	K—B6	61. B—N2	

There is no choice.

61. ...	P × B	69. K—R3	K—B6
62. P—R4	K × P	70. K—N4	K × P
63. P—R5	K—R7	71. K × P	K—K6
64. P—R6	P—N6	72. P—Q5	P × P +
65. P—R7	P—N7	73. K × P	P—B5
66. P—R8 = Q	P—N8 = Q +	74. P—B4	P—B6
67. K × P	Q—N7 + !	75. P—B5	P—B7
68. Q × Q +	K × Q	76. P—B6	P—B8 = Q

Resigns.

Winning by one tempo. All this was forced from move 44!

A great ending. White was not in the same class as Nimzowitsch but he fought steadily and with resource and forced his Grandmaster opponent to give of his best.

GYGLI–NIMZOWITSCH, Winterthur, 1931. *Nimzo-Indian Defence*
If I were asked to concoct a typical Nimzowitsch game the end-product would probably bear a close resemblance to the following encounter. This game highlights in striking fashion so many of the ideas we associate with Nimzowitsch; for example: early infliction of a doubled pawn on the enemy; play on both wings to restrict hostile possibilities of activity (epic restraint);* a blockading knight; a sequence of mysterious, prophylactic rook moves leading to the doubling of Black's rooks on a closed file; a strategic king march in the notes; a phase of manœuvring (*lavieren* or 'tacking', literally) inducing a blunder from the harassed victim, and, finally, a winning variation carried out strictly on squares of one colour.

1. P—Q4	N—KB3	5. N—B3	P—QN3
2. P—QB4	P—K3	6. P—KN3	B—N2
3. N—QB3	B—N5	7. B—N2	B × N +
4. Q—N3	Q—K2		

In Nimzowitsch's eyes it is White who squanders a tempo by playing P—QR3 to force this exchange rather than Black who wastes a move by exchanging bishop for knight without provocation.

8. P × B?
Of course, given the present state of our theoretical knowledge, we now realise that White should recapture with the queen. Gygli was probably seduced by the possibility of placing his QB on a3 *vis-à-vis* Black's queen.

---

* As opposed to localised restraint.

8. ... N—B3
Heading for a5 whence it will place the maximum strain on White's front doubled pawn.

9. B—QR3
As planned with his previous move, but the embarrassment caused to Black is of purely temporary duration. The doubled pawns are permanent.

9. ...	**P—Q3**	**12. P—K4**	**P—K4**
10. Q—R4	**Q—Q2**	**13. 0—0**	**KR—K1**
11. N—Q2	**0—0**		

Nimzowitsch pointed out an interesting possibility at this point which would have led to an unclear position with Black having several pawns for a piece: 13. ... N × QP; 14. Q × Q, N—K7 + ; 15. K—R1, N × Q; 16. N—N1!, B—R3; 17. R—K1, B × P; 18. B—KB1, N × P + ; 19. RP × N, B × B; 20. R × B. However, this adventure would have run counter to Nimzowitsch's strategic designs, therefore he avoided it.

14. B—N2	**N—QR4**	**15. Q—B2**	**P—B4**

Fixing the doubled pawn complex as a permanent target. Black intends to bring further latent pressure to bear on the c4 pawn by means of ... QR—B1 (threatening ... BP × QP) when White will be obliged to release the pressure with P—Q5 thus reducing the mobility of his own central pawns to zero.

16. P—B4 QR—B1
Now White has to sidestep the possibility of: 17. ... BP × P; 18. P × QP, N × BP followed by ... B—R3.

17. BP × P	**QP × P**	**19. Q—Q3**	**B—R3**
18. P—Q5	**Q—K2**	**20. QR—K1**	

White has no possibility of creating mobility for his pawns, so there is nothing for him to undertake apart from aimless manœuvres with his pieces. This type of situation, where one side completely runs out of constructive plans, often occurs in Nimzowitsch games.

20. ... QR—Q1
A mysterious rook move of the first water.

21. R—K3 R—KB1
The spectre of the blockading knight looms up (... N—K1—Q3).

22. R(1)—K1	**N—K1**	**24. Q—B2**	**Q—Q2**
23. KB—B1	**N—Q3**	**25. B—B1**	**P—B3**

With two bad bishops White can only sit and wait. Meanwhile

Black prepares to store up energy for a rainy day by doubling his rooks on the KB file.

26. R—B3   R—B2
27. R—B2   R(1)—KB1‡
28. Q—Q1   B—B1

Capturing on c4 would represent a brutal procedure quite alien to Nimzowitsch. Rather than sate his appetite on a humble pawn Nimzowitsch rightly prefers to torment his opponent by embarking on grand manœuvres ('lavieren') designed to wear down psychological resistance. In fact 28. ... N (either) × QBP would lead to a nasty self-pin against the Ba6, while 28. ... B × P; 29. N × B would unnecessarily release *la Belle au Bois dormant* (Bf1) from its slumbers. Naturally Black does not object to the exchange of his QB for White's KB since, in that case, the front QBP could be devoured in safety.

29. B—Q3   Q—N5   31. B—Q3   Q—K1
30. B—K2   Q—Q2

There is no hurry. White's position is petrified and Black cannot dissipate his advantage without the contribution of a gross blunder on his part.

32. B—K2   B—Q2   33. B—Q3

White refuses to be intimidated, for the moment.

33. ...   Q—B1   36. B—Q3   Q—Q2
34. B—B1   B—N5   37. Q—Q1   B—N5
35. Q—B2   B—R6   38. Q—B2

And what would have been Nimzowitsch's explanation for his last nine, seemingly purposeless, moves? The rationale is to be found in the pages of *My System* where he writes (apropos the difficulties facing the chess student in his efforts to grasp the essence of position play): 'This kind of manœuvring corresponds in a way to the accompaniment in music. Many people hold both this manœuvring and accompaniment as things which may be dispensed with; many lovers of chess go so far as to characterise this moving to and fro as a fruit of decadence. In reality, however, this manœuvring often enough provides the only strategical—be it noted strategical not merely psychological—way of throwing in the scale a slight advantage in terrain and the consequent capacity of moving our troops more quickly from one wing to the other.'

K

However, it should not be overlooked that in the case under review the White player's acute awareness of being involved in a cat and mouse situation contributed in no small way to his sudden collapse.

38. ... P—R4

This move prepares a victorious onslaught against the white king involving a preliminary king-march (39. ... R—K2 followed by K—B2—K1—Q1—B2—N2—R1) in conjunction with P—N3, R—KR2 and P—R5. With no adequate counter-measure and dazed by the *lavieren* White is now ready to blunder. The end of this game must have come as something of a relief to White.

39. N—B1	N(4) × P		**41. Q—N3**	N—Q3
40. B × N	N × B		**42. P—B4**	P—B4

The deluge.

43. N—Q2 N × KP

White resigns. Of course White is hopelessly weak on the light squares after 44. N × N, P × N; 45. R × R, Q × R; 46. Q—K3, B—R6 and he would certainly lose this position, but he could have played on to witness the final demonstration. I suspect that Gygli was demoralised in the extreme and therefore spared himself the ultimate phase.

NIMZOWITSCH–FLOHR, Bled (Veldes), 1931. *Silly Defence*

1. P—QB4	N—KB3	**3. P—K4**	P—Q3?
2. N—QB3	P—K3		

There is no good reason for Black to choose this move which positively encourages White to establish an advantage both in time and in space. The text is rendered even less comprehensible by the realisation that Black has two perfectly playable alternatives in 3. ... P—Q4 and 3. ... P—B4. A modern example of the latter move is Rajkovic–Larsen, Hastings, 1972–1973: **3. ... P—B4; 4. P—K5** (was Flohr scared of this? there was no need to be since the advance also loosens White's position), **4. ... N—N1; 5. P—Q4, P × P; 6. Q × P, N—QB3; 7. Q—K4, P—Q3; 8. N—B3, Q—R4!** (also possible is 8. ... N × P; 9. N × N, N—B3 and 10. ... P × N with approximate equality); **9. P × P, B × P; 10. B—Q3, N—B3; 11. Q—R4, N—K4!** (centralisation—all according to Nimzowitsch!); **12. N × N, Q × N +; 13. B—K3, B—Q2; 14. 0—0—0, B—B3** and Black has satisfactorily overcome the problems of the opening.

Flohr might have emulated one of Nimzowitsch's own classic victories. The game in question was from London, 1927, and Bogoljubow was White: **3. ... P—B4; 4. P—KN3, P—Q4; 5. P—K5, P—Q5; 6. P × N, P × N; 7. QP × P, Q × P; 8. N—B3, P—KR3;**

9. B—N2, B—Q2; 10. N—Q2, B—B3; 11. N—K4, Q—N3; 12. Q—K2, B—K2 (12. ... P—B4?; 13. B—B3!); **13. 0—0, 0—0; 14. P—KR4?** (14. P—B4, N—Q2; 15. B—Q2 =. I have never been able to understand the point of Bogoljubow's 14th move. It does not even contain a threat. Anyway, Nimzowitsch rapidly reduces White's idea—whatever it may have been—*ad absurdum* with a few powerful strokes.) **14. ... P—B4; 15. N—Q2, B × B; 16. K × B, N—B3; 17. N—B3, P—B5; 18. R—K1, R—B3; 19. Q—K4, P × P; 20. P × P, B—Q3; 21. P—KN4, Q × Q; 22. R × Q, QR—KB1; 23. R—K3, R—B5; 24. P—N5, R—N5 + ; 25. K—R1, P × P; 26. P × P, K—B2; 27. N—N1, R—R1 + ; 28. N—R3, K—K2; 29. P—N3, B—B5; 30. R—B3, N—K4. 0–1.** A débâcle of the first order for the man who was to be the first official challenger to Alekhine's World Championship title.

4. P—Q4   P—K4
The dismal corollary to his last feeble move.

5. KN—K2
Nimzowitsch steers for the so-called Sämisch variation of the King's Indian Defence which had been gaining favour with him in recent games (e.g. versus Tartakower, page 233), but Flohr refuses to oblige. This decision on the part of the (then) young Czech Master is no great surprise, since (with a missing tempo) 5. ... P—KN3 could lead to a holocaust after 6. P × P, P × P; 7. Q × Q + , K × Q; 8. B—N5, followed by P—B4 and 0—0—0. However, 5. ... QN— Q2, and only then ... P—KN3, might almost have been playable.

5. ...   B—K2   7. B—K3   Q—B2
6. P—B3   P—B3
After this Black really does run out of constructive plans. I suggest that Black's last chance of staying in the game resided in an immediate exchange on d4 (7. ... P × P) followed by a determined effort to play ... P—Q4 himself. Whether this would have been successful is another matter, but it could hardly have been less promising than the text.

8. Q—Q2   QN—Q2   9. P—Q5!
An important move. Closing the centre reduces Black's counterplay to a minimum. Thus, after 9. ... 0—0, White could permit himself the luxury of playing for mate by means of 10. P—KN4; 11. N—N3, etc., and Black would be in no state to organise any effective resistance.

9. ...   N—N3
A wretched square for the poor beast but Black was afraid to castle.

10. N—N3   B—Q2
10. ... P×P; 11. BP×P, N—B5?; 12. N—N5 and wins.

11. P—N3
An insurance policy against any projected hostile invasion via the c4 square. After this Black has no useful moves left, so he allows himself a series of rather nonsensical ones instead, of which the only point can be to provoke White into some unsound sacrifice. We might compare Black's next few moves (11–18) with Nimzowitsch's provocation play versus Spielmann (page 189) from New York, 1927. In that case Nimzowitsch's provoking moves also served a subsidiary strategic purpose (Q side expansion). Flohr's provocation tactics here, on the other hand, are of minimal positional value; their only justification is a hopeful lack of faith in Nimzowitsch's ability to control his violent instincts. 'Hope springs eternal in the human breast . . .' but in this case Black's prayers remain unanswered.

Nimzowitsch does indeed resort to violence, but a violence grounded firmly in accuracy and garnished with finesse.

11. ...   P—KR4?!   13. 0—0   N—R2
12. B—Q3   P—N3   14. P—QR4
Nimzowitsch refuses to be hurried. Of course, he will eventually smash open lines towards Black's king, but first of all he ensures himself of an additional advantage on the Q side.

14. ...   P—R5   16. P—B4
15. KN—K2   P—QB4
The normal thrust to penetrate Black's shattered lines of defence.

16. ...   P×P   17. R×P   P—N4
Or 17. ... B—KN4; 18. R—B2, B×B; 19. Q×B, P—N4; 20. QR—KB1, P—B3; 21. P—K5 with play similar to the game.

18. R—B2   P—B3
19. P—K5!‡
This sacrificial operation frees 'a whole host of men in the rear'. Of such typical sacrificial situations Nimzowitsch had written: 'So powerful is the pawn's desire to press on here, to expand (of which fact indeed visible recognition is given in the way the officers, laying aside all pride of caste, picturesquely group themselves round this simple foot soldier), that our pawn often seems ready to advance on his own account, when to do so will cost him his life—and now

of a sudden the forces in the rear come to life' (*My System*, Chapter IV).

All this (written years before his game with Flohr) applies perfectly to the position after 19. P—K5!, which would have provided a superb practical example for a later edition of *My System*, had Nimzowitsch lived to write it. (The final revision was in 1927.)

19. ... QP × P

If 19. ... BP × P; 20. B—N6 +, K—Q1; 21. R—B7 with a decisive penetration, e.g. 21. ... N—KB1; 22. R × B, N × B; 23. N—N5, Q—N1; 24. B × NP, N × R; 25. B × N +, followed by Q—N5 + and Q—N6 + winning. The capture of the text puts up more fight and Nimzowitsch still has to provide an elegant display of tactics before he can count on the full point.

20. B—N6 + K—Q1 21. N—K4

'Again, the clearing of a square for one of his own knights is a very special characteristic of an advance of this kind' (i.e. 19. P—K5) (*ibid.*).

21. ...	**N—QB1**	**23. N × KBP**	**R—N2**
22. B × N	**R × B**	**24. B × NP**	**N—Q3**

Amidst the carnage Black still finds the strength to fight back, but Nimzowitsch refutes this last hope with a combination which would surely have found pride of place in the chapter on the 'Pin', had *My System* been written after Bled, 1931.

25. B × P	**N—B4**	**28. Q × Q +**	**B × Q**
26. R × N!	**B × R**	**29. N—R5 +**	**R—K2**
27. P—Q6	**Q × P**	**30. R—KB1**	**B—Q6**

The remainder is easy to comprehend. The most beautiful variations arise after 30. ... B—N3: 31. R—B8 +, B—K1; 32. N—N7 (Black is maintaining a precarious existence in a pin-cushion), 32. ... K—Q2; 33. B × R, B × B; 34. R × B, R × R; 35. N × R, K × N; 36. N—B3 with a winning ending—extra pawn plus light square grip.

31. R—B8 +, K—Q2; 32. R × R, B × N; 33. B × R (the final link in the combination commencing 25. B × P), 33. ... B × B; 34. N—N3, B—Q8; 35. N—B5, B—Q1; 36. R × P, K—B3; 37. R—R8, K—Q2; 38. N—K3, B × P; 39. K—B2, P—K5; 40. R × B +, K × R; 41. P—R5, B—R7; 42. P—N4. Black resigns.

NIMZOWITSCH–MAROCZY, Bled, 1931. *Nimzowitsch Attack* (Notes to this game are by Nimzowitsch, translated from Danish)

1. N—KB3 N—KB3 2. P—QN3 P—Q4

3. B—N2	P—K3	6. N—B3	0—0
4. P—K3	QN—Q2	7. Q—B2	P—B3
5. P—B4	B—Q3	8. R—B1	

The point of this is that he should be able to utilise the square d4 as a piece square (by means of N—Q4, but not P—Q4). The rook-move played ought, as one will soon be able to see, to be understood as a sort of waiting move.

| 8. ... | Q—K2 |
| 9. N—Q4! | B—R6‡ |

Played without finesse, for now the dark squares become weak. Black should have prepared ... e6–e5, either through 9. ... N—B4 or through the dauntless ... P—KN3. By playing as he does, he has to contend with difficulties.

| 10. B × B | Q × B | 12. N—R4! |
| 11. P × P | KP × P | |

The dark squares c5 and d4 are now in White's possession.

12. ...   N—K5?

To provoke one or other weakening pawn-move. But the white position continues to be compact even *with* a pawn-move: Maroczy's style of play can no longer be regarded as being abreast of the modern theories. Instead of the move chosen he ought to have played ... N—K4 followed by ... B—Q2 in conjunction with a retreat of the queen to e7 or d6. There was no longer any reason to struggle against the occupation of the square c5, seeing that he *himself* on his 9th move has laid the foundation for such an occupation. *The ability to accept the consequences of his own mistakes is characteristic of the modern chessmaster.*

13. P—B3!

Of course! The pawn-formation d2, e3, f3 is anything but weak. And especially as d4 and c5 are in White's hands, in such a manner that '... b7–b6 plus ... c6–c5' cannot even be dreamt of. Black has simply lost two tempi, that is all.

13. ...   N(K5)—B3

Here we have the two tempi.

| 14. B—Q3 | R—K1 | 16. Q—B3 | P—QR4? |
| 15. 0—0 | P—KR3 | | |

Weakens the point b6, or, one should rather say, increases the complex of dark-square weaknesses, which henceforth includes d4, c5 and b6. Correct was 16. ... Q—K2 with a defensive position.

17. B—B5!

Well played. All pieces which are not 'dark-squared' are to be exchanged with such enemy men as are. Only in this manner can the superiority be retained.

17. ...	Q—N5	19. R × Q	B × B
18. B × N	Q × Q	20. KR—B1	P—KN3

A beautiful example of dark-square domination.

21. P—KN4	R—K2
22. P—R4	N—K1
23. K—B2	N—Q3
24. N—QB5	B—K1‡
25. N—R4	

White takes his time; the opponent can, in any case, not undertake the least thing.

25. ...	B—Q2
26. R—KN1	K—R2
27. N—QB5	B—K1
28. R(B3)—QB1!	

For the move 28. ... P—N3 is not possible, by reason of: 29. N—R4!, P—QB4; 30. N × NP, R—N1; 31. N × P, etc.

28. ...	R—Q1	31. N—N6	R—R3
29. N—R4	R—R1	32. N—R4	R—R1
30. P—N5	P—R4	33. P—Q3!	

Now it becomes serious! There threatens 34. P—K4, P × P; 35. QP × P with a pawn-majority on the king's wing, also the d-file then offers a chance for White.

33. ...	N—B4!	35. N—B3!	
34. N × N	P × N		

With the threat Nc3—e2—f4 × h5.

35. ...	B—Q2	36. N—K2	P—R5!

On 36. ... QR—K1 comes 37. N—B4, R × P; 38. N × RP or also 38. R(N1)—K1 with advantage for White. The text move is the best possible and not easy to parry.

37. R—QR1!

On 37. P—N4 there would have come 37. ... QR—K1;

38. N—B4, R × P. Black eventually offers a piece on d7, but gets a lot of pawns in compensation.*

37. ...   P—B4

A little better, perhaps, was 37. ... P—B3. The continuation could then be 38. P × BP, R—B2; 39. R—N5, P × P; 40. QR—KN1, R × BP; 41. R—N7 +, K—R3; 42. R × B, P × P; 43. R—QR1, and White ought to win, albeit not entirely with ease (43. ... P—N4; 44. R—QN7 followed by N—B1).

38. N—B4	B—K3	41. P—R5	R(K2)—R2
39. N × RP	P—N4	42. R(R1)—QB1	
40. N—B4	P—N5		

For now an enemy rook may gladly come to a2, it no longer does anything.

42. ...	P × P	46. K—N3	P × P
43. P × P	P—Q5	47. R—K1	P—K7
44. N × B	P × N	48. R—K5	Resigns.
45. R × P	R—R7 +		

A game played in good tournament style by White.

It was in his notes to his other encounter with Maroczy from Bled (which eventually ended in a draw after Nimzowitsch's first offer to split the point had been rejected) that Nimzowitsch exhorted the International Chess Federation to pass legislation to the effect that any rejection of a draw offer should be couched in a 'thoroughly amicable tone', so as to avoid hurting the feelings of the spurned initiator of the peace proposal.   RDK

SPIELMANN–NIMZOWITSCH, Bled, 1931. *Caro Kann Defence*

1. P—K4	P—QB3	4. N × P	N—B3
2. N—KB3	P—Q4	5. N—N3	
3. N—B3	P × P		

I think 5. N × N + would be the automatic choice of most players at the present time, but that may well be a matter of taste or fashion rather than a conclusive testimony to the strength of 5. N × N +, since Bronstein, Wade and Andersson have been achieving good results with the recapture 5. ... KP × N.

* Nimzowitsch's note here may not appear quite consistent with his dismissal of 36. ... QR—K1. The difference between the two lines is that in the latter case Black's advanced QRP is more of a danger while P—QN4 by White represents a slight weakening of his Q side pawns. After 37. P—N4 Maroczy gave: ... QR—K1; 38. N—B4, R × P; 39. N × RP, R—K7 +; 40. K—B1 (to keep Black's R under attack), R/1—K6; 41. N—B6 +, K—R1; 42. N × B, R × RP; 43. R—N2, R × P +; 44. K—N1, R × R +; 45. K × R, R × P, with good counter-chances
                                                                       RDK

5. ... P—B4

Inviting the ending from his games versus Ahues and Thomas. Spielmann avoids this simplification, presumably on the grounds that the position would then tend towards an aridity distasteful to his style.

6. B—B4 P—QR3   7. P—QR4 N—B3

Black has achieved the desired imbalance and prevented the advance P—Q4. However, he has also made some positional concessions in that his QBP may become exposed to a White attack by means of P—Q3 and B—K3, when the reply ... P—QN3 will invite the permanent threat of P—QR5, breaking up Black's Q side pawn structure. However, as Nimzowitsch put it himself: 'If you want to play to win you must be prepared to create weaknesses, not only in your opponent's camp, but also in your own!'

8. P—Q3 P—KN3

Quite provocative. Black actually develops his KB away from the protection of his QBP, which was possible by means of 8. ... P—K3, etc....

9. B—K3 B—N2

Relying on ... Q—R4 + to salvage his QBP.

10. 0—0   P—N3   12. P—R3 B—N2
11. P—B3 0—0   13. Q—K2 N—QR4

The instructive decentralisation in the interests of the centralisation on move 14.

14. B—R2 B—Q4

Nimzowitsch was torn between this move and 14. ... N—Q4. The plan, in any case, is to consolidate his extreme right wing from the direction of the centre. 14. ... B—Q4 also strikes a subtle blow at the light squares which actually fall entirely into Black's hands after Spielmann's error of judgement on move 24.

15. N—Q2

Coming to c4 whence it will support the disruptive thrust P—QR5.

15. ...   B × B   17. N—B4 N—QB3
16. R × B N—Q4

Recentralisation. 17. ... N × N; 18. P × N, N × B; 19. Q × N (threat: P—R5), ... P—QR4 would relieve White of all his light square worries.

18. P—R5‡

The culmination of White's opening strategy. With this temporary pawn sacrifice he succeeds in eliminating his weakness on d3 in exchange for Black's QBP; in addition he lures several of Black's pieces away from the K side which is Spielmann's secret objective.

18. ...	P—QN4		
19. N—N6!	N × N		
20. P × N	Q × NP	**22.** N × P	P—QR4
21. N—K4	Q—B2	**23.** P—Q4	KR—N1

The position before us looks rather good for Black for the following reasons: (*a*) he has a minority attack in motion supported by a powerful fianchettoed bishop. In view of this White's pawn chain (b2/c3/d4) represents a static target for the undermining blows . . . P—QR5—R6 and . . . P—QN5. (*b*) Black has a noticeable, although not yet powerful, hold on the light-square complex comprising the a2–e6 and f3–d5 diagonals. The intersecting point d5 is an especially beckoning post for a Black knight.

However, the White position too is not without its resources and Spielmann could have maintained the balance by combining light-square prophylaxis with dark-square counter-attack, thus: 24. Q—B3!, P—K3 (intending as in the game, . . . N—K2—Q4); 25. N—K4 threatening B—B4 or B—N5 followed by the entry of a White minor piece at KB6. Nimzowitsch regarded that course as leading to equality.

What Spielmann now does leads to disaster and there are two possible, but conflicting, explanations for his actual choice of 24th move: (i) he completely overestimated his own position after he had successfully lured Black's pieces away from the proximity of his king, and therefore felt he was justified in committing an act of extreme violence against the opposing monarch; (ii) he suddenly panicked and lost all confidence in his position and therefore inaugurated a desperation, bluff offensive in the hope of confusing the issue. Nimzowitsch refutes the attack with such masterly poise that it now looks as if explanation (ii) is the more likely, but in the heat of the conflict nothing is so clear and simple as it looks afterwards to the annotator so explanation (i) could equally well be the correct one.

24. P—KB4?

A pseudo-aggressive, loosening advance which wrecks his chances

of controlling the light squares. In order to pursue his attack White
will be obliged to loosen his position even more by advancing his
KNP, thus exposing his position to a vicious counterpunch. We can
say this now, but was it so obvious at the time?

If, in fact, explanation (ii) was the correct one for this move then
this particular case is covered by Nimzowitsch in *Chess Praxis*:
'Sins of omission committed in the central area—such errors are to
be ascribed not only to insufficient knowledge of the principles of
central strategy [hardly the case with Spielmann! RDK], but also to a
certain mood of panic. And the moral? Well, even in apparently
critical positions a consolidation emanating from the centre is often
sufficient; therefore, centralise and *nil desperandum*!'

24. ... P—K3
Of course, Black prepares ... N—K2—Q4 and also invites White
to compromise himself even further with P—KN4.

25. R/2—R1
The reserve rook scurries back for the K side assault, but it is
never given the time to complete its journey.

| **25. ...** | **N—K2** | **27. R—B3** | **P—R5** |
| **26. P KN4** | **N—Q4** | **28. B—Q2** | **Q—B3** |

Increasing the pressure along the a2–e6 and (now) h1–c6
diagonals exerted by the Black pieces.

29. N—K4 P—N5
30. P—B5‡

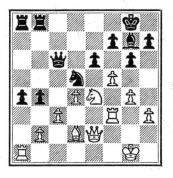

This cannot succeed (if White
had been granted the tempo to place
his QR on KB1 the matter would
be quite different!) and Nimzowitsch now annihilates Spielmann's
overextended structure.

Note the aesthetic picture of co-
operation created by the Black forces.
All the pieces support the minority
attack, yet they all stand ready to
divert their attention at a moment's
notice to a counter-offensive against White's king, which is shielded
by an ominous vacuum. Black's Q in particular glares balefully
along the h1–a8 diagonal towards the hostile potentate.

30. ...	**KP × P**	**33. P—B6**	**P × B!**
31. NP × P	**P – R6!**	**34. P × B**	**R – K1!**
32. NP × P	**P × QBP**	**35. Q—Q3**	**R × N!**

Crushing the final traces of resistance by the elimination of White's most active piece. 35. ... N—N5, on the other hand, would fail to 36. Q—N3.

36. Q × R   R – K1   37. Q – R4

Or 37. Q—Q3, R—K8 + ; 38. R—B1, Q—B8; 39. R—N1, N—K6 - +. A most piquant variation with four major pieces lined up on White's back rank.

37. ...   N—B6   38. R/3—B1   Q—Q4

Dominating the board. White took this opportunity to resign. White is curiously helpless, not so much against the immediate ... P—Q8 = Q but against ... R—K7. Nimzowitsch justifies White's abandonment of the struggle with the line: 39. P—R4 (what else?), ... R—K5; 40. Q—B2, R—K7; 41. Q—B3, Q × Q; 42. R × Q, R—K8 + ; 43. R—B1, R × QR; 44. R × R, N—K7 + !; 45. K—B2, N—B8, and the pawn promotes.

Had Black played 38. ... R—K5? at once White would have struck back with 39. Q—Q8 +, K × P; 40. R × P + !

'A good game which shows just how difficult it is to win at the present high level of chess' (Nimzowitsch).

GAMES, 1932–1935

The Final Years

COPENHAGEN, 1933

		1	2	3	4	5	6	7	8	
1	Nimzowitsch	–	½	1	1	0	1	1	1	5½
2	Stoltz	½	–	½	½	1	1	½	1	5
3	Stahlberg	0	½	–	½	½	1	1	½	4
4	Andersen	0	½	½	–	1	½	½	1	4
5	J. Enevoldsen	1	0	½	0	–	1	½	1	4
6	J. Nielsen	0	0	0	½	0	–	½	1	2
7	B. Nielsen	0	½	0	½	½	½	–	0	2
8	Gemzøe	0	0	½	0	0	0	1	–	1½

STOCKHOLM, February, 1934

		1	2	3	4	5	6	
1	Lundin	—	10	10	1½	11	11	7½
2	Nimzowitsch	01	—	10	1½	½1	11	7
3	Stoltz	01	01	—	1½	½½	11	6½
4	Danielson	0½	0½	0½	—	½1	1½	4½
5	Bergkvist	00	½0	½½	0½	—	½1	3½
6	Dahlkvist	00	00	00	½0	½0	—	1

ZÜRICH, July 14–28, 1934

		1	2	3	4	5	6	7	8	9	10	11	12	13	14	15	16	
1	Alekhine	–	0	½	½	1	1	1	1	1	1	1	1	1	1	1	1	13
2	Euwe	1	–	½	1	0	1	½	½	1	1	1	1	½	1	1	1	12
3	Flohr	½	½	–	½	½	½	½	1	1	1	1	1	1	1	1	1	12
4	Bogoljubow	½	0	½	–	1	½	½	½	1	1	1	1	1	1	1	1	11½
5	Dr. Lasker	0	1	½	0	–	1	0	0	½	1	1	1	1	1	1	1	10
6	Bernstein	0	0	½	½	0	–	½	1	½	½	½	1	1	1	1	1	9
7	Nimzowitsch	0	½	½	½	1	½	–	½	0	0	1	1	½	1	1	1	9
8	Stahlberg	0	½	0	½	1	0	½	–	½	1	0	1	1	½	1	½	8
9	H. Johner	0	0	0	0	½	½	1	½	–	0	1	1	1	1	½	½	7½
10	Henneberger	0	0	0	0	0	½	1	0	1	–	0	0	1	0	1	1	5½
11	Gygli	0	0	0	0	0	½	0	1	0	1	–	½	0	½	½	1	5
12	Rosselli	0	0	0	0	0	0	0	0	0	1	½	–	½	1	1	½	4½
13	Grob	0	½	0	0	0	0	½	0	0	0	1	½	–	0	½	1	4
14	Müller	0	0	0	0	0	0	0	½	0	1	½	0	1	–	0	1	4
15	Naegeli	0	0	0	0	0	0	0	0	½	0	½	0	½	1	–	½	3
16	Joss	0	0	0	0	0	0	0	½	½	0	0	½	0	0	½	–	2

COPENHAGEN, August 18–26, 1934

An 8-round Swiss tournament with 18 players, prizes being
awarded to the first six places

1	Nimzowitsch	$6\frac{1}{2}$
2	Lundin	6
3	Stahlberg	$5\frac{1}{2}$
4	J. Enevoldsen	5
5/6	Stoltz	$\Big\}$ $4\frac{1}{2}$
	Gemzøe	

This was the last tournament in which Nimzowitsch participated.

NIMZOWITSCH–BJØRN NIELSEN, Copenhagen, 1933. *English Opening*
(Notes to this game are by Nimzowitsch, translated from Danish)

1. P—QB4	**N—KB3**	**3. P—K4**	**P—Q4**
2. N—QB3	**P—K3**	**4. P—K5**	**P—Q5**

At this point it is to be observed that this gives an equal game, an
observation which by some will be understood as being extremely
'realistic'. Personally, however, I am far from inclined to understand
the concept of 'realism' (*Saglighed*) so narrowly. When I now say,
that the following expansion of the pawn from e5 (or e2) to g7, which
ploughs on parallel and yet in the opposite direction to *Red's*
(Black's) expansion of the pawn from d4 (or d7) to d2, *bears to a
great extent the stamp of our times,* and that it brings to mind the
expansion of the Soviet and Nazi states, ploughing on in parallel and
yet opposite directions, then *I* understand this observation as being
realistic. And what is most important, this image will set the imagination in motion and assist the readers to be well and truly able to
assimilate the dramatic events of the next moves.

5. P × N
'The burning of the Reichstag'!

5. ... P × N
'The bourgeoisie are decimated'.

6. P × NP
'The parties are dissolved'.

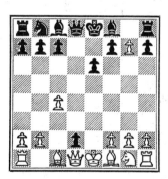

6. ... P × P + ‡
'The mensheviks—and Trotsky
too—are exiled'.

7. B × P   B × P
Both White and 'Red' have now
'come to rest' (?) and are delighted—
each for himself!—with their 'ideal
form of state'!!

8. Q—B2	**N—B3**	
9. N—B3	**N—Q5!**	

This fine exchange aims at the formation 'Bd4' and 'Qf6', in other
words: Black will double on the diagonal h8–a1 with *the bishop in
front of the queen.* Otherwise after B—B3 and ... B × B, Q × B
White would have *conquered* the disputed diagonal.

10. N × N	**B × N**	**11. B—Q3**

Or 11. B—B3, Q—B3!; 12. B × B, Q × B; 13. R—Q1, Q—K4 + ;

14. Q—K2 (or 14. B—K2, B—Q2 and it is Black who gets the diagonal c6–g2 with the help of the bishop at c6), 14. ... Q—R4 + ! (not 14. ... Q × Q + because of B × Q and B—B3); 15. Q—Q2, Q × Q + ; 16. R × Q it is again Black who gets the diagonal to g2, though, to be sure, that would not signify anything, e.g. 16. ... B—Q2; 17. B—K2, B—B3; 18. P—B3, K—K2; 19. K—B2, QR—Q1; 20. KR—Q1 and now it is rather Black who must take care, because his pawn-formation (the pawn at h7) is the less compact. The move played in the game is an innovation, which I wanted to try out on this occasion.

11. ... Q—B3   12. 0—0 B—Q2
There was no joy in ... B × NP; 13. QR—N1, B—Q5; 14. B—K4, P—B3; 15. R—N3, with excellent play for White.

13. B—K4 0—0—0   14. B—QB3 P—K4
A small and yet very excusable mistake. Black should instead be bold and play 14. ... B × B!; 15. P × B, P—K4, for example 16. QR—N1, B—B3; 17. B × B, Q × B; 18. Q—B5 +, Q—K3!; 19. Q × Q +, P × Q; 20. KR—K1, R—Q6 with equalisation. After the move played in the game White gets a microscopic advantage.

15. B × B P × B   16. Q—Q3
Blockade!

16. ... B—B3   17. P—B3! P—KR4
As 17. ... B × B; 18. P × B would open the f-file against the pawn at f7. But perhaps it was none the less correct to go in for that line, there were in any case enough drawing chances. Now, however, White strengthens the pressure.

18. QR—K1 P—R5   20. P—QN4 R—R4
19. B—B5+ K—N1
He will force the bishop to a declaration.

21. B—N4! R/R4—R1
22. P—N5 B—Q2
23. B × B R × B
24. P—R4‡
White may well take the liberty of staging a flank attack. Why? we ask. Yes indeed, because he is in possession of the e-file and of a centralisation quite beyond reproach. And the centralisation entitles him to a little adventure on the flanks.

24. ... Q—KN3

Looks good, but the rook ending is still not *quite* good for Black. Into consideration came 24. ... Q—QN3 to halt the pawn-rush.

25. Q × Q P × Q	**26. R—K6 R—N1**

On 26. ... P—Q6; 27. R × P, R—Q5 there comes simply 28. R—N4.

27. K—B2 P—Q6	**29. R—Q2**
28. R—Q1 P—N3	

And again the d-pawn is blockaded: (strategical) law is law and law shall be kept! And the law says: 'A passed pawn shall be blockaded'.

29. ... P—N4	**31. K—K3 R—Q5**
30. P—R3 R/N1—Q1	

Allows an exchange of rooks, whereafter the loss of the d-pawn can no longer be stopped. But also after 31. ... K—N2; 32. R—K5, R—Q5; 33. R × NP, R × P; 34. R—N4 the loss of the pawn was inevitable.

32. R—K8 R × R +	**35. R × P R—K7**
33. K × R R—Q1 +	**36. R—Q2 R—K6 +**
34. K—B3 R—K1	**37. K—Q4 R—K8**

On 37. ... R—K1 there comes 38. R—KB2 (threatening to play P—B4), R—KB1; 39. K—K5.

38. K—Q5

To play R—Q4—N4.

38. ... P—B4

He does everything he can to save the game!

39. K—Q6 K—N2

39. ... R—QB8 is parried by means of 40. K—B6, K—B1; 41. R—Q7, R × P; 42. R × P.

40. R—Q5 R—QB8	**42. R—N7 + K—B1**
41. R × NP R × P	

Not 42. ... K—N1 because of 43. K—B6.

43. R × P. 1–0

That was stiff resistance!

STAHLBERG–NIMZOWITSCH, Göteberg, 1934—1st Match Game
QP Nimzo-Indian Defence

1. P—Q4 P—K3

Inviting transposition to a French Defence, but Stahlberg politely declines.

2. P—QB4 N—KB3   4. Q—N3
3. N—QB3 B—N5

The Spielmann variation which was Stahlberg's favourite line at the time and which he employed consistently in this match.

4. ... N—B3

Rejecting 4. ... P—B4 which had brought Nimzowitsch such a resounding success versus Bogoljubow at San Remo. Nimzowitsch probably feared that Stahlberg had prepared some improvements for White over this famous game. In the third and fifth games of this match Nimzowitsch did adopt 4. ... P—B4 and his fears turned out to be quite justifiable, since Stahlberg won on both occasions!

5. P—K3 0—0

In game 7 of the Match Nimzowitsch chose the immediate 5. ... P—QR4?! and there followed: 6. B—Q2!, P—K4; 7. P—Q5, N—K2; 8. B—Q3, P—Q3; 9. KN—K2, N—Q2; 10. Q—Q1, N—B4; 11. B—B2, B—N5 (preparing to exchange all of his bishops for enemy knights); 12. 0—0, B × QN; 13. B × B, P—QN4; 14. P × P, B × N; 15. Q × B, N × P; 16. B × KP!, P × B; 17. KR—Q1, Q—Q3; 18. Q—B3, 0—0—0; 19. P—K4, Q—KB3; 20. Q—QR3, N—N3; 21. Q × N, with a winning position for White, although Nimzowitsch put up tremendous resistance and lasted until move 72.

6. B—Q3 P—QR4   7. N—K2

As we have seen 7. B—Q2 would be best, inhibiting Black's following thrust.

7. ... P—R5   9. P—QN3?
8. Q—Q1 P—R6

After this White's Q side forfeits any mobility factor it may once have possessed. After his error on move 7 the most promising course available to White was to permit the isolation of his QRP in order to gain compensation in the centre, thus: 9. P × P, B × P; 10. B × B, R × B; 11. N—N5 followed by P—K4.

9. ... P—Q4!

Going into a position characteristic of a Queen's Gambit but where Black has several advantages over the normal situations generated from that opening, to wit: (i) Black's pawn on QR6 deprives White's QB of the useful development square QN2; (ii) White's QRP is a potential weakness for the endgame; (iii) Black's restraint of White's Q side pawns has eliminated any future possibility of a minority attack from that sector.

10. O—O	P—QN3	13. N—N5	B × B
11. B—Q2	B—N2	14. Q × B	N—QN5
12. R—B1	Q—K2		

Another plus for Black: his QN5 square represents a permanent and unassailable outpost for a N which will menace the White QRP in perpetuity. White's N on b5, however, is fated to be chased back to its stable in no time at all.

15. P × P
And not 15. P—B5? on account of ... N × B!; 16. Q × N, B—R3 with a deadly pin.

15. ...	KN × P	16. B—K4

Threatening 17. N × BP. Interesting is 16. P—K4, but after 16. ... N × B; 17. Q × N, N—N5; 18. Q—Q2, P—QB3; 19. N/5—B3, KR—Q1 Black has the threat of ... B—R3 in addition to his prospects of operating in the Q file against White's shaky centre.

16. ...   P—QB3
The moment of truth.

17. B × N
17. N/5—B3 may well have been stronger. The text leads by force to a position characteristic of a minority attack where Black has the traditional K side counterplay but White has no minority attack!

17. ...   KP × B!
The half-open K file is essential to Black's attacking plans.

18. N/5—B3   B—R3
Black's B is a good piece so it might seem strange to prepare its exchange for a White knight. However, Nimzowitsch wants to reduce White's possibilities by removing a potential blockader of Black's K side pawns.

19. N—R4	B × N	20. Q × B	Q—R2

Coming round to support his N.

21. KR—Q1	QR—K1!

The right rook. Nimzowitsch's army now splits up into two detachments (cf. his game versus Yates, London, 1927, page 59) which operate independently of each other. On the K side Black's rooks prepare a break-through by means of ... P—KB4—B5; meanwhile the Q and N on the opposite wing are occupied with the restraint of White's counter-chances against a3 or c6. As these army corps gradually increase their contact and co-operation White's position evinces a marked and steady deterioration—in other words:

White is caught in a strategic pincer-movement, which appears in a particularly plastic form.

22. Q—Q2   Q—R4   24. N—K2   R—B3
23. N—B3   P—KB4   25. K—R1!

A good try. Stahlberg wants to manœuvre his N to K5 (via KN1 and KB3) whence it will shield his position from frontal assault.

25. ...   P—R3
26. N—N1
Overlooking or underestimating Black's excellent reply. He should have played 26. P—N3.

26. ...   P—B5!‡
A very fine pawn sacrifice which completely cuts across White's projected defence. If White does not accept the offer (e.g. 27. N—B3) then 27. ... P×P; 28. P×P, R/1—KB1 will prove most unpleasant.

27. P×P   R—K5
An outpost in the open file seized by a rook rather than by a N, which would be slightly more normal, according to the postulates of the 'System'.

28. P—N3
Or 28. N—B3, R/5×BP, and the poor knight cannot go any further in its pilgrimage towards Jerusalem (here square K5). In lieu of any obvious relief operation White resolves to cling grimly to his spoils.

28. ...   Q—N4
Very good. Henceforth R—K1 is foiled by a cavalry invasion of d3 while N—B3 loses to a rook invasion of e2. The separate corps begin to make contact.

29. R—B3   P—B4
Another fine move. The pawns which now come into being at c5 and d5 are hanging indeed but White is in no position to attack them. What is more, the Black QP will soon be transformed into a veritable Mjöllnir, a reference which Stahlberg, being a Scandinavian, would have appreciated. The remainder of the game could serve as an ideal demonstration of 'Die Expansionslust der Bauern'.

30. P×P   P×P   32. R—K3   R/3—K3
31. R/1—QB1   R—B3   33. R×R

If 33. R/3—QB3, hoping for repetition, ... R—Q5! would neatly trap White's Q in the middle of her own position—(if 34. R × P, Q × R wins).

33. ... R × R	34. P—B3

White is almost paralysed.

34. ... R—K1	35. R—K1

There is little else White can undertake against the imminent advance of Black's QP. After the exchange of rooks White does at least threaten perpetual check for one move (37. Q—K6 +, etc.).

35. ... R × R	37. Q—QB1 P—Q5
36. Q × R Q—Q2	

The decisive advance.

38. N—K2 Q—N4	39. Q—K1 Q—Q6

Already there were many alternatives sufficient to win. White's case is hopeless.

40. N—B1 Q × P +	42. Q—B2 Q—K5
41. K—N1 K—B2	

Centralisation even now!

43. Q—B1 P—Q6	45. K—N2 and White resigned,
44. Q—Q1 Q—K6 +	

(e.g. 45. ... P—Q7; 46. N—K2, N—Q6 threatening ... N—N7).

Nimzowitsch's handling, in this game, of the difficult major pieces plus knight versus major pieces plus knight situation was superlative. His best games from his later period were outstanding in many respects, and it is tragic that he did not live to the regulation biblical total of three score years and ten. In that case the chess public would have been treated to many subsequent revisions of *My System* and *Chess Praxis* containing these later masterpieces. Perhaps that would also have made this book rather unnecessary!?

NIMZOWITSCH–STAHLBERG, Göteborg, 1934—4th Match Game
Queen's Gambit Declined

1. P—Q4

In his later years Nimzowitsch turned increasingly towards 1. P—Q4 and 1. P—QB4 as his favourite opening weapons.

1. ... P—Q4	4. N—B3 B—K2
2. P—QB4 P—K3	5. B—B4
3. N—QB3 N—KB3	

More usual is the forcing 5. B—N5. Nimzowitsch must have had pleasant memories of the relatively unpretentious developing move chosen here from his game with Naegeli, played at Winterthur, 1931. Then Black had played **4.** ... **QN—Q2** (instead of ... B—K2), and there followed: **5. P×P, P×P; 6. B—B4, P—B3; 7. P—K3, B—K2; 8. B—Q3, 0—0; 9. R—QB1, R—K1; 10. 0—0, N—B1; 11. N—K5, B—Q3; 12. B—N3, Q—K2; 13. P—B4, KN—Q2; 14. P—K4!, P×P; 15. B—B4, N—K3; 16. N×KBP!, K×N; 17. P—B5, N—B3; 18. B—R4, K—N1; 19. N×P, R—B1; 20. P×N, B×P; 21. N×N+, R×N; 22. B×R, P×B; 23. Q—N4+, K—B2; 24. KR—K1.** 1–0.

5. ... **P—B4**

Black seeks to clear up matters in the centre in order to avoid the cramp from which Naegeli suffered after his interpretation of the opening.

It is a matter of taste whether one willingly accepts isolated QP's in this fashion. Nimzowitsch tended to avoid IQP's in his own camp, while Stahlberg, on the contrary, was a staunch supporter of the Tarrasch defence to the Queen's Gambit, which positively invites the IQP.

6. QP×P B×P

The immediate recapture of the pawn with 6. ... P×P would lead to grave difficulties after 7. Q×Q+, K×Q (7. ... B×Q releases the pressure from White's QBP); 8. 0—0—0+ and N—QN5, while the attempt to regain the pawn with the QN would also confer an advantage on White: 6. ... N—R3; 7. B—Q6!, N×P; 8. B×B, Q×B; 9. P×P, P×P; 10. P—K3, 0—0; 11. B—K2, N/4—K5; 12. Q—Q4 with domination of the vital blockading square d4.

7. P—K3 N—B3

7. ... P×P; 8. Q×Q+, etc., would still represent a most unwise course for Black.

8. B—Q3

If White wishes to inflict an '*isolani*' on his opponent, now is surely the time to do so—the most accurate move order is 8. P×P, P×P; 9. B—K2 or 9. B—Q3 with possibilities of transposing into the text.

8. ... **0—0**

Here Black could have reduced his problems with the simplifying manœuvre 8. ... P×P and 9. ... Q×Q as, indeed, he actually played in a later game of the match (with the difference that in the later game Black had played 7. ... 0—0 instead of 7. ... N—B3).

9. 0—0 P—QR3

For this game, at least, Stahlberg had decided as a matter of policy to avoid the move ... QP × BP. In fact 9. ... P × P was still possible, and, although White would retain a small plus in the position without queens, Black should not lose. After the move played White turns, at last, to the theme of the IQP.

10. P × P   P × P

Black could continue capturing on d5 with pieces so as to avoid any structural weaknesses, but after 10. ... N × P; 11. N × N, Q × N White has a number of strong continuations at his disposal, e.g. 12. Q—K2, threatening to centralise the rooks on Q1 and QB1 with gain of time, or the more speculative 12. Q—B2 which adds the threats of B—K4 and B × P + to those already mentioned. True, 12. Q—B2 involves the sacrifice of a piece, but Black hardly dare accept it: 12. ... N—N5; 13. B × P +, K—R1; 14. Q—N1, P—KN3; 15. B × P, P × B; 16. Q × P intending 17. B—K5 +. If now 16. ... N—B3 then 17. B—R6 (doubtless White also has other powerful possibilities at his disposal), 17. ... R—KN1; 18. Q— B6 +, K—R2; 19. N—N5 +, but not 19. B—B4? (threatening mate on KR6), R—N3!; 20. Q—B7 +, R—N2; 21. N—N5 +, Q × N! and White loses material in a most undignified fashion.

11. B—N5

Threatening 12. B × N, P × B; 13. N × P and Black cannot capture the bold N in view of B × P + netting his Q.

11. ...   B—K3   12. N—K2

A flexible move. White can either play this N to f4 with the intention of attacking the QP or to d4 in order to blockade it. As Nimzo-witsch frequently pointed out—the disadvantage of an isolated pawn resides just as much in the weakness of the square directly in front of it (which can be occupied with impunity by hostile pieces) as in the vulnerability of the pawn itself. In this game, as a matter of fact, we observe an illustration of the second case—the pawn's vulnerability to attack.

12. ...   P—R3   13. B—R4   B—KN5

Hoping to deter White from a positive plan of campaign by the threat to weaken his K side pawns. However, this threat turns out to be illusory and, after the Black QB has captured the White KN, the Black IQP dies through its master's sheer inability to lend it adequate protection. Hence Black should have maintained the B at its defensive post on K3 and continued development with, e.g., ... R—B1.

14. R—B1   B—K2

The B must retire in this direction otherwise the pin becomes unbearable. The possibility of ... P—KN4 (as an alternative method of clearing the pin) hardly comes into consideration.

15. Q—N3　B × N

Consistent but faulty. Better was ... Q—Q2 followed by withdrawal of the B to K3.

16. P × B　Q—Q2

Or 16. ... N—K4; 17. N—Q4 parrying all the threats and emphasising White's positional advantage. After 17. ... N × B; 18. Q × N White's control of his KB5 square and the possibility of N—B5 would even make it worth his while to consider a plan involving K—R1, R—KN1 and the build-up of pressure in the KN file against Black's KN2 square.

17. KR—Q1　QR—B1
18. B × N!　B × B
19. B—K4　N—K2‡

His best chance was the active 19. ... P—Q5!; 20. B × N, R × B; 21. N × P, B × N; 23. P × B with some play against White's scattered pawns to make up for White's extra material. However, the passed QP should eventually decide the game in White's favour.

After the defensive text Nimzowitsch plays with wonderful precision to bring about an ending which is lost for Black, despite initial appearances to the contrary.

20. R × R　R × R　　　　21. N—B4!

Much better than the immediate capture. White retains the KB which will be very powerful in the coming ending.

21. ...　Q—N4

There is no really satisfactory alternative. With this move Black pins his hopes on the drawing propensity of the opposite bishops.

22. Q × Q　P × Q　　　　24. R × N　R—R1
23. N × P　N × N

24. ... B × P; 25. R × P would simply shed a second pawn. Now after 25. R × P, R × P; 26. P—N3, B—R5! grants Black excellent counter-chances, while 25. P—QR3?, B × P; 26. R × P, B × P; 27. R × P would make the win, if indeed there is a win, a most arduous process. The efficient method by which Nimzowitsch solves this technical problem is most impressive.

25. R—QB5!

Facilitating the entry of the rook to the 7th rank. Note that the

immediate 25. R—Q7? fails to ... R×P! Now 25. ... R×P??
would allow mate.

25. ...   K—B1

It makes little difference whether Black plays ... B×P at once or
prefaces it with this move. After all, Black must waste a move somewhere to deal with the mate threat.

26. B—Q5

Realising another facet of 25. R—QB5, which made way for this
powerful centralisation, which plans to decide the game by a direct
attack against Black's king. Incidentally, this move also extends some
much-needed protection to the QRP.

26. ...   P—N5

White was actually threatening to capture the QNP by this stage.

27. R—B7

Black is helpless and could already capitulate with a clear conscience. He is bound to lose three pawns. Not even the presence of
opposite bishops can avail him much against this disaster.

27. ...	B×P	**30. R×KNP**	B×R
28. R×P+	K—K1	**31. B×R**	Resigns.
29. R×QNP	B—B6		

LUNDIN–NIMZOWITSCH, Stockholm, 1934. *Queen's Pawn*
(Notes to this game are by Nimzowitsch, translated from Danish)

1. P—Q4	P—Q4	**4. P—K3**	P—QB3
2. N—KB3	B—B4!	**5. B—Q3**	B—N5+!
3. P—B4	P—K3		

Quite an amusing thought. Black will play ... KN—K2. Why? Is
the knight not better placed on f6? The answer is given in the following note.

6. N—B3   KN—K2

The normal moves Q—B2 or Q—K2, with the aim of carrying
through P—K4, could now be parried as follows: 7. Q—B2?, P×P!
and the bishop at f5 is defended. Also 7. Q—K2, B×N+!; 8. P×B,
Q—R4; 9. B—Q2, B×B; 10. Q×B, Q—R3! That was the idea
behind the development ... KN—K2.

7. 0—0   0—0   8. N—K2

Or 8. Q—K2, B×N; 9. P×B, Q—R4; 10. B×B, N×B;
11. P×P, BP×P and Black stands well.

8. ...	B—Q3	**10. B—N2**	Q—N1
9. P—QN3	N—Q2		

To hinder N—K5.

11. N—N3   B—N3   12. P × P

The prelude to an interesting combination, whereby Lundin aims
nevertheless to get a knight firmly planted on e5.

12. ...   KP × P   13. B × B   BP × B

Or 13. ... N × B; 14. N—B5.

14. P—K4   P × P!

Herewith begins a *light-square* campaign of counterplay, which,
without the opponent committing any greater errors, slowly forces
him to his knees. On the other hand, it would have been dangerous
for Black to engage in 14. ... B × N; 15. BP × B, P × P; 16. N—N5,
N—B3; 17. B—R3.

15. N × P   N—Q4

The first 'light' square, soon more will follow.

16. N × B   Q × N   17. N—K5

The goal of the combination (see the note to the 12th move) is
attained. The e5 point is occupied. But Black is at an advantage all
the same—'Nd5' against 'Bb2' means a clear plus for Black.

17. ...   N—B5!

Played in scientific style: new 'light' squares are to be made
vulnerable (e.g. if P—KN3 and P—B4 is provoked, there arises
a new square on e4, which can later be occupied).

18. P—N3   N—R6 +   20. P—B4   Q—Q4 +
19. K—N2   N—N4   21. N—B3   N—K3

Better than ... N—K5. Now there is a threat of ... P—KN4.

22. K—N1   QR—Q1   23. Q—B2

A little better was Q—Q2.

23. ...   Q—KB4!‡

After Q × f5 the e4 point becomes
easy prey for Black.

24. Q × Q   P × Q
25. KR—K1   KR—K1
26. QR—Q1   N—B2
27. N—K5   N—B3
28. P—KR3   N/B2—Q4
29. P—R3   P—KR4

Foils the intended g3–g4 and pro-
cures a threat of ... P—R5.

30. P—KR4   N—KN5   32. R × R   RP × N
31. N × N   R × R +   33. R—K5

This stationing of the rook forms White's last hope—should Black later exchange on e5, then the endgame after d4 × e5 is not clearly won for him. However, the win is easy, if the exchange of rooks takes place *on a square other than e5.*

33. ...   P—KN3   34. K—B1   K—N2
A finesse, one rather expects 34. ... K—B2. But the case is this, that on 35. P—R5 Black reserves for himself the manœuvre 35. ... R—KR1; 36. P × P, R—R8 + ; 37. K—N2, R—QN8 with conspicuous advantage.

35. K—K2   K—B2
Now that can well be played, for on 36. P—R5 winning is 36. ... R—KR1; 37. P × P +, K × P, and the black rook presses in anyway.

36. K—Q3	**N—B3**	**40. K—B4**	**N—Q2**
37. B—B3	**R—Q4**	**41. R—K3**	**R—K3**
38. B—K1	**P—N3**	**42. R × R**	**K × R**
39. P—R4	**R—Q3**	**43. B—B3**	

The attempt 43. P—Q5 +, P × P + ; 44. K—N5 founders on 44. ... N—N1; 45. B—B3, K—Q2; 46. B—K5, K—B1 and ... K—N2, etc.

43. ...   N—B3   45. P—N4
44. B—K1   N—K5
Now 45. P—Q5 + is parried by means of, among other things, 45. ... P × P + ; 46. K—N5, K—Q3; 47. K—R6, N—B4 + ; 48. K × P, K—B3, e.g. 49. B—B2, N × NP; 50. B × P, P—Q5; 51. P—R5, P—Q6; 52. B—K3, N × P.

45. ...	**N—Q3 +**	**47. P—R5**	**N—K5**
46. K—Q3	**K—Q4**	**48. P × P**	**P × P**

White resigns
A true positional game!

DR. EMMANUEL LASKER–NIMZOWITSCH, Zürich, 1934
French Defence

1. P—K4	**P—K3**	**3. N—QB3**	**B—N5**
2. P—Q4	**P—Q4**	**4. P—K5**	

By 1934 the Prosecution (White) had largely abandoned its case based on the insipid 4. P × P, mainly as a result of Nimzowitsch's successful advocacy of the Black position. However, 4. P × P was revived thirty years later by Maître Larsen in his game versus Portisch from the 1964 Interzonal. The sequel was 4. ... P × P; 5. Q—B3!? (the fresh evidence), 5. ... N—QB3; 6. B—QN5, N—K2; 7. B—KB4, 0—0; 8. 0—0—0, N—R4; 9. N/1—K2,

P—QB3; 10. B—Q3, P—QN4; 11. P—KR4!, N—B5; 12. P—R5, P—B3; 13. P—KN4, and Black was sent to the guillotine. It did not take long to elaborate the correct defence which resides in: 5. ... Q—K2 + ! when, oddly enough, White lacks a decent method of parrying the check. An example of what could follow is the amusing miniature Corden–Moles, Oxford, 1970: 6. N—K2 (or 6. B—K3, N—KB3; 7. B—Q3, P—B4!); 6. ... N—QB3; 7. B—K3 (7. Q × QP, N—B3, with excellent compensation for the pawn), 7. ... N—B3; 8. 0—0—0?, B × QN; 9. P × B, B—N5!; 10. Q—B4, P—KN4! 0-1. If 11. Q × NP, B × N; 12. B × B, Q—R6 + ; 13. K— Q2, N—K5 + or 13. K—N1, N—K5 × QBP + and mate.

    4. P × P in conjunction with 5. Q—B3!? enjoyed a short vogue after Larsen's successful prosecution of Portisch but, apart from that, 4. P—K5 has become the almost universal choice in contemporary master practice.

    4. ...   P—QB4   5. B—Q2

Very popular at the time since it prevented the doubling of White's QBP's and prepared to extend White's dark square influence by means of N—QN5, e.g. 5. ... P × P; 6. N—N5, B—B4; 7. P— QN4 and Black is in serious trouble. Nowadays we prefer the more dynamic 5. P—QR3 inviting the infliction of doubled pawns but hoping, thereby, to generate compensating energy in the White position. In particular the retention of White's QB on its original square offers this piece the possibility of fruitful action along the a3-f8 diagonal (P—QR4—B—QR3, etc.). A typical follow-up to 5. P—QR3 would be 5. ... B × N + ; 6. P × B, Q—B2; 7. N—B3 (7. Q—N4, P—B3!; 8. N—B3, P—B5! = +, an idea of the American Grandmaster Robert Byrne which is quite in accordance with Nimzowitsch's theories) ... N—K2; 8. P—QR4, QN—B3; 9. B— Q3, B—Q2; 10. 0—0, P—B5; 11. B—K2, P—B3 with a sharp struggle (Fischer–Larsen, 1st Match Game, Candidates', 1971).

    5. ...   N—K2   6. N—N5

The key move of White's opening variation. Lasker follows Alekhine's famous victory over Nimzowitsch from San Remo, 1930. The alternative is 6. P—QR3, e.g. ... B × N; 7. B × B, QN—B3; 8. N—B3, P × P (or 8. ... P—B5!?; 9. B—K2, P—QN4; 10. 0—0, B—Q2; 11. Q—Q2, P—QR4, Bernstein–Nimzowitsch, also from Zürich, 1934); 9. N × P, N × P!; 10. N × P, B × N; 11. B × N, 0—0; 12. B—Q3, N—B3; 13. B—N3, Q—B3, with a good game for Black—Tringov–Uhlmann, Skopje, 1972.

    6. ...   B × B +   8. P—QB3
    7. Q × B   0—0

As Alekhine played, but Nimzowitsch has prepared some improvements over the intervening three years. White dare not loosen his centre with 8. P×P in view of ... N—Q2; 9. Q—B3, P—QR3; 10. N—Q6, Q—B2; 11. P—QN4, P—QN3 and White's structure begins to crumble. It is interesting that the necessity of defending his centre in such lines prevents White from making use of his ostensibly impressive outpost on Q6.

8. ... N—B4(!)
Another move that is well playable is 8. ... QN—B3. Against Alekhine Nimzowitsch found 8. ... P—QN3?

9. P—KN4!?‡
We have already referred to the 'odds-giving style', and this move constitutes a further example. In *My System* Nimzowitsch wrote: 'Lasker plays by preference—and with inimitable virtuosity—this style. It is this that might make people believe that the heel of Achilles lay for Lasker in his treatment of the opening. But such a judgement rests on an entire misconception.'

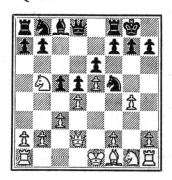

Indeed, 9. P—KN4 is, objectively speaking, a rather weak move which disjoints White's K side pawn constellation in return for the nebulous gain of postponing (not preventing) the undermining thrust ... P—B3. However, the number of games won by Lasker after a supposedly 'inferior' treatment of the opening phase was legion, so P—KN4 cannot really be blamed. This move is the introduction to a genuine struggle and it was Lasker's bad luck that Nimzowitsch conducted the struggle on this particular day with a virtuosity and sense of determination that were sadly absent in most of his other games from Zürich.

A more sedate alternative to 9. P—KN4 is 9. B—Q3, e.g. ... B—Q2; 10. N—B3, B×N; 11. B×B, Q—N3; 12. B—Q3, N—B3 = Stoltz–Nimzowitsch, Match, 1934.

9. ... N—R5!   10. P—N5
Alekhine gave the less uncompromising 10. 0—0—0, P—B3; 11. P—KB4, as a possible improvement.

10. ... P×P   12. 0—0—0 Q—R4
11. P×P N—B3
Thwarting White's aggressive intentions against the Black king (by, for example, Q—B4 ... N—N3, Q—N3 followed by the advance

of the KRP). White can hardly allow 13. N—QB3, B—Q2; 14.
Q—B4, N—N3; 15. Q—N3, KR—B1, when Black's attack is the
more virulent, so he must acquiesce in the transposition to an
ending where Black has good prospects of exploiting the dislocated
nature of White's K side pawns.

13. K—N1
In the endgame White's king would develop greater activity in the
centre rather than tucked away on QN1, hence 13. Q × Q would
have been more accurate.

13. ...	**Q × Q**	**15. NP × P**	**P × P**
14. R × Q	**P—B3!**	**16. B—R3**	

Seeking salvation (or more?) in a tactical skirmish. Note that
White's outpost on Q6 has weighed less heavily than Black's attack
against the opposing pawn chain.

16. ...	**P × P**	**17. N—B7**

And now he abandons Q6 altogether.

17. ...	**R—N1**	**18. N × KP**

This liquidation of the central pawns looks very promising for
White, but he still has the problem to face of how he should develop
his K side pieces. In subsequent play Nimzowitsch actually concentrates on blotting out White's KN and his domination (with
minimum means) of the poor beast in the N + P ending which arises
(from move 36 onwards) is most impressive.

18. ...	**R—B3**
19. N—B7	**B × B**
20. N × B	**N—B6**
21. R/2—Q1	**P × P**
22. N × P	**R—B4**
23. N/5—B4	**QR—KB1**
24. N—Q3‡	

An interesting case of the trans-
mutation of an advantage. White's
weak centre has all but vanished (the
KBP is heavily defended) while
Black's passed QP, although a poten-
tial menace, is held in check for the moment by White's pieces.
Black's real post-skirmish advantage lies not so much in the respective pawn formations but in the superior activity of his pieces. If we
study the diagrammed position (which, incidentally, in its unit group-
ings presents an unusual geometric spectacle with the column of
Black pieces in the KB file and the White men arranged at a distance

of a N's move around the KBP) it will become clear that the majority of White's reasonable moves consist of retreats to the first rank!

24. ...   N/3—K4   26. N—N1
25. N × N   R × N
Where else can it go?

26. ...   N—N4
26. ... N—R5 was also very strong.

27. P—KR4
27. R × P?, R—K8 + ; 28. K—B2, R × P + ; 29. R—Q2, R × R + ; 30. K × R, N—B6 + − + .

27. ...   N—K3   28. R—R2   R—K5?
He should have brought the less active R into play. With 28. ... R—B5! Black would have won quite quickly. The difference is that White can now force Black to abandon either the K file or his attack on White's KRP, which would not have been the case after ... R—B5!

29. P—B3!   R—K6   30. R—K2   R—B5
Black's position remains excellent, but it is no longer overwhelming.

31. R × R   P × R   33. R × P   N—Q5
32. R—Q3   R × RP
Commencing, in a minor key, the restriction of White's N which will eventually bring him victory. The threat is 34. ... R—R8; 35. R—K1, P—KR4, and White is helpless since his N has no moves.

34. R—K4
Parrying the threat and, in addition, forcing the exchange of Black's active R. Black cannot reply
34. ... N × P? in view of 35. R—
K8 +, K—B2; 36. N × N, R—R8 + ;
37. R—K1! + −, a typically artful
Lasker resource.

34. ...   R × R
35. P × R   K—B2‡
Can this ending be won by Black?
He has three advantages which
should amount to a win: (i) the
outside passed pawn. This means

that White will not be able to offer or allow the exchange of N's;
(ii) White's N (see note to move 18) is most limited in its scope, partly
by virtue of the threatened advance of the Black KRP, of course.
But note too that a Black N at e6 and a Black P at h5 virtually
eliminate any productive moves by a White N on h3, and the N must
emerge into play via h3, if it is going to emerge at all, since the Black
N on Q5 denies access to the other egress squares e2 and f3; (iii)
White's KP is isolated. But this is not to say that the P is weak,
although it does eventually fall. The real significance of the 'isolani' is
quite otherwise: 'It is not only the isolani itself that tends to become
a weakness, but also the complex of squares surrounding it. In this
the principal evil is to be found' (*My System*, Part II, Chapter 3).

In the course of this ending Black's control over the e5 square
assumes paramount importance and is absolutely essential to his
plans for victory.

36. K—B1   K—B3   37. K—Q2   K—K4(!)

His Black Majesty occupies himself by keeping the vital square
warm for his good friend the knight, who pays him the honour of
a visit there some 12 moves later.

38. K—K3   P—KR4   39. P—R3

Reinfeld in *Hypermodern Chess* claims that White missed a draw
here with 39. N—R3!, N—B7 + ; 40. K—B3, N—N5; 41. N—B4!
I cannot believe this. Why not 39. N—R3, N—K3! when Black
achieves the ideal restrictive position I outlined above?, e.g. 40. N—
B2, N—B5; 41. K—B3, P—R4! (and not 41. ... N—K3; 42. K—
K3, N—B4; 43. P—N4!); 42. P—R4 (42. K—K3, P—N4;
43. K—B3, N—K3; 44. K—K3, N—B4), 42. ... N—K3; 43. K—
K3, N—B4 – +.

39. ...   P—R4   40. N—R3   N—B7 +

A tease. If 41. K—Q2 then ... N—Q5; 42. K—K3, hoping for
repetition, Black would have to play 42. ... N—K3, which is
actually very strong. In fact, Nimzowitsch could have played
... N—K3 on move 40.

41. K—Q3   N—K8 +   43. K—B3
42. K—K2   N—N7

Not 43. K—Q3?, N—B5 + ; 44. N × N, K × N; 45. K—Q4,
P—KR5; 46. P—K5, N—B4; 47. K—Q5, P—R6, and promotes
with check.

43. ...   N—R5 +   44. K—K3   N—N3

The point of Nimzowitsch's N manœuvre was to get this piece into
contact with e5. It looks now as if White's N has some freedom, but
this freedom is illusory.

45. N—N5

He jumps at the chance after his years of imprisonment.

| 45. ... | K—B3 | 47. N—N5 | K—B3 |
| 46. N—R7 + | K—N2 | 48. N—R7 + | K—K2! |

If now 49. K—Q4, N—B1!; 50. N—N5, N—K3 + - +. A fine example of the principle: *reculer pour mieux sauter.*

49. N—N5   N—K4

Threatening ... N—B5.

50. K—Q4   K—Q3   51. N—R3

Home again. Now both of White's pieces are tied down: the N must keep a sharp eye on the KRP while the K must attempt to fend off the projected invasion of his Q side.

| 51. ... | P—QR5 | 53. N—R3 | P—N3! |
| 52. N—B4 | P—R5 | | |

A vital loss of tempo. Even now haste on Black's part could spoil everything: 53. ... P—N4?; 54. N—B4, N—B3 + ; 55. K—B3, K—K4; 56. N—N6 +, and resistance continues.

| 54. N—B4 | P—N4 | 56. K—K3 | K—B4 |
| 55. N—R3 | N—B3 ǀ | 57. K—Q3 | |

Or 57. K—B4, K—Q5; 58. K—B5, N—K4; 59. N—B2, N—B5 - + and if in this line 58. N—N5 still ... N—K4!, e.g. 59. N—K6 +, K—B5 (threatening ... N—Q6); 60. K × N, P—R6 - +. Lasker adheres to the policy of defending his left flank with his K rather than trying for a reckless counter-attack.

57. ...   P—N5

White must capture on b4 otherwise Black would himself play ... P × P followed by ... N—K4 and ... N—B5.

58. P × P +   K × P

Gradually increasing his control of territory.

59. K—B2   N—Q5 +
60. K—N1

To defend his jeopardised Q wing from QR2.

60. ...   N—K3!‡

Dominating his opposite number. The theme of restriction introduced so early in the game finally reaches its climax. White's N can no longer move at all in view of ... N—B5 or ... N4 and the victorious advance

L

of the KRP, e.g. 61. K—B2, K—B5; 62. N—B2, N—N4 – +.

61. K—R2   K—B5
A change of front. Black will win on the K side after all.

62. K—R3	**K—Q5**	**64. P—N4**	**K—B6**
63. K × P	**K × P**	**65. P—N5**	**K—N7**

Black is overcome by humane considerations and at last resolves to put the White N out of its misery.

White resigned. The variations are now quite simple: 66. P—N6, K × N; 67. P—N7, N—B4 + or 66. N—B4 +, N × N; 67. P—N6, N—K3; 68. K—N5, N—Q1.

Nimzowitsch's handling of the difficult N + P ending which came into being after move 35 has all the precision and satisfying ineluctable logic of the solution to a complex mathematical problem.

TAILPIECE

To end with, as my publisher is showing distress at the increasing length of my book, I give seven games without much comment. They have not appeared in English notation before and show Nimzowitsch at his best, but frankly I include them simply because I like them.

Game played at odds of the queen. Remove White's Q from the board and also Black's KN. Played at Riga, 19??

Nimzowitsch–Leelaus. *Nimzowitsch Attack ?!*

1. P—QN3, P—K4; 2. B—N2, P—KB3; 3. P—K4 (compare Nimzowitsch's game versus Winter, page 196), 3. ... P—B3; 4. N—QB3, B—N5; 5. 0—0—0, B × N; 6. P × B, 0—0; 7. B—R3, R—K1; 8. B—Q6, Q—N3; 9. N—B3, Q × BP; 10. P—KR4, P—KR3; 11. B—B4 +, K—R2; 12. P—R5, P—QN4; 13. B—KB7, R—K3; 14. N—R4, R × B; 15. R × R, Q—QB4; 16. KR—Q1, Q × P; 17. R/1—Q3, Q—K8 + ; 18. K—N2, Q × N; 19. B—N6 +, K—N1; 20. R—K6! 1–0. It is interesting to speculate on the particular point from which White had sufficient compensation for his huge material disadvantage.

From a privately arranged blindfold display over three boards, Bergen, 1921.

Nimzowitsch (without sight of the board)–Jokstad. *Caro Kann*
(by transposition)

1. P—K4, P—Q4; 2. P × P, N—KB3; 3. P—QB4, P—B3; 4. P—Q4, P × P; 5. N—QB3, N—B3; 6. N—B3, B—N5; 7. P × P, KN × P; 8. Q—N3 (cf. page 55 for Nimzowitsch's game versus Alekhine from Bled, 1931, with 8. B—QN5), 8. ... B × N; 9. P × B, N—N3; 10. B—K3, P—K3; 11. P—Q5, P × P; 12. B × N, P × B; 13. 0—0—0, P—Q5; 14. B—B4, Q—N4 + ; 15. K—N1, Q—B4 + ; 16. N—K4, B—B4; 17. KR—N1, 0—0; 18. R—N5, Q—B5; 19. QR—N1, P—N3; 20. R/1—N4, Q × RP; 21. R—R5, Q—B2; 22. P—B4, N—R4; 23. R × P + !, P × R; 24. Q—KR3, P × R; 25. N—B6 +, K—N2; 26. Q—N2 +, K × N; 27. Q—N5. Mate.

Game played at odds of QN. Remove White's QN from the board.

Nimzowitsch–Anderssen, Vidtskne, 1923. Comments by Nimzowitsch from Kagan's magazine where this game was published under the heading:

The Factotum Bishop. *King's Gambit*

1. P—K4, P—K4; **2.** P—KB4, P×P; **3.** N—KB3, N—KB3; **4.** P—K5, N—R4; **5.** Q—K2, B—K2; **6.** P—Q4, 0—0; **7.** B—Q2, P—Q3; **8.** 0—0—0, B—K3; **9.** P—KN4, P×P e.p.; **10.** RP×P, N×P; **11.** Q—R2, N×R; **12.** B—Q3, P—KN3; **13.** R×N, P—KR4; **14.** R—N1, B—N5; **15.** R×B, P×R; **16.** Q—R6, Q—K1 (16. ... P×N!; 17. B×P=); **17.** B—QB4, P×N; **18.** Q×P+, K—R1; **19.** Q—R6+, K—N1; **20.** B—Q3, P—KB4; **21.** B—QB4+. (The double employment of the bishop on the two diagonals has a most amusing effect. To me it seems that this bishop has the same versatility as, for example, the shoeshiner in a small country hotel who, all of a sudden, turns into the porter simply by putting on a different cap, only to reappear as the shoeshiner as soon as you call for him by that name.) **21.** ... R—B2; **22.** Q—N6+, K—R1; **23.** B×R. 1–0.

From a series of simultaneous displays given by Nimzowitsch in Norway January, February, 1925, in which he made the score of +672 =78 −42.

Siebke–Nimzowitsch. *KP Nimzowitsch Defence*

1. P—K4, N—QB3; **2.** P—Q4, P—Q4; **3.** P—K5, B—B4; **4.** B—N5/b5, Q—Q2; **5.** N—KB3, P—K3; **6.** 0—0, P—QR3; **7.** B×N, Q×B; **8.** P—B3, QB—N5; **9.** B—K3, N—K2; **10.** QN—Q2, N—B4; **11.** R—B1, P—QN4; **12.** N—N3, P—QR4; **13.** P—KR3, B×N; **14.** Q×B, P—R5; **15.** N—Q2, P—R4; **16.** P—B4!, NP×P; **17.** R×P, Q—Q2; **18.** R—B2, B—N5; **19.** KR—B1, B—R4; **20.** P—KN3, B—N3; **21.** N—B4, B×P; **22.** N—Q6+, P×N; **23.** R—B7, B×B; **24.** R×Q, B×R; **25.** R—B7, B×P; **26.** Q—K2!, B×P; **27.** Q—N5+, K—B1; **28.** Q—Q7, N—R3; **29.** R—B8+, R×R; **30.** Q×R+, K—K2; **31.** Q×R, P—R6!† (The storm has blown away most of Black's position but what remains is sufficiently solid to stave off disaster.) **32.** Q—QN8, B—N7; **33.** Q—B7+, K—B3; **34.** Q×QP, P—N3; **35.** Q—B4+, K—N2; **36.** P—N4, P×P; **37.** P×P, N—N1; **38.** P—N5, N—K2; **39.** K—B1, N—B4; **40.** Q—B3, N—Q3; **41.** K—K2?, N—K5! (Now it is Black who has winning chances.) **42.** Q—B4, N—B6+; **43.** K—Q3, N×P;

44. K—B2, N—B8; **45.** Q—B3, P—
Q5? (... K—N1!); **46.** Q—B6+,
K—N1; **47.** Q—Q8+, K—R2;
48. Q—KB8, P—Q6+; **49.** K—Q1,
P—R7; **50.** Q×P+, B—N2; **51.**
Q×KP!, P—R8=Q; **52.** Q—R3+,
K—N1; **53.** Q—K6+? (The wrong
check. A draw was possible with
53. Q—B8+, B—B1; 54. Q—K6+,
K—N2; 55. Q—Q7+, K—R1; 56.
Q—R3+=.) **53.** ... K—B1; **54.**

Q—Q6+, K—K1; **55.** Q×P+, K—
K2; **56.** Q—K4+, Q—K4; **57.** Q×Q+, B×Q; **58.** K×N, B—
B5+. 0–1.

Nimzowitsch–Pirc, Frankfort, 1930. *Caro Kann*

1. P—K4, P—QB3; **2.** N—QB3, P—Q4; **3.** N—B3, P×P;
4. N×P, N—B3; **5.** N—N3?!, B—N5; **6.** B—K2, P—K3; **7.** 0—0,
B—Q3; **8.** P—Q4, QN—Q2; **9.** P—B4, Q—B2; **10.** B—Q2, 0—0;
11. B—B3, KR—Q1; **12.** N—N5!, B×B; **13.** Q×B, P—B4;
14. P×P, B×N; **15.** RP×B, Q×BP; **16.** N—K4!, Q—B3 (appar-
ently a strange decision, since White can now smash Black's K side;
but if 16. ... Q—B2; 17. Q—N4 is highly unpleasant while 16. ...
QR—N1; 17. QR—Q1 is similarly unappealing); **17.** N×N+,
N×N; **18.** B×N, P×B; **19.** Q—N4+, K—R1; **20.** Q—R4,
P—K4; **21.** QR—Q1, K—N2; **22.** P—N3, P—N3; **23.** Q—N4+,
K—R1; **24.** Q—B5, Q—K3; **25.** Q—K4, QR—N1; **26.** R—Q5,
R×R; **27.** P×R, Q—Q2; **28.** R—Q1, R—QB1; **29.** R—Q3,
K—N2; **30.** P—KN4!, P—KR3; **31.** R—R1, R—Q1; **32.** Q—K3,
R—KR1; **33.** Q—Q2, Q—Q3; **34.** P—N4, P—R3; **35.** P—R3,
K—N3?! (losing a pawn or surrendering it for counterplay? But
moves are already hard to come by—35. ... P—N4; 36. K—R1,
K—N3; 37. R—QB3, R—Q1; 38. R—B5+ -); **36.** Q—Q3+,
K—N2; **37.** Q×P, Q×QP; **38.** Q×P, P—R4; **39.** K—R2,
Q—Q8; **40.** P—B3, Q—Q5; **41.** Q×Q, P×Q; **42.** P×P, P—Q6;
43. K—N3, R—R1; **44.** K—B2, R×P; **45.** P—R6+, K—R2;
46. K—K3, R—N6; **47.** R—R4, P—B4; **48.** K—Q2, R—R6;
49. R—R5, R—N6; **50.** R×P, R×P; **51.** R×P+, K×P; **52.** K×P,
K—N4; **53.** K—K3, R—N6+; **54.** K—B2, R—R6; **55.** P—N4,
R—N6; **56.** R—B5+, K—N3; **57.** K—N3, R—R6; **58.** R—Q5. 1–0.

Sämisch–Nimzowitsch, Frankfurt, 1930. *Queen's Gambit Declined*
(by transposition)

1. P—Q4, N—KB3; **2.** P—QB4, P—K3; **3.** P—QR3?! (Uninspiring, but hard to refute.) **3. ... P—Q4** (3. ... P—B4; 4. P—K3 is nothing special for Black); **4. N—QB3, QN—Q2; 5. B—N5, P—KR3; 6. B—R4, B—K2; 7. P—K3, 0—0; 8. R—B1, P—QN3; 9. P × P, P × P; 10. B—Q3, P—B4; 11. N—B3, B—N2; 12. 0—0, N—K5; 13. B—N3** (playing to isolate Black's QP. It looks better to inflict hanging pawns with 13. B × B, Q × B; 14. P × P), **13. ... N × B; 14. RP × N, B—KB3; 15. R—K1, R—K1; 16. B—N1, P × P; 17. KN × P, N—K4; 18. Q—B2, P—N3; 19. QR—Q1, QR—B1; 20. B—R2, N—B5; 21. B × N, R × B; 22. Q—Q2, Q—K2; 23. N/3 —K2, R/1—QB1; 24. R—QB1, P—R3; 25. KR—Q1, K—N2; 26. Q—K1, P—KR4; 27. R—Q2, P—R5; 28. P × P, B × P; 29. R/1—Q1, R—KR1; 30. N—QB3, Q—B2; 31. P—KN3, B— KB3; 32. Q—K2, Q—Q2; 33. Q—B3, Q—R6; 34. Q—N2, Q—R4; 35. N/3—K2, R/5—B1; 36. N—B4, Q—R3; 37. K—B1** (a king march which doesn't work), **37. ... P—R4; 38. K—K1?!** (Now the K is cut off. Perhaps he should have retraced his steps.) **38. ... B— R3; 39. P—B3, R/KR1—K1; 40. K—B2, Q—N4; 41. Q—N1, Q—K4; 42. N—N2, P—R5; 43. R—QB1, B—B5; 44. Q—Q1, P—QN4; 45. P—B4** (White fears an eventual ... P—QN5 and tries to gain some space), **45. ... Q—K5; 46. Q—N4, R—KR1; 47. R—KN1, B—Q6; 48. Q—B3, B × N!; 49. Q × Q, B × Q; 50. P × B, R—R7; 51. K—K3, R—K1; 52. K—B2, P—N4; 53. P × P, K—N3; 54. R—K2, R—K3; 55. P—KN4, K × P; 56. K—N3, R/3—KR3; 57. K—B2, R/3—R6.** 0–1.

Nimzowitsch-Voellmy, Bern, 1931. *Nimzowitsch Attack*
1. N—KB3, P—Q4; 2. P—QN3, N—KB3; 3. B—N2, B—B4; 4. P—K3, QN—Q2; 5. P—B4, P—K3; 6. N—B3, P—B3; 7. B— K2, B—Q3; 8. 0—0, Q—K2; 9. P × P, KP × P; 10. R—B1, N—K4; 11. N—Q4!, B—Q2; 12. Q—B2, N—N3; 13. N—B5, B × N; 14. Q × B, B—R6; 15. Q—B2, B × B; 16. Q × B, 0—0; 17. N—R4, KR—K1; 18. Q—Q4, Q—K4; 19. Q × Q, R × Q; 20. N—B5,

R—K2; 21. P—QN4, P—QR3; 22. P—QR4, N—K5; 23. N—N3, N— Q3; 24. R—R1, QR—K1; 25. KR— B1, N—K4; 26. P—N5!‡ (A typical Q Gambit minority attack but without the QP on d4. If Black accepts the pawn sacrifice offered by White's last move he must emerge a pawn down.) **26. ... RP × P; 27. P × P, N × P; 28. B × N, P × B; 29. R—B5, R—Q2; 30. R × NP, N—B3; 31. N— B5, R—B2; 32. N × P.** (Observe the energy displayed by White's N in this game. At the moment it is engaged in a raid on Black's Q side pawns; after this its task is to dash home to guard the K from b7–f1 in record speed; but, once again, the N thirsts for adventure and returns to harass the foe—by express from f1–e8.) 32. ... R—N1; 33. N—Q6, R—Q1; 34. N—B5, P—N3; 35. N—N3, N—K2; 36. P—Q4 (at last), 36. ... R/1—QB1; 37. N—B1, R—B7; 38. P—N4!, R/1—B2; 39. R—N8 +, K—N2; 40. R/1—R8, P—N4; 41. N—N3, K—B3; 42. N—R5 +, K—K3; 43. N—N7 +, K—Q2; 44. R—Q8 +, K—B3; 45. N—K8, R—N2; 46. R—Q6 +, K—N4; 47. R—KB6, R—N3; 48. R × P, N—N3; 49. R—R1, R/N—QB3; 50. R—N1 +, K—B5; 51. R × P, N—R5; 52. R—QB7, R × R; 53. N × R, N—B6 + ; 54. K—N2, N—Q7; 55. R—Q1, N—K5; 56. R—KB1, N—Q7; 57. N—K6! (The final finesse. White sacrifices the exchange to eliminate Black's vestiges of counterplay.) 57. ... N × R; 58. K × N, K—Q6; 59. N × P, R—B8 + ; 60. K—N2, K—K7; 61. N—R3, K—Q6; 62. K—B3. 1–0.

He has no desire to spectate as White's armada of pawns sails down the board. It is impressive to see the way in which White has managed to preserve his K side and central pawns intact.

CHAPTER VII

A PARODY BY HANS KMOCH

After all these genuine games by Nimzowitsch my collection concludes with a bogus one!

This witty parody of a Nimzowitsch game, with mock Nimzowitsch notes, first appeared in 1927 in German. The author was Hans Kmoch, incidentally a great admirer of Nimzowitsch. Far from taking offence Nimzowitsch was himself highly amused by Kmoch's effort. As with all good parodies the spirit of the original does shine through, in distorted fashion of course. Concealed in the humour are clear indications both of Nimzowitsch's egocentricity and of the paradoxes that lie beneath his system. The version which appears here is Kmoch's own translation which first appeared in English in 1951 in the American Magazine *Chess Review*.

A MASTERLY EXAMPLE OF MY SYSTEM

By Hans Kmoch

Anderssen started the sacrificial style, Morphy and Grünfeld the pure attacking style, Steinitz the positional style, Tarrasch the scientific style, Lasker the style of styles, Capablanca the mechanical style, Alekhine a style as brilliant as sunlight. But it is a generally known fact that originality and modernism were introduced by me as my own personal inventions, and enthusiastically imitated (without being fully understood) by the whole world of chess. For the ridiculously small sum of ten marks, the reader can confirm all this in my monumental work *My System*, published by B. Kagan.

Before my time chess was so naïve and undistinguished! One or two brutal opening moves, each one involving a vulgar, obvious threat, a common, banal sacrifice, a painfully elementary, bestially raw checkmate—such, more or less, was the course of chess games before my heyday set in.

Then I appeared on the scene and the chess world paid heed. The hegemony of matter was shattered at a stroke and the era of the spiritual began. Under my creative guidance, the chessmen, hitherto nothing but highwaymen, pirates, and butcher boys, became sensitive artists and subtle instruments of immeasurable profundity.

But why waste words!—come, soar to the dizzy heights of the following game:

FRENCH DEFENCE
Copenhagen, 1927

Notes by me

White	Black
Nimzowitsch	Sistemsson

1. P—K4 P—K3 2. P—KR4!!

My very oldest and latest thought in this opening! To the chess addict nurtured on spineless convention, this move comes as a punch in the face—but calmly, calmly, reader; after all, you cannot be expected to understand such moves. (Forgive me—it is not your fault, until now no one has opened your eyes and ears.) Wait just a little while and there will pass before you a miracle of over-protection of more than earthly beauty. (I assume that I rightly assume that you are quite familiar with my theory of over-protection.)

2. ... P—Q4

Black of course has no suspicion of what is coming and continues serenely in classical style.

3. P—K5!

A move of elemental delicacy. (We detest, as a matter of principle, such words as 'power' and 'strength'; in the first place, such banal expressions make us uncomfortable, and in the second place, we like even less the brutalising tendency which such words imply.)

Wherein lies the beauty of 3. P—K5 ...? Why is this move strong?

The answer is as simple as it is astonishing. The move is strong because it is weak! Weak, that is, only in the traditional sense! In reality, that is to say, it is not the move P—K5, but the pawn on K5 that is weak—a tremendous difference! In former times, it is true, it was customary to reject any move which created a weakness. Today, thanks to me, this view is obsolete. The fact that the pawn on K5 is weak, obliges White to protect the pawn more and more until at last the state of over-protection arises as it were of itself. But as we have seen (cf. *My System*), over-protection is practically equivalent to victory. Hence it follows automatically that the 'weak' move 3. P—K5 is a certain road to triumph. The rest is more or less a matter of technique.

3. ... P—QB4

All according to famous precedent.

4. P—Q4

Here it is quite clear that it is more profitable for White to provoke ... P—QB4 and then play P—Q4, rather than the other way round, which is the customary course. For if White first plays P—Q4, there follows ... P—QB4 and White's queen pawn is under attack. But my clever transposition of moves changes the situation completely. For now Black's queen bishop pawn is suddenly attacked by White's queen pawn!

4. ... P × P

What else can Black do?

5. P—R5!

All very clever, original, and decisive! Of course the ordinary run of people who envy me every spark of my genius but cannot follow my line of reasoning for even three paces, outdo themselves in sneering at me with the poison dripping epithet 'bizarre'.

The text move creates confusion in the whole Black army and prepares for the annihilating invasion by the queen eighteen moves later.

5. ... Q—N3

Naturally not 5. ... N—QB3?; 6. B—QN5!, etc. Why should Black play the French Defence only to allow the Ruy Lopez bishop move after all?!

6. P—R6!

An avaricious dullard would never hit on this deeply considered pawn sacrifice.

6. ... N × P

After 6. ... P × P White has an even more comfortable game.

7. Q—R5!!

The reason for this becomes clear after White's next move.

7. ... P—N3

Threatens to begin a successful siege of the weakling at K5 with ... B—N2. But White forestalls this.

8. Q—R2!!‡

To every fair-minded observer this move must come as a revelation! All the previous manœuvres now become clear! White has completed his development brilliantly and proceeds to over-protect K5. Against this Black is helpless.

8. ... N—B4   **9. B—Q3**

Note the splendid co-operation of White's forces: while the king pawn and the king bishop completely blockade Black's position, the development of the over-protective forces takes place behind the broad backs of these sturdy blockaders.

9. ... N—B3   **10. N—KB3**

As a rule this is a routine move. But here it is strikingly original and as such occupies a place in the storehouse of my intellectual property.

10. ... P—KR4

Old stuff!

11. P—QN3

A deep trap, as will soon become apparent!

11. ... B—N2

How Black must have rejoiced when he anticipated his formidable opponent's occupation of the long diagonal. But . . .

12. B—KB4!!

. . . how bitterly disappointed he must have been to realise that 11. P—QN3 had only been a trap and B—N2 had not been intended at all. The position of Black's bishop at KN2 is now quite pointless. 11. ... B—K2 would have been relatively better.

12. ... B—Q2   **13. QN—Q2 QR—B1**

Black no longer has any good moves!

14. K—K2!!

An extraordinarily deep move. He sees through Black's plans, and in addition he prepares a particularly powerful continuation of his over-protection strategy.

14. ... N—N5

Just what White was waiting for.

15. N—K1!!

This was the point of his previous move! Black is now forced to exchange off the attacking bishop at Q3. But in that event White's king knight enters the fray with fearful effect at Q3, while the square KB3 becomes available to the queen knight. Surely a grandiose piece of strategy. The fact is that I'm a marvellous player, even if the whole chess world bursts with envy.

15. ... N × B   **16. N × N!**

Naturally not 16. P × N? which would have been quite inconsistent. The pawn on QB2 is unimportant, and Black only wastes precious time by capturing it.

16. ...   R × P   17. QR—K1!!
White continues his over-protection without much ado.

17. ...   P—R4
This counter-attack has no punch. Black would naturally like to get a passed pawn plus a rook on the seventh, but it is too late for that.

18. K—Q1!
Now the menaced rook must scurry back, for capture on R7 would be much too dangerous.

18. ...   R—B3!!
At last Black gets the right idea: over-protecting his pawn at K3. But it is already too late.

19. R—K2   K—K2
Introduced into tournament play by me. See the note to White's 14th move. The king over-protects K3.

20. KR—K1   R—K1!
21. N—B3!‡
Completing the over-protection of K5 and thus deciding the fate of the game. Black has no defence. Note the aesthetic effect created by White's position.

21. ...   B—KB1
Now Black threatens to complete the over-protection of K3 by playing ... N—N2. But White has prepared a brilliant combination.

22. P—KN4!!
Much stronger than the obvious B—N5 +, etc.

22. ...   P × P   23. Q—R7!!
Now one clearly realises the masterly understanding of position which went into White's eighth move (Q—R2!!).

23. ...   P × N
Had Black continued over-protecting by 23. ... N—N2 there would have followed 24. B—N5 +, P—B3; 25. B × P +, K—B2; 26. N—N5. Mate. Black's basic error was that he started over-protecting much too late.

24. B—N5 mate

One of my best games! I am proud of it if only because Herr
Sistemsson is one of the strongest Scandinavian players. The game
made an overwhelming impression on the players and spectators as
well as on my opponent. The game has become famous in Denmark
as 'the immortal over-protection game!'

CHAPTER VIII

A SELECTION OF ENTERTAINING POSITIONS FROM NIMZOWITSCH'S GAMES, 1902–1934

I would suggest that you set up each of the following positions on your board and come to your own conclusions before consulting the actual conclusions of each game.

N.–Lange, Berlin, 1902

(1) White to play. How should he proceed?

N.–Hoffer, Nuremburg, 1904

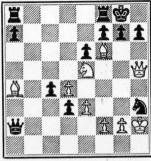

(2) White to play has a straightforward method of winning, but can you discover Nimzowitsch's?

N.–Another, Vienna, 1905

(3) White to play. How would you continue?

N.–Flüss, Zürich, 1906

(4) White to play. Can he capture Black's knight?

N.-Tchigorin, Carlsbad, 1907

(5) Should Black (to move) play 53. . . . K—K3 or 53. . . . K—B3 ?

Duras.-N., Sebastian, 1912

(6) This ending looks unwinnable but Nimzowitsch found a way of wearing his opponent down.

N.-Bogoljubow, Match, 1920

(7) White to play. What should he do about his knight?

Brinckmann-N., Match, 1923

(8) Starting with . . . N × KP Nimzowitsch introduced an exchanging combination that gained material. What was it?

N.-J. Bernstein, Carlsbad, 1923

(9) A technical win for White? Maybe, but Nimzowitsch forced a decision in just four moves.

Steiner-N., Kecskemet, 1927

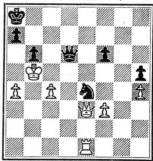

(10) Black to play. Evaluate this position.

Kmoch–N., Niendorf, 1927

(11) Can Black (on the move) lift White's dark-square blockade?

N.–Euwe, Carlsbad, 1929

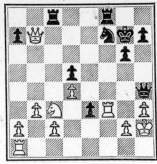

(12) Black to play. Should he capture the knight?

Grau–N., San Remo, 1930

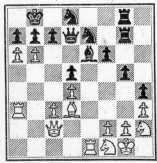

(13) Black to play. Whose attack is more dangerous?

N.–List, Frankfurt, 1930

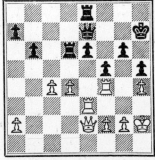

(14) White to play. How should he proceed with his attack?

N.–W. Nielsen, Simultaneous, Copenhagen, 1930

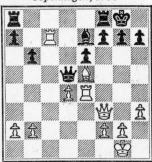

(15) Here Black played ... B—Q3. White then forced a three move win. How?

Asztalos–N., Bled, 1931

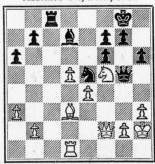

(16) How did Nimzowitsch (to move) take the White position by storm?

Bogoljubow–N., Bled, 1931

E. Andersen–N., Copenhagen, 1933

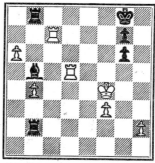

(17) Nimzowitsch has compensation for the exchange in the shape of an extra pawn and a powerful bishop. Is this sufficient? How would you assess this position? It is Black's move.

(18) Black to move. Can he win? He has an extra piece but his own pawns are unimpressive to a degree and White's Q side is menacing. If Black plays ... B × P then R/5—Q7 makes the win out of the question for Black.

SOLUTIONS

(1) 1 N—B6 + !, P × N; 2. R—N1 +, K—B1; 3. B—R7, Q—K1;
4. Q—B5 + and Black is mated. Nimzowitsch missed this and found
the highly ingenious 4. Q—B7?!, Q × Q; 5. P × P, but after 5. ...
Q—B8 + ; 6. R × Q, B—Q5!; 7. B × B, P—K4; 8. B—R7, QR—B1;
9. R—N1, K—Q1 Black's king scurried away from the mating net.
(2) The clear-cut way is 1. Q—N4, P—N3; 2. Q × N, Q—K7 (or
... P—KR4; 3. Q—N3, K—R2; 4. B—Q1); 3. N—B3, P—KR4;
4. Q—N3, K—R2; 5. B—B6, P—Q7; 6. B—K4, P—Q8 = Q;
7. Q—N5 and wins. Black is curiously helpless to prevent the mate in
this line. What Nimzowitsch actually played was a typical example
of a 'combination which no one else would even have thought of':
1. B—K8!!?, QR × B?; 2. Q—R6, P × Q? (... P × B; 3. N—N4,
Q × P!); 3. N—N4 and mates.
(3) Nimzowitsch defeated his anonymous victim thus: 1. R—B6
threatening R × NP, Q × P + and R—R6 mate. 1. ... Q—K4;
2. R × NP, Q—K5 + ; 3. N—B3, Q × R; 4. N—K5, Q—K5 + ;
5. P—B3, Q × N; 6. P—N6. 1–0. If 3. ... Q × N + ; 4. K—R2,
N—B4; 5. P × N, Q × P f5; 6. R × KP + –.
(4) 15. P × N!, B × P; 16. N × B!, R × Q; 17. KR × R, P × N;
18. P—B5!, R—N1; 19. QR—N1, and Black cannot escape the
mate. That was the conclusion of the game. I leave it to you to find
how White wins against 15. ... R—R3.
(5) The game concluded from this position:

53. ...	K—K3?	56. P × P	P—Q5
54. K—B5!	P—B4	57. K × P	K—Q3
55. P—R3!	P × P	58. P—B5	Resigns.

Black should have played: 53. ... K—B3! which draws, e.g.:

(i) 54. P—R4, K—Q3; 55. P—R5, K—K3!; 56. K—B5, P—B4;
57. P—N5, P × P; 58. P—R6, K—B2!; 59. P × P, P—B5 =.

(ii) 54. P—R3, K—Q3; 55. P—R4, K—B3 (not 55. ... K—K3;
56. K—B5, P—B4; 57. P—N5 + –).
(a) 56. P—N5, BP × P; 57. BP × P, P × P; 58. P—R5, P—N5;
59. P—R6, P—N6; 60. K—K3, P—Q5 + !; 61. K—B3,
P—Q6 =. Or 59. K—K3, K—B4!; 60. P—R6, P—Q5 + ;
61. K—B2, P—Q6; 62. P—R7, P—N6 + =.
(b) and this is most probably the line that caused Tchigorin to
abandon 53. ... K—B3!; 56. P—R5, K—Q3; 57. P—
N5, BP × P; 58. P × P, K—K3!!; 59. P—N6, K—B3;

60. K × P, K—N2; 61. K—K6, K—N1; 62. K—B6, K—B1 =, so long as Black keeps the opposition he cannot lose, even though White possesses an extra protected, passed pawn. Tchigorin may have rejected this automatically, overlooking the little trick that helps him to save the ½ point from an ostensibly hopeless situation.

(6) *Lavieren!* 32. R—R7, K—B3; 33. R—N7, R—R4; 34. K—N2, R—R1; 35. K—B3, R—K1; 36. R—N5, K—N3; 37. R—N5 +, K—R3; 38. R—R5, R—K2. Note that Nimzowitsch does not compromise his chances of victory by an injudicious advance of his pawns. 39. R—QN5, R—R2; 40. R—QB5, R—R6 + ; 41. K—K2, R—R2; 42. K—B3, R—N2; 43. R—R5, R—N6 + ; 44. K—K2, R—N2; 45. K—B3, R—B2; 46. R—QN5, R—B6 + ; 47. K—K2, R—B2; 48. K—B3, R—Q2; 49. K—K3!. Cleverly spoiling Black's plan of giving check on QR6, QN6, QB6 and Q6. 49. ... R—Q8; 50. R—R5, K—N3; 51. R—N5 +, K—R3; 52. R—R5, R—QN8; 53. R—QB5, R—QR8. Hoping for the automatic R—R5? However, the ever alert Duras perceives this hidden possibility and avoids it. 54. R—QN5!, R—R5; 55. R—QB5, R—R1; 56. R—QN5, R—R1!!; 57. R—N5, White cannot keep pace with Black's deep manœuvres but there was no longer a satisfactory defence in any case. 57. ... P—B4!; 58. K—B4, R—R1; 59. K—K5, R—R3; 60. K—B4, R—R5 + ; 61. K—K5, R—K5 + ; 62. K—Q6, P—N3; 63. P—B3, R—K6; 64. P—N4, BP × P; 65. P × P, R—KN6; 66. P × P, R × R; 67. P × R +, K × RP. 0–1.

(7) Leave it where it is! Nimzowitsch concluded the game with a sharp combination. 19. B × KP, Q × N; 20. R—B4, B—N5; 21. Q × B, B × B; 22. R × N +. 1–0. If Black plays 19. ... B × B then 20. N—N6 is in White's favour. This was the shortest game Nimzowitsch ever won against Bogoljubow. Perhaps it made him overconfident since Bogoljubow took the next three games to win the match 3–1.

(8) 17. ... N × KP; 18. R × R, Q × R; 19. N × N, P × N; 20. B × RP, B × P; 21. B × P, B × B; 22. R × B, Q—R1; 23. Q—Q4, R—Q1; 24. Q—K3, B—B8! 0–1.

(9) 46. K—N2! threat: R—R1 +. 46. ... N—B3; 47. R—R1 +, N—R4; 48. B × N, P × B; 49. R/1—R1!! 1–0. There is no way to avoid mate.

(10) It is drawn if Black plays 46. ... N—B6 +, e.g. 47. Q × N, Q—B4 + and ... Q—B1 +. Instead of this Nimzowitsch produced the amazing 46. ... P—B4?! and the game still ended in a draw after 47. P × N (P—B5!?), P—R3 + ; 48. K × P, Q—N5; 49. Q × P, Q × RP + ; 50. Q—R5, Q—B3 +.

(11) Indeed he can. Nimzowitsch's startling solution to the

problem was: 50. ... R—N5!!; 51. P×R, P—R5; 52. P—N5+, K×P; 53. B—R3, P—B6; 54. R—N1, K—B5; 55. P—B4, K×P; 56. K—B2, K—B5; 57. K—K1, P—Q5; 58. K—K2, K—Q4; 59. K—B3. B—N2; 60. R—K1, K—B5 dis.+; 61. K—B2, P—N7; 62. P—B5, KP×P; 63. P—K6, B—B3. 0–1.

(12) Decidedly not! However, Euwe, in desperate time trouble, could not resist the temptation. 23. ... R×N?; 24. QR—KB1, P—K7; 25. R×N+, R×R; 26. Q×R+, K—R3; 27. Q—B8+. 1–0. Correct was 23. ... Q×QP! and it is Black who stands better— e.g. 24. QR—KB1, Q—K4+; 25. K—R1, R—B2 or 24. R×N+, R×R; 25. Q×R/B8, Q—K4+; 26. K—N1, P—K7; 27. R—K1, R—B8+; 28. R×R, Q—K6+.

(13) The game continued: 21. ... BP×P; 22. P×P, N/1—B3; 23. B—N5, P—N5; 24. P×P, B×P; 25. Q—Q2, Q—Q3; 26. R—R2, B—K7! 0–1. The start position has all the characteristics of an Exchange French as, indeed, it was. Note Nimzowitsch's challenging asymmetrical handling of this drawing line with ... 0—0—0.

(14) 34. R×BP!, Q×P+ (... NP×R allows Q×P+ and R—N3+); 35. R—R3, KP×R; 36. Q×R, Q—Q1; 37. Q—B7+, K—R3; 38. P—Q5, Q—Q2; 39. Q—B8+, K—N4; 40. K—N3!! 1–0.

(15) 20. ... B—Q3; 21. R—Q7, QR—Q1; 22. R×B!, R×R; 23. Q—B6! 1–0. (... P×Q; 24. R—N4+ and B×P. Mate.)

(16) Black is better since White's Q side pawns can be exposed to attack. The game continued: 48. ... P—B6!; 49. P×P, B—B5; 50. K—Q4, R×RP; 51. R—Q6, R—R8; 52. K—B5, P—R6; 53. P—R4+, K—R4; 54. R/2—Q4, R—KB8; 55. R—Q8, P—B5!; 56. R—QR8, P—R7; 57. R×BP, R×R; 58. P×R, K—N5; 59. K—Q6, B—N6; 60. R—R3, K×BP; 61. K—K7, K—K5; 62. K—B6, K—Q6; 63. K×P, K×P; 64. P—R5, K—N7; 65. R—R8, B—R5. 0–1. A stylish display by Nimzowitsch.

This little-known game was the last decisive encounter between Nimzowitsch and Bogoljubow.

(17) 28. ... R—B8!; 29. R—Q2 (29. R×R, N×B or 29. B—B2, R×R; 30. B×R, N—Q6; 31. Q—K2, B×N; 32. Q×N, Q—B5+), 29. ... P—KN3; 30. N—K3 (if 30. N—N3?, N—N5+!–+), 30. ... B×P!; 31. B—B1 (31. P×B, N—B6+; 32. Q×N, Q—N8 mate), 31. ... B—Q2; 32. K—N1, B—N4; 33. R—Q1, Q×N!; 34. Q×Q, R×R; 35. Q—N6, N—N5; 36. P—N3, B×B. 0–1.

One of Nimzowitsch's most elegant and powerful combinations.

(18) Nimzowitsch extracted the full point by creating threats against the White king: 32. ... R—B1+!; 33. K—N3 (33. K—K3, R—K7+; 34. K—Q4, R—Q7+ followed by the exchange of rooks

when ... B×P can occur in safety), 33. ... B—B8!; 34. P—B4, R—N6 + ; 35. K—B2 (35. K—N4, B×P; 36. R/5—Q7, B—B1 – +), 35. ... R×P + ; 36. K—K1, B×P; 37. R—Q8 +, K—R2; 38. R/8—Q7, R—K5 + ; 39. K—Q2, R—K7 + ; 40. K—B1, B—Q6; 41. R×P +, K—R1! 0–1.

EPILOGUE

'Nimzowitsch had a restless temperament, accompanied by a suspiciousness that amounted to a disease and a nervousness that now and again in the heat of the struggle had an almost painful expression. An egocentric of the purest water, he often blew his own trumpet when annotating his games. 'One of my best games of recent years' was a frequently recurring expression by which Nimzowitsch the annotator gave ample recognition to Nimzowitsch the grandmaster and thus encouraged the latter almost to the same degree that he offended most chess enthusiasts.

But few masters—perhaps none—were so fond of the game of chess as Nimzowitsch. The often childish expression of his vanity should not be allowed to obscure or falsify for us the picture of a valiant seeker after truth. His original and rich intellect gave many a jewel to the treasure-chest of the chess historian, and made clear to many that subtle beauty of the game which is so hard to define. Chess was the great interest of his life, not because it became his profession, but because from his childhood onwards he cherished it more than anything else.'

Gideon Stahlberg in *Chess and Chessmasters*

INDEX OF OPENINGS

All numbers refer to pages.

INDEX OF PLAYERS

Index of Nimzowitsch's opponents in complete games and positions.
Numerals refer to pages; those in heavy type indicate that the
opponent played white.

Index of Complete Games and Positions not involving Nimzowitsch.
Numbers refer to pages.